妙法蓮華経

後秦龜茲國三藏法師
鳩摩羅什奉　詔譯

Title calligraphy by
Nisso Uchino, Archbishop of Nichiren Shu

Cover Art: Statues of Śākyamuni Buddha and Many-Treasures Buddha, as described in the Lotus Sūtra. These were made by Jōkei in wood with polychrome, gold pigment and kirikane cut gold leaf with crystal eyes, and dated Jōji 5, CE 1366. The height of the Śākyamuni figure is 69.5 cm (27.36") and that of Many-Treasures is 68.2 cm (26.85"). They are preserved at the Honkoku-ji Temple in Kyoto which has graciously given permission for their use. Image: Tokyo National Museum Image Archives.

THE LOTUS SUTRA

THE SUTRA OF THE LOTUS FLOWER OF THE WONDERFUL DHARMA

Translated from the Chinese
by SENCHU MURANO

THE LOTUS SUTRA

THE SUTRA OF THE LOTUS FLOWER OF THE WONDERFUL DHARMA

Translated from Kumārajīva's version of
THE SADDHARMAPUṆḌARĪKA-SŪTRA

by

SENCHU MURANO

FORMER PROFESSOR OF BUDDHISM
RISSHO UNIVERSITY

Second Edition revised by
Daniel B. Montgomery

Third Edition revised by
Shinkyo Warner

NICHIREN SHU

Linguistic Advisors

English: R. H. Blyth, L. M. Pruden, Zonjo Ishikawa;

Chinese: Kogyo Toda; *Japanese:* Shoko Kabutogi;

Sanskrit: Keisho Tsukamoto, Ryugen Taga, Takao Maruyama,

Kwansei Tamura, Shinkai Oikawa, Ryoko Mochizuki.

Layout and design by Alan Rowe.

Gaiji custom kanji characters created by Yoshihide Okazawa.

First Edition: 1974
Second Edition: 1991
Third Edition: 2012

Published by NBIC

Nichiren Buddhist International Center
29490 Mission Blvd., Hayward, CA 94544
www.nichiren-shu.org

ISBN 978-0-9719645-6-3

CONTENTS

Preface to the First Edition i
Preface to the Second Edition iii
Preface to the Third Edition iv
Introduction vii
Translator's Note xvii
Chapter I Introductory 1
Chapter II Expedients 24
Chapter III A Parable 52
Chapter IV Understanding by Faith 90
Chapter V The Simile of Herbs 108
Chapter VI Assurance of Future Buddhahood 118
Chapter VII The Parable of a Magic City 129
Chapter VIII The Assurance of Future Buddhahood of the Five Hundred Disciples 157
Chapter IX The Assurance of Future Buddhahood of the Śrāvakas Who Have Something More to Learn and of the Śrāvakas Who Have Nothing More to Learn 169
Chapter X The Teacher of the Dharma 176
Chapter XI Beholding the Stūpa of Treasures 186
Chapter XII Devadatta 200
Chapter XIII Encouragement for Keeping this Sūtra 209
Chapter XIV Peaceful Practices 216
Chapter XV The Appearance of Bodhisattvas from Underground 234
Chapter XVI The Duration of the Life of the Tathāgata 247
Chapter XVII The Variety of Merits 256
Chapter XVIII The Merits of a Person Who Rejoices at Hearing This Sūtra 269

Chapter XIX The Merits of the Teacher of the Dharma 275
Chapter XX Never-Despising Bodhisattva 291
Chapter XXI The Supernatural Powers of the Tathagāta 298
Chapter XXII Transmission 303
Chapter XXIII The Previous Life of Medicine-King Bodhisattva 305
Chapter XXIV Wonderful-Voice Bodhisattva 315
Chapter XXV The Universal Gate of World-Voice-Perceiver Bodhisattva 323
Chapter XXVI Dhāraṇīs 332
Chapter XXVII King Wonderful-Adornment as the Previous Life of a Bodhisattva 337
Chapter XXVIII The Encouragement of Universal-Sage Bodhisattva 343

English/Sanskrit Glossary
Sanskrit Words, English Buddhist Terms and Translated Proper Names Given in This Translation 351

Chinese/Japanese Glossary
Important Chinese Buddhist Terms Given in the Lotus Sutra 373

Index 408
Bibliography 416

PREFACE TO THE FIRST EDITION

A unique interest attaches to this fresh English translation of the Lotus Sutra, more fully entitled *The Sutra of the Lotus Flower of the Wonderful Dharma.* Not only does it correspond to Kumarajiva's classic Chinese text, with the important later additions. It also represents the dedicated work of a Buddhist priest of the Nichiren Sect in Japan. This Sect reveres the Lotus Sutra as its one sacred book, and reverences its truth as the supreme object of devotion. This translation, therefore, results from a motive essentially religious—the motive to "transmit the Dharma" in the contemporary generation.

Heretofore, the Lotus Sutra as cherished in the Far East has been represented in English chiefly through general descriptions, selected passages in anthologies, abbreviated summaries, or quotations of sayings drawn from various parts of the scripture. These have been useful for conveying first impressions, but of necessity they have all been partial, affording scant knowledge of the total impact of the work. Now the entire sutra lies before us in all its surprising dimensions, abundant imagery and cumulative insights. Meaning and spirit can be more adequately apprehended.

It should be noted that in literary form the Lotus Sutra is a vast apocalypse. The setting of its events is cosmic. Numerical indications are astronomic. Shakyamuni is still the central figure, but he is pictured as imparting his wisdom to an enormous assemblage of beings, superhuman, human and subhuman. He also is shown conversing with other great teachers of enlightenment drawn from an infinity of other worlds in the far reaches of the universe spread out in space and time. He has attained perfect enlightenment. His compassion for living beings is boundless. His duration is eternal. By countless expedients in story, parable, allegory and symbolic metaphor he appeals to every degree of aspiration for deliverance from the bonds of ignorance, error and suffering. Both prose and verse are used to carry the weight of imagery involved. Through it all the translator has been careful to preserve the ethical and spiritual values of the Mahayana teachings thus expressed.

For full appreciation of all it contains, the Lotus Sutra must be read in its entirety. In making this possible for English-speaking readers, Senchu Murano has rendered notable service in his appointed task of furthering "transmission of the Dharma" in the modern world.

CLARENCE H. HAMILTON
Winchester, Massachusetts, 1974.

PREFACE TO THE SECOND EDITION

The most conspicuous difference of the second edition of the Lotus Sutra from its first edition is adoption of the original Sanskrit word *Dharma* as the expression of the Chinese translation *Fa* (Japanese Hō). As was stated in the Translator's Note of the first edition, my policy is, with a few exceptions, to translate into English every word translated into Chinese from Sanskrit, and *Fa* was translated in the first edition as "the Law" when it stands for the Truth or the teaching of the Buddha. In the Chinese version by Kumārajīva, Buddha and Saṃgha are in most cases transliterated, not translated, but Dharma is invariably translated as *Fa*, not transliterated except in dhāraṇīs. In Christianity, the Law is used as the revelation of the will of God; therefore, it is assumed that the expression "Law of the Buddha" is not far from the Buddha-Dharma.

In the modern usage, however, the word *Law* is associated with laws made by men so far that it hardly preserves the purity of the highest truth revealed through the enlightenment of the Buddha, or the meaning of the fundamental existence of the world inclusive of all living and non-living beings. In order to save the word from unnecessary connotations, I have recovered the original Sanskrit form of the word with the result that the full title of the sutra itself has been radically changed to the "Sūtra of the Lotus Flower of the Wonderful Dharma."

The Dharma does not necessarily mean the Truth or the teaching of the Buddha. Sometimes it simply means "a thing" or "practice." In such cases, the *Fa* is translated into an English word proper to the meaning involved.

On this occasion of issuing the second edition of the Lotus Sutra, I wish to express my heartfelt gratitude to the Very Reverend Daniel B. Montgomery, who kindly assisted me in revising the first edition with his ample knowledge of Christianity and Buddhism and his wonderful caliber in English writing.

SENCHU MURANO
Kamakura, Japan, 1991.

PREFACE TO THE THIRD EDITION

Soon after I took up Nichiren Shu Buddhism, a dear friend suggested an addition to my practice. He noted that by reading a chapter a day from the Lotus Sutra, after a month one will have completed all 28 chapters. Doing this month after month would help any reader absorb many different aspects of the Sutra, and truly make it part of their life.

For fifteen some-odd years now I have been following this practice. It does not get old. Each time I read the Sutra, something new appears. Of course it could be that as the circumstances of life change, different aspects of the Sutra become more important. However I still do not feel I have fully plumbed the depths of this amazing and wonderful work.

In some months of those years, I explored translations other than Bishop Murano's. But I always came back, and it remains my favorite. Burton Watson's is arguably the most famous, but I did not find in it the same emphasis on the Bodhisattva practice that Bishop Murano's rendition provides. Other translations from Bukkyō Dendō Kyōkai and Risshō Kōsei-Kai are as precise and scholarly, but they do not have the poetic rhythm and beauty that Bishop Murano has produced. Not since reading Vladimir Nabokov had I encountered another author, for whom English is not his native language, who has produced a work in English of such elegance and poise.

On the other hand, Bishop Murano's translation is not without its flaws. Legend has it that Japanese typesetters not fluent in English laid out the second edition. One could barely read more than five pages without running into a typographical error, either in the English or Sanskrit words. There also seems to be confusion between British English and American English spellings. One could find both flavor and flavour sprinkled throughout.

Some have questioned the additions and comments provided by Bishop Murano, all of which he was very careful to either bracket within the text or provide as footnotes. His insertions to the text are often crucial to making any sense of this book in English. Then again, comments such as his footnote in Chapter Thirteen stating that, "A woman must change herself into a man in order to become a Buddha," have sparked lively discussion in many study groups.

There is also the way Bishop Murano uses the term "Brahman" in his translation. In the Hindu cosmology, Brahman is an impersonal, all encompassing foundation, essence or background of existence. Even describing Brahman is difficult since to assert either its being or non-being limits it. On the other hand, "Brahma" is the name conventionally used to denote a creator god. Unlike the creator in Judeo-Christian accounts of reality, there can be many Brahmas and thus many creations.

The Lotus Sutra does not mention Brahman as an all encompassing entity. It does mention several creator gods, traveling from their worlds to hear the Buddha teach the Lotus Sutra and vowing to protect both the Sutra itself and those who uphold it. In this translation, Bishop Murano names these beings "Brahman." While this is correct by the rules of Sanskrit grammar, it can create confusion for those who expect to see the name "Brahma" applied to creator gods.

Finally, there are the glossaries at the end of the book. One gets the impression that these were not written for an English audience, rather for Japanese who have some knowledge of English. To find the definition of an English or Sanskrit term, you had to start with the first glossary, which then gave the corresponding Japanese term. You would then have to go to the second glossary to find the meaning of this Japanese term, an extra step that most English readers found tedious and unnecessary.

In this third edition of Bishop Murano's translation, we have set three goals:

1. Fix typographical errors.

2. Move to a consistent American English spelling. The choice of American over British was not entirely arbitrary, since all those who helped on this project speak American English.

3. Reorganize the glossaries so that someone looking up an English or Sanskrit term can find the meaning directly without going through a Japanese term. We have maintained the glossary of important Chinese Buddhist terms since it contained far

more terms than the English/Sanskrit Glossary. However, the long definitions in it have been replaced with references to the English/Sanskrit Glossary.

The footnotes and bracketed additions are left intact. We did not change the names of the beings referred to as "Brahman" to "Brahma." After all, this is Bishop Murano's translation. Out of gratitude for his work to put this together, we have chosen to leave it as close to his intention as possible, whether or not we completely understand that intention.

Even with the extra polish we have given to this revision, there is still something to be said for reading something with flaws. From the very first chapter, the Lotus Sutra invites questioning. It encourages us to speak up when something doesn't make sense, whether a small typo or a big concept.

A careful and patient reading of the Lotus Sutra, using Nichiren's writings as a guide, will show how to understand it. More importantly, the Sutra shows how to practice it, how to make it real in our lives. For those of us who have English as our native language, Bishop Murano's translation is an essential gate into this wonderful teaching, into the mind of the Buddha who is always thinking, "How shall I cause all living beings to quickly become Buddhas?"

As the Heavenly Brahma Kings declared in Chapter Seven: "May the merits we have accumulated by this offering be distributed among all living beings, and may we and all other living beings attain the enlightenment of the Buddha."

Namu Myoho Renge Kyo

Shinkyo Will Warner
Tampa, Florida, 2012.

INTRODUCTION

The Sūtra of the Lotus Flower of the Wonderful Dharma is an English translation of the Kasuga edition of the *Myōhōrengekyō*. The *Myōhōrengekyō* is a Chinese translation of a Sanskrit text of the *Saddharmupuṇḍarīka-sūtra* by Kumārajīva in 406. In this Introduction, the *Saddharmupuṇḍarīka-sūtra* is abbreviated to the Lotus Sūtra for convenience's sake.

Recent investigations disclose that the Sanskrit text of the Lotus Sūtra used by Kumārajīva differed from the Kasuga edition in the following points:

1. Kumārajīva's text did not contain Chapter XII of the Kasuga edition. This chapter was translated by Fa-i in 490 and inserted into Kumārajīva's version probably at the beginning of the sixth century.

2. Kumārajīva's text did not contain the part of Chapter XXV of the Kasuga edition covering from the 24th line of p. 327 to the last line of p. 331. This part of the chapter was translated by Jñānagupta and inserted in the *Myōhōrengekyō* sometime between 561 and 601.

The contents of this sūtra may be summarized as follows:

In Chapter I, the Buddha finishes expounding the Sūtra of the Innumerable Teachings and emits a ray of light from the white curls between his eyebrows. It is said that at that instant eighteen thousand worlds in the east become visible. From this we see that the Buddha was sitting facing the east at that time.

Maitreya Bodhisattva asks Mañjuśrī Bodhisattva why the Buddha displayed this wonder. Mañjuśrī answers that the Buddha will expound the Lotus Sūtra because Sun-Moon-Light Buddha (Nichigattōmyō, Candrasūryapradīpa. See *Translator's Note* and *Glossaries*) displayed the same wonder before he expounded the Lotus Sūtra.

In Chapter II, the Buddha expounds the Dharma to Śāriputra and others. He says that the teaching of Nirvāṇa was expounded as an expedient for the purpose of leading people to the Great Vehicle, and that the teaching of the Three Vehicles was expounded for the purpose of revealing the One Vehicle.

In Chapter III, Śāriputra tells the Buddha that he understands the Dharma. The Buddha assures him of his future Buddhahood. At the request of Śāriputra, the Buddha expounds the Dharma again to the bhikṣus with the parable of a burning house. He says that the Three Vehicles: the Śrāvaka-Vehicle, Pratyekabuddha-Vehicle and Buddha-Vehicle were expounded only for the purpose of saving all living beings by the Great Vehicle.

In Chapter IV, Subhūti, Mahā-Kātyāyana, Mahā-Kāśyapa and Mahā-Maudgalyāyana express their understanding of the Dharma with the parable of a poor son.

In Chapter V, the Buddha repeats the expounding of the Dharma with the simile of herbs.

In Chapter VI, the Buddha assures Subhūti, Mahā-Kātyāyana, Mahā-Kāśyapa and Mahā-Maudgalyāyana of their future Buddhahood.

In Chapter VII, the Buddha says that, when he was a Bodhisattva in his previous existence, he heard the Lotus Sūtra from Great-Universal-Wisdom-Excellence Buddha (See *Glossaries*) and expounded that sūtra after the extinction of that Buddha. He tells the bhikṣus the parable of a magic city and says that the teaching of Nirvāṇa was expounded in order to give people a rest on the way to the wisdom of the Buddha.

In Chapter VIII, Pūrṇa-Maitrāyaṇīputra, Ājñāta-Kauṇḍinya, Uruvilvā-Kāśyapa, Gayā-Kāśyapa, Nadī-Kāśyapa, Kālodāyin, Aniruddha, Revata, Kapphina, Bakkula, Cunda, Svāgata, and other Arhats, five hundred altogether, express their understanding of the Dharma with the parable of the gem inside a garment. The Buddha assures them of their future Buddhahood.

In Chapter IX, the Buddha assures Ānanda, Rāhula and two thousand Śrāvakas of their future Buddhahood. When the Buddha assured Ānanda of his future Buddhahood, eight thousand Bodhisattvas complained, saying that even great Bodhisattvas had not yet been assured of their future Buddhahood. The Buddha explained the reason by telling them of his relation to Ānanda in his previous existence.

In Chapter X, the Buddha encourages Medicine-King Bodhisattva to keep this sūtra. This is the first chapter that carries the address of the Buddha to a Bodhisattva except Chapter IX in which the Buddha addressed the eight thousand Bodhisattvas to meet their complaint.

New conceptions are presented in Chapter XI. First, the conception of the replicas of Śākyamuni Buddha is introduced. It is held that Śākyamuni Buddha can manifest his replicas by his supernatural powers. The statement at the beginning of this chapter that his replicas were called back from the worlds of the ten quarters to the Sahā-World (p. 188 ff.) implies that the Buddha manifested his replicas and dispatched them to the worlds of the ten quarters before the composition of this chapter. It has already been conceived in the previous chapters that there are Buddhas in the worlds of the ten quarters, and that a world is a Buddha-world in which lives one Buddha and no more. There is no statement that the number of the Buddhas of the worlds of the ten quarters was doubled after the dispatch of the replicas of Śākyamuni Buddha. Here we see that the dispatch of the replicas of Śākyamuni Buddha means nothing but an interpretation of the Buddhas of the worlds of the ten quarters as the replicas of Śākyamuni Buddha. Prior to this chapter, Śākyamuni Buddha behaved himself as one of the present Buddhas. But here in this chapter, all the present Buddhas other than Śākyamuni, that is, the Buddhas of the worlds of the ten quarters, are regarded as the replicas of Śākyamuni Buddha; and Śākyamuni Buddha, as their original. Thus the Buddhas of the worlds of the ten quarters are subordinated to Śākyamuni Buddha.

Second, Many-Treasures Buddha (Prabhūtaratna) is introduced in this chapter. Although he is a past Buddha, Many-Treasures Buddha is very active. He can hear the voice of the Buddha of any other world from afar. He can move. He can say anything but expound the Dharma. Many thousands of billions of kalpas ago, he appeared in a world at the distance of many thousands of billions of asaṃkhyas of worlds to the east of the Sahā-World. He made a vow to come to any expounder of the Lotus Sūtra to praise him and to hear the Dharma directly from him. He rejoiced at hearing the Lotus Sūtra expounded by Śākyamuni Buddha who was living on Mt. Gṛdhrakūṭa of the Sahā-World. Here we see that Śākyamuni Buddha was regarded as the first Buddha to expound the Lotus Sūtra.

The stūpa containing the perfect body of Many-Treasures Buddha came all the way from his world to the sky below the Sahā-World, entered the Sahā-World from underneath, sprang up from underground, and hung in the sky before Śākyamuni Buddha. Many-Treasures Buddha praised Śākyamuni Buddha from within the stūpa and said that he had come to hear the Dharma directly from Śākyamuni Buddha. Great-Eloquence Bodhisattva asked Śākyamuni Buddha to open the door of the stūpa. Śākyamuni Buddha told him that Many-Treasures Buddha had made a vow to see the replicas of the expounder of the Lotus Sūtra collected before the opening of the door of the stūpa. The Bodhisattva asked Śākyamuni Buddha to collect his replicas. Thereupon Śākyamuni Buddha emitted rays of light from the white curls between his eyebrows. This emitting of light stood for the order that all his replicas should come back to the Sahā-World. Śākyamuni Buddha purified the Sahā-World by eliminating all the mountains and seas, except Mt. Gṛdhrakūṭa, to make seats for his replicas. Finding that the Sahā-World was too small to receive all his replicas, he purified two hundred billion nayuta worlds of each of the eight quarters surrounding the Sahā-World, and amalgamated those worlds with the Sahā-World into one Buddha-world. Finding again that this expanded Buddha-world was not yet large enough to receive all of them, the Buddha again purified two hundred billion more nayuta worlds of each of the eight quarters surrounding the expanded world, and amalgamated those worlds with the expanded world into one Buddha-world. Now all the replicas of Śākyamuni Buddha seated themselves in the twice expanded Buddha-world. Each replica was accompanied by a Bodhisattva. Śākyamuni Buddha went up to the sky and opened the door of the stūpa. Many-Treasures Buddha moved sideways. Śākyamuni Buddha entered the stūpa, and sat by the side of Many-Treasures Buddha. The congregation wished to be raised up high enough to be with the two Buddhas. Śākyamuni Buddha raised them up, and said that he was wishing to transmit this sūtra to someone.

Here we see a newly-established arena of the expounding of the Dharma of Śākyamuni Buddha. The stūpa of Many-Treasures Buddha is hanging in the sky above Mt. Gṛdhrakūṭa. The two Buddhas are sitting side by side in the stūpa. The congregation is in the sky. The Buddhas of the worlds of the ten quarters are sitting on the ground of the expanded Buddha-world, each accompanied by a Bodhisattva. This expanded world is, however, not treated as one world in the later chapters. The Sahā-World not amalgamated with the neighboring worlds is recovered in Chapter XII, and no more mentioning of the purified worlds surrounding the Sahā-World is found in the following chapters. Mt. Sumeru is given in the verses at the end of Chapter XI, and the mountains and seas of the Sahā-World are referred to without any remark of recovery in Chapter XIX. This shows that the mountains and seas of the Sahā-World as well as of the worlds surrounding the Sahā-World have already been restored before the verses at the end of Chapter XI. But even after the mountains and seas are restored, the replicas of Śākyamuni Buddha continue staying in the once-purified worlds until the end of Chapter XXII.

As we shall see later, Many-Treasures Buddha and the replicas of Śākyamuni Buddha have no important role after Chapter XI. Before he came to the Sahā-World, Many-Treasures Buddha knew that Śākyamuni Buddha was the original of the Buddhas of the worlds of the ten quarters, that is, that the Buddhas of the worlds of the ten quarters were the replicas of Śākyamuni Buddha. The Buddhas of the worlds of the ten quarters followed the order of Śākyamuni Buddha because they knew that they were his replicas. Many-Treasures Buddha and the Buddhas of the worlds of the ten quarters came to the Sahā-World for no other purpose than to reveal the truth that Śākyamuni Buddha is the Original and Supreme Buddha as far as the present Buddhas are concerned.

Chapter XII, which is an insertion, betrays discrepancies from Chapter XI in the following points.

1. Śākyamuni Buddha and Many-Treasures Buddha are on Mt. Sacred Eagle (Gṛdhrakūṭa), not in the stūpa hanging in the sky.

2. Many-Treasures Buddha came from the nadir, not from the east.

3. Many-Treasures Buddha is accompanied by a Bodhisattva.

4. At the beginning of this chapter, Mañjuśrī Bodhisattva is at the palace of Dragon-King Sāgara in the sea.

5. There is no response to the wish of the Buddha to transmit this sūtra to someone.

This chapter has two different topics. In the first part of this chapter, the Buddha assures Devadatta of his future Buddhahood. The fact that no word of thanks to the Buddha is given by Devadatta shows that Devadatta is considered to be already dead at the time of the assurance of his future Buddhahood.

In the second part of this chapter, Accumulated-Wisdom Bodhisattva, who is accompanying Many-Treasures Buddha, requests Many-Treasures Buddha to go home with him. Śākyamuni Buddha checks them, saying that Mañjuśrī is coming. Mañjuśrī comes from the sea with innumerable Bodhisattvas. Accumulated-Wisdom asks Mañjuśrī how many people he saved in the sea. Mañjuśrī summons innumerable Bodhisattvas from the sea and says that these Bodhisattvas were saved by him. Here the difference between the Bodhisattvas who came with him and the Bodhisattvas who were summoned by him is not explained.

Accumulated-Wisdom asks Mañjuśrī whether anyone is qualified to become a Buddha quickly. Mañjuśrī introduces to him an eight-year-old girl from among the Bodhisattvas whom he summoned, and says that she is so qualified. Accumulated-Wisdom does not believe him. The girl comes to Śākyamuni Buddha, and offers him a gem. Here we see that the presence of Many-Treasures Buddha is ignored.

Śākyamuni Buddha receives the gem immediately. The girl asks both Accumulated-Wisdom and Śāriputra whether the Buddha received her gift quickly or not. Both of them answer that he did it quickly. She says that she will become a Buddha more quickly. Thereupon she changes herself into a man, goes to the Spotless World in the south, and becomes a Buddha. Here we see that Śāriputra, who was regarded as the wisest disciple of the Buddha in the previous chapters, is treated with less respect. A southern world designated as the destination of a Bodhisattva is given only in this chapter as far as the Lotus Sūtra is concerned.

In Chapter XIII, Medicine-King Bodhisattva and Great-Eloquence Bodhisattva vow to expound this sūtra. This vow of theirs is followed by the Buddha's assurance of the future Buddhahood of Mahā-Prajāpatī, Yaśodharā, and six thousand other bhikṣuṇīs. These bhikṣuṇīs and other Śrāvakas also vow to expound this sūtra. These Śrāvakas say, however, that they will expound this sūtra in worlds other than the Sahā-World in which the people are too evil to save. Here we see that the Śrāvakas are considered to be less competent than the Bodhisattvas.

The Buddha encourages the Bodhisattvas to expound this sūtra. The Bodhisattvas vow to expound it not only in the Sahā-World but also in the worlds of the ten quarters. They request the Buddha to transmit this sūtra to them. They say that they will criticize ignorant people and arrogant bhikṣus and that, even when they are spoken ill of, struck with swords or sticks, or driven out of their monasteries, they will endure all this, and not spare even their lives.

In Chapter XIV, at the request of Mañjuśrī Bodhisattva, the Buddha teaches him the peaceful practices by which one can expound this sūtra without being spoken ill of, struck with swords or sticks, or driven out of his monastery.

In Chapter XV, we see the presence of innumerable Bodhisattvas from the other worlds in the congregation. They are not the Bodhisattvas accompanying the replica-Buddhas sitting on the ground. It is not stated when they joined the congregation.

The Bodhisattvas from the other worlds also vow to expound this sūtra in this Sahā-World, and request the Buddha to transmit this sūtra to them. Contrary to the expectation of the Bodhisattvas not only of the Sahā-World but also of the other worlds, however, the Buddha refuses their request, saying that there are other Bodhisattvas who will expound this sūtra after his extinction. At that instant many thousands of billions of Bodhisattvas spring up from underground, and join the congregation. Maitreya Bodhisattva asks the Buddha who they are. The Buddha says that they are his disciples, and that they have been living in the sky below this Sahā-World for the past innumerable kalpas. Maitreya Bodhisattva says that it is unbelievable that the Buddha taught them innumerable kalpas ago because the Buddha attained enlightenment only forty and odd years ago.

In Chapter XVI, the Buddha says that he became the Buddha innumerable kalpas ago, and that he has been teaching the living beings not only of this world but also of innumerable worlds outside this world since then. He also says that during this time he gave various names to himself, for instance, Burning-Light Buddha (Dīpaṃkara). Here we see that all the past Buddhas are regarded as the different names of Śākyamuni Buddha. Thus Śākyamuni Buddha is established as the original not only of the present Buddhas but also of the past Buddhas.

In this chapter the Buddha says that he will stay in this Sahā-World forever. Here Śākyamuni Buddha is established also as the Eternal Buddha.

In Chapter XVII, the Buddha tells Maitreya Bodhisattva of the merits of those who understand the longevity of the Buddha and expound this sūtra after his extinction.

In Chapter XVIII, the Buddha tells Maitreya Bodhisattva of the merits of those who rejoice at hearing this sūtra.

In Chapter XIX, the Buddha tells Constant-Endeavor Bodhisattva of the merits of the teacher of the Dharma.

In Chapter XX, the Buddha tells Great-Power-Obtainer Bodhisattva (Mahāsthāmaprāpta) the story of his previous life in which he was Never-Despising Bodhisattva. (Sadāparibhūta, literally, "Always-Despised." See *Glossaries*.)

In Chapter XXI, the Bodhisattvas from underground vow to expound this sūtra after the extinction of the Buddha, and request the Buddha to transmit this sūtra to them. He consents to their request.

In Chapter XXII, Śākyamuni Buddha gets out of the stūpa, descends on to the ground and sits. Then he rises from his seat, and tells all the Bodhisattvas that he will transmit this sūtra to them. He tells the Buddhas of the worlds of the ten quarters that they may be where they wish to be. They return to their home worlds. Śākyamuni Buddha tells Many-Treasures Buddha that his stūpa may be where it was. We see the presence of Many-Treasures Buddha, however, in Chapters XXIII, XXIV and XXV. The

Bodhisattvas of the other worlds are present in Chapter XXIII, but no mention of their presence is found after that. Neither have we any mention of the presence of the Bodhisattvas from underground in and after Chapter XXIII as far as the Chinese version is concerned. (See *Viśiṣṭacāritra* in the *Index*.)

It is clearly seen that Chapter XXII has the contents of the closing chapter of a sūtra. It is most probable that the oldest part of this sūtra is Chapters II to IX, in which Śrāvakas have the leading role in the dialogues of the Buddha. In Chapters X to XXII, Bodhisattvas are active while Śrāvakas seldom speak. It may be safely said that Chapters X to XXII are the second oldest part of this sūtra. Chapter XII should be treated separately. Chapter I may have been composed at the outset, but it is considered that some parts of it may have been added or revised in the course of the making of the later chapters.

The arena of the expounding of the Dharma by Śākyamuni Buddha changes from time to time. In Chapter I to X, the Buddha expounds the Dharma on Mt. Gṛdhrakūṭa. In Chapter XI, Many-Treasures Buddha comes riding in his stūpa to the sky above Mt. Gṛdhrakūṭa. The Buddhas of the worlds of the ten quarters come and sit in the expanded Buddha-world composed of the Sahā-World and the worlds adjacent to the Sahā-World. Śākyamuni Buddha enters the stūpa of Many-Treasures Buddha, and raises up the congregation to the sky. The Bodhisattvas of the other worlds come and join the congregation. Śākyamuni Buddha expounds the Dharma from within the stūpa. Then he gets out of the stūpa, descends on to the ground, and expounds the Dharma.

Chapters XXIII to XXVIII are additions, constituting the newest part of this sūtra except Chapter XII and the part of Chapter XXV as previously stated. We can find no conception of the replicas of Śākyamuni Buddha in these chapters. The presence of Many-Treasures Buddha in Chapters XXIII, XXIV, and XXV can be dispensed with. His presence in these chapters may have been introduced to give these chapters the appearance of a continuation of the foregoing chapters. The Bodhisattvas from the other worlds, whose presence is given in Chapter XXIII, must have returned home by the end of that chapter because Wonderful-Voice Bodhisattva came from an eastern world and returned to that world in Chapter XXIV. The supremacy of Śākyamuni Buddha, which was elaborately established in the second oldest part of this sūtra, is overshadowed by his statement in Chapter XXIII that the woman who acts according to this sūtra will be reborn in the World of Amitāyus Buddha, and also by the statement of Pure-Flower-Star-King-Wisdom Buddha in Chapter XXIV that Śākyamuni Buddha is shorter in stature than he.

The bulk of these added chapters is dedicated to enhancing the virtues of Bodhisattvas. Medicine-King Bodhisattva is praised in Chapter XXIII. The living beings of the Sahā-World are benefited by Wonderful-Voice Bodhisattva of another world in Chapter XXIV. The calling of the name of World-Voice-Perceiver Bodhisattva is recommended rather than the keeping of this sūtra in Chapter XXV. Those who know the names of Medicine-King Bodhisattva and Medicine-Superior Bodhisattva are honored in Chapter XXVII. The Buddha says that he will protect anyone who keeps the name of Universal-Sage Bodhisattva in Chapter XXVIII.

Medicine-King Bodhisattva, Brave-In-Giving Bodhisattva, two of the kings of the four quarters, rākṣasīs, Hārītī, and her children and attendants utter dhāraṇīs in Chapter XXVI; and Universal-Sage Bodhisattva, in Chapter XXVIII. This shows an influence of mysticism which later developed into Esoteric Buddhism. The statement of Universal-Sage Bodhisattva in Chapter XXVIII that the person who keeps this sūtra will be reborn in the Tuṣita Heaven where Maitreya Bodhisattva lives, discloses the fact that this chapter was composed much later than the second oldest part of this sūtra in which Maitreya Bodhisattva was active as a questioner. Chapters XXIII to XXVIII have each a *raison d'être* of its own, but logical sequence can hardly be detected from them.

SENCHU MURANO

TRANSLATOR'S NOTE

1. This is a translation of the *Myōhōrengekyō,* not a revision of it by comparison with the extant Sanskrit text of the *Saddharmapuṇḍarīka-sūtra.*

2. The Chinese words are given in the Japanese pronunciation. There are only two Chinese words used in this translation: *ryo,* a unit of the Chinese gold coinage, and *shu,* a unit of the Chinese weights. The Chinese words in footnotes and glossaries are also given in the Japanese pronunciation.

3. The Japanese pronunciation is also used for the dhāraṇīs given in Chapters XXVI and XXVIII.

4. All the Sanskrit words translated into Chinese, including proper names, are translated into English with the following exceptions:

(a) The words which have no suitable equivalents in English: Tathāgata (Nyorai), Śrāvaka (Shōmon), Dharma (Hō), Karma (Gō), and āsrava (Ro or Uro). For Dharma, see *Preface to the Second Edition.*

(b) Sūtra, which is accepted as an English word.

(c) Jīvakajīvaka, of which the translation *myōmyō* loses the onomatopoetical character of the original word.

5. All the Sanskrit words transliterated into Chinese characters are given in Sanskrit with the exception of *shutara,* a transliteration of *sūtra. Shutara,* which is used only as one of the *kubuhō* or nine elements of sūtras, is translated as prose.

6. The compounds of Sanskrit and Chinese words are given in the combinations of transliterations and translations with the following exceptions:

(a) The compounds of which either of the components is omitted because of redundancy: *tōji* (a stūpa or a monastery), *hyōsetsu* (a yaṣṭi), *aku-rasetsu* (a rākṣasa), and *sōbō* (a monastery).

(b) *Rasetsunyo* is rendered as rākṣasī because it is more natural that the Sanskrit component of the word should follow its own declension.

7. The Sanskrit proper names are not affected by declension when followed by other Sanskrit words: e.g., Amitāyus Buddha.

8. The transliterations of Sanskrit sentences are given according to the Sanskrit grammar; Namubutsu (Namo Buddhāya), Namu Shakamunibutsu (Namaḥ Śākyamunaye Buddhāya).

9. *Gaṅgā* is given according to the modernized spelling *Ganges.*

10. The following words begin with capital letters:

(a) Proper names and their appositions and titles.

(b) The epithets of the Buddha.

(c) The Sanskrit words connected with enlightenment; Buddha, Bodhisattva, Pratyekabuddha, Śrāvaka, Arhat, Anāgāmin, Sakṛdāgāmin, Srota-āpanna, Bodhi, Nirvāṇa, and Parinirvāṇa.

(d) The Way, which stands for spiritual direction or practice.

11. The parts enclosed with brackets are supplements deemed necessary for the understanding of the sentences concerned.

12. The lines of verses enclosed with parentheses should be considered to be excluded from the words of the person who sings the verses. Parentheses are used only in verses.

13. The verses are translated in the same number of lines as given in the Chinese translation in which one line is made of four or five characters. Efforts have been made to make four or six lines as a stanza. When one or two or three lines complete a meaning, they are attached to the preceding or succeeding line or lines to make a stanza of four or six lines. A stanza is marked off by a blank line, but sometimes two or more stanzas are put together to make clear the contents of the verses concerned. All the Chinese verses have lines of even numbers except the first set of verses in Chapter XIV.

14. The spellings and accents of the Sanskrit words are given according to Wogihara's *Saddharmapuṇḍarīka-sūtram.*

ACKNOWLEDGEMENT FOR THE FIRST EDITION

The translator wishes to express his heartfelt gratitude to Bollingen Foundation for their offer of a fellowship to assist him in translating the Chinese version of the *Saddharmapuṇḍarīka* during 1960-1964 through the recommendation of Dr. Clarence H. Hamilton.

April 28, 1974

ACKNOWLEDGEMENT FOR THE SECOND EDITION

I wish to express my wholehearted appreciation and gratitude to Rev. Senchu Murano, Chief Priest of Myochoji Temple at Kamakura-shi, Kanagawa-ken, and Rev. Gyosei Kamatani, Chief Priest of Myokoji Temple at Kashiba-cho, Nara-ken, for their financial support toward our publication of the second edition of the Lotus Sutra.

Tsumyo Ito
Chief Administrator
Nichiren Shu
April 28, 1991

ACKNOWLEDGEMENT FOR THE THIRD EDITION

Regardless of the Buddha's injunction in Chapter Fourteen to not praise people by name, we need to acknowledge several whose contributions to this revision project were crucial as a small token of gratitude to them. Deanna Wooddy faithfully transcribed chapters of the book into electronic form in the days before OCR. The Nichiren Shu Sangha in Indonesia provided searchable PDF files of the second edition which we were then able to proofread and correct. Nichiren Shu Shimbun Co. Ltd., publishers of the second edition of this book, assisted with preparations for layout and design of this edition. Rev. Myokei Caine-Barrett and Rev. Ryuei McCormick contributed their proofreading skills.

We are also pleased to acknowledge the consulting and proofreading support given by Professor Shinjo Hara, Dean of Buddhist Studies, Rissho University, and his fellow faculty members: Professor Hirohisa Toda and Associate Professor Kanji Tamura. Additionally, both Rissho University and the Nichiren Buddhist International Center provided financial support for this publication.

Most of all, we are thoroughly grateful to Bishop Senchu Murano himself, and the support of his family estate for this third edition. Bishop Murano's wit, his patience, his wisdom, and his dedication to making the Lotus Sutra accessible to the English-speaking world are an inspiration to all of us who aspire to grow the seeds of the Wonderful Dharma.

Shobin Watanabe
Chief Administrator
Nichiren Shu
September 26, 2012

THE SUTRA OF THE LOTUS FLOWER OF THE WONDERFUL DHARMA

THE SUTRA OF THE LOTUS FLOWER OF THE WONDERFUL DHARMA

CHAPTER I

INTRODUCTORY

Thus have I heard.[1] The Buddha once lived on Mt. Gṛdhrakūṭa[2] in the City of King-House.[3] He was accompanied by twelve thousand great bhikṣus. They were Arhats. They had already eliminated āsravas, and had no illusions. They had already benefited themselves, broken off the bonds of existence [in the world of birth and death], and obtained liberty in their minds. They included Ājñāta-Kauṇḍinya, Mahā-Kāśyapa, Uruvilvā-Kāśyapa, Gayā-Kāśyapa, Nadī-Kāśyapa, Śāriputra, Great Maudgalyāyana, Mahā-Kātyāyana, Aniruddha, Kapphina, Gavāṃpati, Revata, Pilindavatsa, Bakkula, Mahā-Kauṣṭhila, Nanda, Sundarananda, Pūrṇa who was the son of Maitrāyaṇī, Subhūti, Ānanda, and Rāhula. They were great Arhats well known to the multitude.

There were also two thousand [Śrāvakas], some of whom had something more to learn while others had nothing more to learn.[4] Mahā-Prajāpatī Bhikṣuṇī was present with her six thousand attendants. Yaśodharā Bhikṣuṇī, the mother of Rāhula, was also present with her attendants.

There were also eighty thousand Bodhisattva-mahāsattvas. They never faltered in [seeking] Anuttara-samyak-saṃbodhi. They had already obtained dhāraṇīs, turned the irrevocable wheel of

---

1 It is held that sūtras were recited by Ānanda.

2 For Sanskrit words and other Buddhist terms, see the English/Sanskrit Glossary.

3 For translated proper names, see the English/Sanskrit Glossary.

4 See *Śaikṣa* and *Aśaikṣa* in the English/Sanskrit Glossary.

the Dharma with eloquence according to the wishes [of all living beings], made offerings to many hundreds of thousands of Buddhas, and planted the roots of virtue under those Buddhas, by whom they had always been praised. They had already trained themselves out of their compassion towards others, entered the Way to the wisdom of the Buddha, obtained great wisdom, and reached the Other Shore so that their fame had already extended over innumerable worlds. They had already saved many hundreds of thousands of living beings. They included Mañjuśrī Bodhisattva, World-Voice-Perceiver Bodhisattva, Great-Power-Obtainer Bodhisattva, Constant-Endeavor Bodhisattva, Never-Resting Bodhisattva, Treasure-Palm Bodhisattva, Medicine-King Bodhisattva, Brave-In-Giving Bodhisattva, Treasure-Moon Bodhisattva, Moon-Light Bodhisattva, Full-Moon Bodhisattva, Great-Power Bodhisattva, Immeasurable-Power Bodhisattva, Transcending-Triple-World Bodhisattva, Bhadrapāla Bodhisattva, Maitreya Bodhisattva, Accumulated-Treasure Bodhisattva, and Leading-Teacher Bodhisattva. Eighty thousand Bodhisattva-mahāsattvas such as these were present.

Śakra-Devānām-Indra was also present. Twenty thousand gods were attending on him. There were also Beautiful-Moon God, Universal-Fragrance God, Treasure-Light God, and the four great heavenly-kings. Ten thousand gods were attending on them. Freedom God and Great-Freedom God were also present. Thirty thousand gods were attending on them. Brahman Heavenly-King who was the lord of the Sahā-World, Great Brahman Śikhin, and Great Brahman Light were also present. Twelve thousand gods were attending on them.

There were also the eight dragon-kings: Nanda Dragon-King, Upananda Dragon-King, Sāgara Dragon-King, Vāsuki Dragon-King, Takṣaka Dragon-King, Anavatapta Dragon-King, Manasvin Dragon-King, and Utpalaka Dragon-King, each accompanied by hundreds of thousands of attendants. There were also the four kiṃnara-kings: Dharma Kiṃnara-King, Wonderful-Dharma Kiṃnara-King, Great-Dharma Kiṃnara-King, and Dharma-Keeping Kiṃnara-King, each accompanied by hundreds of thousands of attendants.

There were also the four gandharva-kings: Musical[5] Gandharva-King, Musical-Voice Gandharva-King, Beautiful Gandharva-King, and Beautiful-Voice Gandharva-King, each accompanied by hundreds of thousands of attendants.

There were also the four asura-kings: Balin Asura-King, Kharaskandha Asura-King, Vemacitrin Asura-King, and Rāhu Asura-King, each accompanied by hundreds of thousands of attendants.

There were also the four garuḍa-kings: Great-Power-Virtue Garuḍa-King, Great-Body Garuḍa-King, Great-Fulfillment Garuḍa-King, and Free-At-Will Garuḍa-King, each accompanied by hundreds of thousands of attendants.

King Ajātaśatru, who was the son of Vaidehī, was also present with his hundreds of thousands of attendants. They each worshipped the feet of the Buddha, retired, and sat to one side.

Thereupon the four kinds of devotees, who were surrounding the World-Honored One, made offerings to him, respected him, honored him, and praised him. The World-Honored One expounded a sūtra of the Great Vehicle called the "Innumerable Teachings, the Dharma for Bodhisattvas, the Dharma Upheld by the Buddhas." Having expounded this sūtra, the Buddha sat cross-legged [facing the east], and entered into the samādhi for the purport of the innumerable teachings. His body and mind became motionless.

Thereupon the gods rained mandārava-flowers, mahā-mandārava-flowers, mañjūṣaka-flowers, and mahā-mañjūṣaka-flowers upon the Buddha and the great multitude. The world of the Buddha quaked in the six ways. The great multitude of the congregation, which included bhikṣus, bhikṣuṇīs, upāsakas, upāsikās, gods, dragons, yakṣas, gandharvas, asuras, garuḍas, kiṃnaras, mahoragas, men, nonhuman beings, the kings of small countries, and the wheel-turning-holy-kings, were astonished. They rejoiced, joined their hands together [towards the Buddha], and looked up at him with one mind.

---

5 楽 Gaku. The name of the Chinese symbol for this Ghandarva-King was once pronounced gyō, meaning "to wish."

Thereupon the Buddha emitted a ray of light from the white curls between his eyebrows, and illumined all the corners of eighteen thousand worlds in the east,[6] down to the Avīci Hell of each world, and up to the Akaniṣṭha Heaven of each world. The congregation saw from this world the living beings of the six regions of those worlds. They also saw the present Buddhas of those worlds. They also heard the Dharma expounded by those Buddhas. They also saw the bhikṣus, bhikṣuṇīs, upāsakas and upāsikās of those worlds who had already attained [the various fruits of] enlightenment by their various practices. They also saw the Bodhisattva-mahāsattvas [of those worlds] who were practicing the Way of Bodhisattvas [in various ways] according to the variety of their karmas which they had done in their previous existence, and also according to the variety of their ways of understanding [the Dharma] by faith.[7] They also saw the past Buddhas [of those worlds] who had already entered into Parinirvāṇa. They also saw the stūpas of the seven treasures which had been erected to enshrine the śariras of those Buddhas after their Parinirvāṇa.

Thereupon Maitreya Bodhisattva thought:

"The World-Honored One is now displaying a wonder[, that is, a good omen]. Why is he displaying this good omen? The Buddha, the World-Honored One, has entered into a samādhi. Whom shall I ask why he is displaying this inconceivable, rare thing? Who can answer my question?"

He thought again:

"This Mañjuśrī, the son of the King of the Dharma, has already met innumerable Buddhas and made offerings to them in his previous existence. He must have seen this rare thing before. Now I will ask him."

At that time the bhikṣus, bhikṣuṇīs, upāsakas, upāsikās, gods, dragons, and other supernatural beings thought, "Whom shall we ask why the Buddha is emitting this ray of light, that is, why he is displaying this wonder?"

---

6 From this we see that the Buddha was sitting facing the east.

7 種種因縁種種信解種種相貌 Literally means, "various causes, various ways of understanding by faith, various appearances."

At that time the congregation included the four kinds of devotees: bhikṣus, bhikṣuṇīs, upāsakas and upāsikās. They also included gods, dragons, and other supernatural beings. Maitreya Bodhisattva, wishing to have his doubts removed, and also understanding the minds of the congregation, asked Mañjuśrī:

"Why is the World-Honored One displaying this good omen, this wonder? Why is he emitting a great ray of light, illumining eighteen thousand worlds to the east, and causing us to see those beautifully-adorned[8] worlds of the Buddhas?"

Thereupon Maitreya Bodhisattva, wishing to repeat what he had said, asked him in gāthās:

Mañjuśrī!
Why is the Leading Teacher
Emitting a great ray of light
From the white curls between his eyebrows?

[The gods] rained mandārava-flowers
And mañjūṣaka-flowers.
A breeze carrying the fragrance of candana
Is delighting the multitude.

Because of this, the ground has become
Beautiful and pure;
And this world quaked
In the six ways.

The four kinds of devotees
Are joyful.
They are happier than ever
In body and mind.

The light from [the white curls]
Between the eyebrows of the Buddha illumines

---

8 The worlds are adorned with the four kinds of devotees, Bodhisattvas, and stūpas of the seven treasures.

Eighteen thousand worlds to the east.
Those worlds look golden-colored.

I see from this world
The living beings of the six regions
Extending down to the Avīci Hell,
And up to the Highest Heaven
Of each of those worlds.
I see the region to which each living being is to go,
The good or evil karmas he is doing,
And the rewards or retributions he is going to have.

I also see the Buddhas,
The Saintly Masters, the Lion-like Ones,
Who are expounding
The most wonderful sūtra
With their pure and gentle voices,
And teaching
Many billions of Bodhisattvas.
The brahma voices of the Buddhas
Are deep and wonderful,
Causing people to wish to hear them.

I also see the Buddha of each of those worlds
Expounding his right teachings to all living beings
In order to cause them to attain enlightenment.

He explains his teachings
With stories of previous lives,
And with innumerable parables and similes.

To those who are confronted with sufferings,
And tired of old age, disease, and death,
The Buddha expounds the teaching of Nirvāṇa,
And causes them to eliminate these sufferings.

To those who have merits,
Who have already made offerings to the past Buddhas,
And who are now seeking a more excellent teaching,
The Buddha expounds [the Way of] cause-knowers.

To the Buddha's sons
Who are performing various practices,
And who are seeking unsurpassed wisdom,
The Buddha expounds the Pure Way.

Mañjuśrī!
I see and hear
Hundreds of thousands of millions of things
Such as these
From this world.
I will tell you briefly some more of them.

I see as many Bodhisattvas of those worlds
As there are sands in the River Ganges,
Who are seeking the enlightenment of the Buddha
[In various ways] according to their environments.[9]

Some of them practice almsgiving.
They joyfully give treasures
Such as gold, silver,
Pearls, maṇis, shells, agates, and diamonds.
They also give menservants and maidservants,
Vehicles and palanquins adorned with treasures.

They proceed to the enlightenment of the Buddha
By the merits obtained thereby,
Wishing to obtain this vehicle,[10]
The most excellent vehicle
In the triple world,
The vehicle praised by the Buddhas.

---

9 種種因緣 Literally means, "various causes."

10 This implies the Buddha-Vehicle.

Some Bodhisattvas give
Jeweled chariots yoked with four horses,
Equipped with railings and flower-canopies,
And adorned on all sides.

I also see some Bodhisattvas
Offering their flesh or their limbs
Or their wives or their children
In order to attain unsurpassed enlightenment.

I also see some Bodhisattvas
Joyfully offering
Their heads or their eyes or their bodies
In order to attain the wisdom of the Buddha.

Mañjuśrī!
I see some kings coming to a Buddha,
And asking him about unsurpassed enlightenment.
They have renounced the world of pleasures,
Left their palaces,
Parted from their ministers and women,
And shaved their beard and hair.
They now wear monastic robes.

I also see some Bodhisattvas
Becoming bhikṣus,
Living alone in retired places,
And joyfully reciting sūtras.

I also see some Bodhisattvas
Zealously and courageously
Entering remote mountains, and pondering
The enlightenment of the Buddha.

I also see some of them having given up desires,
And living in retired places,

Entering deep into dhyāna-concentration,
And obtaining the five supernatural powers.

I also see some Bodhisattvas finding peace in dhyāna,
Joining their hands together [towards the Buddha],
And praising the King of the Dharma
With tens of millions of gāthās.

I also see some Bodhisattvas resolute in mind.
They have obtained profound wisdom
By questioning the Buddha.
And now they remember what they heard from him.

I also see some sons of the Buddha
Concentrating their minds, having wisdom,
Expounding the Dharma to the multitude
With innumerable parables and similes,
Expounding the Dharma with joy,
Teaching [other] Bodhisattvas,
Defeating the army of Māra,
And beating the drum of the Dharma.

I also see some Bodhisattvas
Being tranquil and peacefully calm,
Not delighting in being respected
By gods or dragons.

I also see some Bodhisattvas
Living in forests, and emitting rays of light
In order to save the denizens in hell,
And cause them to enter the Way to Buddhahood.

I also see some sons of the Buddha
Walking about forests without sleeping
In order to attain
The enlightenment of the Buddha.

I also see some of them
Observing the precepts with due deportment,
And keeping purity like that of gems,
In order to attain the enlightenment of the Buddha.

I also see some sons of the Buddha
Enduring abuse
Or blows with sticks
Inflicted by arrogant people
In order to attain
The enlightenment of the Buddha.

I also see some Bodhisattvas
Giving up wanton pleasures,
Parting from foolish companions,
Approaching men of wisdom,
Controlling their minds from distraction,
And concentrating their minds in hills or forests
For thousands of billions of years
In order to attain the enlightenment of the Buddha.

I also see some Bodhisattvas
Offering delicious food and drink
And hundreds of kinds of medicines
To the Buddha and the Saṃgha.

Some offer garments and beautiful robes
Worth tens of millions
Or beyond monetary value
To the Buddha and the Saṃgha.

Some offer thousands of billions
Of jeweled houses made of candana
And wonderful bedding
To the Buddha and the Saṃgha.

Some offer pure gardens and forests
Abounding in flowers and fruits,
And furnished with rivers, springs,
and pools for bathing,
To the Buddha and the Saṃgha.

I see those Bodhisattvas
Making offerings of those wonderful things
Joyfully and untiringly
In order to attain unsurpassed enlightenment.

Some Bodhisattvas expound
The truth of tranquil extinction,
And with various expedients,
Teach innumerable living beings.

I also see some Bodhisattvas
Who attained the following truth:
"The nature of things is not dual.
It is [formless] like the sky."

I also see some sons of the Buddha
Having no attachment in their minds.
They seek unsurpassed enlightenment
With this wonderful wisdom.

Mañjuśrī!
Some Bodhisattvas make offerings
To the śarīras of a Buddha
After his extinction.

I also see some sons of the Buddha
Adorning the world of the Buddha
With as many stūpa-mausoleums
As there are sands in the River Ganges.

Those stūpas of treasures are
Lofty and wonderful.
They are five thousand yojanas high,
And two thousand yojanas wide and deep.

Each of the stūpa-mausoleums has
One thousand pairs of banners and streamers.
It also has curtains adorned with gems.
It also has jeweled bells ringing.

Gods, dragons, men, and nonhuman beings
Constantly offer incense, flowers, and music
[To the stūpa-mausoleums].
Mañjuśrī!
Those sons of the Buddha
Adorn the stūpa-mausoleums
And offer the adornments
To the śarīras [of the Buddha].

The worlds [of the Buddha] naturally become
As wonderful and as beautiful
As the [flowers] of the kingly tree
In full bloom on the top of Mt. Sumeru.

The multitude of this congregation and I
Can see the various wonderful things
Of those worlds
By the ray of light of the Buddha [of this world].

The supernatural powers of the Buddha
And his wisdom are rare.
He is illumining innumerable worlds
By emitting a pure ray of light.
We were astonished
At seeing [those worlds].

Mañjuśrī, Son of the Buddha!
Remove our doubts!
The four kinds of devotees
Are looking up with joy at you and me,
Wishing to know why this ray of light is emitted
By the World-Honored One.

Son of the Buddha, answer me!
Remove our doubts and cause us to rejoice!
For what purpose is the Buddha
Emitting this ray of light?

Does he wish to expound the Wonderful Dharma
Which he attained when he was sitting
At the place of enlightenment?
Does he wish to assure us of our future Buddhahood?

He shows us the worlds of the Buddhas
Adorned with many treasures.
We can see the Buddhas of those worlds.
This cannot be for some insignificant reason.

Mañjuśrī, know this!
The four kinds of devotees and the dragons
Are looking at you, thinking:
"What is he going to say?"

Thereupon Mañjuśrī said to Maitreya Bodhisattva-mahasāttva and the other great men:

"Good men! I think that the Buddha, the World-Honored One, wishes to expound a great teaching, to send the rain of a great teaching, to blow the conch-shell horn of a great teaching, to beat the drum of a great teaching, and to explain the meaning of a great teaching.

"Good men! I met many Buddhas in my previous existence. At that time I saw the same good omen as this. Those Buddhas emitted the same ray of light as this, and then expounded a great teaching.

Therefore, know this! I think that this Buddha also is emitting this ray of light, and showing this good omen, wishing to cause all living beings to hear and understand the most difficult teaching in the world to believe.

"Good men! Innumerable, inconceivable, asaṃkya kalpas ago, there lived a Buddha called Sun-Moon-Light, the Tathāgata, the Deserver of Offerings, the Perfectly Enlightened One, the Man of Wisdom and Practice, the Well-Gone, the Knower of the World, the Unsurpassed Man, the Controller of Men, the Teacher of Gods and Men, the Buddha, the World-Honored One. He expounded the right teachings. His expounding of the right teachings was good at the beginning, good in the middle, and good at the end. The meanings of those teachings were profound. The words were skilful, pure, unpolluted, perfect, clean, and suitable for the explanation of brahma practices. To those who were seeking Śrāvakahood, he expounded the teaching of the four truths, a teaching suitable for them, saved them from birth, old age, disease, and death, and caused them to attain Nirvāṇa. To those who were seeking Pratyekabuddhahood, he expounded the teaching of the twelve causes, a teaching suitable for them. To Bodhisattvas, he expounded the teaching of the six pāramitās, a teaching suitable for them, and caused them to attain Anuttara-samyak-saṃbodhi, that is, to obtain the knowledge of the equality and differences of all things.

"After his extinction there appeared a Buddha also called Sun-Moon-Light. After his extinction there appeared another Buddha also called Sun-Moon-Light. In the same manner, twenty thousand Buddhas appeared in succession, all of them being called Sun-Moon-Light with the surname Bharadvāja.

"Maitreya, know this! All those Buddhas were called Sun-Moon-Light with the ten epithets. Their expounding of the Dharma was good at the beginning, good in the middle, and good at the end. The last Sun-Moon-Light Buddha was once a king. He had eight sons born to him before he renounced the world. The first son was called Having-Intention; the second, Good-Intention; the third, Infinite-Intention; the fourth, Treasure-Intention; the fifth, Increasing-Intention; the sixth, Doubts-Removing-Intention; the seventh, Resounding-Intention; and the eighth, Dharma-Intention. These eight princes had unhindered powers and virtues. Each of them was the ruler of the four continents [of a Sumeru-world].[11] Having heard that their father had renounced the world and attained Anuttara-samyak-saṃbodhi, they abdicated from their thrones, and followed their father. They renounced the world, aspired for the Great Vehicle, performed brahma practices, and became teachers of the Dharma. They had already planted the roots of good under ten million Buddhas in their previous existence.

"Thereupon the last Sun-Moon-Light Buddha expounded a sūtra of the Great Vehicle called the 'Innumerable Teachings, the Dharma for Bodhisattvas, the Dharma Upheld by the Buddhas.' Having expounded this sūtra, he sat cross-legged [facing the east] in the midst of the great multitude, and entered into the samādhi for the purport of the innumerable teachings. His body and mind became motionless.

"Thereupon the gods rained mandārava-flowers, mahā-mandārava-flowers, mañjūṣaka-flowers, and mahā-mañjūṣaka-flowers upon the Buddha and the great multitude. The world of the Buddha quaked in the six ways. The great multitude of the congregation, which included bhikṣus, bhikṣuṇīs, upāsakas, upāsikās, gods, dragons, yakṣas, gandharvas, asuras, garuḍas, kiṃnaras, mahoragas, men, nonhuman beings, the kings of small countries, and the wheel turning-holy kings, were astonished. They rejoiced, joined their hands together [towards the Buddha], and looked up at him with one mind.

"Thereupon the Tathāgata emitted a ray of light from the white curls between his eyebrows, and illumined all the corners of eighteen thousand Buddha-worlds in the east just as this Buddha is illumining the Buddha-worlds as we see now.

"Maitreya, know this! There were two thousand million Bodhisattvas in that congregation. They wished to hear the Dharma. They were astonished at seeing the Buddha-worlds illumined by this ray of light. They wished to know why the Buddha was emitting this ray of light.

11 See *Sumeru-World* in the English/Sanskrit Glossary.

"At that time there was a Bodhisattva called Wonderful-Light. He had eight hundred disciples. Sun-Moon-Light Buddha emerged from his samādhi, and expounded the sūtra of the Great Vehicle to Wonderful-Light Bodhisattva and others without rising from his seat for sixty small kalpas. It was called the 'Lotus Flower of the Wonderful Dharma, the Dharma for Bodhisattvas, the Dharma Upheld by the Buddhas.' The hearers in the congregation also sat in the same place for sixty small kalpas, and their bodies and minds were motionless. They thought that they had heard the Buddha expounding the Dharma for only a mealtime. None of them felt tired in body or mind. Having completed the expounding of this sūtra at the end of the period of sixty small kalpas, Sun-Moon-Light Buddha said to the Brahmans, Māras, śramaṇas, brāhmaṇas, gods, men, and asuras, 'I shall enter into the Nirvāṇa-without-remainder at midnight tonight.'

"At that time there was a Bodhisattva called Virtue-Store. Sun-Moon-Light Buddha assured him of his future Buddhahood. The Buddha said to the bhikṣus, 'This Virtue-Store Bodhisattva will become a Buddha immediately after me. He will be called Pure-Body, the Tathāgata, the Arhat, the Samyak-saṃbuddha.'

"Having assured him of his future Buddhahood, the Buddha then entered into the Nirvāṇa-without-remainder at midnight. After his extinction, Wonderful-Light Bodhisattva kept the Sūtra of the Lotus Flower of the Wonderful Dharma, and expounded it to men for eighty small kalpas. The eight sons of Sun-Moon-Light Buddha became his disciples. He taught them and caused them to resolve to attain Anuttara-samyak-saṃbodhi. They made offerings to many hundreds of thousands of billions of Buddhas, and then attained the enlightenment of the Buddha [one after another]. The son who became a Buddha last was called Burning-Light. One of the eight hundred disciples [of Wonderful-Light] was called Fame-Seeking. He was attached to gain. He read and recited many sūtras, but did not understand them. He forgot many parts of those sūtras. Therefore, he was called Fame-Seeking.[12] But he [later] planted the

12 The reason for the name is not adequate here. The reason given in the following verses is more convincing. This is evidence that the verses were composed earlier than the prose section for this chapter.

roots of good, and became able to see many hundreds of thousands of billions of Buddhas. He made offerings to them, respected them, honored them, and praised them.

"Maitreya, know this! Wonderful-Light Bodhisattva at that time was no one but myself; and Fame-Seeking Bodhisattva, no one but you. This good omen we see now is not different from what I saw at that time. Therefore, I think that the Tathāgata of today also will expound the sūtra of the Great Vehicle called the 'Lotus Flower of the Wonderful Dharma, the Dharma for Bodhisattvas, the Dharma Upheld by the Buddhas.' "

Thereupon Mañjuśrī, wishing to repeat what he had said, sang in gāthās in the midst of the great multitude:

According to my memory,
Innumerable, countless kalpas ago,
There lived a Buddha, a Man of the Highest Honor,
Called Sun-Moon-Light.

That World-Honored One expounded the Dharma,
And caused innumerable living beings
And many hundreds of millions of Bodhisattvas
To enter the Way to the wisdom of the Buddha.

Seeing the Great Saint
Who had renounced the world,
The eight sons born to him when he was a king
Followed him, and performed brahma practices.

The Buddha expounded
To the great multitude
A sūtra of the Great Vehicle
Called the 'Innumerable Teachings.'

Having expounded this sūtra, the Buddha sat cross-legged
On the seat of the Dharma [facing the east],
And entered into the samādhi
For the purport of the innumerable teachings.

The gods rained mandārava-flowers.
Heavenly drums sounded by themselves.
The gods, dragons, and other supernatural beings
Made offerings to the Man of the Highest Honor.

The worlds of the Buddhas quaked much.[13]
The Buddha emitted a ray of light
From between his eyebrows,
And showed things rarely to be seen.

This ray of light illumined
Eighteen thousand Buddha-worlds in the east.
It showed the region
To which each living being was to go by his karmas.

The worlds of the Buddhas were
Adorned with many treasures,
And given the colors of lapis lazuli and crystal.
I saw all this by the light of the Buddha.

I also saw the gods, men, dragons, yakṣas,
Gandharvas, and kiṃnaras of those worlds.
Each of them made offerings
To the Buddha by whom he was taught.

I also saw the Tathāgatas of those worlds
Who had attained enlightenment by themselves.
The color of their bodies was as beautiful
And as wonderful as that of the golden mountains,
Or as that of a golden image
Put in a shrine of pure lapis lazuli.

Those World-Honored Ones explained to the
great multitudes
The meaning of the profound teaching.

---

13 This plurality of the worlds is not consistent with the foregoing prose section. See page 3.

There were innumerable Śrāvakas
In the worlds of those Buddhas.
All those great multitudes were seen
By the light of the Buddha.

The bhikṣus were living in mountains and forests.
They made endeavors,
And observed the pure precepts
As carefully as one keeps brilliant gems.

As many Bodhisattvas
As there are sands in the River Ganges
Performed almsgiving, patience, and other practices.
I saw all this by the light of the Buddha.

I also saw some Bodhisattvas
Who entered deep into dhyāna-concentrations,
And became tranquil and motionless in body and mind,
In order to attain unsurpassed enlightenment.

I also saw some Bodhisattvas,
Who realized the tranquil extinction of all things,
And expounded the Dharma to [the people of] their worlds
In order to attain the enlightenment of the Buddha.

The four kinds of devotees
Of the world of Sun-Moon-Light Buddha
Also saw the Buddha displaying this great wonder.
They had great joy.
They asked one another:
"Why is he doing this?"

He who was honored by gods and men
Emerged from his samādhi,
And praised Wonderful-Light Bodhisattva, saying:
"You are the eyes of the world.

You are believed and relied on
By all living beings.
You are keeping the store of the Dharma.
Only you will understand the Dharma which
I shall expound."

Having praised Wonderful-Light
And caused him to rejoice,
That World-Honored One expounded
The Sūtra of the Lotus Flower of the Wonderful Dharma.
He never rose from his seat for sixty small kalpas.
Wonderful-Light, the Teacher of the Dharma,
Kept the Wonderful Dharma
Expounded by that World-Honored One.

Having expounded the Sūtra
Of the Lotus Flower of the Wonderful Dharma,
And caused the multitude to rejoice,
The Buddha told the gods and men
At that moment on that day,
"I have already expounded to you
The truth of the reality of all things.
I shall enter into Nirvāṇa[14] at midnight tonight.
Make efforts with all your hearts!
Leave the life of license!
It is difficult to see a Buddha, who can be seen
Only once in hundreds of millions of kalpas."

Having heard that the Buddha would enter into Nirvāṇa,
Those sons of the World-Honored One
Were filled with sorrow.
They said, "How quickly the Buddha is gone!"

The Saintly Master, the King of the Dharma,
Consoled the countless living beings, saying:

14 *Nirvāṇa* stands for Parinirvāṇa.

"Although I shall pass away,
You must not worry.
This Virtue-Store Bodhisattva has already understood
The truth of the reality [of all things]
[To be attained by the wisdom] without āsravas.
He will become a Buddha immediately after me.
He will be called Pure-Body.
He will save innumerable living beings."

The Buddha passed away that night
Just as fire dies out when wood is gone.
His śarīras were distributed.
Countless stūpas were erected to enshrine them.

As many bhikṣus and bhikṣuṇīs
As there are sands in the River Ganges
Redoubled their endeavors
In order to attain unsurpassed enlightenment.

Wonderful-Light, the Teacher of the Dharma,
Kept the store of the Dharma of the Buddha, and expounded
The Sūtra of the Lotus Flower of the Wonderful Dharma
For eighty small kalpas.

Led by Wonderful-Light, those eight princes resolved
To attain unsurpassed enlightenment.
[Wonderful-Light said to them:]
"You will be able to see countless Buddhas."

Having made offerings to [countless] Buddhas,
Those princes followed them, practiced the Great Way,
And became Buddhas in succession.
Each of them assured another of his future Buddhahood.

The last God of Gods
Was called Burning-Light Buddha.

As the leader of seers,
He saved innumerable living beings.

There was a lazy man
Among the disciples
Of Wonderful-Light, the Teacher of the Dharma.
[The lazy man] was attached to fame and gain.

Always seeking fame and gain,
He often visited noble families.
He did not understand what he had recited,
Gave it up, and forgot it.
Because of this,
He was called Fame-Seeking.

But he [later] did many good karmas,
And became able to see innumerable Buddhas.
He made offerings to them,
Followed them, practiced the Great Way,
And performed the six pāramitās.
Now he sees the Lion-Like One of the Śākyas.

He will become a Buddha
In his future life.
He will be called Maitreya.
He will save innumerable living beings.

The lazy man who lived after the extinction
Of [Sun-Moon-] Light Buddha was
No one but you.
Wonderful-Light, the Teacher of the Dharma, was I.

The ray of light of [Sun-Moon-] Light Buddha,
That is, the good omen, was the same as what I see now.
Judging from this, the present Buddha also will expound
The Sūtra of the Lotus Flower of the Wonderful Dharma.

The good omen I see now is like that of old.
This is an expedient employed by the Buddhas.
The present Buddha is also emitting a ray of light
In order to reveal the truth of the reality [of all things].

[Mañjuśrī said to the multitude:]

All of you, know this, join your hands together,
And wait with one mind!
The Buddha will send the rain of the Dharma
And satisfy those who seek enlightenment.

The Buddha will remove
Any doubt of those who seek
The teaching of the Three Vehicles.
No question will be left unresolved.

CHAPTER II

EXPEDIENTS

Thereupon the World-Honored One emerged quietly from his samādhi, and said to Śāriputra:

"The wisdom of the [present] Buddhas is profound and immeasurable. The gate to it is difficult to understand and difficult to enter. [Their wisdom] cannot be understood by any Śrāvaka or Pratyekabuddha because the [present] Buddhas attended on many hundreds of thousands of billions of [past] Buddhas, and practiced the innumerable teachings of those Buddhas bravely and strenuously to their far-flung fame until they attained the profound Dharma which you have never heard before, [and became Buddhas,] and also because [since they became Buddhas] they have been expounding the Dharma according to the capacities of all living beings in such various ways that the true purpose of their [various] teachings is difficult to understand.

"Śāriputra! Since I became a Buddha, I [also] have been expounding various teachings with various stories of previous lives, with various parables, and with various similes. I have been leading all living beings with innumerable expedients in order to save them from various attachments, because I have the power to employ expedients and the power to perform the pāramitā of insight.

"Śāriputra! The insight of the Tathāgatas is wide and deep. [The Tathāgatas] have all the [states of mind towards] innumerable [living beings,] unhindered [eloquence,] powers, fearlessness, dhyāna-concentrations, emancipations, and samādhis. They entered deep into boundlessness, and attained the Dharma which you have never heard before.

"Śāriputra! The Tathāgatas divide [the Dharma] into various teachings, and expound those teachings to all living beings so skillfully and with such gentle voices that living beings are delighted. Śāriputra! In short, the Buddhas attained the innumerable teachings which you have never heard before. No more, Śāriputra, will I say because the Dharma attained by the Buddhas is the highest Truth, rare [to hear] and difficult to understand. Only the Buddhas attained [the highest Truth, that is,] the reality of all things[1] in regard to their appearances as such, their natures as such, their entities as such, their powers as such, their activities as such, their primary causes as such, their environmental causes as such, their effects as such, their rewards and retributions as such, and their equality as such [despite these differences].

Thereupon the World-Honored One, wishing to repeat what he had said, sang in gāthās:

The [wisdom of the] World-Heroes is immeasurable.
None of the living beings in the world,
Including gods and men,
Knows the [wisdom of the] Buddhas.

No one can measure the powers, fearlessness,
Emancipations, samādhis,
And other properties of the [present] Buddhas,
Because they, in their previous existence,
Followed innumerable Buddhas
And practiced the teachings of those Buddhas.

The profound and wonderful Dharma
Is difficult to see and difficult to understand.
I practiced the teachings of the [past] Buddhas
For many hundreds of millions of kalpas,
And became a Buddha at the place of enlightenment.
I have already attained the Dharma.

1 諸法 "All things" here apparently denotes living beings, judging from the nine factors of them given below. But the all-inclusiveness of this expression gave room to the rise of the philosophy that non-living beings also have these nine factors.

I know the various effects, rewards and retributions,
Natures and appearances of all things.[2]
The Buddhas of the worlds of the ten quarters
Also know all this.

The Dharma cannot be shown.
It is inexplicable by words.
No one can understand it
Except the Buddhas
And the Bodhisattvas
Who are strong in the power of faith.

Even the Buddhas' disciples who made offerings
To the [past] Buddhas in their previous existence,
[Even the disciples] who eliminated all āsravas,
[Even the disciples] who are now at the final stage
Of their physical existence,
Cannot understand [the Dharma].

As many people as can fill the world,
Who are as wise as you, Śāriputra, will not be able
To measure the wisdom of the Buddhas,
Even though they try to do so with their combined efforts.

As many people as can fill the worlds of the ten quarters,
Who are as wise as you, Śāriputra,
Or as many other disciples of mine
As can fill the kṣetras of the ten quarters,
Will not be able to know [the wisdom of the Buddhas]
Even though they try to do so with their combined efforts.

As many Pratyekabuddhas as can fill
The worlds of the ten quarters, or as many as
bamboo groves,
Who are wise enough to reach

2 大果報種種性相義 Literally means, "great effects, rewards, various natures and appearances."

The final stage of their physical existence without āsravas,
Will not be able to know
Even a bit of the true wisdom of the Buddhas
Even though they continue trying to do so with all
their hearts
For many hundreds of millions of kalpas.

As many Bodhisattvas as rice-plants, hemps, bamboos
or reeds,
Or as can fill the kṣetras of the ten quarters,
Who have just begun to aspire for enlightenment,
Who made offerings to innumerable Buddhas in their
previous existence,
Who understand the meanings of the Dharma [in their
own ways],
And who are expounding the Dharma [as they
understand it],
Will not be able to know the wisdom of the Buddhas
Even though they continue trying to do so with
all their hearts
And with all their wonderful wisdom
For as many kalpas as there are sands in the River Ganges.

As many never-faltering Bodhisattvas
As there are sands in the River Ganges
Will not be able to know the wisdom of the Buddhas
Even though they try to do so with all their hearts.

(He said to Śāriputra again:)
I have already attained
The profound and wonderful Dharma,
The Dharma without āsravas, the inconceivable Dharma.
It is known only to me
And to the Buddhas of the worlds of the ten quarters.

Śāriputra, know this!
The Buddhas do not speak differently.

Have great power of faith
In the Dharma expounded by the Buddhas!
As a rule, the World-Honored Ones expound the
true teaching
Only after a long period [of expounding
expedient teachings].

(He said to the Śrāvakas
And to those who were seeking the vehicle
of cause-knowers:)
I saved all living beings
From the bonds of suffering,
And caused them to attain Nirvāṇa.
I showed to them
The teaching of the Three Vehicles as an expedient
In order to save them from various attachments.

The great multitude at that time included Śrāvakas. [They also included] Ājñāta-Kauṇḍinya, and other Arhats, twelve hundred[3] altogether, who had already eliminated āsravas. [They also included] the bhikṣus, bhikṣuṇīs, upāsakas, and upāsikās, [that is, the four kinds of devotees] who had already aspired for Śrāvakahood or Pratyekabuddhahood. All of them thought:

"Why does the World-Honored One extol so enthusiastically the power of the Buddhas to employ expedients? Why does he say that the Dharma attained by him is profound and difficult to understand, and that the true purpose of his teachings is too difficult for Śrāvakas and Pratyekabuddhas to know? He expounded to us the teaching of emancipation. We obtained this teaching and reached Nirvāṇa. We do not know why he says all this."

Thereupon Śāriputra, seeing the doubts of the four kinds of devotees, and also because he, himself, did not understand [why the Buddha had said this], said to the Buddha:

"World-Honored One! Why do you extol so enthusiastically [what you call] the highest [Truth, and the power of the Buddhas

3 "Twelve hundred" is given as "twelve thousand" in Chapter I.

to employ] expedients? [Why do you extol] the Dharma which [you say] is profound, wonderful, and difficult to understand? I have never heard you say all this before. The four kinds of devotees also have the same doubts. World-Honored One! Explain all this! Why do you extol so enthusiastically the Dharma which [you say] is profound, wonderful, and difficult to understand?"

Thereupon Śāriputra, wishing to repeat what he had said, sang in gāthās:

Sun of Wisdom, Great Honorable Saint!
You expound the Dharma for the first time
after a long time.
You say that you obtained
The powers, fearlessness, samādhis,
Dhyāna-concentrations, emancipations,
And other inconceivable properties [of a Buddha].

No one asks you about the Dharma you attained
At the place of enlightenment.
[The Dharma] is too difficult for me to measure.
[So it is for others; therefore,] no one asks you.

Although you are not asked, you extol the teachings
[Of the past Buddhas] which you practiced.
Your wisdom is wonderful.
It is the same wisdom that the other Buddhas obtained.

The Arhats-without-āsravas
And those who are seeking Nirvāṇa
Are now in the mesh of doubts, wondering:
"Why does the Buddha say all this?"

Those who are seeking the vehicle of cause-knowers,
And the bhikṣus, bhikṣuṇīs, gods, dragons,
Gandharvas, and other supernatural beings,
Are exchanging glances of perplexity.

They are looking up at you, at the Honorable Biped
Thinking:
"What is this for?
Buddha! Explain all this!"

You once said to me:
"You are the most excellent Śrāvaka."
With all my wisdom, however, I now doubt.
I do not understand
Whether the Truth I attained is final or not,
Whether the teachings I practiced are true or not.

Your sons born from your mouth are looking up at you
With their hands joined together, entreating:
"With your wonderful voice,
Explain all this as it really is!"

As many gods and dragons
As there are sands in the River Ganges,
And the eighty thousand Bodhisattvas
Who are seeking Buddhahood,
And the wheel-turning-holy-kings
Of billions of worlds
Are joining their hands together respectfully,
Wishing to hear the Perfect Way.

Thereupon the Buddha said to him, "No, no, I will not. If I do, all the gods and men in the world will be frightened and perplexed."

Śāriputra said to him again:

"World-Honored One! Explain it, explain it! The many hundreds of thousands of billions of asaṃkhyas of living beings in this congregation have active functions of mind and clear wisdom because they have seen the [past] Buddhas in their previous existence. If they hear you, they will respect and believe you."

Thereupon Śāriputra, wishing to repeat what he had said, sang in a gāthā:

King of the Dharma, Most Honorable One!
Explain it! Do not worry!
The innumerable living beings in this congregation
Will respect and believe you.

The Buddha checked him again, saying, "No. If I do, all the gods, men and asuras in the world will be frightened and perplexed, and arrogant bhikṣus will fall into a great pit."

Thereupon the Buddha repeated this in a gāthā:

No, no, I will not say any more.
My teaching is wonderful and inconceivable.
If arrogant people hear me,
They will not respect or believe me.

Thereupon Śāriputra said to him again:

"World-Honored One! Expound the Dharma, expound the Dharma! The hundreds of thousands of billions of living beings in this congregation like me followed the [past] Buddhas and received their teachings in their consecutive previous existences. They will respect and believe you. They will be able to have peace after the long night and obtain many benefits."

Thereupon Śāriputra, wishing to repeat what he had said, sang in gāthās:

Most Honorable Biped!
Expound the Highest Truth!
I am your eldest son.
Expound the Dharma!

The innumerable living beings in this congregation
Will respect and believe the Dharma.
They have been taught by the [past] Buddhas
In their consecutive previous existences.
They are joining their hands together [towards you],
Wishing with all their hearts to hear
and receive your words.

Expound the Dharma
To us twelve hundred men,
And also to the other people
Who are seeking Buddhahood!
We shall be very glad to hear the Dharma.
The other people will also.

Thereupon the World-Honored One said to him:

"You asked me three times with enthusiasm. How can I leave the Dharma unexpounded? Listen to me attentively, and think over my words! Now I will expound [the Dharma] to you."

When he had said this, five thousand people among the bhikṣus, bhikṣuṇīs, upāsakas, and upāsikās of this congregation rose from their seats, bowed to the Buddha, and retired because they were so sinful and arrogant that they thought that they had already obtained what they had not yet, and that they had already understood what they had not yet. Because of these faults, they did not stay. The World-Honored One kept silence and did not check them.

Thereupon the World-Honored One said to Śāriputra:

"Now this congregation has been cleared of twigs and leaves, only sincere people being left. Śāriputra! Those arrogant people may go. Now listen to me attentively! I will expound [the Dharma] to you."

Śāriputra said, "Certainly, World-Honored One! I wish to hear you."

The Buddha said to him:

"The Buddhas, the Tathāgatas, expound this Wonderful Dharma as rarely as the udumbara-flower blooms. Śāriputra! Believe what I am going to say! My words are not false.

"Śāriputra! The purpose of the various teachings that the Buddhas expound according to the capacities of all living beings is difficult to understand. I also expound various teachings with innumerable expedients, that is to say, with stories of previous lives, parables, similes and discourses. [The purpose of the various teachings of the Buddhas is difficult to understand] because the Dharma cannot be understood by reasoning. Only the Buddhas know the Dharma because the Buddhas, the World-Honored Ones, appear in the worlds only for one great purpose.

"Śāriputra! What is the one great purpose for which the Buddhas, the World-Honored Ones, appear in the worlds? The Buddhas, the World-Honored Ones, appear in the worlds in order to cause all living beings to open [the gate to] the insight of the Buddha, and to cause them to purify themselves. They appear in the worlds in order to show the insight of the Buddha to all living beings. They appear in the worlds in order to cause all living beings to obtain the insight of the Buddha. They appear in the worlds in order to cause all living beings to enter the Way to the insight of the Buddha. Śāriputra! This is the one great purpose for which the Buddhas appear in the worlds."

The Buddha said to Śāriputra:

"The Buddhas, the Tathāgatas, teach only Bodhisattvas. All they do is for one purpose, that is, to show the insight of the Buddha to all living beings, to cause them to obtain the insight of the Buddha.

"Śāriputra! I also expound various teachings to all living beings only for the purpose of revealing the One Buddha-Vehicle. There is no other vehicle, not a second or a third. Śāriputra! All the present Buddhas of the worlds of the ten quarters also do the same.

"Śāriputra! All the Buddhas in the past expounded various teachings to all living beings with innumerable expedients, that is to say, with stories of previous lives, parables, similes and discourses, only for the purpose of revealing the One Buddha-Vehicle. The living beings who heard those teachings from those Buddhas finally obtained the knowledge of the equality and differences of all things.

"Śāriputra! All the Buddhas who will appear in the future also will expound various teachings to all living beings with innumerable expedients, that is to say, with stories of previous lives, parables, similes and discourses, only for the purpose of revealing the One Buddha-Vehicle. The living beings who hear those teachings from those Buddhas also will finally obtain the knowledge of the equality and differences of all things.

"Śāriputra! The present Buddhas, the present World-Honored Ones, of many hundreds of thousands of billions of Buddha-worlds of the ten quarters benefit all living beings, and give them peace. These Buddhas also expound various teachings with innumerable expedients, that is to say, with stories of previous lives, parables, similes and discourses, only for the purpose of revealing the One Buddha-Vehicle. The living beings who hear the teachings from these Buddhas will also finally obtain the knowledge of the equality and differences of all things.

"Śāriputra! These [present] Buddhas teach only Bodhisattvas because they wish to show the insight of the Buddha to all living beings, to cause them to obtain the insight of the Buddha, and to cause them to enter the Way to the insight of the Buddha.

"Śāriputra! So do I. I know that all living beings have various desires. I also know that they have attachments deep in their minds. Therefore, I expound various teachings to them with stories of previous lives, parables, similes and discourses, that is to say, with various expedients according to their natures.

"Śāriputra! I do all this for the purpose of causing them to realize the teaching of the One Buddha-Vehicle, that is, to obtain the knowledge of the equality and differences of all things. Śāriputra! There is not a second vehicle in the worlds of the ten quarters. How can there be a third?

"Śāriputra! The Buddhas appear in the evil worlds in which there are the five defilements. The worlds are defiled by the decay of the kalpa, by illusions, by the deterioration of the living beings, by wrong views, and by the shortening of lives. Śāriputra! When a kalpa is in decay, the living beings [in that kalpa] are so full of illusions, so greedy, and so jealous that they plant many roots of evil. Therefore, the Buddhas divide the One Buddha-Vehicle into three as an expedient.

"Śāriputra! Some disciples of mine, who think that they are Arhats or Pratyekabuddhas, will not be my disciples or Arhats or Pratyekabuddhas if they do not hear or know that the Buddhas, the Tathāgatas, teach only Bodhisattvas.

"Śāriputra! Some bhikṣus and bhikṣuṇīs do not seek Anuttara-samyak-saṃbodhi because they think that they have already attained Arhatship, that they have already reached the final stage of their physical existence, and that the Nirvāṇa attained by them is the final one. Know this! They are arrogant because it cannot be that the bhikṣus who attained Arhatship do not believe the Dharma. Some bhikṣus who live in a period in which no Buddha lives after my extinction may not believe the Dharma after they attain Arhatship because in that period it will be difficult to meet a person who keeps, reads, and recites this sūtra, and understands the meanings of it. They will be able to understand the Dharma when they meet another Buddha.

"Śāriputra and all of you present here! Understand the Dharma by faith with all your hearts! There is no vehicle other than the One Buddha-Vehicle."

Thereupon the World-Honored One, wishing to repeat what he had said, sang in gāthās:

Some bhikṣus and bhikṣuṇīs
Were arrogant.
Some upāsakas were self-conceited.
Some upāsikās were unfaithful.
Those four kinds of devotees
Were five thousand in number.

They could not see their own faults.
They could not observe all the precepts.
They were reluctant to heal their own wounds.
Those people of little wisdom are gone.
They were the dregs of this congregation.
They were driven away by my powers and virtues.

They had too few merits and virtues
To receive the Dharma.
Now there are only sincere people here.
All twigs and leaves are gone.

Śāriputra, listen attentively!
The Buddhas, having attained the Dharma,
Expound it to all living beings
By their immeasurable power to employ expedients.

I caused all living beings to rejoice
By telling them stories of previous lives,
Parables, similes and discourses,
That is to say, by employing various expedients
Because I knew their thoughts,
The various teachings they were practicing,
Their desires, their natures,
And the good and evil karmas they have previously done.

The sūtras were composed of prose, gāthās, and geyas.
The contents of them were
Miracles, parables, similes, upadeśas,
And stories of the previous lives
Of Buddhas and of their disciples.
The reasons why the sūtras were expounded
were also given.[4]

I expounded the teaching of Nirvāṇa to the dull people
Who wished to hear the teachings of the Lesser Vehicle,
Who were attached to birth and death,
And who were troubled by many sufferings
Inflicted on them because they have not practiced
The profound and wonderful teachings under
innumerable Buddhas.

I expounded this expedient teaching in order to cause them
To enter the Way to the wisdom of the Buddha.
I never said to them:
"You will be able to attain the enlightenment of the
Buddha." I never said this
Because time was not yet ripe for it.
Now is the time to say it.
I will expound the Great Vehicle definitely.
I expounded various sūtras of the nine elements

4 或説修多羅伽陀及本事本生未曾有亦説於因縁譬喩井祇夜優婆提舎経 Literally means, "There were given prose or gāthās or stories of the previous lives of Bodhisattvas or stories of the previous lives of Buddhas or miracles or reasons or parables or similes or geyas or upadeśas."

According to the capacities of all living beings.
I expounded various sūtras
Because those sūtras were a basis for the Great Vehicle.

Some sons of mine are pure in heart, gentle and wise.
They have practiced the profound and wonderful teachings
Under innumerable Buddhas
[In their previous existence].
I will expound this sūtra of the Great Vehicle to them,
And assure them of their future Buddhahood, saying:
"You will attain the enlightenment of the Buddha
In your future lives."

Deep in their minds they are thinking of me,
And observing the pure precepts.
Therefore, they will be filled with joy
When they hear they will become Buddhas.
I know their minds.
Therefore, I will expound the Great Vehicle to them.

Any Śrāvaka or Bodhisattva
Who hears even a gāthā
Of this sūtra which I am to expound
Will undoubtedly become a Buddha.

There is only one teaching, that is, the One Vehicle
In the Buddha-worlds of the ten quarters.[5]
There is not a second or a third vehicle
Except when the Buddhas teach expediently.

The Buddhas lead all living beings
By tentative names [of vehicles]
In order to expound their wisdom.
They appear in the worlds
Only for the One Vehicle.

---

5 Here the worlds of the ten quarters include the Sahā-World. This usage is often seen hereafter.

Only this is true; the other two are not.
The Buddhas do not save living beings by
  the Lesser Vehicle.
They dwell in the Great Vehicle.
The Dharma they attained is adorned
With the power of concentration of mind
And with the power of wisdom.
They save all living beings by the Dharma.

I attained unsurpassed enlightenment,
The Great Vehicle, the Truth of Equality.
If I lead even a single man
By the Lesser Vehicle,
I shall be accused of stinginess.
It is not good at all to do this.

I do not deceive
Those who believe me and rely on me.
I am not greedy or jealous
Because I have eliminated all evils.
Therefore, in the worlds of the ten quarters,
I am fearless.

I am adorned with the physical marks of a Buddha.
I am illumining the world with my light.
To the countless living beings who honor me,
  I will expound
The seal of the truth, that is, the reality of all things.

Know this, Śāriputra!
I once vowed that I would cause
All living beings to become
Exactly as I am.

That old vow of mine
Has now been fulfilled.

I lead all living beings
Into the Way to Buddhahood.

Seeing people of no wisdom, I thought:
"If I teach them only the Way to Buddhahood,
They will be distracted.
They will doubt my teaching, and not receive it.
I know that they did not plant
The roots of good in their previous existence.
They are deeply attached to the five desires.
They suffer because of stupidity and cravings.
Because they have many desires,
They will fall into the three evil regions,
Or go from one to another of the six regions
Only to undergo many sufferings.
Through their consecutive previous existences,
Their small embryos have continued to grow up
To become men of few virtues and merits.
They are now troubled by many sufferings.
They are in the thick forests of wrong views.
They say "Things exist,"
Or "Things do not exist."
They are attached to sixty-two wrong views.
They are deeply attached to unreal things.
They hold them firmly, and do not give them up.
They are arrogant, self-conceited,
Liable to flatter others, and insincere.
They have never heard of the name of a Buddha
Or of his right teachings
For thousands of billions of kalpas.
It is difficult to save them."

Therefore, Śāriputra!
I expounded an expedient teaching
In order to eliminate their sufferings.
That was the teaching of Nirvāṇa.

The Nirvāṇa which I expounded to them
Was not true extinction.[6]

All things are from the outset
In the state of tranquil extinction.
The Buddhas' sons who complete the practice of the Way
Will become Buddhas in their future lives.

I expounded the teaching of the Three Vehicles
Only as an expedient.
All the other World-Honored Ones also
Expound the teaching of the One Vehicle [with expedients].

The great multitude present here
Shall remove their doubts.
The Buddhas do not speak differently.
There is only one vehicle, not a second.

The number of the Buddhas who passed away
During the past innumerable kalpas was
Hundreds of thousands of billions,
Uncountable.

All those World-Honored Ones expounded
The truth of the reality of all things
With various stories of previous lives, parables and similes,
That is to say, with innumerable expedients.

All those World-Honored Ones expounded
The teaching of the One Vehicle,
And led innumerable living beings [with expedients]
Into the Way to Buddhahood.

All those Great Saintly Masters
Who knew the deep desires

---

6 滅 Extinction. This is a translation of Nirvāṇa.

Of the gods, men, and other living beings
Of all the worlds,
Revealed the Highest Truth
With various expedients.

Those who met a past Buddha,
Who heard the Dharma from him,
And who obtained various merits and virtues
By almsgiving or by observing the precepts
Or by patience or by making endeavors
Or by dhyāna or by wisdom,
Have already attained
The enlightenment of the Buddha.

Those who, after the extinction of a Buddha,
Were good and gentle,[7]
Have already attained
The enlightenment of the Buddha.

Those who, after the extinction of a Buddha,
Erected billions of stūpas,
And who purely and extensively adorned [those stūpas]
With treasures
Such as gold, silver, crystal,
Shell, agate, ruby, and lapis lazuli,
And who offered those adornments to his śarīras;
Or those who made the mausoleum [of the Buddha]
With stone, bricks, or clay,
Or with many kinds of wood,
Such as candana, aloes, or agalloch;
Or those who made the mausoleum of the Buddha
With heaps of earth
In the wilderness;

7 This and the following lines, in which easy practices are given as the ways to attain the enlightenment of the Buddha, emphasize the importance of faith rather than of practice.

Or the boys who made the stūpa of the Buddha
With heaps of sand by playing,
Have already attained
The enlightenment of the Buddha.

Those who carved an image of the Buddha
With the [proper] physical marks in his honor
Have already attained
The enlightenment of the Buddha.

Those who made an image of the Buddha
With the seven treasures;
Or those who made it
Of copper, copper-gold alloy, nickel,
Pewter, lead, tin, iron, wood, or clay;
Or those who made it in plaster work,
Have already attained
The enlightenment of the Buddha.

Those who drew or caused others to draw in color
A picture of the Buddha adorned with his physical marks,
Each mark representing one hundred merits,
Have already attained the enlightenment of the Buddha.

The boys who by playing drew
A picture of the Buddha
With a piece of grass or wood,
Or with a brush,
Or with the back of their fingernails,
Became able to accumulate merits one by one.
Having great compassion towards others,
They attained the enlightenment of the Buddha,
Taught only Bodhisattvas,
And saved many living beings.

Those who respectfully offered
Flowers, incense, streamers, and canopies

To the image or picture of the Buddha
Enshrined in a stūpa-mausoleum;
Or those who caused men to make music
By beating drums, by blowing horns and conches,
And by playing reed-pipes, flutes, lyres, harps,
Lutes, gongs, and copper cymbals,
And offered the wonderful sounds produced thereby
To the image or picture of the Buddha;
Or those who sang joyfully in praise of him for his virtues;
Or those who just murmured [in praise of him],
Have already attained
The enlightenment of the Buddha.

Those who, without concentrating their minds,
Offered nothing but a flower to the picture of the Buddha,
Became able to see
Innumerable Buddhas one after another.

Those who bowed to the image of the Buddha,
Or just joined their hands together towards it,
Or raised only one hand towards it,
Or bent their heads a little towards it
And offered the bending to it,
Became able to see innumerable Buddhas one after another.
They attained unsurpassed enlightenment,
Saved countless living beings,
And entered into the Nirvāṇa-without-remainder
Just as fire dies out when wood is gone.

Those who entered a stūpa-mausoleum
And said only once "Namo Buddhāya,"
Without even concentrating their minds,
Have already attained the enlightenment of the Buddha.

Those who heard the Dharma
In the lifetime of a past Buddha

Or after his extinction
Have already attained the enlightenment of the Buddha.

The World-Honored Ones in the future
Will be countless in number.
Those Tathāgatas also
Will expound the Dharma with expedients.

The Tathāgatas save all living beings
With innumerable expedients.
They cause all living beings to enter the Way
To the wisdom-without-āsravas of the Buddha.
Anyone who hears the Dharma
Will not fail to become a Buddha.

Every Buddha vows at the outset:
"I will cause all living beings
To attain the same enlightenment
That I attained."

The future Buddhas will expound many thousands
Of myriads of millions of teachings
For just one purpose,
That is, for the purpose of revealing the One Vehicle.

The Buddhas, the Most Honorable Bipeds,
Expound the One Vehicle because they know:
"All things are devoid of substantiality.
The seed of Buddhahood comes from
dependent origination."

The Leading Teachers expound the Dharma
with expedients
After realizing at the place of enlightenment:
"This is the abode of the Dharma and the position
of the Dharma.
The reality of the world is permanently as it is."

Gods and men are making offerings
To the present Buddhas of the worlds of the ten quarters.
The Buddhas as many as there are sands in the
River Ganges
Who appeared in these worlds,
Are expounding the Dharma
For the purpose of giving peace to all living beings.

They know the Highest Truth of Tranquil Extinction.
They have the power to employ expedients.
Although they expound various teachings,
Their purpose is to reveal the Buddha-Vehicle.

Knowing the deeds of all living beings,
And their thoughts deep in their minds,
And the karmas they have done in their previous existence,
And their desires, natures, and powers to make efforts,
And also knowing whether each of them is keen or dull,
The Buddhas expound the Dharma according to
their capacities,
With various stories of previous lives, parables, similes
and discourses,
That is to say, with various expedients.

I also do the same.
I show the enlightenment of the Buddha
With various teachings
In order to give peace to all living beings.

I know the natures and desires of all living beings
By the power of my wisdom.
Therefore, I expound various teachings expediently,
And cause all living beings to rejoice.

Śāriputra, know this!
Seeing with the eyes of the Buddha
The living beings of the six regions, I thought:

"They are poor, and devoid of merits and wisdom.
They incessantly suffer because they are taken
To the rough road of birth and death.
They cling to the five desires
Just as a yak loves its tail.
They are occupied with greed and cravings,
And blinded by them.
They do not seek the Buddha who has great power.
They do not seek the Way to eliminate sufferings.
They are deeply attached to wrong views.
They are trying to stop suffering by suffering."

My great compassion was aroused towards them.
I for the first time sat at the place of enlightenment[,]
[And attained enlightenment].
For three weeks afterwards,
I gazed on the tree,
Or walked about, thinking:
"The wisdom I obtained is
The most wonderful and excellent.
The living beings [of the six regions]
Are dull, attached to pleasures,
And blinded by stupidity.
How shall I save them?"

On that occasion King Brahman,
Heavenly-King Śakra,
The four heavenly world-guardian kings,
Great-Freedom God, and other gods [of each world],
And thousands of millions of their attendants
Joined their hands together [towards me] respectfully,
Bowed to me,
And asked me to turn the wheel of the Dharma.

I thought:
"If I extol only the Buddha-Vehicle,
The living beings [of the six regions] will not believe it

Because they are too much enmeshed in sufferings
to think of it.
If they do not believe but violate the Dharma,
They will fall into the three evil regions.
I would rather enter into Nirvāṇa[8] quickly
Than expound the Dharma to them."

But, thinking of the past Buddhas
who employed expedients,
I changed my mind and thought:
"I will expound the Dharma which I attained
By dividing it into the Three Vehicles."

The Buddhas of the worlds of the ten quarters
Appeared before me when I had thought this.
They consoled me with their brahma voices:
"Good, Śākyamuni, Highest Leading Teacher!
You attained the unsurpassed Dharma.
You have decided to expound it with expedients
After the examples of the past Buddhas.
We also expound the Three Vehicles
To the living beings
Although we attained
The most wonderful and excellent Dharma.
Men of little wisdom wish to hear
The teachings of the Lesser Vehicle.
They do not believe that they will become Buddhas.
Therefore, we show them
Various fruits of enlightenment.
Although we expound the Three Vehicles,
Our purpose is to teach only Bodhisattvas."

Śāriputra, know this!
Hearing the deep, pure, and wonderful voices
Of the Lion-Like Saints,
I joyfully called out, "Namo Buddhāya!"

---

8 "Nirvāṇa" means "Parinirvāṇa."

I thought:
"I appeared in the defiled world.
Just like the other Buddhas,
I will expound the Dharma
According to the capacities of all living beings."
Having thought this, I went to Vārāṇasī,
And expounded the Dharma to the five bhikṣus
With expedients
Because the state of tranquil extinction of all things
Is inexplicable by words.

That was my first turning
Of the wheel of the Dharma.
Thus the words: Nirvāṇa, Arhat, Dharma,
and Saṃgha
Came into existence.

I said to them:
"For the past innumerable kalpas
I have been extolling the teaching of Nirvāṇa
In order to eliminate the sufferings of birth
and death."

Śāriputra, know this!
Then I saw many sons of mine,
Thousands of billions in number,
Seeking the enlightenment of the Buddha.
They came to me respectfully.
They had already heard
Expedient teachings
From the past Buddhas.

I thought:
"I appeared in this world
In order to expound my wisdom.
Now is the time to do this."

Śāriputra, know this!
Men of dull capacity and of little wisdom cannot
believe the Dharma.
Those who are attached to the appearances of things
are arrogant.
They cannot believe it, either.

I am now joyful and fearless.
I have laid aside all expedient teachings.
I will expound only unsurpassed enlightenment
To Bodhisattvas.

The Bodhisattvas who hear the Dharma
Will be able to remove the mesh of doubts.
The twelve hundred Arhats also
Will become Buddhas.

All the Buddhas in the past, present, and future
Expounded, are expounding, and will expound
In the same manner the Dharma beyond comprehension.
I also will expound it in the same manner.

The Buddhas seldom appear in the worlds.
It is difficult to meet them.
Even when they do appear in the worlds,
They seldom expound the Dharma.

It is difficult to hear the Dharma
Even during innumerable kalpas.
It is also difficult to meet a person
Who listens to the Dharma attentively.
It is as difficult as seeing an udumbara-flower.
This flower, loved by all living beings,
And treasured by gods and men,
Blooms only once in a long time.

Anyone who rejoices at hearing the Dharma
And utters even a single word in praise of it
Should be considered to have already made offerings
To the past, present, and future Buddhas.
Such a person is rarely seen,
More rarely than the udumbara-flower.

[The Buddha said to the great multitude:]

All of you, do not doubt me!
I am the King of the Dharma.
I say to you:
"I will expound the teaching of the One Vehicle
Only to Bodhisattvas.
There is no Śrāvaka among my disciples."

Śāriputra, other Śrāvakas, and Bodhisattvas!
Know this!
This Wonderful Dharma is
The hidden core of the Buddhas.

The living beings
In the evil world of the five defilements
Are attached to many desires.
They do not seek the enlightenment of the Buddha.

Evil people in the future will doubt the One Vehicle
When they hear it from a Buddha.
They will not believe or receive it.
They will violate the Dharma, and fall into the evil regions.

Extol the teaching of the One Vehicle
In the presence of those who are modest,
Who are pure in heart,
And who are seeking the enlightenment
of the Buddha!

Śāriputra [and others], know this!
As a rule, the Buddhas expound the Dharma
With billions of expedients as stated above,
According to the capacities of all living beings.

Those who do not study the Dharma
Cannot understand it.
You have already realized
The fact that the Buddhas, the World-Teachers,
    employ expedients,
According to the capacities of all living beings.
Know that, when you remove your doubts,
And when you have great joy,
You will become Buddhas!

[Here ends] the First Volume of the Sūtra of the Lotus Flower of the Wonderful Dharma.

CHAPTER III

A PARABLE

Thereupon Śāriputra, who felt like dancing with joy, stood up, joined his hands together, looked up at the honorable face, and said to the Buddha:

"Hearing this truthful voice of yours, I feel like dancing [with joy]. I have never felt like this before. Why is that? We [Śrāvakas and the Bodhisattvas] heard this Dharma before. [At that time] we saw that the Bodhisattvas were assured of their future Buddhahood, but not that we were. We deeply regretted that we were not given the immeasurable insight of the Tathāgata.

"World-Honored One! I sat alone under a tree or walked about mountains and forests, thinking, 'We [and the Bodhisattvas] entered the same world of the Dharma. Why does the Tathāgata save us only by the teachings of the Lesser Vehicle?'

"Now I understand that the fault was on our side, not on yours, because if we had waited for your expounding of the Way to Anuttara-samyak-saṃbodhi, we would have been saved by the Great Vehicle. When we heard your first teaching, we did not know that that teaching was an expedient one expounded according to our capacities. Therefore, we believed and received that teaching at once, thought it over, and attained the enlightenment [to be attained by that teaching].

"World-Honored One! I reproached myself day and night [after I saw that the Bodhisattvas were assured of their future Buddhahood]. Now I have heard from you the Dharma that I had never heard before. I have removed all my doubts. I am now calm and peaceful in body and mind. Today I have realized that I am your son, that I was born from your mouth, that I was born in [the world of] the Dharma, and that I have obtained the Dharma of the Buddha."

Thereupon Śāriputra, wishing to repeat what he had said, sang in gāthās:

Hearing this truthful voice,
I have the greatest joy
That I have ever had.
I have removed all the mesh of doubts.

You have taught us the Great Vehicle
 without a break from of old.
Your voice is rare to hear.
It dispels the sufferings of all living beings.
I once eliminated āsravas.
Hearing this voice of yours,
I have now removed all sorrows.

I walked about mountains and valleys,
Or sat under a tree in a forest, thinking this over.
I reproached myself with a deep sigh:
"Why was I deceived?
We also are sons of the Buddha
[Just as the Bodhisattvas are].
We entered the same [world]
[Of the] Dharma-without-āsravas.
But we shall not be able to expound
Unsurpassed enlightenment in the future.
We are in the same [world of the] Dharma.
But we shall not be given
The golden body with the thirty-two marks,
The ten powers, and the emancipations [of the Buddha].
We are deprived of the hope
To have the eighty wonderful marks,
The eighteen unique properties
And the other merits [of the Buddha]."

[Sitting] in the midst of the great multitude,
You benefited all living beings.
Your fame extended over the worlds of the ten quarters.
When I was walking alone,
I saw all this, and thought:
"I am not given this benefit. I have been deceived."

I thought this over day and night,
And wished to ask you,
"Am I disqualified
[From having this benefit] or not?"

I always saw you praising the Bodhisattvas.
Therefore, I thought this over day and night.
Now hearing from you,
I understand that you expound the Dharma
According to the capacities of all living beings.
You lead all living beings
To the place of enlightenment
By the Dharma-without-āsravas, difficult to understand.

I once was attached to wrong views,
And became a teacher of the aspirants
 for the teaching of Brahman.
You expounded to me the teaching of Nirvāṇa,
And removed my wrong views because
 you understood me.
I gave up all those wrong views,
And attained the truth that nothing is substantial.

At that time I thought
That I had attained extinction.[1]
But now I know
That the extinction I attained is not the true one.
When I become a Buddha in the future,
I shall be adorned with the thirty-two marks,

1 This is Nirvāṇa.

And respected
By gods, men, yakṣas, and dragons.
Only then I shall be able to say
That I have eliminated all [illusions].

In the midst of the great multitude,
You said to me, "You will become a Buddha."
Hearing this truthful voice,
All my doubts are gone.

When I had heard this from you,
I was much frightened and perplexed; I thought:
"The Buddha troubles me.
Isn't he Māra in the form of a Buddha?"

You skillfully expound the Dharma
    with various parables and similes,
And with various stories of previous lives.
Now my mind is as peaceful as the sea.
Hearing you, I have removed the mesh of doubts.

You said:
"The innumerable Buddhas in the past
Expounded the Dharma with expedients.
The numberless Buddhas at present
Also expound the Dharma
With expedients.
So will the countless Buddhas
In the future."

You appeared in this world,
Left your home, attained enlightenment,
And now turn the wheel of the Dharma,
Also with expedients.

You expound the true teaching;
Pāpīyas does not.

Therefore, I know
That you are not a transformation of Māra.
I thought that the Dharma was expounded by Māra
Because I was in the mesh of doubts.

I hear your gentle voice.
Your voice is deep and wonderful.
You expound the Pure Dharma.
My heart is filled with great joy.
All my doubts are gone.
I have obtained true wisdom.

I shall become a Buddha without fail.
I shall be respected by gods and men.
I will turn the wheel of the unsurpassed Dharma,
And teach Bodhisattvas.

Thereupon the Buddha said to Śāriputra:

"Now I will tell you in the presence of this great multitude including gods, men, śramaṇas, and brāhmaṇas. Under two billion Buddhas in the past, I always taught you in order to cause you to attain unsurpassed enlightenment. You studied under me in the long night. I led you with expedients. Therefore, you have your present life under me.

"Śāriputra! I caused you to aspire for the enlightenment of the Buddha in your previous existence. You forgot all this, and thought that you had already attained extinction.[2] In order to cause you to remember the Way you practiced under your original vow, I now expound to the Śrāvakas this sūtra of the Great Vehicle called the 'Lotus Flower of the Wonderful Dharma, the Dharma for Bodhisattvas, the Dharma Upheld by the Buddhas.'

"Śāriputra! After a countless, inconceivable number[3] of kalpas from now, you will be able to make offerings to many thousands of billions of Buddhas, to keep their right teachings, to practice the Way which Bodhisattvas should practice, and to become

2 This is Nirvāṇa.

3 In spite of the expression, this is a finite number.

a Buddha called Flower-Light, the Tathāgata, the Deserver of Offerings, the Perfectly Enlightened One, the Man of Wisdom and Practice, the Well-Gone, the Knower of the World, the Unsurpassed Man, the Controller of Men, the Teacher of Gods and Men, the Buddha, the World-Honored One. The world of that Buddha will be called Free-From-Taint. That world will be even, pure, adorned, peaceful, and fertile, where gods and men will prosper. The ground of that world will be made of lapis lazuli; the roads will fan out from the center to the eight directions. Those roads will be marked off by ropes of gold, and the trees of the seven treasures on the roadsides will always bear flowers and fruit. Flower-Light Tathāgata will also lead the living beings [of his world] by the teaching of the Three Vehicles.

"Śāriputra! Although the world in which he appears will not be an evil one, that Buddha will expound the teaching of the Three Vehicles according to his original vow. The kalpa in which he appears will be called Great-Treasure-Adornment. Why will it be called Great-Treasure-Adornment? It is because in that world Bodhisattvas will be regarded as great treasures. The number of the Bodhisattvas [in that world] will be countless, inconceivable, beyond any mathematical calculation, beyond inference by any parable or simile. No one will know the number except the Buddha who has the power of wisdom. When those Bodhisattvas wish to go somewhere, jeweled flowers will receive their feet and carry them. Those Bodhisattvas will not have just begun to aspire for enlightenment. A long time before that they will have already planted the roots of virtue, performed the brahma practices under many hundreds of thousands of billions of Buddhas, received the praises of the Buddhas, studied the wisdom of the Buddhas, obtained great supernatural powers, and understood all the teachings of the Buddhas. They will be upright, honest, and resolute in mind. The world of that Buddha will be filled with such Bodhisattvas.

"Śāriputra! The duration of the life of Flower-Light Buddha will be twelve small kalpas excluding the period in which he was a prince and had not yet attained Buddhahood. The duration of the life of the people of his world will be eight small kalpas.

At the end of his life of twelve small kalpas, Flower-Light Tathāgata will assure Resolution-Fulfillment Bodhisattva of his future attainment of Anuttara-samyak-saṃbodhi, saying to the bhikṣus, 'This Resolution-Fulfillment Bodhisattva will become a Buddha immediately after me. He will be called Flower-Foot-Easy-Walking, the Tathāgata, the Arhat, the Samyak-saṃbuddha. His world will be like mine.'

"Śāriputra! After the extinction of Flower-Light Buddha, his right teachings will be preserved for thirty-two small kalpas. After that the counterfeit of his right teachings will be preserved also for thirty-two small kalpas."

Thereupon the World-Honored One, wishing to repeat what he had said, sang in gāthās:

Śāriputra! In your future life you will become
A Buddha, an Honorable One of Universal Wisdom,
Called Flower-Light,
And save innumerable living beings.

You will make offerings to innumerable Buddhas.
You will perform the Bodhisattva practices.
You will obtain the ten powers and the other merits,
And attain unsurpassed enlightenment.

The kalpa [of that Buddha] will come
after innumerable[4] kalpas from now.
It will be called Great-Treasure-Adornment.
The world [of that Buddha] will be called Free-From-Taint.
It will be pure and undefiled.
Its ground will be made of lapis lazuli.
Its roads will be marked off by ropes of gold.
Its trees of the various colors of the seven treasures
Will always bear flowers and fruit.

The Bodhisattvas of that world
Will always be resolute in mind.

4 This "innumerable" is finite.

They will have already obtained
The supernatural powers and the pāramitās.
They will have already studied the Way of Bodhisattvas
Under innumerable Buddhas.
Those great people will be taught
By the Flower-Light Buddha.

That Buddha will appear in his world at first as a prince.
The prince will give up his princeship and worldly fame.
He will renounce the world at the end of his life
as a layman,
And attain the enlightenment of the Buddha.

The duration of the life of Flower-Light Buddha
Will be twelve small kalpas.
The duration of the life of the people of his world
Will be eight small kalpas.

After the extinction of that Buddha,
His right teachings will be preserved
For thirty-two small kalpas.
All living beings will be saved [by his right teachings].

After the end of the period of his right teachings,
The counterfeit of them will last for thirty-two
[small kalpas].
His śarīras will be distributed far and wide.
Gods and men will make offerings to them.

These will be the deeds
Of Flower-Light Buddha.
That Honorable Biped will be
The most excellent one without a parallel.
You will be he.
Rejoice!

At that time the great multitude included bhikṣus, bhikṣuṇīs, upāsakas and upāsikās, that is, the four kinds of devotees; and gods, dragons, yakṣas, gandharvas, asuras, garuḍas, kiṃnaras and mahoragas. When they saw that Śāriputra was assured of his future attainment of Anuttara-samyak-saṃbodhi by the Buddha, they danced with great joy. They took off their garments and offered them to the Buddha. Śakra-Devānām-Indra, the Brahman Heavenly-King, and innumerable other gods also offered their wonderful heavenly garments and the heavenly flowers of mandāravas and mahā-mandāravas to the Buddha. The heavenly garments, which had been released from the hands of the gods, whirled in the sky. The gods simultaneously made many thousands of millions of kinds of music in the sky, and caused many heavenly flowers to rain down.

They said, "The Buddha turned the first wheel of the Dharma at Vārāṇasī a long time ago. Now he turns the wheel of the unsurpassed and greatest Dharma."

Thereupon the gods, wishing to repeat what they had said, sang in gāthās:

The Buddha turned the wheel of the teaching
  of the Four Truths
At Vārāṇasī a long time ago.
He taught that all things are composed
  of the five aggregates
And that they are subject to rise and extinction.

Now he turns the wheel of the Dharma,
The most wonderful, unsurpassed, and greatest.
The Dharma is profound.
Few believe it.
So far we have heard
Many teachings of the World-Honored One.
But we have never heard
Such a profound, wonderful, and excellent teaching as this.
We are very glad to hear this
From the World-Honored One.

Śāriputra, a man of great wisdom,
Was assured of his future Buddhahood.
We also shall be able
To become Buddhas,
And to receive
The highest and unsurpassed honor
in the world.

The Buddha expounds his enlightenment,
difficult to understand,
With expedients according to the capacities
of all living beings.
We obtained merits by the good karmas
which we did
In this life of ours and in our previous existence.
We also obtained merits by seeing the Buddha.
May we attain the enlightenment of the Buddha
by these merits!

Thereupon Śāriputra said to the Buddha:

"World-Honored One! Now my doubts are gone. You assured me of my future attainment of Anuttara-samyak-saṃbodhi. These twelve hundred people now have freedom of mind. When they had something more to learn, [that is to say, when they had not yet completed their study for Arhatship,] you taught them, saying, 'My teaching is for the purpose of causing you to emancipate yourselves from birth, old age, disease, and death, and to attain Nirvāṇa.' The [two thousand] people, including those who have something more to learn and those who have nothing more to learn, also think that they attained Nirvāṇa because they emancipated themselves from such a view as 'I exist,' or 'I shall exist forever,' or 'I shall cease to exist.' But [both the twelve hundred people and the two thousand people] are now quite perplexed because they have heard from you [the Dharma] which they had never heard before. World-Honored One! In order to cause the four kinds of devotees to remove their doubts, explain why you said all this to them! "

Thereupon the Buddha said to Śāriputra:

"Did I not tell you, 'The Buddhas, the World-Honored Ones, expound the Dharma with expedients, that is, with various stories of previous lives, with various parables, with various similes, and with various discourses only for the purpose of causing all living beings to attain Anuttara-samyak-saṃbodhi'? All these teachings of the Buddhas are for the purpose of teaching Bodhisattvas. Śāriputra! Now I will explain this with a parable. Those who have wisdom will be able to understand the reason if they hear the following parable.

"Śāriputra! Suppose there lived a very rich man in a certain country, in a certain village, in a certain town. He was old. His wealth was immeasurable. He had many paddy fields, houses, and servants. His manor house was large, but had only one gate. In that house lived many people, numbering a hundred or two hundred or five hundred. The buildings were in decay, the fences and walls corrupt, the bases of the pillars rotten, and the beams and ridgepoles tilting and slanted.[5]

"All of a sudden fires broke out at the same time from all sides of the house, and it began to burn. In this house lived children of the rich man, numbering ten or twenty or thirty. The rich man was very frightened at the great fires breaking out from the four sides of the house. He thought, 'I am able to get out of the gate of the burning house safely, but my children are still inside. They are engrossed in playing. They do not know that the fires are coming towards them. They are not frightened or afraid. They are about to suffer, but do not mind. They do not wish to get out.' Śāriputra! He also thought, 'I am strong-muscled. I will put them in a flower-plate or on a table and bring them out.'

"But he thought again, 'This house has only one gate. Worse still, the gate is narrow and small. My children are too young to know this. They are attached to the place where they are playing. They may fall [out of the plate or table] and get burned. I had better tell them of the danger. This house is already burning. They must come out quickly so as not to be burned to death.'

---

5 The house represents the realities of the triple world. It does not reflect the wealth of the owner.

"Having thought this, he said to his children as he had thought, 'Come out quickly!' He warned them with these good words out of his compassion towards them, but they were too much engrossed in playing to hear the words of their father. They were not frightened or afraid. They did not wish to come out. They did not know what a fire was, what a house was, and what they would lose. They ran about happily. They only glanced at their father occasionally.

"Thereupon the rich man thought, 'This house will be burned down soon by this great fire. If they and I do not get out at once,[6] we shall be burned. I will save them from this danger with an expedient.'

"An idea came to his mind that his children would be attracted by the various toys which they wished to have. He said to them, 'The toys you wish to have are rare and difficult to obtain. You will be sorry if you do not get them now. There are sheep-carts, deer-carts, and bullock-carts outside the gate. You can play with them. Come out of this burning house quickly! I will give you any of them according to your wishes.'

"Hearing of the toys from their father, the children rushed quickly out of the burning house, pushing one another, and striving to be first, because they thought that they could get what they each wished to have. The rich man, who saw them having come out safely and sitting in the open on the crossroad with no more hindrance, felt relieved and danced with joy. They said to their father, 'Father! Give us the toys! Give us the sheep-carts, deer-carts, and bullock-carts you promised us!'

"Śāriputra! Then the rich man gave each of them a large cart of the same size. The cart was tall, wide and deep, adorned with many treasures, surrounded by railings, and having bells hanging on the four sides. A canopy adorned with rare treasures was fixed on the top of it. Garlands of flowers, tied with jeweled ropes, were hanging from the canopy. In the cart were quilts spread one on another, and a red pillow. The cart was yoked with white bullocks. The color of the skin of the white bullocks was bright; their build, beautiful and stout; and their pace, regular. They

---

6 It is understood that the father was in the house at that time.

could run as swift as the wind. The cart was guarded by many attendants. [This great rich man gave one of these carts to each of his children] because his wealth was so immeasurable that his various storehouses were full [of treasures]. He thought, 'My treasures are limitless. I should not give inferior, smaller carts to them. They are all my children. Therefore, I love them without partiality. I have a countless number of these large carts of the seven treasures. I gave one of these to each of my children equally. There should be no discrimination. The large carts are numerous enough to be given to all the people of this country. Needless to say, I can give them to my sons. [Therefore, I did.]'

"The children rode in the large carts, and had the greatest joy that they had ever had because they had never expected to get them. Śāriputra! What do you think of this? Do you think that the rich man was guilty of falsehood when he gave his children the large carts of treasures?"

Śāriputra said:

"No, World-Honored One! He saved his children from the fire and caused them to survive. [Even if he had not given them anything,] he should not have been accused of falsehood because the children should be considered to have already been given the toys [they had wished to have] when they survived. He saved them from the burning house with the expedient. World-Honored One! Even if he had not given them the smallest cart, he should not have been accused of falsehood because he thought at first, 'I will cause them to get out with an expedient.' Because of this, he should not. Needless to say, he was not guilty of falsehood when he remembered his immeasurable wealth and gave them the large carts in order to benefit them."

The Buddha said to Śāriputra:

"So it is, so it is. It is just as you say. Śāriputra! The same can be said of me. [I thought, ']I am the father of the world. I eliminated fear, despondency, grief, ignorance and darkness. I obtained immeasurable insight, powers and fearlessness. I have great supernatural powers, the power of wisdom, the pāramitā of expedients, the pāramitā of wisdom, great compassion, and great loving-kindness. I am not tired of seeking good things or of benefiting all living beings. I have appeared in the triple world, which can be likened to the rotten and burning house, in order to save all living beings from the fires of birth, old age, disease, death, grief, sorrow, suffering, lamentation, stupidity, darkness, and the three poisons, to teach all living beings, and to cause them to attain Anuttara-samyak-saṃbodhi. I see that all living beings are burned by the fires of birth, old age, disease, death, grief, sorrow, suffering and lamentation. They undergo various sufferings because they have the five desires and the desire for gain. Because they have attachments and pursuits, they have many sufferings in their present existence, and will suffer in hell or in the world of animals or in the world of hungry spirits in their future lives. Even when they are reborn in heaven or in the world of humans, they will still have many sufferings such as poverty or parting from their beloved ones or meeting with those whom they hate. Notwithstanding all this, however, they are playing joyfully. They are not conscious of the sufferings. They are not frightened at the sufferings or afraid of them. They do not dislike them or try to get rid of them. They are running about this burning house of the triple world, and do not mind even when they undergo great sufferings.[']

"Śāriputra! Seeing all this, I [also] thought, 'I am the father of all living beings. I will eliminate their sufferings, give them the pleasure of the immeasurable wisdom of the Buddha, and cause them to enjoy it.'

"Śāriputra! I also thought, 'If I extol my insight, powers, and fearlessness in the presence of those living beings only by my supernatural powers and by the power of my wisdom, that is to say, without any expedient, they will not be saved because they have not yet been saved from birth, old age, disease, death, grief, sorrow, suffering and lamentation, but are burning up in the burning house of the triple world. How can they understand the wisdom of the Buddha?'

"Śāriputra! The rich man did not save his children by his muscular power although he was strong enough. He saved them from the burning house with a skilful expedient and later gave them each a large cart of treasures.

"In the same manner, I save all living beings from the burning house of the triple world, not by my powers or fearlessness, but with a skillful expedient. I expounded the teaching of the Three Vehicles: the Śrāvaka-Vehicle, Pratyekabuddha-Vehicle, and Buddha-Vehicle, as an expedient. I said, 'Do not wish to live in the burning house of the triple world! Do not crave for inferior forms, sounds, smells, tastes or things tangible! If you cling to them and crave for them, you will be burned by them. Get out of the triple world quickly and obtain the teaching of the Three Vehicles: the Śrāvaka-Vehicle, Pratyekabuddha-Vehicle, and Buddha-Vehicle! I now assure you that you will never fail [to obtain those vehicles]. Exert yourselves, make efforts!'

"With this expedient, I caused them to advance. I said to them again, 'Know this! This teaching of the Three Vehicles is extolled by the saints.[7] This teaching saves you from any attachment or bond or desire. Ride in these Three Vehicles, eliminate āsravas, obtain the [five] faculties, the [five] powers, the [seven] ways to enlightenment, and the [eight right] ways, and practice dhyāna-concentrations, emancipations, and samādhis so that you may be able to enjoy immeasurable peace and pleasure!'

"Śāriputra! Those who have intelligence, who receive the Dharma by faith after hearing it from the Buddha, from the World-Honored One, and who seek Nirvāṇa with strenuous efforts in order to get out of the triple world, are called Śrāvakas. They may be likened to the children who left the burning house in order to get the sheep-carts. Those who receive the Dharma by faith after hearing it from the Buddha, from the World-Honored One, who seek the self-originating wisdom with strenuous efforts, who wish to have good tranquility in seclusion, and who perfectly understand the causes of all things, are called Pratyekabuddhas. They may be likened to the children who left the burning house in order to get the deer-carts. Those who receive the Dharma by faith after hearing it from the Buddha, from the World-Honored One, who

7 "The saints" stands for the Buddhas.

strenuously seek the knowledge of all things, the wisdom of the Buddha, the self-originating wisdom, the wisdom to be obtained without teachers, and the insight and powers and fearlessness of the Tathāgata, who give peace to innumerable living beings out of their compassion towards them, and who benefit gods and men, that is to say, who save all living beings, are called men of the Great Vehicle. Bodhisattvas are called Mahāsattvas because they seek this vehicle. They may be likened to the children who left the burning house in order to get the bullock-carts.

"Śāriputra! Seeing that all his children had come out of the burning house safely and reached a carefree place, the rich man remembered that he had immeasurable wealth. So without partiality, he gave them each a large cart. I am also a father, the father of all living beings. Seeing that many hundreds of thousands of millions of living beings have come out of the painful, fearful and rough road of the triple world through the gate of the teachings of the Buddha, and obtained the pleasure of Nirvāṇa, I thought, 'I have the store of the Dharma in which the immeasurable wisdom, powers and fearlessness of the Buddhas are housed. These living beings are all my children. I will give them the Great Vehicle. I will not cause them to attain extinction[8] by their own ways. I will cause them to attain the extinction of the Tathāgata.'

"To those who have left the triple world, I will give the dhyāna-concentrations and emancipations of the Buddhas for their pleasure. These things are of the same nature and of the same species. These things are extolled by the saints[9] because these things bring the purest and most wonderful pleasure.

"Śāriputra! The rich man persuaded his children to come out at first by promising them the gifts of the three kinds of carts. But the carts which he gave them later were the largest and most comfortable carts adorned with treasures. In spite of this, the rich man was not accused of falsehood. Neither am I. I led all living beings at first with the teaching of the Three Vehicles. Now I will save them by the Great Vehicle only. Why is that? It is because, if

---

8 This is Nirvāṇa.

9 "The saints" stands for the Buddhas.

I had given them the teaching of the Great Vehicle at first directly from my store of the Dharma in which my immeasurable wisdom, powers and fearlessness are housed, they would not have received all of the Dharma. Śāriputra! Therefore, know this! The Buddhas divide the One Buddha-Vehicle into three by their power to employ expedients."

Thereupon the Buddha, wishing to repeat what he had said, sang in gāthās:

I will tell you a parable.
A rich man had a manor house.
It was old, rotten,
Broken and ruined.
The house was about to collapse.
The lower parts of the pillars were rotten;
The beams and ridge-poles, tilting and slanted;
The foundation and steps, broken;
The fences and walls, corrupt;
The plaster of the walls, peeling;
The rush thatched on the roof, falling;
The rafters and eaves, slipping out of each other;
The hedges around the house, bent;
And refuse and debris, scattered all over.

In this house lived
Five hundred people.[10]
Kites, owls, crested eagles,
Eagles, crows,
Magpies, doves, pigeons,
Lizards, snakes, vipers, scorpions,
Millipedes, wall lizards, centipedes,
Weasels, badgers, mice, rats,
And poisonous vermin
Were moving about.

10 This is inconsistent with "a hundred or two hundred or five hundred" previously.

Maggots and other vermin
Assembled on the excretions
Scattered all over
In the house.

Foxes, wolves, and small foxes
Were crawling on corpses,
Biting them, chewing them,
And dismembering them.

Many dogs were scrambling for their prey.
Weak and nervous from hunger,
They were seeking food here and there.
They were fighting with each other,
Snapping at each other,
And barking at each other.
The house was
So dreadful, so extraordinary.

Mountain spirits, water spirits,
Yakṣas and other demons
Lived here and there.
They fed on people and poisonous vermin.

Wild birds and beasts
Hatched their eggs,
Suckled or bred.
They protected their offspring.
Yakṣas scrambled for their young,
Took them, and ate them.
Having eaten to their hearts' content,
They became more violent.
They fought with each other.
Their shrieks were dreadful.

The demons called kumbhāṇḍas
Crouched on the ground

Or jumped a foot or two above the ground.
They walked to and fro
And played at their will.
They seized dogs by the legs,
Or hit them
Until they lost their voices,
And held their feet against their necks.
They enjoyed seeing them frightened.

Some demons,
Tall, large,
Naked, black, and thin,
Lived in the house.
They were crying for food
With loud and evil voices.

The necks of some demons
Were as slender as needles.
The heads of some demons
Were like that of a cow.
They ate people or dogs.
Their hair was disheveled
Like mugworts.
They were cruel and dangerous.
Always hungry and thirsty,
They were running about, shrieking.

Yakṣas, hungry spirits,
And wild birds and beasts
Were unbearably hungry.
They were looking out of the windows
In all directions for food.
The house was so dangerous, so dreadful.

This old and rotten house
Was owned by a man.

Shortly after he went out
To a place in the neighborhood,[11]
Fires broke out suddenly
In the house.

Raging flames came out
Of all sides at the same time.
The ridges, rafters,
Beams and pillars
Burst, quaked, split, broke and fell.
The fences and walls also fell.

All the demons yelled.
The eagles, crested eagles,
And other birds, and kumbhāṇḍas
Were frightened and perplexed.
They did not know
How to get out of the house.
The wild beasts and poisonous vermin
Hid themselves in holes.

In that house also lived
Demons called piśācakas.
Because they had few merits and virtues,
They suffered from the fire.
They killed each other,
Drank blood, and ate flesh.

The small foxes were
Already dead.
Large wild beasts
Rushed at them and ate them.
Ill-smelling smoke rose
And filled the house.

---

11 This is inconsistent with the foregoing prose section in which it is understood that he was in the house when the fires broke out and because he thought, 'I am able to get out of the gate of the burning house...'

The centipedes, millipedes,
And poisonous snakes
Were driven out of their holes
By the fire,
And eaten
By the kumbhāṇḍa-demons.

The hair of the hungry spirits caught fire.
With hunger, thirst and burning,
The spirits ran about
In agony and dismay.

The house was so dreadful.
[In that house] there were
Poisonings, killings and burnings.
There were many dangers, not just one.

At that time the house-owner
Was standing outside the gate.
He heard a man say to him:
"Some time ago
Your children entered this house to play.[12]
They are young and ignorant.
They are engrossed in playing."
Hearing this,
The rich man was frightened.
He rushed into the burning house.

In order to save them
From burning to death,
He told them
Of the dangers of the house:
"There are demons and poisonous vermin here.
Flames have already spread all over.

12 This is inconsistent with the foregoing prose section in which it says that the children "are still inside."

Many sufferings are coming
One after another endlessly.
There are poisonous snakes,
Lizards, vipers,
Yakṣas, kumbhāṇḍa-demons,
Small foxes, foxes, dogs,
Crested eagles, eagles,
Kites, owls and centipedes here.
They are unbearably hungry and thirsty.
They are dreadful.
These sufferings are difficult to avoid.
Worse still, there is a big fire."

Though the children heard his warning,
They were still engrossed in playing.
They did not stop playing
Because they were ignorant.

The rich man
Thought:
"They are ignorant.
My anxiety deepens
There is nothing pleasant
In this house.
But they are engrossed
In playing.
They do not listen to me.
They will be burned to death."

At the time
He thought of an expedient.
He said to them:
"I have many kinds of toys.
They are beautiful carts
Made of wonderful treasures.

They are sheep-carts, deer-carts,
And large[13] bullock-carts.
They are outside the gate.
Come out!
I made those carts
For you.
Play with them
As you like!"

Hearing of the carts from him,
They ran out,
Striving to be first,
And reached an open place.
They were now free
From the sufferings.

Seeing them come out
Of the burning house
To the safe crossroad,
He sat on the lion-like seat,
And said to others with joy:
"I am happy.
These children are difficult to bring up.
They are young and ignorant.
They entered the dangerous house.
In that house were
Many poisonous vermin
And many dangerous mountain spirits.
Raging flames of big fires rose
From the four sides of the house
At the same time.
But my children were
Engrossed in playing.
Now I saved them

13 In the foregoing prose section the bullock-carts as one of the three kinds of carts are not modified with the adjective "large."

From the dangers.
Therefore, I am happy."

The children saw their father
Sitting in peace.
They came to him,
And said:
"Give us
The three kinds of jeweled carts
That you promised us!
You said:
"Come out, and I will give you
The three kinds of carts as you like."
Now is the time for that.
Give them to us now!"

He was a very rich man.
He had many storehouses.
He made many large carts
Adorned with treasures,
Such as gold, silver,
Lapis lazuli, shell and agate.

[The carts] were beautifully adorned.
Railings were put around them.
Bells were hanging on the four sides
With ropes of gold.

[The carts] were roofed
With nets of pearls.
Garlands of golden flowers
Were hanging on all sides.

Other ornaments of fabrics
Of divers colors
Encircled the bodies of the carts.
Bedding was made of soft cloth.

[The bedding] was covered
With the most wonderful woolen fabrics.
They were bright, white, pure and clean,
Worth hundreds of thousands of millions.

Large white bullocks,
Fat, stout, powerful,
And beautiful in their build,
Were yoked to the jeweled carts.
The carts were also guarded
By many attendants.

[The rich man] gave to each of his children
One of these wonderful carts.
The children
Danced with joy.

They drove these jeweled carts
In all directions.
There were happy and delighted.
Nothing could stop their joy.

(The Buddha said to Śāriputra:)
I am like the father.
I am the Saint of Saints.
I am the father of the world.

All living beings are my children.
They are deeply attached
To the pleasures of the world.
They have no wisdom.

The triple world is not peaceful.
It is like the burning house.
It is full of sufferings.
It is dreadful.

There are always the sufferings
Of birth, old age, disease and death.
They are like flames
Raging endlessly.

I have already left
The burning house of the triple world.
I am tranquil and peaceful
In a bower in a forest.

This triple world
Is my property.
All living beings therein
Are my children.

There are many sufferings
In this world.
Only I can save
[All living beings].

I told this to all living beings.
But they did not believe me
Because they were too much attached
To desires and defilements.

Therefore, I expediently expounded to them
The teaching of the Three Vehicles,
And caused them to know
The sufferings of the triple world.
I opened, showed, and expounded
The Way out of the world.

Those children who were resolute in mind
Were able to obtain
The six supernatural powers
Including the three major supernatural powers,

And to become cause-knowers
Or never-faltering Bodhisattvas.

Śāriputra!
With this parable I expounded
The teaching of the One Buddha-Vehicle
To all living beings.
All of you will be able to attain
The enlightenment of the Buddha
If you believe and receive
These words of mine.

This vehicle is
The purest and most wonderful.
This is unsurpassed by any other vehicle
In all the worlds.
This vehicle is approved with joy by the Buddhas.
All living beings should extol it.
They should make offerings to it,[14]
And bow to it.

The powers, emancipations,
dhyāna-concentrations, wisdom,
And all the other merits [of the Buddhas],
Many hundreds of thousands of millions in number,
Are loaded in this vehicle.

I will cause all my children
To ride in this vehicle
And to enjoy themselves
Day and night for kalpas.

The Bodhisattvas and Śrāvakas
Will be able to go immediately

14 Here the vehicle of the Dharma is regarded as the object of worship.

To the place of enlightenment
If they ride in this jeweled vehicle.

Therefore, even if you try to find another vehicle
Throughout the worlds of the ten quarters,
You will not be able to find any other one
Except those given by the Buddhas expediently.

(The Buddha said to Śāriputra:)
All of you
Are my children.
I am your father.

You were under the fires of many sufferings
For the past innumerable kalpas.
Therefore, I saved you
From the triple world [with expedients].

I once told you that you had attained extinction.
But you eliminated only birth and death
[By that extinction].
The extinction you attained was not the true one.
What you should do now is
Obtain the wisdom of the Buddha.

The Bodhisattvas in this multitude
Should hear
With one mind
The true teaching of the Buddhas.

The Buddhas, the World-Honored Ones,
Say only expediently [that some are not Bodhisattvas]
To tell the truth,
All living beings taught by them are Bodhisattvas.

---

15 This is Nirvāṇa.

[I said:]
"To those who have little wisdom,
And who are deeply attached to sensual desires,
The Buddhas expound the truth that all is suffering.
Those [who hear this truth]
Will have the greatest joy that they have ever had.
The statement of the Buddhas that all is suffering
Is true, not false.
To those who are ignorant
Of the cause of all sufferings,
And who are too deeply attached
To the cause of suffering
To give it up even for a moment,
The Buddhas expound
The [eight right] ways[16] as expedients.

The cause of suffering is greed.
When greed is eliminated,
There is nothing to be attached to.
The extinction of suffering
Is called the third truth.
In order to attain this extinction,
The [eight right] ways must be practiced.
Freedom from the bonds of suffering[,]
[That is, from illusions] is called emancipation."

From what illusions can one be emancipated, however,
[By the practice of the eight right ways]?
He can be emancipated only from unreal things
[That is, from the five desires] thereby.
He cannot be emancipated from all illusions.
The Buddhas say
That he has not yet attained
The true extinction[17]

---

16 See *Eight Right Ways* in the English/Sanskrit Glossary.

17 This is Nirvāṇa.

Because he has not yet attained
Unsurpassed enlightenment.
I also do not think that I have led him
To the [true] extinction thereby.

I am the King of the Dharma.
I expound the Dharma without hindrance.
I appeared in this world
In order to give peace to all living beings.

Śāriputra!
I expound this seal of the Dharma
In order to benefit
[All living beings] of the world.
Do not propagate it carelessly
At the place where you are!

Anyone who rejoices at hearing this sūtra,
And who receives it respectfully,
Know this, has already reached
The stage of avaivartika.

Anyone who believes and receives this sūtra
Should be considered
To have already seen the past Buddhas,
Respected them, made offerings to them,
And heard the Dharma from them
In his previous existence.

Anyone who believes what you expound
Should be considered
To have already seen all of us,
That is, you and me,
And the Saṃgha of bhikṣus,
And the Bodhisattvas.

I expound only to people of profound wisdom
This Sūtra of the Lotus Flower of the Wonderful Dharma
Because men of little wisdom would doubt this sūtra,
And not understand it even if they heard it.
No Śrāvaka
Or Pratyekabuddha
Can understand
This sūtra.

Even you, Śāriputra,
Have understood this sūtra
Only by faith.
Needless to say,
The other Śrāvakas cannot do otherwise.
They will be able to follow this sūtra
Only because they believe my words,
Not because they have wisdom.

Śāriputra!
Do not expound this sūtra
To those who are arrogant and idle,
And who think that the self exists!

Do not expound it to men of little wisdom!
They would not be able to understand it
Even if they heard it
Because they are deeply attached to the five desires.

Those who do not believe this sūtra
But slander it,
Will destroy the seeds of Buddhahood
Of all living beings of the world.

Some will scowl at this sūtra
And doubt it.
Listen! I will tell you
How they will be punished.

In my lifetime or after my extinction
Some will slander this sūtra,
And despise the person
Who reads or recites
Or copies or keeps this sūtra.
They will hate him,
Look at him with jealousy,
And harbor enmity against him.
Listen! I will tell you
How they will be punished.

When their present lives end,
They will fall into the Avīci Hell.
They will live there for a kalpa,
And have their rebirth in the same hell.
This rebirth of theirs will be repeated
For innumerable kalpas.

After that they will be reborn
In the world of animals.
Some of them will become dogs or small foxes.
They will be bald, thin and black.
They will suffer from mange and leprosy
Men will treat them mercilessly,
And hate and despise them.
They will always suffer from hunger and thirst.
Their bones will project; their flesh sag.
They will always suffer in their present existence.
After their death, they will be put
Under pieces of tile or stones.
Those who destroy the seeds of Buddhahood
Will be punished like this.

Some of them will become
Camels or asses.
They will always be heavily loaded,
And beaten with sticks or whips.

They will think of nothing
But water and hay.
Those who slander this sūtra
Will be punished like this.

Some of them will become small foxes.
They will suffer
From mange and leprosy.
They will have only one eye
When they come to a town,
They will be struck by boys.
Some of them
Will be beaten to death.
After they die
They will become boas.
Their bodies will be large,
Five hundred yojanas long.
They will be deaf and stupid.

They will wriggle along without legs.
They will be bitten
By many small vermin.
They will suffer day and night.
They will have no time to take a rest.
Those who slander this sūtra
Will be punished like this.

Some of them will become men again.
They will be foolish, short, ugly,
Crooked, crippled, blind, deaf,
And hunchbacked.
No one will believe their words.
They will always have fetid breath.
They will be possessed by demons.
Poverty-stricken and mean,
They will be employed by others.

Worn-out, thin,
And subject to many diseases,
They will have no one to rely on.
Anyone who employs them
Will not take care of them.
They will lose before long
What little they may have earned.
When they study medicine,
And treat a patient with a proper remedy,
The patient will have another disease
Or die.
When they are ill in health,
No one will cure them.
Even when they take a good medicine,
They will suffer all the more.
They will be attacked by others,
Or robbed or stolen from.
Their sins will incur these misfortunes.
These sinful people will never be able to see
The Buddha, the King of the Saints,
Who expounds the Dharma
And teaches all living beings.
They will always be reborn
In the places of difficulty
[In seeing the Buddha].
They will be mad, deaf or distracted.
They will never be able to hear the Dharma.
For as many kalpas
As there are sands in the River Ganges,
They will be deaf and dumb.
They will not have all the sense organs.
Accustomed to living in hell,
They will take it for their playground.
Accustomed to living in other evil regions,
They will take them for their homes.
They will live
Among camels, asses, wild boars, and dogs.

Those who slander this sūtra
Will be punished like this.

When they are reborn in the world of men,
Deafness, blindness, dumbness,
Poverty, and many other defects
Will be their ornaments;
Dropsy, diabetes, mange,
Leprosy, carbuncles, and many other diseases
Will be their garments.
They will always smell bad.
They will be filthy and defiled.
Deeply attached to the view
That the self exists,
They will aggravate their anger.
Their lust will not discriminate
Between [humans,] birds or beasts.
Those who slander this sūtra
Will be punished like this.

(The Buddha said to Śāriputra:)
A kalpa will not be long enough to describe
The punishments to be inflicted
Upon those who slander this sūtra.

Therefore,
I tell you.
Do not expound this sūtra
To people of no wisdom!

Expound it to clever people
Who have profound wisdom,
Who hear much,
Who remember well,
And who seek
The enlightenment of the Buddha!

Expound it to those who have seen
Many thousands of myriads
Of millions of Buddhas
And planted the roots of good
In their previous existence,
And who are now resolute in mind!

Expound it
To those who make efforts,
Who have compassion towards others,
And who do not spare their lives!

Expound it to those
Who respect others,
Who have no perfidy in them,
Who keep away from ignorant people,
And who live alone
In mountains or valleys!

Śāriputra!
Expound it to those
Who keep away
From evil friends,
And who approach
Good friends!

Expound it to the Buddha's sons
Who keep the precepts
As cleanly and as purely
As they keep gems,
And who seek
The sūtra of the Great Vehicle!

Expound it to those
Who are not angry
But upright, gentle,
Compassionate

Towards all others,
And respectful to the Buddhas!

Expound it to the Buddha's sons
Who expound the Dharma without hindrance
To the great multitude
With their pure minds
By telling them
Various stories of previous lives,
Parables and similes,
And also by giving them various discourses!

Expound it to the bhikṣus
Who seek the Dharma in all directions
In order to obtain
The knowledge of all things,
Who join their hands together
Towards the sūtra of the Great Vehicle,
Who receive it respectfully,
Who keep it with joy,
And who do not receive
Even a gāthā of any other sūtra!

Expound it to those
Who seek this sūtra
As eagerly as they seek
The śarīras of the Buddha!

[Expound it to those]
Who receive [this sūtra]
And put it on their heads,
And who do not seek
Any other sūtra
Or think of the books of heresy!

(The Buddha said to Śāriputra:)
Those who seek the enlightenment of the Buddha
Are as various as previously stated.
A kalpa will not be long enough
To describe the variety of them.
They will be able to understand [this sūtra] by faith.
Expound to them
The Sūtra of the Lotus Flower of the Wonderful Dharma!

CHAPTER IV

UNDERSTANDING BY FAITH

Thereupon the men living the life of wisdom: Subhūti, Mahā-Kātyāyana, Mahā-Kāśyapa, and Mahā-Maudgalyāyana felt strange because they heard the Dharma from the Buddha that they had never heard before, and because they heard that the World-Honored One had assured Śāriputra of his future attainment of Anuttara-samyak-saṃbodhi. They felt like dancing with joy, rose from their seats, adjusted their robes, bared their right shoulders, put their right knees on the ground, joined their hands together with all their hearts, bent themselves respectfully, looked up at the honorable face, and said to the Buddha:

"We elders of the Saṃgha were already old and decrepit [when we heard of Anuttara-samyak-saṃbodhi]. We did not seek Anuttara-samyak-saṃbodhi because we thought that we had already attained Nirvāṇa, and also because we thought that we were too old and decrepit to do so.[1] You have been expounding the Dharma for a long time. We have been in your congregation all the while. We were already tired [when we heard of Anuttara-samyak-saṃbodhi]. Therefore, we just cherished the truth that nothing is substantial, the truth that nothing is different from any other thing, and the truth that nothing more is to be sought. We did not wish to perform the Bodhisattva practices, that is, to purify the world of the Buddha and to lead all living beings [to Buddhahood] by displaying supernatural powers because you had already led us out of the triple world and caused us to attain Nirvāṇa. Neither did we wish at all to attain Anuttara-samyak-saṃbodhi, which you were teaching to Bodhisattvas, because we were already too old and

1 They thought that energy was necessary for seeking Anuttara-samyak-saṃbodhi.

decrepit to do so. But now we are very glad to hear that you have assured a Śrāvaka of his future attainment of Anuttara-samyak-saṃbodhi. We have the greatest joy that we have ever had. We have never expected to hear such a rare teaching all of a sudden. How glad we are! We have obtained great benefits. We have obtained innumerable treasures although we did not seek them.

"World-Honored One! Allow us to explain our understanding by telling a parable. Suppose there lived a man [in a certain country]. When he was a little boy, he ran away from his father. [The boy] lived in another country for a long time, say, for ten, twenty or fifty years. As time passed by, he became poorer. He wandered about all directions, seeking food and clothing.

"While wandering here and there, he happened to walk towards his home country. At that time his father stayed in a city [of that country]. He had been vainly looking for his son ever since. He was now very rich. He had innumerable treasures. His storehouses were filled with gold, silver, lapis lazuli, coral, amber and crystal. He had many servants, clerks, and secretaries. He also had countless elephants, horses, carts, cows, and sheep. He invested his money in all the other countries, and earned interest. He dealt with many merchants and customers.

"The poor son, having wandered from town to town, from country to country, from village to village, came to the city where his father was living. The father had been thinking of him for more than fifty years since he had lost him, but never told others [that he had a missing son]. He was alone, pining for his son. He thought, 'I am old and decrepit. I have many treasures. My storehouses are filled with gold, silver, and other treasures. But I have no son [other than the missing one]. When I die, my treasures will be scattered and lost. I have no one to transfer my treasures to. Therefore, I am always yearning for my son.' The father thought again, 'If I can find my son and give him my treasures, I shall be happy and peaceful, and have nothing more to worry about.'

"World-Honored One! At that time the poor son, who had worked at various places as a day worker, happened to come to the house of his father. Standing by the gate of the house, he saw his father in the distance. His father was sitting on a lion-like seat, putting his feet on a jeweled footstool. Brāhmaṇas, kṣatriyas, and householders surrounded him respectfully. He was adorned with a necklace of pearls worth ten million. The secretaries and servants were standing on either side of him, holding insect-sweepers made of white hairs. Above him was a jeweled awning, from which streamers of flowers were hanging down. Perfume was sprayed and beautiful flowers were strewn on the ground. He was exhibiting treasures and engaging in trade. Adorned with these various things, he looked extraordinarily powerful and virtuous.

"Seeing the exceedingly powerful father, the poor son was frightened. He regretted that he had come there. He thought, 'Is he a king or someone like a king? This is not the place where I can get something by labor. I had better go to a village of the poor, where I can work to get food and clothing easily. If I stay here any longer, I shall be forced to work.'

"Having thought this, the poor son ran away. The rich man, who was sitting on the lion-like seat, recognized him at first sight as his son. He was delighted. He thought, 'Now I have found the person to whom I can transfer my treasures and storehouses. I have been thinking of my son all this time, but I have had no way to find him. Now he has come by himself all of a sudden. This is just what I wanted. I am old, but not too old to lose any attachment [to my treasures].'

"He immediately dispatched a man standing beside him to quickly bring back the poor son. The messenger ran up to the poor son and caught him. The poor son was frightened. He cried, 'You Devil! I have done nothing wrong. Why do you catch me?'

"The messenger pulled him by force. The poor son thought, 'I am caught though I am not guilty. I shall be killed.' More and more frightened, the poor son fainted and fell to the ground. Seeing all this in the distance, the father said to the messenger, 'I do not want him any more. Do not bring him forcibly! Pour cold water on his face and bring him to himself! Do not talk with him any more!'

"The father said this because he had realized that his son was too base and mean to meet a noble man [like his father]. He knew that the man was his son, but expediently refrained from telling to others that that was his son. [The messenger poured water on the son. The son was brought to himself.] The messenger said to him, 'Now you are released. You can go anywhere you like.'

"The poor son had the greatest joy that he had ever had. He stood up and went to a village of the poor to get food and clothing. Thereupon the rich man thought of an expedient to persuade his son to come to him. He [wished to] dispatch messengers in secret. He said to two men looking worn-out, powerless and virtueless, 'Go and gently tell the poor man that he will be employed here for a double day's pay. If he agrees with you, bring him here and have him work. If he asks you what work he should do, tell him that he should clear dirt and that you two also will work with him.'

"The two messengers looked for the poor son. Having found him, they told him what they had been ordered to tell. The poor son [came back with them,] drew his pay in advance, and cleared dirt with them. Seeing him, the father had compassion towards him, and wondered [why he was so base and mean]. Some days later he saw his son in the distance from the window. The son was weak, thin, worn-out, and defiled with dirt and dust. The father took off his necklace, his garment of thin and soft cloth, and other ornaments. He put on tattered and dirty clothing, smeared himself with dust, and carried a dirt-utensil in his right hand. He looked fearful. He [came to the workers and] said, 'Work hard! Do not be lazy!'

"With this expedient the father came to his son. He said to him, 'Man! Stay here and work! Do not go anywhere else! I will pay you more. Do not hesitate to take trays, rice, flour, salt and vinegar as much as you need! You can have an old servant if you want to. Make yourself at home! I feel like your father. Do not worry any more! I am old, and you are young. When you work, you do not deceive [the other workers]. You are not lazy. You do not get angry [with the other workers], or reproach them. You are not like the other workers who do these evil things. From now on I will treat you as my son.'

"The rich man gave him a name and called him son. The poor son was glad to be treated kindly, but still thought that he was a humble employee. Therefore, the rich man had him clear dirt for twenty years. After that the father and son trusted each other. Now the son felt no hesitation in entering the house of his father, but still lodged in his old place.[2]

"World-Honored One! Now the rich man became ill. He knew that he would die soon. He said to the poor son, 'I have a great deal of gold, silver, and other treasures. My storehouses are filled with them. You know the amounts of them. You know what to take, and what to give. This is what I have in mind. Know this! You are not different from me in all this. Be careful lest the treasures be lost!'

"Thereupon the poor son obeyed his order. He took custody of the storehouses of gold, silver, and other treasures, but did not wish to take anything worth even a meal from them. He still stayed in his old lodging. He could not yet give up the thought that he was base and mean.

"After a while the father noticed that his son had become more at ease and peaceful, that he wanted to improve himself, and that he felt ashamed of the thought that he was base and mean. The time of the death of the father drew near. The father told his son to call in his relatives, the king, ministers, kṣatriyas, and householders. When they all assembled, he said to them, 'Gentlemen, know this! This is my son, my real son. He ran away from me when I lived in a certain city, and wandered with hardships for more than fifty years. His name is so-and-so; mine, so-and-so. When I was in that city, I anxiously looked for him. I happened to find him [years ago]. This is my son. I am his father. All my treasures are his. He knows what has been taken in and what has been paid out.'

"World-Honored One! At that time the poor son was very glad to hear these words of his father. He had the greatest joy that he had ever had. He thought, 'I never dreamed of having this store of treasures myself. It has come to me unexpectedly.'

"World-Honored One! The great rich man is you. We are like [his son, that is,] your sons because you always tell us that we are your sons. World-Honored One! We once had many troubles

---

2 He lodged in the hut outside the gate.

in the world of birth and death because of the three kinds of sufferings.[3] We were so distracted and so ignorant that we clung to the teachings of the Lesser Vehicle. At that time you caused us to think over all things and to clear away the dirt of fruitless discussions about them. We made strenuous efforts according to the teachings [of the Lesser Vehicle] and attained Nirvāṇa as a day's pay. Having attained it, we had great joy, and felt satisfied [with the attainment of it]. We said, 'We have obtained much because we made efforts according to the teachings of the Buddha.' But when you saw that we clung to mean desires and wished to hear only the teachings of the Lesser Vehicle, you left us alone. You did not tell us that we had the treasure-store, that is, the insight of the Tathāgata. You expounded the wisdom of the Buddha[, that is, the Great Vehicle] with expedients, but we did not aspire for that vehicle because, when we had obtained the day's pay of Nirvāṇa from the Buddha, we thought that we had already obtained enough. We did not wish to have what you had showed and expounded to the Bodhisattvas by your wisdom. You expounded the Dharma to us with expedients according to our capacities because you knew that we wished to hear the teachings of the Lesser Vehicle. We did not know that we were your sons. Now we know that you do not grudge your wisdom to anyone. Although we were your sons then as we are now, we wished to hear only the teachings of the Lesser Vehicle. If we had aspired for the teaching of the Great Vehicle, you would have already expounded it to us. Now you expound only the One Vehicle in this sūtra. You once reproached us Śrāvakas in the presence of the Bodhisattvas because we wished to hear the teachings of the Lesser Vehicle. [At that time we thought that you had taught us only the Lesser Vehicle,] but now we know that you have been teaching us the Great Vehicle from the outset. Therefore, we say that the great treasures of the King of the Dharma have come to us although we did not seek them, and that we have already obtained all that the sons of the Buddha should obtain."

---

3 See *Three Kinds of Suffering* and other enumerated conceptions in the English/Sanskrit Glossary.

Thereupon Mahā-Kāśyapa, wishing to repeat what they had said, sang in gāthās:

Hearing your teaching of today,
We are dancing with joy.
We have never had
Such joy before.

You say:
"The Śrāvakas will be able to become Buddhas."
We have obtained unsurpassed treasures
Although we did not seek them.

Suppose there lived a boy.
He was young and ignorant.
He ran away from his father
And went to a remote country.
He wandered from country to country
For more than fifty years.

The father anxiously sought him
In all directions.
Finally tiring of looking for him,
He settled in a certain city.

He built a house,
And enjoyed satisfaction
Of the five desires.
He was very rich.
He had a great deal of gold, silver,
Shell, agate, pearl and lapis lazuli;
And many elephants, horses,
Cows, sheep,
Palanquins, carts,
Farmers and attendants.

He invested his money in all the other countries,
And earned interest.
Merchants and customers
Were seen everywhere [around him].

Thousands of billions of people
Surrounded him respectfully.
He was favored by the king,
And respected
By the ministers,
And by the powerful families.

Many people came to see him
For various purposes.
Because he was rich,
He was very powerful.
As he became older,
He thought more of his son.
He thought from morning till night:
"I shall die before long.
It is more than fifty years
Since my ignorant son left me
What shall I do
With the things in the store-houses?"

At that time the poor son
Wandered from village to village,
From country to country,
Seeking food and clothing.
Sometimes he got what he wanted,
At other times he could not.
Getting thinner from hunger,
He had scabs and itches on his skin.
Wandering from one place to another,
He came to the city of his father.

Employed at places from day to day,
He came to the house of his father.

At that time the rich man was sitting
On the lion-like seat
Under the great awning of treasures
Inside the gate of the house.
Many attendants were surrounding him.
Many people were on his guard.

Some of his attendants were counting
Gold, silver, and other treasures.
Some were keeping accounts;
Others, writing notes and bills.

Seeing his father noble and honorable,
The poor son thought:
"Is he a king,
Or someone like a king?"

Frightened and scared,
He wondered:
"Why did I come here?"
He thought:
"If I stay here any longer,
I shall be forced to work."

Having thought this, he ran away.
He asked someone
For the way to a village of the poor
In order to get a job.

From his lion-like seat,
The rich man saw the poor son in the distance,
And recognized him as his son.
But he did not tell this to the others.

He immediately dispatched a messenger
To chase, catch, and bring him back.
The poor son cried out with fright,
And fell to the ground in agony, thinking:
"He caught me.
I shall be killed.
What use was it coming here
For food and clothing?"

The rich man thought:
"He is ignorant, narrow-minded, and mean.
If I tell him that I am his father,
He will not believe me."

He thought of an expedient.
He called
Some squint-eyed, short, ugly,
powerless and virtueless men,
And said to them:
"Go and tell him:
'You will be employed
To clear away dirt and dust.
You can get a double day's pay.'"

Hearing this from them,
The poor son came joyfully with them.
He cleared away dirt and dust,
And cleaned the buildings.

The rich man saw him from the window.
He thought:
"He is ignorant.
He willingly does mean work."
Thereupon the rich man
Put on old and dirty clothes,
Picked up a dirt-utensil,
And walked towards his son.

With this expedient he came to his son,
And told him to work on, saying:
"I will pay you more.
You can use twice as much oil for your feet.
You can take food and drink as you like.
You can use more matting to warm yourself with."

Sometimes he chided him, saying:
"Work hard!"
At other times he coaxed him, saying:
"I will treat you as my son."

By his wisdom the rich man succeeded
In leading his son into his household.
Twenty years after that
He had his son manage his house.

The son was entrusted
With the keeping of the accounts
Of gold and silver,
And of pearl, crystal, and so on.
But he still lodged
In the hut outside the gate, thinking:
"I am poor.
None of these treasures are mine."

Seeing the mind of his son
Becoming less mean and more noble,
The father called in
His relatives, the king, ministers,
Kṣatriyas, and householders,
In order to give his treasures to his son.

He said to the great multitude:
"This is my son.
He was gone
For fifty years.

I found him
Twenty years ago.
I missed him
When I was in a certain city.
I wandered, looking for him,
And came here.
Now I will give him
All my houses and men.
He can use them
As he likes."

The son thought:
"I was poor, base and mean.
Now I have obtained
The treasures, houses,
And all the other things
From my father.
Never before
Have I been so happy."

You are like the father.
Knowing that we wished
To hear the Lesser Vehicle,
You did not say to us,
  "You will become Buddhas."
You said of us to others:
"Though they are my disciples,
  they are Śrāvakas.
They eliminated āsravas,
But attained only the Lesser Vehicle."

You said to us:
"Expound the most excellent Way
  [to Bodhisattvas]!
Those who practice the Way
Will be able to become Buddhas."

By this order of yours
We expounded the unsurpassed Way
To the great Bodhisattvas
With various stories of previous lives,
With various parables and similes
And with various discourses.[4]

Hearing the [Way, that is, the] Dharma from us,
Those sons of yours
Thought it over day and night,
And practiced it strenuously.

Thereupon the Buddha assured them
Of their future Buddhahood, saying to them:
"You will become Buddhas
In your future lives."

You expounded the real thing,
That is, the store
Of the hidden core of the Buddhas
Only to the Bodhisattvas.
You did not expound
This truth to us.

The poor son came to his father,
And took custody
Of the things of his father,
But wished to take none of them.

The same can be said of us.
We did not wish to have the treasure-store
Of the teachings of the Buddhas
Although we expounded it [to the Bodhisattvas].

---

4 According to this, the Buddha has the Śrāvakas assist him in teaching Bodhisattvas. It was considered that the Śrāvakas were too old to perform the Bodhisattva practices, but still competent enough to teach Bodhisattvas.

We were satisfied with the elimination
Of illusions within ourselves.
What we accomplished was that elimination.
We did nothing more.

You told us
To purify the world of the Buddha
And teach all living beings.
We heard this, but did not wish to do so
Because we had already attained the truth:
"All things are void and tranquil.
Nothing appears or disappears.
Nothing is larger or smaller.
Nothing has āsravas.
Nothing is subject to cause and effect."
Having thought this, we did not wish
To do [the Bodhisattva practices].

In the long night
We did not care
For the wisdom of the Buddha.
We did not wish to have it.
We thought:
"The Dharma we attained is perfect."

Having studied the truth of the Void in the long night,
We emancipated ourselves
From the sufferings of the triple world,
Attained the Nirvāṇa-with-remainder,
And reached the final stage
Of our physical existence.

You said [to us]:
"When you attain enlightenment infallibly,
You will have already repayed
The favors I gave you."

Although we expounded to the sons of the Buddha
The teachings for Bodhisattvas in order to cause them
To seek the enlightenment of the Buddha,
We did not wish to attain
The same enlightenment for ourselves.
You, our Leader, left us alone because you knew this.
You did not persuade us
To seek the enlightenment of the Buddha.
You did not say
That we should be able to have real benefits.

The rich man knew
That his son was base and mean.
Therefore, he made him nobler
With expedients,
And then gave him
All his treasures.

In the same manner,
You knew that we wished
To hear the Lesser Vehicle.
Therefore, you did a rare thing.
You prepared us with expedients,
And then taught us the great wisdom.

Today we are not what we were then.
We have obtained
What we did not expect
To obtain
Just as the poor son obtained
The innumerable treasures.

World-Honored One!
We have attained enlightenment, perfect fruit.
We have secured pure eyes
With which we can see the Dharma-without-āsravas.

We observed the pure precepts of the Buddha
In the long night.
Today we have obtained the effects and rewards
[Of our observance of the precepts].
We performed the brahma practices for long
According to the teachings of the King of the Dharma.
Now we have obtained the great fruit
Of the unsurpassed Dharma-without-āsravas.

We are Śrāvakas in this sense of the word.[5]
We will cause all living beings
To hear the voice telling
Of the enlightenment of the Buddha.

We are Arhats
In the true sense of the word.
All gods and men,
All Māras and Brahmans
In the worlds
Should make offerings to us.

You, the World-Honored One, are the great benefactor.
By doing this rare thing,
You taught and benefited us
Out of your compassion towards us.

No one will be able to repay your favors
Even if he tries to do so
For many hundreds of millions of kalpas.
No one will be able to repay your favors
Even if he bows to you respectfully,
And offers you his hands, feet or anything else.

No one will be able to repay your favors
Even if he carries you on his head or shoulders

---

5 Here a Śrāvaka is interpreted as a person who causes others to hear.

And respects you from the bottom of his heart
For as many kalpas
As there are sands in the River Ganges,
Or even if he offers you
Delicious food, innumerable garments of treasures,
Many beddings, and various medicines,
Or even if he erects a stūpa-mausoleum
Made of the cow-head candana,
And adorns it with treasures,
Or even if he covers the ground
With garments of treasures
And offers them to the Buddha
For as many kalpas
As there are sands in the River Ganges.

The Buddhas have
Great supernatural powers.
Their powers are rare, immeasurable,
Limitless and inconceivable.

The Buddhas are the Kings of the Dharma
They are free from āsravas, from cause and effect.
The Buddhas practice patience
In order to save inferior people.
They expound the Dharma according to the capacities
Of the ordinary people who are attached to forms.

The Buddhas expound the Dharma
In perfect freedom.
Knowing the various desires and dispositions
Of all living beings,
They expound the Dharma
With innumerable parables
And with innumerable similes
According to their capacities.

Some living beings planted the roots of good
In their previous existence.
Some of the roots have fully developed.
Seeing all this, the Buddhas understand
The capacities of all living beings,
And divide the teaching of the One Vehicle into three,
According to the capacities
Of all living beings.

[Here ends] the Second Volume of the Sūtra of the Lotus Flower of the Wonderful Dharma.

CHAPTER V

THE SIMILE OF HERBS

Thereupon the World-Honored One said to Mahā-Kāśyapa and other great disciples:

"Excellent, excellent! You spoke of my true merits very well. My true merits are just as you said. In reality, however, I have more merits. They are innumerable, asaṃkhya. You will not be able to describe all of them even if you try to do so for many hundreds of millions of kalpas.

"Kāśyapa, know this! I, the Tathāgata, am the King of the Dharma. Nothing I say is false. I expound all teachings with expedients by my wisdom in order to lead all living beings to the stage of knowing all things. I know what region a living being will be taken to by what teaching, and what a living being has deep in his mind. I am not hindered by anything in knowing all this. I know all things clearly, and show my knowledge of all things to all living beings.

"Kāśyapa! Suppose the various trees and grasses of the one thousand million Sumeru-worlds[1] including herbs growing in the thickets, forests, mountains, ravines and valleys, on the ground, and by the rivers, all these plants being different in names and forms, were covered with a dark cloud, and then watered by a rainfall at the same time. The small, middle and large roots, stems, branches and leaves of the trees and grasses including herbs growing in the thickets and forests were watered. So were the tall and short trees, whether they were superior or middle or inferior. Those plants were given more or less water by the same rain from the same cloud, and grew differently according to their species. They obtained different

1 See *One Thousand Million Sumeru-Worlds* in the English/Sanskrit Glossary.

flowers and fruits although they grew on the same ground and received water from the same rain.

"Kāśyapa, know this! I, the Tathāgata, am like the cloud. I appeared in this world just as the large cloud rose. I expounded the Dharma to gods, men and asuras of the world with a loud voice just as the large cloud covered all the one thousand million Sumeru-worlds. I said to the great multitude, 'I am the Tathāgata, the Deserver of Offerings, the Perfectly Enlightened One, the Man of Wisdom and Practice, the Well-Gone, the Knower of the World, the Unsurpassed Man, the Controller of Men, the Teacher of Gods and Men, the Buddha, the World-Honored One. I will cause all living beings to cross [the ocean of birth and death] if they have not yet done so. I will cause them to emancipate[2] themselves [from suffering] if they have not yet done so. I will cause them to have peace of mind if they have not yet done so. I will cause them to attain Nirvāṇa if they have not yet done so. I know their present lives as they are, and also their future lives as they will be. I know all. I see all. I know the Way. I have opened the Way. I will expound the Way. Gods, men and asuras! Come and hear the Dharma!'

"Thereupon many thousands of billions of people came to hear the Dharma from me. Having seen them, I knew which were clever, which were dull, which were diligent, and which were lazy. Therefore, I expounded to them an innumerable variety of teachings according to their capacities in order to cause them to rejoice and receive benefits with pleasure. Having heard these teachings, they became peaceful in their present lives. In their future lives, they will have rebirths in good places, enjoy pleasures by practicing the Way, and hear these teachings again. After hearing these teachings again, they will emancipate themselves from all hindrances, practice the teachings according to their capacities, and finally enter the Way, just as the grasses and trees in the thickets and forests, which were watered by the rain from the same large cloud, grew differently according to their species.

"The various teachings I expound are of the same content, of the same taste. Those who emancipate themselves [from the bonds of existence,] from illusions, and from birth and death, will finally

2 解 May also be interpreted as "to understand [the Dharma]."

obtain the knowledge of the equality and differences of all things. But those who hear or keep my teachings or read or recite the sūtras in which my teachings are expounded, or act according to my teachings, do not know the merits that they will be able to obtain by these practices. Why is that? It is because only I know their capacities, appearances, entities and natures. Only I know what teachings they have in memory, what teachings they have in mind, what teachings they practice, how they memorize the teachings, how they think of the teachings, how they practice the teachings, for what purpose they memorize the teachings, for what purpose they think of the teachings, for what purpose they practice the teachings, and for what purpose they keep what teachings. Only I see clearly and without hindrance that they are at various stages [of enlightenment]. I know this, but they do not know just as the trees and grasses including herbs in the thickets and forests do not know whether they are superior or middle or inferior. My teachings are of the same content, of the same taste. Those who emancipate themselves [from the bonds of existence,] from illusions, and from birth and death, will finally attain Nirvāṇa, that is, eternal tranquility or extinction. They will be able to return to the state of the Void.

"Although I knew the equality and differences of all things, I refrained from expounding it to them in order to protect them because I saw their [various] desires.

"Kāśyapa, and all of you present here! It is an extraordinarily rare thing to see that you have understood, believed and received the Dharma which I expounded variously according to the capacities of all living beings because it is difficult to understand the Dharma which the Buddhas, the World-Honored Ones, expound according to the capacities of all living beings."

Thereupon the World-Honored One, wishing to repeat what he had said, sang in gāthās:

As the destroyer of the bonds of existence,
I, the King of the Dharma, have appeared in this world.
Since then I have expounded the Dharma variously
According to the desires of all living beings.

I am honorable, and my wisdom is profound.
Therefore, I have been reticent on this truth[,]
[That is, the reality of all things,] for a long time.
I did not make haste to expound it to all living beings.

If they had heard it [without expedients],
Men of ignorance would have had doubts,
And lost their way [to enlightenment] forever,
Though men of wisdom would have understood it by faith.

Therefore, Kāśyapa, I expounded [the Dharma]
With various expedients to all living beings
According to their capacities
In order to cause them to have the right view.

Kāśyapa, know this!
Suppose a large cloud rose in the sky,
And covered everything on the earth.
The cloud was so merciful
That it was about to send a rainfall.
Lightning flashed,
And thunder crashed in the distance,
Causing people to rejoice.

The cloud covered the sun,
And cooled the earth.
It hung down
As low as if we could reach it.

Now the rain came down
To all the quarters of the earth.
The rainwater was immeasurable.
It soaked all the earth.
There were many plants
In the retired and quiet places
Of the mountains, rivers and ravines.

They were herbs, cereal-plants, young rice-plants,
Vegetables, sugar canes, and other grasses;
Fruit-trees including vines,
And other trees, tall and short.
They were sufficiently watered by the rain.
So were all the dry lands.
The herbs and trees grew thick by the rain.

All the grasses and trees in thickets and forests
Were watered variously according to their species
By the rain water of the same taste
Coming down from the [same] cloud.

All the trees grew differently
According to their species.
They became superior or middle or inferior
Or tall or short trees.

The roots, trunks, branches, leaves,
Flowers and fruits of the various trees
Were given a fine and glossy luster
By the same rain.

Although watered by the same rain,
Some of them were tall, while others not,
Because they were different
In their entities, appearances and natures.

I am like the cloud.
I appeared in this world
Just as the large cloud covered
Everything on the earth.

Since I appeared in this world,
I have been expounding
The reality of all things
To all living beings.

(The Great Saint,
The World-Honored One,
Said to the multitude
Of gods and men:)

I am the Tathāgata,
The Most Honorable Biped.
I have appeared in this world
Just as the large cloud rose.

All living beings are dying of thirst.
I will water them.
I will save them from suffering.
I will give them the pleasure of peace,
The pleasure of the world,
And the pleasure of Nirvāṇa.

All gods and men!
Listen to me with one mind!
Come here and see me,
Who am the Most Honorable One!

I am the World-Honored One.
I am not surpassed by anyone.
I have appeared in this world
To give peace to all living beings.

I will expound the Dharma as pure as nectar
To you all in this great multitude.
My teachings are of the same taste.
They are for emancipation, that is, for Nirvāṇa.

I will expound these teachings [of mine]
With a wonderful voice.
My purpose is
To reveal the Great Vehicle.

I see all living beings equally.
I have no partiality for them.
There is not 'this one' or 'that one' to me.
I transcend love and hatred.

I am attached to nothing.
I am hindered by nothing.
I always expound the Dharma
To all living beings equally.
I expound the Dharma to many
In the same way as to one.

I always expound the Dharma.
I do nothing else.
I am not tired of expounding the Dharma
While I go or come or sit or stand.
I expound the Dharma to all living beings
Just as the rain waters all the earth.

I am not tired of giving
The rain of the Dharma to all living beings.
I have no partiality for them,
Whether they are noble or mean,
Whether they observe or violate the precepts,
Whether they live a monastic life or not,
Whether they have right or wrong views,
Whether they are clever or dull.

Those who hear the Dharma from me
Will reach various stages
[Of enlightenment]
According to their capacities.

Those who live among gods and men,
Or those who live with a wheel-turning-holy-king,
Or with King Śakra or with King Brahman,
May be likened to the small herbs.

Those who know the Dharma-without-āsravas,
Who attained Nirvāṇa,
And who obtained the six supernatural powers,
Including the three major supernatural powers,
May be likened to the middle herbs.
So may those who live alone in mountains or forests,
Who practice dhyāna-concentrations,
And who attained the enlightenment of cause-knowers.

Those who seek the stage of the World-Honored One,
Who practice endeavors and concentration of mind,
And who wish to become Buddhas,
May be likened to the large herbs.

My sons [, that is, the Bodhisattvas]
Who seek
The enlightenment of the Buddha exclusively,
Who believe that they will become Buddhas definitely,
And who have compassion towards others,
May be likened to the short trees.

The Bodhisattvas
Who turn the irrevocable wheel of the Dharma
By their supernatural powers,
And who save many thousands of myriads
Of millions of living beings,
May be likened to the tall trees.

Although my teachings are of the same content to anyone
Just as the rain is of the same taste,
The hearers receive my teachings differently
According to their capacities
Just as the plants receive
Different amounts of the rain water.

I now expediently reveal the Dharma with this simile.
I expound one truth with various discourses.

This simile is only one of the expedients
Employed by my wisdom,
Just as a drop of sea water is
Part of the great ocean.

Though I water all living beings of the world
With the same rain of the Dharma,
They practice the teachings
Of the same taste differently
According to their capacities,
Just as the herbs and trees
In thickets and forests
Grew gradually according to their species.

The Buddhas always expound
The teachings of the same taste
In order to cause all living beings of the world
To understand the Dharma.
Those who practice the teachings continuously
Will obtain [various fruits of] enlightenment.

Both the Śrāvakas and the cause-knowers,
Who live in mountains or forests,
Who have reached the final stage
 of their physical existence,
And who have attained enlightenment
 by hearing the Dharma,
May be likened to the herbs
Which have already grown up.

The Bodhisattvas
Who resolve to seek wisdom,
Who understand the triple world,
And who seek the most excellent vehicle,
May be likened to the short trees
Which have already grown up.

Those who practice dhyāna,
Who have supernatural powers,
Who have great joy
When they hear that all things are insubstantial,
And who save all living beings
By emitting innumerable rays of light,
May be likened to the tall trees
Which have already grown up.

As previously stated, Kāśyapa, I expound the Dharma
And lead human flowers
[To the fruits of Buddhahood]
Just as the large cloud waters all flowers
By a rain of the same taste
And causes them to bear their fruits.

Kāśyapa, know this!
I reveal the enlightenment of the Buddha
With various stories of previous lives,
With various parables and similes,
That is, with various expedients.
All the other Buddhas do the same.

Now I will tell you [, Śrāvakas,]
The most important truth.
You, Śrāvakas,
Have not yet attained [true] extinction.
What you are now practicing is
The Way of Bodhisattvas.
Study and practice it continuously,
And you will become Buddhas.

CHAPTER VI

ASSURANCE OF FUTURE BUDDHAHOOD

Thereupon the World-Honored One, having sung these gāthās, said to the great multitude [of bhikṣus]:

"This Mahā-Kāśyapa, a disciple of mine, will see three hundred billions of Buddhas, of World-Honored Ones, make offerings to them, respect them, honor them, praise them, and expound an innumerable number of their great teachings in his future life. After that, on the final stage of his physical existence, he will become a Buddha, called Light, the Tathāgata, the Deserver of Offerings, the Perfectly Enlightened One, the Man of Wisdom and Practice, the Well-Gone, the Knower of the World, the Unsurpassed Man, the Controller of Men, the Teacher of Gods and Men, the Buddha, the World-Honored One. His world will be called Light-Virtue; and the kalpa in which he will become that Buddha, Great-Adornment. The duration of the life of that Buddha will be twelve small kalpas. His right teachings will be preserved for twenty small kalpas, and the counterfeit of his right teachings will be preserved also for twenty small kalpas. His world will be adorned, and not be defiled with tile-pieces, rubble, thorns or dirt. The ground [of his world] will be even, and devoid of pits and mounds. It will be made of lapis lazuli. Jeweled trees will stand in lines, and the roads will be marked off by ropes of gold. Jeweled flowers will be strewn all over the ground, and the ground will be purified. Many hundreds of thousands of millions of Bodhisattvas and innumerable Śrāvakas will live in that world. Although Māra and his followers also will live there, they will not do any evil but protect the teachings of the Buddha."

Thereupon the World-Honored One, wishing to repeat what he had said, sang in gāthās:

I will tell you, bhikṣus.
I see this Kāśyapa
With the eyes of the Buddha.
He will become a Buddha
In his future life
After innumerable[1] kalpas from now.

He will see in his future life
Three hundred billions
Of Buddhas, of World-Honored Ones.
He will make offerings to them,
And perform brahma practices
To obtain the wisdom of the Buddha.
Having made offerings
To the Most Honorable Bipeds,
He will study and practice
Unsurpassed wisdom,
And become a Buddha on the final stage
Of his physical existence.

The ground [of his world] will be pure.
It will be made of lapis lazuli.
Many jeweled trees
Will stand on the roadsides.
The roads will be marked off by ropes of gold.
Anyone will rejoice at seeing them.

Fragrance will be sent forth from the trees;
And beautiful flowers will be strewn
On the ground, which will be adorned
With various wonderful things.
The ground will be even,
And devoid of mounds and pits.

---

1 This is finite.

The number of the Bodhisattvas
Will be beyond calculation.
They will be gentle.
They will have great supernatural powers.
They will keep the sūtras of the Great Vehicle
Expounded by the Buddhas.

The Śrāvakas will have already eliminated āsravas,
And reached the final stage of their physical existence.
They will become sons of the King of the Dharma.
Their number also will be beyond calculation.
Even those who have heavenly eyes
Will not be able to count them.

The duration of the life of that Buddha
Will be twelve small kalpas.
His right teachings will be preserved
For twenty small kalpas.
The counterfeit of his right teachings
Will be preserved also for twenty small kalpas.
All this is my prophecy
About the World-Honored One called Light.

Thereupon Great Maudgalyāyana, Subhūti and Mahā-Kātyāyana trembled, joined their hands together with all their hearts, looked up at the World-Honored One with unblenching eyes, and sang in gāthās in unison:

Great Hero, World-Honored One!
King of the Dharma of the Śākyas!
Give us your voice
Out of your compassion towards us!

If you see what we have deep in our minds,
And assure us of our future Buddhahood,
We shall feel as cool and as refreshed
As if we were sprinkled with nectar.

Suppose a man came
From a country suffering from famine.
Now he saw the meal of a great king.
He did not partake of it in doubts and fears.
After he was told to take it by the king,
He took it at once.
We are like that man.
We know the defects of the Lesser Vehicle.
But we do not know how to obtain
The unsurpassed wisdom of the Buddha.

Although we hear you say [to us],
"You will become Buddhas,"
We are still in doubts and fears about it,
Just as that man was about the meal.
If you assure us of our future Buddhahood,
We shall be happy and peaceful.

You, the Great Hero, the World-Honored One,
Wish to give peace to all the people of the world.
If you assure us of our future Buddhahood, we shall be
Like the man who was permitted to take the meal.

Thereupon the World-Honored One, having understood the wishes of the great disciples, said to the bhikṣus:

"In his future life, this Subhūti will see three hundred billion nayutas of Buddhas, make offerings to them, respect them, honor them, praise them, perform brahma practices, complete the Way of Bodhisattvas, and become a Buddha on the final stage of his physical existence. He will be called Beautiful-Form, the Tathāgata, the Deserver of Offerings, the Perfectly Enlightened One, the Man of Wisdom and Practice, the Well-Gone, the Knower of the World, the Unsurpassed Man, the Controller of Men, the Teacher of Gods and Men, the Buddha, the World-Honored One. The kalpa in which he will become that Buddha will be called Having-Treasures;

and his world, Treasure-Born. The ground [of his world] will be even, made of crystal, adorned with jeweled trees, and devoid of mounds, pits, rubble, thorns and dirt. Jeweled flowers will cover the ground to purify it. The people of that world will live in buildings of wonderful treasures. His disciples in Śrāvakahood will be numberless, beyond calculation or comparison. The Bodhisattvas will be many thousands of billions of nayutas in number. The duration of the life of that Buddha will be twelve small kalpas. His right teachings will be preserved for twenty small kalpas. The counterfeit of his right teachings will be preserved also for twenty small kalpas. That Buddha will always stay in the sky, expound the Dharma to the multitude, and save innumerable Bodhisattvas and Śrāvakas.

Thereupon the World-Honored One, wishing to repeat what he had said, sang in gāthās:

Bhikṣus!
Now I will tell you.
Listen to me
With one mind!

Subhūti, a disciple of mine,
Will be able
To become a Buddha
Called Beautiful-Form.

He will make offerings
To many billions of Buddhas, and practice
According to the practices of the Buddhas,
And finally attain great enlightenment.

On the final stage of his physical existence,
He will obtain the thirty-two physical marks,
And become as beautiful and as wonderful
As a mountain of treasures.

The world of that Buddha
Will be the purest.
Anyone will be happy to see it.
That Buddha will save
Innumerable living beings
Of that world.

Many Bodhisattvas
In the world of that Buddha
Will be clever.
They will turn
The irrevocable wheel of the Dharma,
And adorn that world.

The Śrāvakas in that world also
Will be countless.
They will have the six supernatural powers,
Including the three major supernatural powers.
They will have the eight emancipations.
They will be exceedingly powerful and virtuous.

The supernatural powers
Employed by that Buddha
For the expounding of the Dharma
Will be inconceivable.

As many gods and men
As there are sands in the River Ganges
Will join their hands together
And listen to the words of that Buddha.

The duration of the life of that Buddha
Will be twelve small kalpas.
His right teachings will be preserved
For twenty small kalpas.
The counterfeit of his right teachings
Also will be preserved for twenty small kalpas.

Thereupon the World-Honored One said to the bhikṣus:

"Now I will tell you. This Great Kātyāyana will make many offerings to eight hundred thousand millions of Buddhas, attend on them, respect them, and honor them in his future life. After the extinction of each of those Buddhas, he will erect a stūpa-mausoleum a thousand yojanas high, and five hundred yojanas wide and deep. He will make it of the seven treasures: gold, silver, lapis lazuli, shell, agate, pearl and ruby. He will offer flowers, necklaces, incense to apply to the skin, incense powder, incense to burn, canopies, banners and streamers to this stūpa-mausoleum. After that he will make the same offerings to two billions of Buddhas. Having made offerings to those Buddhas, he will complete the Way of Bodhisattvas, and become a Buddha called Jāmbūnada-Gold-Light, the Tathāgata, the Deserver of Offerings, the Perfectly Enlightened One, the Man of Wisdom and Practice, the Well-Gone, the Knower of the World, the Unsurpassed Man, the Controller of Men, the Teacher of Gods and Men, the Buddha, the World-Honored One. The ground [of his world] will be even, made of crystal, and adorned with jeweled trees. The roads will be marked off by ropes of gold, and wonderful flowers will cover the ground to purify it. Anyone will rejoice at seeing it. The four evil regions: hell, the region of hungry spirits, that of animals, and that of asuras, will not exist in that world. Many gods and men will live there. Śrāvakas and Bodhisattvas, many billions in number, also will live there to adorn that world. The duration of the life of that Buddha will be twelve small kalpas. His right teachings will be preserved for twenty small kalpas, and the counterfeit of his right teachings also will be preserved for twenty small kalpas."

Thereupon the World-Honored One, wishing to repeat what he had said, sang in gāthās:

Bhikṣus!
Listen with one mind!
What I say
Is true, not false.

This Kātyāyana
Will make
Wonderful offerings
To the Buddhas.

After the extinction of each of the Buddhas,
He will erect a stūpa of the seven treasures,
And offer flowers and incense to the śarīras
[Of the Buddha enshrined in the stūpa].

On the final stage of his physical existence,
He will obtain the wisdom of the Buddha
And attain perfect enlightenment.
His world will be pure.
He will save many billions of living beings.
All living beings
In the worlds of the ten quarters
Will make offerings to him.

No light will surpass
The light of that Buddha.
The name of that Buddha will be
Jāmbū[nada]-Gold-Light.

Innumerable Bodhisattvas and Śrāvakas
Will live in his world, and adorn that world.
They will have already eliminated
The bonds of existence.

Thereupon the World-Honored One said again to the great multitude:

"Now I will tell you. This Great Maudgalyāyana will make various offerings to eight thousand Buddhas, respect them, and honor them. After the extinction of each of those Buddhas, he will erect a stūpa-mausoleum a thousand yojanas high, and five hundred yojanas wide and deep. He will make it of the seven treasures: gold, silver, lapis lazuli, shell, agate, pearl and ruby. He will offer flowers, necklaces, incense applicable to the skin, incense powder, incense to burn, canopies, banners and streamers to the stūpa-mausoleum. After that he will make the same offerings to two hundred billions of Buddhas. Then he will become a Buddha called Tamālapattracandana-Fragrance, the Tathāgata, the Deserver of Offerings, the Perfectly Enlightened One, the Man of Wisdom and Practice, the Well-Gone, the Knower of the World, the Unsurpassed Man, the Controller of Men, the Teacher of Gods and Men, the Buddha, the World-Honored One. The kalpa in which he will become that Buddha will be called Joyfulness; and his world, Mind-Happiness. The ground [of his world] will be even, made of crystal, adorned with jeweled trees, and purified with strewn flowers of pearls. Anyone will rejoice at seeing it. Innumerable gods, men, Bodhisattvas and Śrāvakas will live there. The duration of the life of that Buddha will be twenty-four small kalpas. His right teachings will be preserved for forty small kalpas, and the counterfeit of his right teachings also will be preserved for forty small kalpas."

Thereupon the World-Honored One, wishing to repeat what he had said, sang in gāthās:

After he gives up his present existence,
This Great Maudgalyāyana, a disciple of mine,
Will see many Buddhas,
Many World-Honored Ones.
He will see eight thousand of them,
And then two hundred billions of them.

In order to attain
The enlightenment of the Buddha,
He will make offerings to them, and respect them.
He will perform brahma practices under those Buddhas,
And keep the teachings of those Buddhas
For innumerable[2] kalpas.

After the extinction of each of those Buddhas,
He will erect a stūpa of the seven treasures.

---

2 This is finite.

There will be a long golden yaṣṭi
On the top of the stūpa.
He will offer flowers, incense and music
To the stūpa-mausoleum of the Buddha.

He will finally complete
The Way of Bodhisattvas,
And become a Buddha
Called Tamāla[pattra]candana-Fragrance
In a world called
Mind-Happiness.

The duration of the life of that Buddha
Will be twenty-four [small] kalpas.
He will expound to gods and men
The enlightenment of the Buddha.

As many Śrāvakas as there are sands in the River Ganges
Will have the six supernatural powers,
Including the three major supernatural powers.
They will be exceedingly powerful and virtuous.

Innumerable Bodhisattvas also will live there.
They will be resolute in mind, and strenuous.
They will never falter
In seeking the wisdom of the Buddha.

After the extinction of that Buddha,
His right teachings
Will be preserved for forty small kalpas.
So will the counterfeit of them.

The five hundred disciples of mine[3]
Are powerful and virtuous.
They also shall be assured
Of their future Buddhahood.

---

3 Five hundred disciples are not given as a group in the foregoing chapters.

They will become Buddhas
In their future lives.

Now I will tell you
About my previous existence
And also about yours.
All of you, listen attentively!

CHAPTER VII

THE PARABLE OF A MAGIC CITY

The Buddha said to the bhikṣus:

"A countless, limitless, inconceivable, asaṃkhya[1] number of kalpas ago, there lived a Buddha called Great-Universal-Wisdom-Excellence, the Tathāgata, the Deserver of Offerings, the Perfectly Enlightened One, the Man of Wisdom and Practice, the Well-Gone, the Knower of the World, the Unsurpassed Man, the Controller of Men, the Teacher of Gods and Men, the Buddha, the World-Honored One. His world was called Well-Composed; and the kalpa in which he became that Buddha, Great-Form.

"Bhikṣus! It is a very long time since that Buddha passed away. Suppose someone smashed all the earth-particles of one thousand million Sumeru-worlds into ink-powder. Then he went to the east[, carrying the ink-powder with him]. He inked a dot as large as a particle of dust [with that ink-powder] on the world at a distance of one thousand worlds[2] from his world. Then he went again and repeated the inking of a dot on the world at every distance of one thousand worlds until the ink-powder was exhausted. What do you think of this? Do you think that any mathematician or any disciple of a mathematician could count the number of the worlds [he went through]?"

"No, we do not, World-Honored One!"

"Bhikṣus! Now all the worlds he went through, whether they were inked or not, were smashed into dust. The number of the kalpas which have elapsed since that Buddha passed away is many

1 This is an adjective, meaning "innumerable."

2 Each of these worlds is considered to be composed of one thousand million Sumeru-worlds.

hundreds of thousands of billions of asaṃkhyas[3] larger than the number of the particles of the dust thus produced. Yet I remember [the extinction of] that Buddha by my power of insight as vividly as if he had passed away today."

Thereupon the World-Honored One, wishing to repeat what he had said, sang in gāthās:

According to my remembrance,
There lived a Buddha, an Honorable Biped,
Called Great-Universal-Wisdom-Excellence,
Countless kalpas ago.

Suppose someone smashed
All the earth-particles
Of one thousand million Sumeru-worlds
Into ink-powder.

He went, [carrying the ink-powder with him,]
And inked a dot as large as a particle of dust
On the world at a distance of one thousand worlds.
He repeated the inking until the ink-powder was exhausted.

Suppose the worlds
Through which he went,
Whether they were inked or not,
Were smashed into dust.

It is innumerable[4] kalpas,
More than the number
Of the particles of dust thus produced,
Since that Buddha passed away.

I remember the extinction of that Buddha
As vividly as if he had passed away just now,

---

3 This is an adjective, meaning "innumerable."

4 This is a finite number.

By my unhindered wisdom; I also remember
The Śrāvakas and Bodhisattvas who lived [with him].

Bhikṣus, know this!
My wisdom is pure, wonderful,
Free from āsravas and from hindrance.
I know those who lived innumerable kalpas ago.

The Buddha said to the bhikṣus:

"The duration of the life of Great-Universal-Wisdom-Excellence Buddha was five hundred and forty billion nayuta kalpas. [Before he attained Buddhahood,] he sat at the place of enlightenment and defeated the army of Māra. He wished to attain Anuttara-samyak-saṃbodhi, but could not because the Dharma of the Buddhas had not yet come into his mind. He sat cross-legged without moving his mind and body for one to ten small kalpas. During all that time the Dharma of the Buddhas did not come into his mind.

"[Before he sat at the place of enlightenment,] the Trāyastriṃśa Gods prepared him a lion-like seat a yojana high under the Bodhi-tree so that he might be able to attain Anuttara-samyak-saṃbodhi on that seat. When he sat on that seat, the Brahman-heavenly-kings rained heavenly flowers on the area extending a hundred yojanas in all directions from that seat. From time to time withered flowers were blown away by fragrant winds and new flowers were rained down. [The Brahman-heavenly-kings] continued this offering to him for fully ten small kalpas. [After he attained Buddhahood also,] they continued raining flowers until he passed away.

"[When he sat on that seat,] the four heavenly-kings beat heavenly drums, and the other gods made heavenly music and offered it to him. They continued these offerings also for fully ten small kalpas. [After he attained Buddhahood also,] they continued these offerings until he passed away.

"Bhikṣus! At the end of the period of ten small kalpas, the Dharma of the Buddhas came into the mind of Great-Universal-Wisdom-Excellence Buddha. Now he attained Anuttara-samyak-saṃbodhi. Before he left home, he had sixteen sons. The first son was called Accumulated-Wisdom. Each of the sons had various playthings. When the sons heard that their father had attained Anuttara-samyak-saṃbodhi, they gave up the playthings, left home, and came to that Buddha.

"[When they were leaving home,] their mothers saw them off, weeping. Not only the wheel-turning-holy-king, who was their grandfather, but also one hundred ministers and hundreds of thousands of billions of subjects surrounded and followed the princes, wishing to come to the place of enlightenment, to see Great-Universal-Wisdom-Excellence Tathāgata, to make offerings to that Buddha, respect him, honor him, and praise him.

"Having come [to that Buddha], the princes worshipped him at his feet with their heads, walked around him, joined their hands together towards him with all their hearts, looked up at the World-Honored One, and praised him in gāthās:

In order to save all living beings,
You, the World-Honored One,
Who have great powers and virtues,
[Made efforts] for many hundreds of millions of years.
Now you have become a Buddha.
You have finally fulfilled your vows. Congratulations!

You, the World-Honored One, are exceptional.
When you were sitting,
You were quiet and peaceful.
You did not move your body, hands or feet
For ten small kalpas.
Your mind was tranquil, not distracted.
You have finally obtained tranquil extinction.
You now dwell peacefully in the Dharma-without-āsravas.

Seeing that you have peacefully attained
The enlightenment of the Buddha,
We, too, have obtained benefits.
Congratulations! How glad we are!
All living beings are suffering.

Being blind, they have no leader.
They do not know how to stop suffering,
Or that they should seek emancipation.
In the long night fewer people go to heaven,
And more people go to the evil regions.
They go from darkness to darkness, and do not hear
Of the names of the Buddhas.

You are the Most Honorable One.
You have obtained the peaceful Dharma-without-āsravas.
Not only we but also all gods and men
Will be able to obtain the greatest benefit.
Therefore, we bow and devote ourselves to you,
The Most Honorable One.

"Thereupon the sixteen princes, having praised the Buddha with these gāthās, begged the World-Honored One to turn the wheel of the Dharma, saying, 'World-Honored One! Expound the Dharma, and give peace and many benefits to gods and men out of your compassion towards them!' They repeated this in gāthās:

You, the Hero of the World, are unequalled.
Adorned with the marks
Of one hundred merits,
You have obtained unsurpassed wisdom.
Expound the Dharma and save us
And other living beings of the world!

Expound the Dharma, reveal the Dharma,
And cause us to obtain that wisdom!
If we attain Buddhahood,
Others also will do the same.

You, the World-Honored One, know
What all living beings have deep in their minds,
What teachings they are practicing,
And how much power of wisdom they have.

You know their desires, the merits they obtained,
And the karmas they did
In their previous existence.
Turn the wheel of the unsurpassed Dharma!

The Buddha said to the bhikṣus:

"When Great-Universal-Wisdom-Excellence Buddha attained Anuttara-samyak-saṃbodhi, five hundred billion Buddha-worlds in each of the ten quarters quaked in the six ways, and all those worlds, including those intercepted from the brilliant rays of light of the sun and the moon by the neighboring worlds, were illumined [by great rays of light], and the living beings of those worlds were able to see each other for the first time. They said to each other, 'How did you appear so suddenly?' The palaces of the gods of those worlds, including the palace of Brahmans, also quaked in the six ways. The great rays of light which illumined all those worlds were brighter than the rays of light emitted by those gods.

"The palaces of the Brahman-heavenly[-kings] of the five hundred billion worlds in the east were illumined twice as brightly as ever. The Brahman-heavenly-kings [of those worlds] each thought, 'My palace has never been illumined so brightly before. Why is that?' They visited each other and discussed the reason. There was a great Brahman-heavenly-king called All-Saving among them. He said to the other Brahmans in gāthās:

Why are our palaces illumined
More brightly than ever?
Let us find [the place]
[From where this light has come].

Did a god of great virtue or a Buddha
Appear somewhere in the universe?
This great light illumines
The worlds of the ten quarters.

"Thereupon the Brahman-heavenly-kings of the five hundred billion worlds went to the west, carrying flower-plates filled with heavenly flowers, in order to find [the place from where the light had come]. Their palaces also moved as they went. They [reached the Well-Composed World and] saw that Great-Universal-Wisdom-Excellence Tathāgata was sitting on the lion-like seat under the Bodhi-tree at the place of enlightenment, surrounded respectfully by gods, dragon-kings, gandharvas, kiṃnaras, mahoragas, men and nonhuman beings. They also saw that the sixteen princes were begging the Buddha to turn the wheel of the Dharma. Thereupon the Brahman-heavenly-kings worshipped the Buddha with their heads, walked around him a hundred thousand times, and strewed heavenly flowers to him. The strewn flowers were heaped up to the height of Mt. Sumeru. The Brahman-heavenly-kings offered flowers also to the ten-yojana-tall Bodhi-tree of the Buddha. Having offered flowers, they offered their palaces to the Buddha, saying, 'We offer these palaces to you. Receive them and benefit us out of your compassion towards us!' In the presence of the Buddha, they simultaneously praised him in gāthās with all their hearts:

You, the World-Honored One, are exceptional.
It is difficult to meet you.
You have innumerable merits.
You are saving all living beings.

As the great teacher of gods and men,
You are benefiting all living beings
Of the worlds of the ten quarters
Out of your compassion towards them.

We have come here from five hundred billion worlds.
We gave up the pleasure
Of deep dhyāna-concentration
Because we wished to make offerings to you.
Our palaces are beautifully adorned
Because we accumulated merits in our previous existence.

We offer [these palaces] to you.
Receive them out of your compassion towards us!

"Thereupon the Brahman-heavenly-kings, having praised the Buddha with these gāthās, said, 'World-Honored One! Turn the wheel of the Dharma and save all living beings! Open the Way to Nirvāṇa!' They simultaneously said in a gāthā with all their hearts:

Hero of the World, Most Honorable Biped!
Expound the Dharma!
Save the suffering beings
By the power of your great compassion!

"Thereupon Great-Universal-Wisdom-Excellence Tathāgata gave his tacit consent to their appeal.

"Bhikṣus! The great Brahman-[heavenly-]kings of the five hundred billion worlds in the southeast, who saw their palaces illumined more brightly than ever, danced with joy. They also wondered why [their palaces were so illumined]. They visited each other and discussed the reason. There was a great Brahman-heavenly-king called Great-Compassion among them. He said to the other Brahmans in gāthās:

Why is it
That we see this light?
Our palaces are illumined
More brightly than ever.

Did a god of great virtue or a Buddha
Appear somewhere in the universe?
We have never seen this [light] before.
Let us do our best to find [the reason].

Let us go even to the end of one thousand billion worlds,
And find the place from where this light has come.

A Buddha may have appeared somewhere in the universe
In order to save the suffering beings.

"Thereupon the Brahman-heavenly-kings of the five hundred billion [worlds] went to the northwest, carrying flower-plates filled with heavenly flowers, in order to find [the place from where the light had come]. Their palaces also moved as they went. They [reached the Well-Composed World and] saw that Great-Universal-Wisdom-Excellence Tathāgata was sitting on the lion-like seat under the Bodhi-tree of the place of enlightenment, surrounded respectfully by gods, dragon-kings, gandharvas, kiṃnaras, mahoragas, men, and nonhuman beings. They also saw that the sixteen princes were begging the Buddha to turn the wheel of the Dharma. Thereupon the Brahman-heavenly-kings worshipped the Buddha with their heads, walked around him a hundred thousand times, and strewed heavenly flowers to him. The strewn flowers were heaped up to the height of Mt. Sumeru. The Brahman-heavenly-kings offered flowers also to the Bodhi-tree of the Buddha. Having offered flowers, they offered their palaces to the Buddha, saying, 'We offer these palaces to you. Receive them and benefit us out of your compassion towards us!' In the presence of the Buddha, they simultaneously praised him in gāthās with all their hearts:

Saintly Master, God of Gods!
Your voice is as sweet as a kalaviṅka's.
You have compassion towards all living beings.
We now bow before you.
You, the World-Honored One, are exceptional.
You appear only once in a very long time.

No Buddha has appeared
For the past one hundred and eighty kalpas.
The three evil regions are crowded;
And the living beings in heaven, decreasing.

Now you have appeared in this world
And become the eye of all living beings.
As their refuge, you are saving them.
As their father, you are benefiting them
Out of your compassion towards them.
We are now able to see you
Because we accumulated merits
In our previous existence.

"Thereupon the Brahman-heavenly-kings, having praised the Buddha with these gāthās, said, 'World-Honored One! Turn the wheel of the Dharma and save all living beings out of your compassion towards them!' Then they simultaneously said in gāthās with all their hearts:

Great Saint, turn the wheel of the Dharma
And reveal the reality of all things!
Save the suffering beings
And cause them to have great joy!

If they hear the Dharma, some will attain enlightenment;
Others will be reborn in heaven.
The living beings in the evil regions will decrease;
And those who do good patiently will increase.

"Thereupon Great-Universal-Wisdom-Excellence Tathāgata gave his tacit consent to their appeal.

"Bhikṣus! The great Brahman-[heavenly-]kings of the five hundred billion worlds in the south, who saw their palaces illumined more brightly than ever, also danced with joy. They wondered why [their palaces were so illumined]. They visited each other and discussed the reason, saying, 'Why are our palaces illumined so brightly?' There was a great Brahman-heavenly-king called Wonderful-Dharma among them. He said to the other Brahmans in gāthās:

Our palaces are illumined so brightly.
There must be some reason.
Let us find [the place]
[From where the light has come].

We have never seen this [light]
For the past one hundred thousand kalpas.
Did a god of great virtue or a Buddha appear
Somewhere in the universe?

"Thereupon the Brahman-heavenly-kings of the five hundred billion [worlds] went to the north, carrying flower-plates filled with heavenly flowers, in order to find [the place from where the light had come]. Their palaces also moved as they went. They [reached the Well-Composed World and] saw that Great-Universal-Wisdom-Excellence Tathāgata was sitting on the lion-like seat under the Bodhi-tree of the place of enlightenment, surrounded respectfully by gods, dragon-kings, gandharvas, kiṃnaras, mahoragas, men and nonhuman beings. They also saw that the sixteen princes were begging the Buddha to turn the wheel of the Dharma. They worshipped the Buddha with their heads, walked around him a hundred thousand times, and strewed heavenly flowers to him. The strewn flowers were heaped up to the height of Mt. Sumeru. The Brahman-heavenly-kings offered flowers also to the Bodhi-tree of the Buddha. Having offered flowers, they offered their palaces to the Buddha, saying, 'We offer these palaces to you. Receive them and benefit us out of your compassion towards us!' In the presence of the Buddha, they simultaneously praised him in gāthās with all their hearts:

It is difficult to see a World-Honored One.
You, the World-Honored One, eliminated all illusions.
We have not seen a World-Honored One
For the past one hundred and thirty kalpas.

Send the rain of the Dharma
On the hungry and thirsty beings!
Possessor of immeasurable wisdom,
We have never seen anyone wiser than you.
You are as rare as an udumbara-flower.
Now we have met you today.

Our palaces are beautifully adorned
With your light.
World-Honored One, receive them
Out of your great compassion towards us!

"Thereupon the Brahman-heavenly-kings, having praised the Buddha with these gāthās, said, 'World-Honored One! Turn the wheel of the Dharma so that Māra, Brahman, the other gods, śramaṇas, and brāhmaṇas of the world may be peaceful, and that they may be saved!' They simultaneously praised the Buddha in gāthās with all their hearts:

Most Honorable of Gods and Men!
Turn the wheel of the unsurpassed Dharma,
Beat the drum of the Great Dharma,
Blow the conch-shell horn of the Great Dharma,
Send the rain of the Great Dharma,
And save innumerable living beings!
Devoting ourselves to you, we beg you.
Resound your profound teaching!

"Thereupon Great-Universal-Wisdom-Excellence Tathāgata gave his tacit consent to their appeal.

"The great Brahman-[heavenly-]kings of the five hundred billion worlds in the southwest, west, northwest, north, northeast, and nadir also did the same. The great Brahman-heavenly-kings of the five hundred billion worlds in the zenith, who saw their palaces illumined more brightly than ever, also danced with joy. They wondered why [their palaces were so illumined]. They visited each other and discussed the reason, saying, 'Why are our palaces illumined so brightly?' There was a great Brahman-heavenly-king called Śikhin among them. He said to the other Brahmans in gāthās:

Our palaces are adorned
More brightly than ever.
Why are they illumined
By this powerful light?

We have never seen nor heard
Of such a wonderful thing as this before.
Did a god of great virtue or a Buddha appear
Somewhere in the universe?

"Thereupon the Brahman-heavenly-kings of the five hundred billion [worlds] went down, carrying flower-plates filled with heavenly flowers, in order to find [the place from where the light had come]. Their palaces also moved as they went. They [reached the Well-Composed World and] saw that Great-Universal-Wisdom-Excellence Tathāgata was sitting on the lion-like seat under the Bodhi-tree of the place of enlightenment, surrounded respectfully by gods, dragon-kings, gandharvas, kiṃnaras, mahoragas, men and non-human beings. They also saw that the sixteen princes were begging the Buddha to turn the wheel of the Dharma. They worshipped the Buddha with their heads, walked around him a hundred thousand times, and strewed heavenly flowers to him. The strewn flowers were heaped up to the height of Mt. Sumeru. The Brahman-heavenly-kings offered flowers also to the Bodhi-tree of the Buddha. Having offered flowers, they offered their palaces to the Buddha, saying, 'We offer these palaces to you. Receive them and benefit us out of your compassion towards us!' In the presence of the Buddha, they simultaneously praised him in gāthās with all their hearts:

How good it is to see a Buddha,
To see the Honorable Saint who saves the world!

He saves all living beings
From the prison of the triple world.

The All-Knower, the Most Honorable One
 of Gods and Men,
Opens the gate of the teachings as sweet as nectar,
And saves all living beings
Out of his compassion towards them.

There has been no Buddha
For the past innumerable kalpas.
Before you appeared,
The worlds of the ten quarters were dark.

The living beings in the three evil regions
And asuras are increasing.
The living beings in heaven are decreasing.
Many fall into the evil regions after their death.

They do not hear the Dharma from a Buddha.
Because they did evils,
Their appearances are getting worse;
And their power and wisdom, decreasing.
Because they did sinful karmas,
They lose pleasures and the memory of pleasures.
They are attached to wrong views.
They do not know how to do good.
They are not taught by a Buddha;
Therefore, they fall into the evil regions.

Now you have appeared for the first time
 after a long time,
And become the eyes of the world.
You have appeared in this world
Out of your compassion towards all living beings,
And finally attained perfect enlightenment.

We are very glad.
All the others also rejoice at seeing you,
Whom they have never seen before.

Our palaces are beautifully adorned
With your light.
We offer them to you.
Receive them out of your compassion towards us!

May the merits we have accumulated by this offering
Be distributed among all living beings,
And may we and all other living beings
Attain the enlightenment of the Buddha!

"Thereupon the Brahman-heavenly-kings of the five hundred billion [worlds], having praised the Buddha with these gāthās, said to him, 'World-Honored One! Turn the wheel of the Dharma so that all living beings may be peaceful, and that they may be saved!' They said in gāthās:

World-Honored One, turn the wheel of the Dharma,
Beat the drum of the Dharma as sweet as nectar,
Save the suffering beings,
And show them the way to Nirvāṇa!

Assent to our appeal!
You studied the Dharma for innumerable kalpas.
Expound it with your exceedingly wonderful voice
Out of your compassion towards us!

"Thereupon Great-Universal-Wisdom-Excellence Tathāgata, having assented to the appeals made by the Brahman-heavenly-kings of the worlds of the ten quarters and also by the sixteen princes, turned the wheel of the teaching [of the four truths] three times, making twelve proclamations altogether. The wheel of this teaching could not be turned by any other one in the world, be he a śramaṇa, a brāhmaṇa, a god, Māra or Brahman. The Buddha said,

'This is suffering. This is the cause of suffering. This is extinction of suffering. This is the Way to extinction of suffering.'

"Then he expounded the teaching of the twelve causes, saying, 'Ignorance causes predisposition. Predisposition causes consciousness. Consciousness causes name-and-form. Name-and-form causes the six sense organs. The six sense organs cause impression. Impression causes feeling. Feeling causes craving. Craving causes grasping. Grasping causes existence. Existence causes birth. Birth causes aging-and-death, grief, sorrow, suffering and lamentation. When ignorance is eliminated, predisposition is eliminated. When predisposition is eliminated, consciousness is eliminated. When consciousness is eliminated, name-and-form is eliminated. When name-and-form is eliminated, the six sense organs are eliminated. When the six sense organs are eliminated, impression is eliminated. When impression is eliminated, feeling is eliminated. When feeling is eliminated, craving is eliminated. When craving is eliminated, grasping is eliminated. When grasping is eliminated, existence is eliminated. When existence is eliminated, birth is eliminated. When birth is eliminated, aging-and-death, grief, sorrow, suffering and lamentation are eliminated.'

"When the Buddha expounded these teachings to the great multitude of gods and men, six hundred billion nayuta men emancipated themselves from āsravas, and obtained profound and wonderful dhyāna-concentrations, the six supernatural powers including the three major supernatural powers, and the eight emancipations because they gave up wrong views.[5] At his second, third and fourth expoundings of these teachings also, thousands of billions of nayutas of living beings, that is, as many living beings as there are sands in the River Ganges, emancipated themselves from āsravas because they gave up wrong views.[6] [They became Śrāvakas.] Those who became Śrāvakas thereafter were also innumerable, uncountable.

"The sixteen princes were young boys at that time. They renounced the world and became śrāmaṇeras. Their sense organs were keen; and their wisdom, bright. They had already

---

5 不受一切法 Literally means, "because they did not receive anything."

6 See footnote 5 above.

made offerings to hundreds of thousands of billions of Buddhas, performed brahma practices, and sought Anuttara-samyak-saṃbodhi in their previous existence. They said to the Buddha simultaneously, 'World-Honored One! All these Śrāvakas of great virtue, many thousands of billions in number, have already done [what they should do]. World-Honored One! Expound to us the teaching of Anuttara-samyak-saṃbodhi! If we hear that teaching, we will study and practice it. World-Honored One! We wish to have the insight of the Tathāgata. You know what we have deep in our minds.'

"Seeing the sixteen princes having renounced the world, eight billion followers of the wheel-turning-holy-king begged the king to allow them to do the same. He conceded to them immediately.

"The Buddha assented to the appeal of the śrāmaṇeras, but it was twenty thousand kalpas afterwards that he expounded to the four kinds of devotees the sūtra of the Great Vehicle called the 'Lotus Flower of the Wonderful Dharma, the Dharma for Bodhisattvas, the Dharma Upheld by the Buddhas.'

"When the Buddha completed the expounding of this sūtra, the sixteen śrāmaṇeras kept, recited and understood this sūtra in order to attain Anuttara-samyak-saṃbodhi. The sixteen śrāmaṇeras, [who were] Bodhisattvas, received this sūtra by faith. Some Śrāvakas understood it by faith, but the other Śrāvakas and other living beings, thousands of billions in number, doubted it.

"It took the Buddha eight thousand kalpas to complete the expounding of this sūtra. During that time he did not take a rest. Having completed the expounding of this sūtra, the Buddha entered a quiet room and practiced dhyāna-concentration for eighty-four thousand kalpas. Seeing him practicing dhyāna-concentration quietly in the room, the sixteen Bodhisattva-śrāmaṇeras each sat on a seat of the Dharma, expounded the Sūtra of the Lotus Flower of the Wonderful Dharma to the four kinds of devotees for eighty-four thousand kalpas, and saved six hundred billion nayutas of living beings, that is, as many living beings as there are sands in the River Ganges. They showed them the Way, taught them, benefited them, caused them to rejoice and to aspire for Anuttara-samyak-saṃbodhi.

"Having practiced dhyāna-concentration for eighty-four thousand kalpas, the Buddha emerged from his samādhi, came back to his seat of the Dharma, sat quietly, and said to the great multitude, 'These sixteen Bodhisattva-śrāmaṇeras are rare. Their sense organs are keen; and their wisdom, bright. In their previous existence, they already made offerings to many hundreds of thousands of billions of Buddhas, performed brahma practices under those Buddhas, kept the wisdom of those Buddhas, showed it to the living beings [of the worlds of those Buddhas], and caused them to enter into it. All of you! Approach these [Bodhisattva-śrāmaṇeras] from time to time and make offerings to them! Why is that? It is because anyone, be he a Śrāvaka or a Pratyekabuddha or a Bodhisattva, who believes this sūtra expounded by these sixteen Bodhisattvas, keeps it, and does not slander it, will be able to attain Anuttara-samyak-saṃbodhi, that is, the wisdom of the Tathāgata.'"

The Buddha said to the bhikṣus:

"These sixteen Bodhisattvas willingly expounded the Sūtra of the Lotus Flower of the Wonderful Dharma. Each of them taught six hundred billion nayutas of living beings, that is, as many living beings as there are sands in the River Ganges. Those living beings were always accompanied by the Bodhisattva[, by whom they were taught,] in their consecutive existences. [In each of their consecutive existences,] they heard the Dharma from him, and understood it by faith. By the merits [they had thus accumulated], they were given a privilege to see four billion Buddhas, that is, four billion World-Honored Ones. They have not yet seen all of them.

"Bhikṣus! Now I will tell you. The sixteen śrāmaṇeras, who were the disciples of that Buddha, have already attained Anuttara-samyak-saṃbodhi. They now expound the Dharma in the worlds of the ten quarters.[7] They have many hundreds of thousands of billions of attendants consisting of Bodhisattvas and Śrāvakas. Two of the śrāmaṇeras are now Buddhas in the east. One of them is called Akṣobhya. He is in the World of Joy. The other is called Sumeru-Peak. Another couple of the śrāmaṇeras are now Buddhas in the southeast, called Lion-Voice and Lion-Form. Another couple of them are now Buddhas in the south, called Sky-Dwelling and

7 Strictly speaking, the quarters are eight, as are shown below.

Eternal-Extinction. Another couple of them are now Buddhas in the southwest, called Emperor-Form and Brahma-Form. Another couple of them are now Buddhas in the west, called Amitāyus and Saving-All-Worlds-From-Suffering. Another couple of them are now Buddhas in the northwest, called Tamālapattracandana-Fragrance-Supernatural-Power and Sumeru-Form. Another couple of them are now Buddhas in the north, called Cloud-Freedom and Cloud-Freedom-King. One of the remaining two is now a Buddha in the northeast called Eliminating-Fear-Of-All-Worlds. The other one, that is, the sixteenth śrāmaṇera is I, Sakyamuni Buddha. I attained Anuttara-samyak-saṃbodhi in this Sahā-World.

"Bhikṣus! When we were śrāmaṇeras, we each taught many hundreds of thousands of billions of living beings, that is, as many living beings as there are sands in the River Ganges. Those living beings who followed me, heard the Dharma from me in order to attain Anuttara-samyak-saṃbodhi. Some of them are still in Śrāvakahood. I now teach them the Way to Anuttara-samyak-saṃbodhi. They will be able to enter the Way to Buddhahood by my teaching, but not immediately because the wisdom of the Tathāgata is difficult to believe and difficult to understand. Those living beings as many as there are sands in the River Ganges, whom I taught [when I was a śrāmaṇera], included you bhikṣus and those who will be reborn as my disciples in Śrāvakahood after my extinction. My disciples who do not hear this sūtra or know the practices of Bodhisattvas, after my extinction will make a conception of extinction by the merits they will have accumulated by themselves, and enter into Nirvāṇa as they conceive it. At that time I shall be a Buddha of another name in another world. Those who will enter into Nirvāṇa as they conceive it will be able [to be reborn] in the world I shall live in, seek the wisdom of the Buddha, and hear this sūtra. They will be able to attain [true] extinction only by the Vehicle of the Buddha in that world because there is no other vehicle except when the Tathāgatas expound the Dharma with expedients.

"Bhikṣus! I will collect Bodhisattvas and Śrāvakas and expound this sūtra to them when I realize that the time of my Nirvāṇa[8] is

8 This stands for Parinirvāṇa.

drawing near, that the living beings have become pure in heart, that they can understand the truth of the Void by firm faith, and that they have already entered deep into dhyāna-concentration. No one in the world can attain [true] extinction by the two vehicles. [True] extinction can be attained only by the One Buddha-Vehicle.

"Bhikṣus, know this! I can enter skillfully deep into the natures of all living beings. Because I saw that they wished to hear the teachings of the Lesser Vehicle and that they were deeply attached to the five desires, I expounded the teaching of Nirvāṇa to them. When they heard that teaching, they received it by faith.

"I will tell you a parable. Once upon a time there was a dangerous, bad road five hundred yojanas long. It was so fearful that no men lived in the neighborhood. Now many people wished to pass through this road in order to reach a place of treasures. They were led by a man, clever, wise, and well informed of the conditions of the dangerous road. He took them along this dangerous road, but halfway the people got tired of walking. They said to him, 'We are tired out. We are also afraid of the danger of this road. We cannot go a step farther. Our destination is still far off. We wish to go back.'

"The leader, who knew many expedients, thought, 'What a pity! They wish to go back without getting great treasures.' Having thought this, he expediently made a city by magic at a distance of three hundred yojanas from the starting-point of this dangerous road. He said to them, 'Do not be afraid! Do not go back! You can stay in that great city, and do anything you like. If you enter that city, you will be peaceful. If you go on afterwards and reach the place of treasures, then you can go home.'

"Thereupon the worn-out people had great joy. They said, 'We have never had such joy as this before. Now we shall be able to get off this bad road and become peaceful.'

"Then they made their way forward and entered the magic city. They felt peaceful, thinking that they had already passed [through the bad road]. Seeing that they had already had a rest and relieved their fatigue, the leader caused the city to disappear, and said to them, 'Now the place of treasures is near. I made this city by magic in order to give you a rest.'

"Bhikṣus! I, the Tathāgata, am like the leader. I am your great leader. I know that the bad road, which is made of birth-and-death and illusions, is dangerous and long, and that we should pass through it and get off it. If you had heard only of the One Vehicle of the Buddha, you would not have wished to see or approach the Buddha, but would have thought, 'The Way to Buddhahood is too long for us to pass through unless we make painstaking efforts for a long time.'

"I knew that you were mean and timid. In order to give you a rest halfway, I expounded expediently to you the teaching of Nirvāṇa by the two vehicles.[9] To those who attained the two [vehicles], I say, 'You have not yet done all that you should do. You are near the wisdom of the Buddha. Think it over and consider it! The Nirvāṇa you attained is not true. I divided the One Vehicle of the Buddha into three only expediently.'

"I say this just as the leader, who saw that his party had had a rest in the great city which he had made by magic in order to give them a rest, said to them, 'The place of treasures is near. This city was not true. I made it by magic.'"

Thereupon the World-Honored One, wishing to repeat what he had said, sang in gāthās;

Great-Universal-Wisdom-Excellence Buddha sat
At the place of enlightenment for ten [small] kalpas.
He could not attain the enlightenment of the Buddha
Because the Dharma of the Buddhas had not yet
  come into his mind.

The gods, dragon-kings,
And asuras rained down
Heavenly flowers,
And offered them to him.

The gods beat heavenly drums,
And made many kinds of music.

---

9 The two vehicles are the Śrāvaka-Vehicle and the Pratyekabuddha-Vehicle.

Withered flowers were swept away by fragrant winds;
And fresh and beautiful flowers were rained down.

After the ten small kalpas elapsed,
He attained the enlightenment of the Buddha.
The gods and men of the world
Felt like dancing with joy.

Surrounded by their followers,
Thousands of billions in number,
The sixteen sons of that Buddha
Came to him.

Worshipping the feet of the Buddha with their heads,
They begged him to turn the wheel of the Dharma, saying:
"Lion-like Saint! Send the rain of the Dharma
On us and on all others also!"

It is difficult to meet a World-Honored One.
He appears only once in a very long time.
When he appears, he causes all the worlds to quake
In order to awaken all living beings.

The palaces of the Brahmans
Of five hundred billion worlds in the east
Were illumined
More brightly than ever.

Traveling to find [the place from where the light had come],
The Brahmans of those worlds came to that Buddha.
They strewed flowers and offered them to him.
They also offered their palaces.

They praised him with gāthās,
And begged him to turn the wheel of the Dharma.
The Buddha sat in silence although he was begged
Because he knew that the time was not yet ripe for that.

The Brahmans came also from the three other quarters,
From the four intermediate quarters, zenith, and nadir.
They strewed flowers, offered their palaces,
And begged the Buddha to turn the wheel
of the Dharma, saying:

"It is difficult to meet you.
Open the gate of the teachings as sweet as nectar
Out of your great compassion towards us,
And turn the wheel of the unsurpassed Dharma!"

Assenting to their appeal,
The World-Honored One of Immeasurable Wisdom
Expounded the various teachings, that is,
The four truths and the twelve causes, saying:
"All the causes, from ignorance to aging-and-death,
Rise one after another.
You should know
All these illusions."

When he expounded these teachings,
Sixty quadrillions of living beings
Eliminated sufferings,
And became Arhats.

At his second expounding of these teachings also,
Tens of millions of living beings, that is,
As many living beings as there are sands
in the River Ganges,
Became Arhats because they gave up wrong views.

Those who attained the enlightenment
[of Arhats] afterwards
Were also innumerable.
No one would be able to count them
Even if he tried to do so for a billion kalpas.

The sixteen princes renounced the world,
And became śrāmaṇeras.
They begged the Buddha to expound the teaching
Of the Great Vehicle, saying:
"We and our attendants wish to attain
The enlightenment of the Buddha.
May we have the purest eyes of wisdom
Just as yours!"

Knowing the wishes of the [princes
who were] young boys
And the practices they performed
in their previous existence,
The Buddha taught them the six pāramitās
And many supernatural things
With innumerable stories of previous lives
And with various parables and similes.

The gāthās of the Sūtra of the Lotus Flower
of the Wonderful Dharma
Were sung [by the Buddha] to expound
the true teaching,
That is, [to expound] the Way which Bodhisattvas
should practice.
The gāthās were as many as there are sands
in the River Ganges.

Having expounded this sūtra, the Buddha
entered a quiet room,
And practiced dhyāna-concentration.
Concentrating his mind, he sat at the same place
For eighty-four thousand kalpas.

Seeing him still in dhyāna,
The śrāmaṇeras wished to expound
The unsurpassed wisdom of the Buddha
To many hundreds of millions of living beings.

They each sat on a seat of the Dharma
And expounded this sūtra of the Great Vehicle.
Also after the peaceful extinction of that Buddha,
They proclaimed this sūtra, and helped propagate it.

They each saved
Six hundred billions of living beings,
That is, as many living beings
As there are sands in the River Ganges.

After the extinction of that Buddha,
Some heard the Dharma [from one of the śrāmaṇeras].
They were reborn in the world of a Buddha,
Accompanied by [the śrāmaṇera, that is,] their teacher.

Those sixteen śrāmaṇeras practiced
  the Way to Buddhahood.
They are now in the worlds of the ten quarters.[10]
They have already attained
Perfect enlightenment [and become Buddhas].

Those who heard the Dharma from those śrāmaṇeras
Are now living under those Buddhas.
To those who are still in Śrāvakahood
[The Buddhas] teach the Way to Buddhahood.

I was one of the sixteen śrāmaṇeras.
You were among those to whom I expounded
  the Dharma.
Therefore, I now lead you with expedients
To the wisdom of the Buddha.

Because I taught you in my previous existence,
I expound the Sūtra of the Lotus Flower
  of the Wonderful Dharma

---

10 Strictly speaking, they are in the worlds of the eight quarters.

In order to lead you into the Way to Buddhahood.
Think it over! Do not be surprised! Do not be afraid!

Suppose there was a bad and dangerous road.
Many wild animals lived in the neighborhood.
No man was there; no water nor grass there.
The road was so fearful.

Many tens of millions of people
Wished to pass through this dangerous road.
The road was very long.
It was five hundred yojanas long.

The people had a leader.
He had a good memory.
He was wise and resolute in mind.
He could save people from dangers.

Getting tired,
The people said to him:
"We are tired.
We wish to go back."

He thought:
'How pitiful they are!
Why do they wish to return
Without getting great treasures?'
Thinking of an expedient, he said to himself:
'I will use my supernatural powers.'

He made a great city by magic,
And adorned it with houses.
The city was surrounded by gardens, forests,
And by ponds and pools for bathing.
Many-storied gates and tall buildings [in that city]
Were filled with men and women.

Having made all this by magic,
He consoled the people, saying:
"Do not be afraid! Enter that city!
And do anything you like!"

They entered that city,
And had great joy.
They felt peaceful,
And thought that they had already passed
[through the road].

Seeing that they had already had a rest,
The leader collected them, and said:
"Go on ahead now!
This is a magic city.
You were tired out halfway.
You wished to go back.
Therefore, I made this city by magic
As an expedient.
Make efforts!
Let us go to the place of treasures!"

I am like the leader.
I am the leader of all living beings.
I saw that halfway some got tired
With the seeking of enlightenment,
And that they could not pass through
the dangerous road
Of birth-and-death and illusions.
Therefore, I expounded to them the teaching
of Nirvāṇa
As an expedient to give them a rest, saying:
"You have already eliminated sufferings.
You have done everything you should do."

Now I see that they have already attained Nirvāṇa
And that they have become Arhats.

Therefore, I now collect the great multitude,
And expound to them the true teaching.

The Buddhas expound the teaching of the Three Vehicles
Only as an expedient.
There is only the One Buddha-Vehicle.
The two [vehicles] were taught only as resting places.

Now I will tell you the truth.
What you attained is not [true] extinction.
Make great efforts in order to obtain
The Buddha's knowledge of all things.
When you obtain the knowledge of all things
And the ten powers of the Buddha,
And the thirty-two physical marks,
You will be able to say that you attained true extinction.
The Buddhas, the Leaders, expound the teaching
of Nirvāṇa
In order to give a rest [to all living beings].
When they see them having already had a rest,
They lead them to the wisdom of the Buddha.

[Here ends] the Third Volume of the Sūtra of the Lotus Flower of the Wonderful Dharma.

CHAPTER VIII

THE ASSURANCE OF FUTURE BUDDHAHOOD OF THE FIVE HUNDRED DISCIPLES

Thereupon Pūrṇa, the son of Maitrāyaṇī having heard from the Buddha the Dharma expounded with expedients by the wisdom [of the Buddha] according to the capacities of all living beings, and having heard that [the Buddha] had assured the great disciples of their future attainment of Anuttara-samyak-saṃbodhi, and also having heard of the previous life of the Buddha, and also having heard of the great, unhindered, supernatural powers of the Buddhas, had the greatest joy that he had ever had, became pure in heart, and felt like dancing [with joy]. He rose from his seat, came to the Buddha, and worshipped him at his feet with his head. Then he retired to one side of the place, looked up at the honorable face with unblenching eyes, and thought:

'The World-Honored One is extraordinary. What he does is exceptional. He expounds the Dharma with expedients by his insight according to the various natures of all living beings of the world, and saves them from various attachments. The merits of the Buddha are beyond the expression of our words. Only the Buddha, only the World-Honored One, knows the wishes we have deep in our minds.'

Thereupon the Buddha said to the bhikṣus:

"Do you see this Pūrṇa, the son of Maitrāyaṇī? I always praise him, saying that he is the most excellent expounder of the Dharma. I also praise him for his various merits. He strenuously protects my teachings, and helps me propagate them. He shows the Way to the four kinds of devotees, teaches them, benefits them and causes them to rejoice. He explains my right teachings perfectly, and gives great benefits to those who are performing brahma practices[1] with him. No one except the Tathāgata excels him in eloquence. Do not say that he protects only my teachings and helps me propagate them! In his previous existence he also protected the right teachings of nine thousand million Buddhas and helped them propagate their teachings. Under those Buddhas also he was the most excellent expounder of the Dharma. He clearly understood the truth of the Void expounded by those Buddhas, and obtained the four kinds of unhindered eloquence. He always expounded the Dharma clearly and purely, with no doubtfulness. Although he had the supernatural powers of Bodhisattvas, he performed brahma practices throughout his previous existence. Therefore, the people of the world of the Buddha [under whom he performed brahma practices] thought that he was a Śrāvaka. He benefited many hundreds of thousands of living beings with this expedient, and also caused innumerable, asaṃkhya people to aspire for Anuttara-samyak-saṃbodhi. He did the work of the Buddha, that is, taught all living beings so that the world of the Buddha might be purified.

"Bhikṣus! Pūrṇa was the most excellent expounder of the Dharma under the seven Buddhas. He is the same under me. He will be the same under the future Buddhas of this Kalpa of Sages. He will protect the teachings of those Buddhas and help them propagate their teachings. After the end of this kalpa also he will protect the teachings of innumerable Buddhas, help them propagate their teachings, teach and benefit innumerable living beings, and cause them to aspire for Anuttara-samyak-saṃbodhi. He will always make efforts to teach all living beings strenuously so that the worlds of those Buddhas may be purified. He will perform the Way of Bodhisattvas step by step for innumerable, asaṃkhya[2] kalpas, and then attain Anuttara-samyak-saṃbodhi in this world. He will be called Dharma-Brightness, the Tathāgata, the Deserver of Offerings, the Perfectly Enlightened One, the Man of Wisdom and Practice, the Well-Gone, the Knower of the World, the Unsurpassed Man, the Controller of Men, the

1 Brahma practices are regarded as the practices of a Śrāvaka.

2 This is finite.

Teacher of Gods and Men, the Buddha, the World-Honored One. The world of that Buddha will be composed of one thousand million Sumeru-worlds, that is, as many Sumeru-worlds as there are sands in the River Ganges. The ground [of that world] will be made of the seven treasures. It will be as even as the palm of a hand. There will be no mountains nor ravines nor ditches. Tall buildings adorned with the seven treasures will be seen everywhere in that world, and the palaces of gods of that world will hang so low in the sky that gods and men will be able to see each other. There will be no evil regions nor women. The living beings of that world will be born without any medium.[3] They will have no sexual desire. They will have great supernatural powers, emit light from their bodies, and fly about at will. They will be resolute in mind, strenuous, and wise. They will be golden in color, and adorned with the thirty-two marks. They will feed on two things: the delight in the Dharma, and the delight in dhyāna. There will be innumerable, asaṃkhya Bodhisattvas, that is, thousands of billions of nayutas of Bodhisattvas. They will have great supernatural powers and the four kinds of unhindered eloquence. They will teach the living beings of that world. There will also be uncountable Śrāvakas there. They will have the six supernatural powers including the three major supernatural powers, and the eight emancipations. The world of that Buddha will be adorned with those innumerable merits. The kalpa [in which Pūrṇa will become that Buddha] will be called Treasure-Brightness; and his world, Good-Purity. The duration of the life of that Buddha will be innumerable, asaṃkhya[4] kalpas, and his teachings will be preserved for a long time. After his extinction, stūpas of the seven treasures will be erected [in his honor] throughout that world."

Thereupon the Buddha, wishing to repeat what he had said, sang in gāthās:

---

3 It means that they will be born not through the medium of a mother or an egg or moisture but by their own karmas. It is held that those who are born without any medium appear in a moment in their adult forms. See *Four Kinds of Birth* in the English/Sanskrit Glossary.

4 This is finite.

Bhikṣus, listen to me attentively!
The Way practiced by my sons
Is beyond your comprehension
Because they learned how to employ expedients.

Knowing that people wish to hear
The teachings of the Lesser Vehicle,
And that they are afraid of having the great wisdom,
[My sons, that is,] the Bodhisattvas transform themselves
Into Śrāvakas or cause-knowers,
And teach the people with innumerable expedients.

Saying to the innumerable living beings, [for instance,]
"We are Śrāvakas.
We are far from the enlightenment of the Buddha,"
They save them, and cause them to attain [Śrāvakahood].
Even the lazy people who wish to hear the Lesser Vehicle
Will become Buddhas with this expedient
in the course of time.

My disciples are performing
The Bodhisattva practices secretly
Though they show themselves in the form of Śrāvakas.
They are purifying my world
Though they pretend to want little
And to shun birth-and-death.[5]
In the presence of the people,
They pretend to have the three poisons and wrong views.
They save them with these expedients.
They change themselves into various forms.
If I speak of all their transformations,
The listeners will doubt me.

Under hundreds of thousands of millions of past Buddhas,
This Pūrṇa practiced strenuously what he should do.

5 Śrāvakas are trying to get rid of the world of birth-and-death, not to purify the world of the Buddha.

He expounded and protected
The teachings of those Buddhas.

In order to obtain unsurpassed wisdom,
He became the most excellent disciple
Of those Buddhas.
He was learned and wise.
He expounded the Dharma without fear,
And made his listeners rejoice.
He was never tired
Of helping those Buddhas do their work.

He obtained great supernatural powers
And the four kinds of unhindered eloquence.
Seeing who was clever, and who was dull,
He always expounded the Pure Dharma.

He expounded the Dharma of the Great Vehicle
To hundreds of thousands of millions of living beings,
And caused them to dwell in the Dharma
So that the worlds of those Buddhas might be purified.

In the future also he will make offerings
To innumerable Buddhas, protect their right teachings,
Help them propagate their teachings,
And purify their worlds.

He will always fearlessly expound the Dharma
With expedients.
He will save countless living beings
And cause them to have the knowledge of all things.

He will make offerings to many Tathāgatas
And protect the treasure-store of the Dharma.
After that he will be able to become a Buddha
Called Dharma-Brightness.

His world will be called Good-Purity.
It will be made of the seven treasures.
His kalpa will be called Treasure-Brightness.
There will be Bodhisattvas [in his world],
Many hundreds of millions in number.
They will have great supernatural powers.
They will be powerful and virtuous.
They will be seen throughout that world.

Innumerable Śrāvakas will organize the Saṃgha.
They will have the three major supernatural powers,
The eight emancipations,
And the four kinds of unhindered eloquence.

The living beings of that world will have no sexual desire.
They will be born without any medium.[6]
They will be adorned with the marks [of the Buddha].
They will not think
Of any other food [than the two kinds of food]:
The delight in the Dharma, and the delight in dhyāna.
There will be neither women nor evil regions
In that world.

Pūrṇa Bhikṣu will be able to obtain
All these merits,
And have his pure world
Inhabited by many sages and saints.
I have innumerable things to say of him.
I have told you only a few of them.

Thereupon the twelve hundred Arhats, who had already obtained freedom of mind, thought:

"We have never been so joyful before. How glad we shall be if we are assured of our future Buddhahood by the World-Honored One just as the other great disciples were!" Seeing what they had in their minds, the Buddha said to Maha-Kāśyapa:

6 See p. 159, footnote 3.

"Now I will assure these twelve hundred Arhats, who are present before me, of their future attainment of Anuttara-samyak-saṃbodhi one after another. My great disciple Kauṇḍinya Bhikṣu, who is among them, will make offerings to six billion and two hundred thousand million Buddhas, and then become a Buddha called Universal-Brightness, the Tathāgata, the Deserver of Offerings, the Perfectly Enlightened One, the Man of Wisdom and Practice, the Well-Gone, the Knower of the World, the Unsurpassed Man, the Controller of Men, the Teacher of Gods and Men, the Buddha, the World-Honored One. The others of the five hundred Arhats, including Uruvilvā-Kāśyapa, Gayā-Kāśyapa, Nadī-Kāśyapa, Kālodāyin, Udāyin, Aniruddha, Revata, Kapphina, Bakkula, Cunda, and Svāgata, also will attain Anuttara-samyak-saṃbodhi, and become Buddhas also called Universal-Brightness."

Thereupon the World-Honored One, wishing to repeat what he had said, sang in gāthās:

Kauṇḍinya Bhikṣu will see
Innumerable[7] Buddhas.
After asaṃkhya[8] kalpas from now,
He will attain perfect enlightenment.

He will emit great rays of light [from his body].
He will have all supernatural powers.
His fame will spread over the worlds of the ten quarters.
Respected by all living beings,
He will expound unsurpassed enlightenment to them.
Therefore, he will be called Universal-Brightness.

His world will be pure.
The Bodhisattvas [of that world] will be brave.
They will go up to the tops of wonderful, tall buildings,
And then go out into the worlds of the ten quarters.

---

7 This is finite.

8 This, too, is finite.

There they will make the best offerings
To the Buddhas of those worlds.

After making offerings, they will have great joy.
They will return to their home world in a moment.
They will be able to do all this
By their supernatural powers.

[Universal-Brightness] Buddha will live for
 sixty thousand kalpas.
His right teachings will be preserved twice as long
 as his life;
And the counterfeit of them, also twice as long
 as his right teachings.
When his teachings are eliminated, gods and men
 will be sad.

The five hundred bhikṣus
Will become Buddhas one after another.
They also will be called Universal-Brightness.
One who has become a Buddha will say to another:
"You will become a Buddha after my extinction.
[The living beings of] the world
To be saved by that Buddha
Will be like those whom I am teaching today."

The beauty of the worlds [of those Buddhas],
And the supernatural powers [of those Buddhas],
And the number of the Bodhisattvas and Śrāvakas
 [of those worlds],
And the number of kalpas of the lives [of those Buddhas],
Of their right teachings, and of the counterfeit of them,
Will be the same [as in the case of Kauṇḍinya].

Kāśyapa! Now you have heard of the future
Of the five hundred Arhats
Who have freedom of mind.

All the other Śrāvakas also will [become Buddhas].
Tell this to the Śrāvakas
Who are not present here!

Thereupon the five hundred Arhats, having been assured by the Buddha of their future Buddhahood, felt like dancing with joy, stood up from their seats, came to the Buddha, worshipped him at his feet with their heads, and reproached themselves for their faults, saying:

"World-Honored One! We thought that we had already attained perfect extinction.[9] Now we know that we were like men of no wisdom because we were satisfied with the wisdom of the Lesser Vehicle although we had already been qualified to obtain the wisdom of the Tathāgata.

"World-Honored One! Suppose a man visited his good friend. He was treated to drink, and fell asleep drunk. His friend had to go out on official business. He fastened a priceless gem inside the garment of the man as a gift to him, and went out. The drunken man did not notice what his friend had given him. After a while he got up, and went to another country. He had great difficulty in getting food and clothing. He satisfied himself with what little he had earned. Some time later the good friend happened to see him. He said, 'Alas, man! Why have you had such difficulty in getting food and clothing? I fastened a priceless gem inside your garment on a certain day of a certain month of a certain year so that you might live peacefully and satisfy your five desires. The gem is still there, and you do not notice it. You are working hard, and worrying about your livelihood. What a fool you are! Trade that gem for what you want! You will not be short of anything you want.'

"You, the Buddha, are like his friend. We thought that we had attained extinction when we attained Arhatship because we forgot that we had been taught to aspire for the knowledge of all things by you when you were a Bodhisattva just as the man who had difficulty in earning his livelihood satisfied himself

9 This is a translation of Nirvāṇa.

with what little he had earned. You, the World-Honored One, saw that the aspiration for the knowledge of all things was still latent in our minds; therefore, you awakened us, saying, 'Bhikṣus! What you had attained was not perfect extinction. I caused you to plant the good root of Buddhahood a long time ago. [You have forgotten this; therefore,] I expounded the teaching of Nirvāṇa as an expedient. You thought that you had attained true extinction when you attained the Nirvāṇa [which I taught you as an expedient].'

"World-Honored One! Now we see that we are Bodhisattvas in reality, and that we are assured of our future attainment of Anuttara-samyak-saṃbodhi. Therefore, we have the greatest joy that we have ever had."

Thereupon Ājñāta-Kauṇḍinya and the others, wishing to repeat what they had said, sang in gāthās:

Your assurance of our future Buddhahood
Gives us unsurpassed peace.
Hearing your voice, we have the greatest joy
  that we have ever had.
We bow to you, to the Buddha of Immeasurable Wisdom.

Now in your presence,
We reproach ourselves for our faults.
The Nirvāṇa we attained was
Only part of the immeasurable treasures of yours.
We were like a foolish man with no wisdom.
We satisfied ourselves with what little we had attained.

Suppose a poor man visited
His good friend, who was very rich.
The friend feasted him
With delicacies.

He fastened a priceless gem
Inside the garment of the man as a gift to him,

And went out without leaving a word.
The sleeping man did not notice [the gift].

The man woke up, and went to another country.
He worked to get food and clothing.
He had much difficulty
In earning his livelihood.

He satisfied himself with what little he earned.
He did not wish to get anything more.
He did not notice the priceless gem
Fastened inside his garment.

The good friend who gave the gem to the poor man
Happened to see him later.
He blamed him severely,
And showed him the gem fastened [inside the garment].

Seeing the gem,
The poor man had great joy.
Now he satisfied his five desires
With many treasures.

We are like the poor man.
In the long night you taught us
Out of your compassion towards us,
And caused us to aspire for unsurpassed [enlightenment].

Because we had no wisdom, we did not notice that.
The Nirvāṇa we attained was only part [of your wisdom].
Satsifying ourselves with it,
We did not wish to attain anything more.

Now you have awakened us, saying:
"What you attained was not true extinction.
When you have the unsurpassed wisdom of the Buddha,
You will attain true extinction."

Hearing from you that we are assured
Of becoming Buddhas one after another,
And that our worlds will be adorned,
We are joyful in body and mind.

CHAPTER IX

THE ASSURANCE OF FUTURE BUDDHAHOOD OF THE ŚRĀVAKAS WHO HAVE SOMETHING MORE TO LEARN AND THE ŚRĀVAKAS WHO HAVE NOTHING MORE TO LEARN

Thereupon Ānanda and Rāhula thought, 'We are always thinking: How glad we shall be if we are assured of our future Buddhahood!' They rose from their seats, came to the Buddha, worshipped his feet with their heads, and said to him:

"World-Honored One! We think that we also are qualified to be assured [of our future Buddhahood]. Only you, the Tathāgata, are our refuge. We are known to all gods, men and asuras of the world. Ānanda always protects the store of the Dharma as your attendant. Rāhula is your son. If you assure us of our future attainment of Anuttara-samyak-saṃbodhi, the wishes not only of us but also of others will be fulfilled."

Thereupon the two thousand disciples [composed of the two kinds of Śrāvakas]: the Śrāvakas who had something more to learn and the Śrāvakas who had nothing more to learn, also rose from their seats, bared their right shoulders, came to the Buddha, joined their hands together with all their hearts, looked up at the World-Honored One, begged him just as Ānanda and Rāhula did, and stood to one side of the place.

Thereupon the Buddha said to Ānanda:

"In your future life you will become a Buddha called Mountain-Sea-Wisdom-Supernatural-Power-King, the Tathāgata, the Deserver of Offerings, the Perfectly Enlightened One, the Man of Wisdom and Practice, the Well-Gone, the Knower of the World, the Unsurpassed Man, the Controller of Men, the Teacher of Gods and Men, the Buddha, the World-Honored One.

You will attain Anuttara-samyak-saṃbodhi [and become that Buddha] after you make offerings to sixty-two hundred million Buddhas and protect the store of their teachings. That Buddha will teach twenty thousand billion Bodhisattvas, that is, as many Bodhisattvas as there are sands in the River Ganges, and cause them to attain Anuttara-samyak-saṃbodhi. The world [of that Buddha] will be called Always-Raising-Banner-Of-Victory. His world will be pure, and the ground of it will be made of lapis lazuli. The kalpa [in which you will become that Buddha] will be called Wonderful-Voice-Resounding-Everywhere. The duration of the life of that Buddha will be many thousands of billions of asaṃkhyas of kalpas. No one will be able to count the number of the kalpas. His right teachings will be preserved for twice as long as his life, and the counterfeit of his right teachings will be preserved for twice as long as his right teachings.

"Ānanda! Mountain-Sea-Wisdom-Supernatural-Power-King Buddha will be praised for his merits by many thousands of billions of Buddhas or Tathāgatas of the worlds of the ten quarters, that is, by as many Buddhas or Tathāgatas as there are sands in the River Ganges."

Thereupon the World-Honored One, wishing to repeat what he had said, sang in gāthās:

> Now I announce to the Saṃgha:
> Ānanda, the keeper of the Dharma,
> Will make offerings to Buddhas,
> And then attain perfect enlightenment.
>
> He will be called
> Mountain-Sea-Wisdom-Supernatural-Power-King.
> His world will be pure, and called
> Always-Raising-Banner-Of-Victory.
>
> He will teach as many Bodhisattvas
> As there are sands in the River Ganges.
> He will be exceedingly powerful and virtuous.
> His fame will extend over the worlds of the ten quarters.

The duration of his life will be immeasurable
Because he has compassion towards all living beings.
His right teachings will be preserved for twice as long
as his life;
The counterfeit of them, for twice as long
as his right teachings.

Under him, as many living beings
As there are sands in the River Ganges
Will obtain the seeds
Of the enlightenment of the Buddha.

There were eight thousand Bodhisattvas[1] who had just resolved to aspire [for Anuttara-samyak-saṃbodhi] in this congregation. They thought, 'As far as we have heard, even great Bodhisattvas have never been assured of their future Buddhahood. Why have these Śrāvakas been so assured?'

Thereupon the World-Honored One, seeing what the Bodhisattvas had in their minds, said to them:

"Good men! Ānanda and I resolved to aspire for Anuttara-samyak-saṃbodhi under the Void-King Buddha at the same time [in our previous existence]. At that time Ānanda always wished to hear much while I always practiced strenuously. Therefore, I have already attained Anuttara-samyak-saṃbodhi[, but he has not yet]. Now he protects my teachings. He also will protect the store of the teachings of future Buddhas, teach Bodhisattvas, and cause them to attain [Anuttara-samyak-saṃbodhi], according to his original vow. Therefore, now he has been assured of his future Buddhahood."

Having heard from the Buddha that he was assured of his future Buddhahood, and that his world would be adorned, Ānanda was able to fulfill his wish. He had the greatest joy that he had ever had. At that moment he recollected the store of the teachings of many thousands of billions of past Buddhas perfectly and without hindrance as if he had heard those teachings just now. He also recollected his original vow.

1 Eight thousand Bodhisattvas are not given as a group in the foregoing chapters.

Thereupon Ānanda sang in gāthās:

You, the World-Honored One, are exceptional.
You reminded me of the teachings
Of innumerable Buddhas in the past
As if I had heard them today.

Having no doubts, I now dwell peacefully
In the enlightenment of the Buddha.
I will expediently become the attendant
Of future Buddhas, and protect their teachings.

Thereupon the Buddha said to Rāhula:

"In your future life you will become a Buddha called Walking-On-Flowers-Of-Seven-Treasures, the Tathāgata, the Deserver of Offerings, the Perfectly Enlightened One, the Man of Wisdom and Practice, the Well-Gone, the Knower of the World, the Unsurpassed Man, the Controller of Men, the Teacher of Gods and Men, the Buddha, the World-Honored One. [Before you become that Buddha,] you will make offerings to as many Buddhas, as many Tathāgatas, as the particles of dust of ten worlds. [Before you become that Buddha,] you will become the eldest son of those Buddhas just as you are now mine.

"The adornments of the world of Walking-On-Flowers-Of-Seven-Treasures Buddha, the number of the kalpas for which that Buddha will live, the number of his disciples, the duration of the preservation of his right teachings, and the duration of the preservation of the counterfeit of his right teachings will be the same as in the case of Mountain-Sea-Wisdom-Supernatural-Power-King Tathāgata.

"After you become the eldest son of the [Mountain-Sea-Wisdom-Supernatural-Power-King] Buddha, you will attain Anuttara-samyak-saṃbodhi[, and become Walking-On-Flowers-Of-Seven-Treasures Buddha]."

Thereupon the World-Honored One, wishing to repeat what he had said, sang in gāthās:

When I was a crown prince,
Rāhula was my eldest son.
When I attained the enlightenment of the Buddha,
He received the Dharma, and became the son
of the Dharma.

In his future life he will see
Many hundreds of millions of Buddhas,
Become the eldest son of those Buddhas, and seek
The enlightenment of the Buddha with all his heart.

Only I know his secret practices.
He shows himself
To all living beings
In the form of my eldest son.

He has many thousands of billions of merits.
His merits are countless.
He dwells peacefully in the Dharma of the Buddha,
And seeks unsurpassed enlightenment.

Thereupon the World-Honored One saw the two thousand Śrāvakas, of whom some had something more to learn while others had nothing more to learn. They were gentle, quiet and pure. They looked up at the Buddha with all their hearts.

The Buddha said to Ānanda, "Do you see these two thousand Śrāvakas, of whom some have something more to learn while others have nothing more to learn?"

"Yes, I do."

"Ānanda! These people will make offerings to as many Buddhas, as many Tathāgatas, as the particles of dust of fifty worlds. They will respect those Buddhas, honor them, and protect the store of their teachings. They will finally go to the worlds of the ten quarters and become Buddhas at the same time. They will be equally called Treasure-Form, the Tathāgata, the Deserver of Offerings, the Perfectly Enlightened One, the Man of Wisdom and Practice, the Well-Gone, the Knower of the World, the Unsurpassed Man, the Controller of Men, the Teacher of Gods and Men, the Buddha, the World-Honored One. They will live for a kalpa. They will be the same in regard to the adornments of their worlds, the number of the Śrāvakas and Bodhisattvas of their worlds, the duration of the preservation of their right teachings, and the duration of the preservation of the counterfeit of their right teachings."

Thereupon the World-Honored One, wishing to repeat what he had said, sang in gāthās:

I assure the future Buddhahood
Of these two thousand Śrāvakas
Who are now present before me.
They will become Buddhas in their future lives.

They will make offerings to as many Buddhas
As the particles of dust as previously stated.
They will protect the store of the teachings
of those Buddhas,
And attain perfect enlightenment.

They will go to the worlds of the ten quarters.
Their [Buddha-]names will be the same.
They will sit at the place of enlightenment
And obtain unsurpassed wisdom at the same time.

Their [Buddha-]names will be Treasure-Form.
[The adornment of] their worlds, [the number
of] their disciples,
[The duration of the period of] their right teachings,
[And that of] the counterfeit of them will be the same.

By their supernatural powers, they will save
The living beings of the worlds of the ten quarters.
Their fame will extend far and wide.
They will enter into Nirvāṇa[2] in the course of time.

2 This stands for Parinirvāṇa.

Thereupon the two thousand Śrāvakas, of whom some had something more to learn while others had nothing more to learn, having heard the Buddha assure them of their future Buddhahood, danced with joy, and sang in a gāthā:

> You, the World-Honored One, are the light of wisdom.
> Hearing from you
> That we are assured of our future Buddhahood,
> We are as joyful as if we were sprinkled with nectar.

CHAPTER X

THE TEACHER OF THE DHARMA

Thereupon the World-Honored One said to Medicine-King Bodhisattva[1] in the presence of the eighty thousand great men:[2]

"Medicine-King! Do you see the innumerable gods, dragon-kings, yakṣas, gandharvas, asuras, garuḍas, kiṃnaras, mahoragas, men, and nonhuman beings, and [the four kinds of devotees:] bhikṣus, bhikṣuṇīs, upāsakas, and upāsikās, and those who are seeking Śrāvakahood or Pratyekabuddhahood or the enlightenment of the Buddha in this great multitude? If in my presence any of them rejoices, even on a moment's thought, at hearing even a gāthā or a phrase of the Sūtra of the Lotus Flower of the Wonderful Dharma, I will assure him of his future Buddhahood, saying to him, 'You will be able to attain Anuttara-samyak-saṃbodhi.'"

The Buddha said to Medicine-King:

"If after my extinction anyone rejoices, even on a moment's thought, at hearing even a gāthā or a phrase of the Sūtra of the Lotus Flower of the Wonderful Dharma,[3] I also will assure him of his future attainment of Anuttara-samyak-saṃbodhi. If anyone keeps, reads, recites, expounds and copies even a gāthā of the Sūtra of the Lotus Flower of the Wonderful Dharma, and respects a copy of this sūtra just as he respects me, and offers flowers, incense, necklaces, incense powder, incense applicable to the skin, incense to burn,

---

1 The Buddha addressed a Bodhisattva or Bodhisattvas for the first time here in this sūtra except in Chapter IX in which he addressed the eight thousand Bodhisattvas to explain the reason why he had assured Ānanda of his future Buddhahood.

2 大士 See *Daiji* in the Chinese/Japanese Glossary.

3 According to this chapter, the Buddha will go to another world after his life in this world, but will appear in any other world to expound the Dharma.

canopies, banners, streamers, garments and music to it, or just joins his hands together respectfully towards it, Medicine-King, know this, he should be considered to have appeared in the world of men out of his compassion towards all living beings, although he already made offerings to ten billion Buddhas and fulfilled his great vow under those Buddhas in a previous existence.

"Medicine-King! If anyone asks you who will become a Buddha in his future life, answer that such a person as previously stated will! Why is that? The good men or women who keep, read, recite, expound and copy even a phrase of the Sūtra of the Lotus Flower of the Wonderful Dharma, and offer flowers, incense, necklaces, incense powder, incense applicable to the skin, incense to burn, canopies, banners, streamers, garments and music to a copy of this sūtra, or just join their hands together respectfully towards it, should be respected by all the people of the world. All the people of the world should make the same offerings to them as they do to me. Know this! These good men or women are great Bodhisattvas. They should be considered to have appeared in this world by their vow to expound the Sūtra of the Lotus Flower of the Wonderful Dharma out of their compassion towards all living beings, although they already attained Anuttara-samyak-saṃbodhi [in their previous existence]. Needless to say, those who keep all the passages of this sūtra and make various offerings to this sūtra [are great Bodhisattvas]. Medicine-King, know this! They should be considered to have given up the rewards of their pure karmas and appeared in the evil world after my extinction in order to expound this sūtra out of their compassion towards all living beings. The good men or women who expound even a phrase of the Sūtra of the Lotus Flower of the Wonderful Dharma even to one person even in secret after my extinction, know this, are my messengers. They are dispatched by me. They do my work. It is needless to say this of those who expound this sūtra to many people in a great multitude.

"Medicine-King! An evil man who speaks ill of me in my presence with evil intent for as long as a kalpa is not as sinful as the person who reproaches laymen or monks with even a single word of abuse for their reading and reciting the Sūtra of the Lotus Flower of the Wonderful Dharma.

"Medicine-King! Anyone who reads and recites the Sūtra of the Lotus Flower of the Wonderful Dharma, know this, will be adorned just as I am. I will shoulder him. Wherever he may be, bow to him! Join your hands together towards him with all your heart, respect him, make offerings to him, honor him, and praise him! Offer him flowers, incense, necklaces, incense powder, incense applicable to the skin, incense to burn, canopies, banners, streamers, garments, food and various kinds of music! Make him the best offerings that you can obtain in the world of men! Strew the treasures of heaven to him! Offer him heaps of the treasures of heaven! Why is that? It is because, while he is expounding the Dharma with joy, if you hear it even for a moment, you will immediately[4] be able to attain Anuttara-samyak-saṃbodhi."

Thereupon the World-Honored One, wishing to repeat what he had said, sang in gāthās:

> If you wish to dwell in the enlightenment of the Buddha,
> And to obtain the self-originating wisdom,
> Make offerings strenuously to the keeper
> Of the Sūtra of the Lotus Flower of the Wonderful Dharma!
>
> If you wish to obtain quickly the knowledge
> Of the equality and differences of all things,
> Keep this sūtra, and also make offerings
> To the keeper of this sūtra!
>
> Anyone who keeps
> The Sūtra of the Lotus Flower of the Wonderful Dharma,
> Know this, has compassion towards all living beings
> Because he is my messenger.
>
> Anyone who keeps
> The Sūtra of the Lotus Flower of the Wonderful Dharma

---

4 即 "Immediately" is used only here in this chapter. The assurance of immediate attainment of Anuttara-samyak-saṃbodhi is inconsistent with the foregoing chapters in which it says that one will become a Buddha after a certain number of kalpas.

Should be considered to have given up his pure world
and come here
Out of his compassion towards all living beings.

Know that he can appear wherever he wishes!
He should be considered
To have appeared in this evil world
In order to expound the unsurpassed Dharma.

Offer flowers and incense of heaven,
Jeweled garments of heaven,
And heaps of wonderful treasures of heaven
To the expounder of the Dharma!

Join your hands together and bow
To the person who keeps this sūtra
In the evil world after my extinction,
Just as you do to me!

Offer delicious food and drink,
And various garments to this son of mine,
And yearn to hear the Dharma [from him]
Even if for only a moment!

Anyone who keeps this sūtra in the future
Should be considered
To have been dispatched by me
To the world of men in order to do my work.

Whoever for as long as a kalpa,
With evil intent and flushed face,
Speaks ill of me,
Will incur immeasurable retributions.
Whoever for even a moment
Reproaches those who read, recite and keep
The Sūtra of the Lotus Flower of the Wonderful Dharma
Will incur even more retributions.

Whoever for as long as a kalpa
Joins his hands together towards me
And praises me with innumerable gāthās
In order to attain the enlightenment of
the Buddha,
Will obtain innumerable merits
Because he praises me.
Whoever praises the keeper of this sūtra
Will obtain even more merits.

For eight thousand million kalpas
Offer to the keeper of this sūtra
The most wonderful things to see,
Hear, smell, taste and touch!

If you make these offerings,
And hear [this sūtra] even for a moment,
You will rejoice and say,
"Now I have obtained great benefits."

Medicine-King! I will tell you.
The Sūtra of the Lotus Flower of the Wonderful Dharma
Is the most excellent sūtra
That I have ever expounded.

Thereupon the Buddha said again to Medicine-King Bodhisattva-mahāsattva:

"I have expounded many sūtras. I am now expounding this sūtra. I also will expound many sūtras in the future. The total number of the sūtras will amount to many thousands of billions. This Sūtra of the Lotus Flower of the Wonderful Dharma is the most difficult to believe and the most difficult to understand.

"Medicine-King! This sūtra is the store of the hidden core of all the Buddhas. Do not give it to others carelessly! It is protected by the Buddhas, by the World-Honored Ones. It has not been expounded explicitly. Many people hate it with jealousy even in my lifetime. Needless to say, more people will do so after my extinction.

"Medicine-King, know this! Anyone who copies, keeps, reads and recites this sūtra, makes offerings to it, and expounds it to others after my extinction, will be covered by my robe. He also will be protected by the present Buddhas of the other worlds. He will have the great power of faith, the power of vows, and the power of roots of good. Know this! He will live with me. I will pat him on the head.

"Medicine-King! Erect a stūpa of the seven treasures in any place where this sūtra is expounded, read, recited or copied, or in any place where a copy of this sūtra exists! The stūpa should be tall, spacious and adorned. You need not enshrine my śarīras in the stūpa.[5] Why not? It is because it will contain my perfect body. Offer flowers, incense, necklaces, canopies, banners, streamers, music and songs of praise to the stūpa! Respect the stūpa, honor it, and praise it! Anyone who, after seeing the stūpa, bows to it, and makes offerings to it, know this, will approach Anuttara-samyak-saṃbodhi.

"Medicine-King! Although many laymen or monks will practice the Way of Bodhisattvas, they will not be able to practice it satisfactorily, know this, unless they see, hear, read, recite, copy or keep this Sūtra of the Lotus Flower of the Wonderful Dharma or make offerings to it. If they hear this sūtra, they will. Anyone who, while seeking the enlightenment of the Buddha, sees or hears this Sūtra of the Lotus Flower of the Wonderful Dharma, and after hearing it, understands it by faith and keeps it, know this, will approach Anuttara-samyak-saṃbodhi.

"Medicine-King! Suppose a man on a plateau felt thirsty and sought water. He dug a hole in order to get water. As long as he saw the dug-out lumps of earth were dry, he knew that water was still far off. He went on digging, and then found the dug-out lumps of earth wet. When he finally found mud, he was convinced that water was near. In the same manner, know this, the Bodhisattvas who have not yet heard, understood or practiced this Sūtra of the Lotus Flower of the Wonderful Dharma, are still far from Anuttara-samyak-saṃbodhi. [The Bodhisattvas] who hear, understand, think

5 The needlessness of enshrining the śarīras of the Buddha in a stūpa is not given in the foregoing chapters.

over, and practice this sūtra, will approach Anuttara-samyak-saṃbodhi. Why is that? It is because Anuttara-samyak-saṃbodhi which all the Bodhisattvas [should attain] is expounded only in this sūtra. This sūtra opens the gate of expedients and reveals the seal of the truth. The store of this Sūtra of the Lotus Flower of the Wonderful Dharma is sound and deep. No one can reach its core. Now I show it to the Bodhisattvas in order to teach them and cause them to attain [Anuttara-samyak-saṃbodhi].

"Medicine-King! The Bodhisattvas who, having been surprised at hearing this Sūtra of the Lotus Flower of the Wonderful Dharma, doubt and fear it, know this, are beginners in Bodhisattvahood. The Śrāvakas who, having been surprised at hearing this sūtra, doubt and fear it, know this, are men of arrogance.

"Medicine-King! How should the good men or women who live after my extinction expound this Sūtra of the Lotus Flower of the Wonderful Dharma to the four kinds of devotees when they wish to? They should enter the room of the Tathāgata, wear the robe of the Tathāgata, sit on the seat of the Tathāgata, and then expound this sūtra to the four kinds of devotees. To enter the room of the Tathāgata means to have great compassion towards all living beings. To wear the robe of the Tathāgata means to be gentle and patient. To sit on the seat of the Tathāgata means to see the voidness of all things. They should do these [three] things and then without indolence expound this Sūtra of the Lotus Flower of the Wonderful Dharma to Bodhisattvas and the four kinds of devotees.

"Medicine-King! Although I shall be in another world [after my extinction], I will manifest men and women [by my supernatural powers], dispatch them [to the expounder of the Dharma], and have them collect people to hear the Dharma from him. I also will manifest monks, nuns and men or women of faith [by my supernatural powers], dispatch them, and have them hear the Dharma from them. These people manifested [by my supernatural powers] will hear the Dharma [from him], receive it by faith, follow it, and not oppose it. If he lives in a retired place, I will dispatch gods, dragons, demigods, gandharvas, asuras, and others to him, and have them hear the Dharma from him. Although I shall be in another world, I will cause him to see me from time to time. If he forgets a phrase of this sūtra, I will tell it to him for his complete [understanding]."

Thereupon the World-Honored One, wishing to repeat what he had said, sang in gāthās:

If you wish to give up all indolence,
Hear this sūtra!
It is difficult to hear this sūtra.
Few receive it by faith.

A man on a plateau, feeling thirsty,
Dug a hole in order to get water.
As long as he saw the dug-out lumps of earth were dry,
He knew that water was still far off.
When he found the earth wet and muddy,
He was convinced that water was near.

In the same manner, Medicine-King, know this!
Those who do not hear
The Sūtra of the Lotus Flower of the Wonderful Dharma
Are far from the wisdom of the Buddha.

In this profound sūtra
The teachings for the Śrāvakas are criticized.
Those who hear
That this sūtra is the king of all the sūtras,
And think over this sūtra clearly after hearing it,
Know this, will approach the wisdom of the Buddha.
If you wish to expound this sūtra,
Enter the room of the Tathāgata,
Wear the robe of the Tathāgata,
Sit on the seat of the Tathāgata,
[And after doing these three things,]
Expound it to people without fear!

To enter the room of the Tathāgata means
to have great compassion.

To wear his robe means to be gentle and patient.
To sit on his seat means to see the voidness
of all things.
Expound the Dharma only after you do these
[three] things!

If anyone speaks ill of you, or threatens you
With swords, sticks, tile-pieces or stones
While you are expounding this sūtra,
Think of me, and be patient!

My body is pure and indestructible.
I will appear in any of many thousands of billions
of worlds
During many hundreds of millions of kalpas,
And expound the Dharma to the living beings.

If a teacher of the Dharma expounds this sūtra
After my extinction,
I will manifest the four kinds of devotees:
Bhikṣus, bhikṣuṇīs, and men and women of pure faith,
And dispatch them to him
So that they may make offerings to him,
And that they may lead many living beings,
Collecting them to hear the Dharma [from him].

If he is hated and threatened
With swords, sticks, tile-pieces or stones,
I will manifest men and dispatch them to him
In order to protect him.

If an expounder of the Dharma
Reads and recites this sūtra
In a retired and quiet place,
Where no human voice is heard,
I will show my pure and radiant body to him.
If he forgets a sentence or a phrase of this sūtra,

I will tell it to him
For his complete understanding.

Anyone who expounds this sūtra to the four kinds
of devotees,
Or reads or recites this sūtra in a retired place,
After doing these [three] virtuous things,
Will be able to see me.

If he lives in a retired place,
I will dispatch gods, dragon-kings, yakṣas,
Demigods, and others to him,
And have them hear the Dharma [from him].

He will expound the Dharma with joy.
He will expound it without hindrance.
He will cause a great multitude to rejoice
Because he is protected by all the Buddhas.

Those who come to this teacher of the Dharma
Will be able to complete the Way of Bodhisattvas quickly.
Those who follow him and study will be able to see
As many Buddhas as there are sands in the River Ganges.

CHAPTER XI

BEHOLDING THE STŪPA OF TREASURES

Thereupon a stūpa of the seven treasures sprang up from underground and hung in the sky before the Buddha. The stūpa was five hundred yojanas high and two hundred and fifty yojanas wide and deep. It was adorned with various treasures. It was furnished with five thousand railings and ten million chambers. It was adorned with innumerable banners and streamers, from which jeweled necklaces and billions of jeweled bells were hanging down. The fragrance of tamālapattra and candana was sent forth from the four sides of the stūpa to all the corners of the world. Many canopies, adorned with streamers, and made of the seven treasures—gold, silver, lapis lazuli, shell, agate, pearl and ruby—were hanging in the sky [one upon another from the top of the stūpa] up to the [heaven of the] palaces of the four heavenly-kings. The thirty-three gods offered a rain of heavenly mandārava-flowers to the stūpa of treasures. Thousands of billions of living beings, including the other gods, dragons, yakṣas, gandharvas, asuras, garuḍas, kiṃnaras, mahoragas, men and nonhuman beings, also offered flowers, incense, necklaces, streamers, canopies and music to the stūpa of treasures, venerated the stūpa, honored it, and praised it.

Thereupon a loud voice of praise was heard from within the stūpa of treasures:

"Excellent, excellent! You, Śākyamuni, the World-Honored One, have expounded to this great multitude the Sūtra of the Lotus Flower of the Wonderful Dharma, the Teaching of Equality, the Great Wisdom, the Dharma for Bodhisattvas, the Dharma

Upheld by the Buddhas. So it is, so it is. What you, Śākyamuni, the World-Honored One, have expounded is all true."

Thereupon the four kinds of devotees [in the congregation], having seen the great stūpa of treasures hanging in the sky, and having heard the voice from within the stūpa, had delight in the Dharma, but wondered why these unprecedented things had happened. They rose from their seats, joined their hands together [towards the stūpa] respectfully, retired, and stood to one side.

Thereupon a Bodhisattva-mahāsattva called Great-Eloquence, having noticed that the gods, men and asuras of the world had doubts, said to the Buddha, "World-Honored One! Why did this stūpa of treasures spring up from underground? Why was that voice heard from within [the stūpa]?"

The Buddha said to him:

"The perfect body of a Tathāgata is in this stūpa of treasures. A long time ago there was a world called Treasure-Purity at the distance of many thousands of billions of asaṃkhyas of worlds to the east [of this world]. In that world lived a Buddha called Many-Treasures. When he was yet practicing the Way of Bodhisattvas, he made a great vow: 'If anyone expounds a sūtra called the Lotus Flower of the Wonderful Dharma in any of the worlds of the ten quarters after I become a Buddha and pass away, I will cause my stūpa-mausoleum to spring up before him so that I may be able to prove the truthfulness of the sūtra and say 'excellent' in praise of him because I wish to hear that sūtra [directly from him]."

"He attained enlightenment[, and became a Buddha]. When he was about to pass away, he said to the bhikṣus in the presence of the great multitude of gods and men, 'If you wish to make offerings to my perfect body after my extinction, erect a great stūpa!'

"If anyone expounds the Sūtra of the Lotus Flower of the Wonderful Dharma in any of the worlds of the ten quarters, that Buddha, by his supernatural powers and by the power of his vow, will cause the stūpa of treasures enshrining his perfect body to spring up before the expounder of the sūtra. Then he will praise [the expounder of the sūtra], saying, 'Excellent, excellent!'

"Great-Eloquence! Now Many-Treasures Tathāgata caused his stūpa to spring up from underground in order to hear the Sūtra of the Lotus Flower of the Wonderful Dharma [directly from me]. Now he praised me, saying, 'Excellent, excellent!' "

Thereupon Great-Eloquence Bodhisattva, resorting to the supernatural powers of [Śākyamuni] Tathāgata, said to him, "World-Honored One! We wish to see that Buddha."

The Buddha said to Great-Eloquence Bodhisattva-mahāsattva:

"Many-Treasures Buddha made another great vow: 'If a Buddha wishes to show me to the four kinds of devotees when my stūpa of treasures appears before him in order that I may be able to hear the Sūtra of the Lotus Flower of the Wonderful Dharma [directly from him], he must call back all the Buddhas of his replicas[1] who will be expounding the Dharma in the worlds of the ten quarters at that time. Then I will show myself [to the four kinds of devotees].' Great-Eloquence! Now I will collect the Buddhas of my replicas who are now expounding the Dharma in the worlds of the ten quarters."

Great-Eloquence said to him, "World-Honored One! We also wish to see the Buddhas of your replicas, bow to them, and make offerings to them."

Thereupon the Buddha emitted a ray of light from the white curls [between his eyebrows, and faced the east]. The congregation saw the Buddhas of five hundred billion nayuta worlds, that is, as many worlds as there are sands in the River Ganges, in the east. The ground of those worlds was made of crystal. Those worlds were adorned with jeweled trees and garments, and filled with many thousands of billions of Bodhisattvas. Jeweled curtains were stretched and jeweled nets were hung over those worlds, where the Buddhas were expounding the Dharma with loud and wonderful voices. The congregation also saw that many thousands of billions of Bodhisattvas, with whom those worlds

---

1 "The Buddhas of his replicas" are the Buddhas who are the replicas of Śākyamuni Buddha. It is held that Śākyamuni Buddha can produce Buddhas in his likeness by his supernatural powers, and dispatch them to the worlds of the ten quarters for the purpose of expounding the Dharma. This means that the Buddhas of the worlds of the ten quarters are the replicas of Śākyamuni Buddha. This idea is first introduced here in this sūtra. The replicas of Śākyamuni Buddha are subject to Śākyamuni Buddha. They must come to him when they are told to do so.

were filled, were expounding the Dharma to the living beings of those worlds.

The Buddha also illumined the worlds of the south, west, north, the four intermediate quarters, zenith, and nadir, with rays of light emitted from the white curls [between his eyebrows]. The worlds of those quarters looked like those of the east.

Thereupon each of the Buddhas of the [worlds of the] ten quarters said to the Bodhisattvas under him, "Good men! Now I will go to Śākyamuni Buddha of the Sahā-World. I also will make offerings to the stūpa of treasures of Many-Treasures Tathāgata."

At that instant the Sahā-World was purified. The ground of the world became lapis lazuli. The world was adorned with jeweled trees. The eight roads were marked off by ropes of gold. The towns, villages, cities, oceans, rivers, mountains,[2] forests and thickets were eliminated. The incense of great treasures was burned; mandārava-flowers, strewn over the ground; and jeweled nets and curtains with jeweled bells, hung over the world. The gods and men were removed to other worlds except those who were in the congregation.

At that time each of the Buddhas was accompanied by an attendant who was a great Bodhisattva. Some of the Buddhas came under the jeweled trees in the Sahā-World. The jeweled trees were five hundred yojanas tall, and adorned with branches, leaves, flowers and fruits. Under the jeweled trees were lion-like seats five yojanas tall, adorned with great treasures. The Buddhas sat cross-legged on the seats [under the jeweled trees]. The seats [under the jeweled trees] in the [Sahā-World composed of] one thousand million Sumeru-worlds were, however, too few to receive all the Buddhas of Śākyamuni Buddha's replicas who were to come from the worlds even of one of the ten quarters. [Seeing this,] Śākyamuni Buddha purified two hundred billion nayuta worlds of each of the eight quarters [neighboring the Sahā-World] to receive all the Buddhas of his replicas. The hells, the regions of hungry spirits, the regions of animals, and the regions of asuras [of those worlds] were eliminated; and the gods and men [of those worlds] were removed to other worlds. The ground of those purified worlds became lapis lazuli. The worlds were adorned with jeweled trees

2 Except Mt. Gṛdhrakūṭa.

five hundred yojanas tall. The trees were adorned with branches, leaves, flowers and fruits. Under the trees were lion-like seats of treasures five yojanas tall, adorned with various treasures. The great oceans, rivers, the Mucilinda Mountains, the Mahā-Mucilinda Mountains, the Surrounding Iron Mountains, the Great Surrounding Iron Mountains, the Sumeru Mountains, and all the other great mountains [of those worlds] were eliminated, and all those worlds were amalgamated into one Buddha-world[3] [that is, into the world of Śākyamuni Buddha]. The jeweled ground of this [expanded] world was even. Jeweled curtains and canopies adorned with streamers were hung over this [expanded] world; the incense of great treasures, burned; and jeweled flowers of heaven, strewn over the ground.

Śākyamuni Buddha again purified two hundred billion nayuta more worlds of each of the eight quarters [neighboring the expanded world] to seat all the Buddhas of his replicas. The hells, the regions of hungry spirits, the regions of animals, and the regions of asuras [of those worlds] were eliminated; and the gods and men [of those worlds] were removed to other worlds. The ground of those purified worlds became lapis lazuli. The worlds were adorned with jeweled trees five hundred yojanas tall. The trees were adorned with branches, leaves, flowers and fruits. Under the trees were lion-like seats of treasures five yojanas tall, adorned with great treasures. The great oceans, rivers, the Mucilinda Mountains, the Mahā-Mucilinda Mountains, the Surrounding Iron Mountains, the Great Surrounding Iron Mountains, the Sumeru Mountains, and all the other great mountains [of those worlds] were eliminated, and all those worlds were amalgamated into one Buddha-world [that is, into the world of Śākyamuni Buddha]. The jeweled ground of this [expanded] world was even. Jeweled curtains and canopies adorned with streamers were hung over this [expanded] world; the incense of great treasures, burned; and jeweled flowers of heaven, strewn over the ground.

Thereupon the Buddhas of the replicas of Śākyamuni Buddha in the worlds of the east, who were expounding the Dharma in those

---

3 The Sahā-World and the four hundred billion nayuta worlds of each of the eight quarters surrounding it are not treated as one world in the following chapters.

worlds numbering hundreds of thousands of billions of nayutas, that is, as many as there are sands in the River Ganges, came [to this expanded world]. So did the Buddhas of the worlds of the nine other quarters. They sat on the seats [under the jeweled trees]. [The Sahā-World and] the four hundred billion nayuta worlds of each of the eight quarters[, which were amalgamated into one Buddha-world,] were filled with those Buddhas, with those Tathāgatas.

Thereupon one of the Buddhas on the lion-like seats under the jeweled trees, wishing to inquire after Śākyamuni Buddha, gave a handful of jeweled flowers to his attendant, and said to him, [wishing to] dispatch him:

"Good man! Go to Śākyamuni Buddha who is now living on Mt. Gṛdhrakūṭa! Ask him on my behalf, 'Are you in good health? Are you peaceful? Are the Bodhisattvas and Śrāvakas peaceful or not?' Strew these jeweled flowers to him, offer them to him, and say, 'That Buddha sent me to tell you that he wishes to see the stūpa of treasures opened.'"

All the other Buddhas also dispatched their attendants in the same way.[4]

Thereupon Śākyamuni Buddha, having seen that all the Buddhas of his replicas had already arrived and sat on the lion-like seats, and also having heard that they had told their attendants of their wish to see the stūpa of treasures opened, rose from his seat, and went up to the sky. All the four kinds of devotees stood up, joined their hands together towards him, and looked up at him with all their hearts. Now he opened the door of the stūpa of the seven treasures with the fingers of his right hand. The opening of the door made a sound as large as that of the removal of the bolt and lock of the gate of a great city. At that instant all the congregation saw Many-Treasures Tathāgata sitting with his perfect and undestroyed body on the lion-like seat in the stūpa of treasures as if he had been sitting in dhyāna-concentration. They also heard him say:

"Excellent, excellent! You, Śākyamuni Buddha, have joyfully expounded the Sūtra of the Lotus Flower of the Wonderful Dharma. I have come to hear this sūtra [directly from you]."

---

4 It is understood here that the attendants went to Śākyamuni Buddha, conveyed the messages of their masters to him, and returned to their masters.

Having seen that the Buddha, who had passed away many thousands of billions of kalpas before, had said this, the four kinds of devotees praised him, saying, "We have never seen [such a Buddha as] you before." They strewed heaps of jeweled flowers of heaven to Many-Treasures Buddha and also to Śākyamuni Buddha.

Thereupon Many-Treasures Buddha in the stūpa of treasures offered a half of his seat to Śākyamuni Buddha, saying, "Śākyamuni Buddha, sit here!"

Śākyamuni Buddha entered the stūpa and sat on the half-seat with his legs crossed. The great multitude, having seen the two Tathāgatas sitting cross-legged on the lion-like seat in the stūpa of the seven treasures, thought, "The seat of the Buddhas is too high. Tathāgata! Raise us up by your supernatural powers so that we may be able to be with you in the sky!"

Thereupon Śākyamuni Buddha raised them up to the sky by his supernatural powers, and said to the four kinds of devotees with a loud voice:

"Who will expound the Sūtra of the Lotus Flower of the Wonderful Dharma in this Sahā-World? Now is the time to do this. I shall enter into Nirvāṇa[5] before long. I wish to transmit this Sūtra of the Lotus Flower of the Wonderful Dharma to someone so that this sūtra may be preserved."

Thereupon the World-Honored One, wishing to repeat what he had said, sang in gāthās:

> The Saintly Master, the World-Honored One,
> Who had passed away a long time ago,
> Came riding in the stūpa of treasures
> To hear the Dharma [directly from me].
> Could anyone who sees him
> Not make efforts to hear the Dharma?
>
> It is innumerable[6] kalpas
> Since he passed away.

---

5 This means Parinirvāṇa.

6 This is finite.

He wished to hear the Dharma at any place
Because the Dharma is difficult to meet.

His original vow was this:
"After I pass away,
I will go to any place
To hear the Dharma."

The Buddhas of my replicas
As innumerable
As there are sands in the River Ganges
Also came here
From their wonderful worlds,
Parting from their disciples,
And giving up the offerings made to them
By gods, men and dragons,
In order to hear the Dharma,
See Many-Treasures Tathāgata, Who passed away
[a long time ago],
And have the Dharma preserved forever.

I removed innumerable living beings from many worlds,
And purified those worlds
By my supernatural powers
In order to seat those Buddhas.

Those Buddhas came under the jeweled trees.
The trees are adorned with those Buddhas
Just as a pond of pure water is adorned
With lotus flowers.

There are lion-like seats
Under the jeweled trees.
Those Buddhas sat on the seats.
The worlds are adorned
With the light of those Buddhas as bright
As a great torch in the darkness of night.

Wonderful fragrance is sent forth
From the bodies of those Buddhas
To the worlds of the ten quarters.
The living beings of those worlds
Smell the fragrance joyfully,
Just as the branches of a tree bend before a strong wind.
Those Buddhas employ these expedients
In order to have the Dharma preserved forever.

(The Buddha said to the great multitude.)
Who will protect
And keep this sūtra,
And read and recite it
After my extinction?
Make a vow before me to do this!

Many-Treasures Buddha,
Who had passed away a long time ago,
Made a loud voice like the roar of a lion
According to his great vow.

Many-Treasures Tathāgata and I
And the Buddhas of my replicas,
Who have assembled here,
Wish to know who will do [all this].

My sons!
Who will protect the Dharma?
Make a great vow
To preserve the Dharma forever!

Anyone who protects this sūtra
Should be considered
To have already made offerings
To Many-Treasures and to me.

Many-Treasures Buddha vowed to go
About the worlds of the ten quarters,
Riding in the stūpa of treasures,
In order to hear this sūtra [directly from the expounder].

Anyone [who protects this sūtra] also
Should be considered to have already made offerings
To the Buddhas of my replicas, who have come here
And adorned the worlds with their light.

Anyone who expounds this sūtra
Will be able to see me,
To see Many-Treasures Tathāgata,
And to see the Buddhas of my replicas.

Good men! Think this over clearly!
It is difficult
[To expound this sūtra].
Make a great vow to do this!

It is not difficult
To expound all the other sūtras
As many as there are sands
In the River Ganges.

It is not difficult
To grasp Mt. Sumeru[7]
And hurl it to a distance
Of countless Buddha-worlds.

It is not difficult to move [a world]
[Composed of] one thousand million Sumeru-worlds

---

7 It should be considered that Mt. Sumeru, which was eliminated earlier, has already been restored before the singing of these gāthās. The existence of the ocean is noticed in the next chapter and all the mountains, forests, rivers and oceans of the one thousand million Sumeru-worlds are seen later in the sūtra. Therefore, it should be considered that the mountains and others, which were eliminated earlier, were restored before the singing of these gāthās although the replicas of Śākyamuni Buddha stayed in those worlds.

With the tip of a toe
And hurl it to another world.

It is not difficult
To stand in the Highest Heaven
And expound innumerable other sūtras
To all living beings.

It is difficult
To expound this sūtra
In the evil world
After my extinction.

It is not difficult
To grasp the sky,
And wander about with it
From place to place.

It is difficult
To copy and keep this sūtra
Or cause others to copy it
After my extinction.

It is not difficult
To put the great earth
On the nail of a toe
And go up to the Heaven of Brahman.

It is difficult
To read this sūtra
Even for a while in the evil world
After my extinction.

It is not difficult
To shoulder a load of hay

And stay unburned in the fire
At the end of the kalpa [of destruction].

It is difficult
To keep this sūtra
And expound it to even one person
After my extinction.

It is not difficult
To keep the store
Of eighty-four thousand teachings
Expounded in the sūtras
Composed of the twelve elements,[8]
And expound it to people,
And cause the hearers to obtain
The six supernatural powers.

It is difficult
To hear and receive this sūtra,
And ask the meanings of it
After my extinction.

It is not difficult
To expound the Dharma
To many thousands of billions of living beings
As many as there are sands
In the River Ganges
So that they may be able
To obtain the benefits:
Arhatship and the six supernatural powers.

It is difficult
To keep
This sūtra
After my extinction.

8 See *Twelve Elements* in the English/Sanskrit Glossary.

Since I attained
The enlightenment of the Buddha,
I have expounded many sūtras
In innumerable worlds.

This sūtra is
The most excellent.
To keep this sūtra
Is to keep me.

Good men!
Who will receive and keep this sūtra,
And read and recite it
After my extinction?
Make a vow before me
[To do all this]!

It is difficult to keep this sūtra.
I shall be glad to see
Anyone keeping it even for a moment.
So will all the other Buddhas.
He will be praised by all the Buddhas.
He will be a man of valor,
A man of endeavor.
He should be considered
To have already observed the precepts,
And practiced the dhūta.
He will quickly attain
The unsurpassed enlightenment
of the Buddha.

Anyone who reads and recites this sūtra in the future
Is a true son of mine.
He shall be considered to live
On the stage of purity and good.

Anyone, after my extinction,
Who understands the meaning of this sūtra,
Will be the eye of the worlds
Of gods and men.

Anyone who expounds this sūtra
Even for a moment in this dreadful world,
Should be honored with offerings
By all gods and men.

[Here ends] the Fourth Volume of the Sūtra of the Lotus Flower of the Wonderful Dharma.

CHAPTER XII

DEVADATTA[1]

Thereupon the Buddha said to the Bodhisattvas, gods, men and the four kinds of devotees:

"[When I was a Bodhisattva] in my previous existence, I sought the Sūtra of the Lotus Flower of the Wonderful Dharma for innumerable kalpas without indolence. I became a king [and continued to be so] for many kalpas. [Although I was a king,] I made a vow to attain unsurpassed Bodhi. I never faltered in seeking it. I practiced alms-giving in order to complete the six pāramitās. I never grudged elephants, horses, the seven treasures, countries, cities, wives, children, menservants, maidservants or attendants. I did not spare my head, eyes, marrow, brain, flesh, hands or feet. I did not spare even my life.

"In those days the lives of the people of the world were immeasurably long. [One day] I abdicated from the throne in order to seek the Dharma[, but retained the title of king]. I entrusted the crown prince with the administration of my country. I beat a drum and sought the Dharma in all directions, saying with a loud voice, 'Who will expound the Great Vehicle to me? If there is anyone, I will make offerings to him, and run errands for him for the rest of my life.'

"Thereupon a seer came to [me, who was] the king. He said, 'I have a sūtra of the Great Vehicle called the Sūtra of the Lotus Flower of the Wonderful Dharma. If you are not disobedient to me, I will expound this sūtra to you.'

1 This chapter was not translated by Kumārajīva. It was inserted into Kumārajīva's version. See Introduction.

"Having heard this, I danced with joy, and immediately became his servant. I offered him anything he wanted. I collected fruits, drew water, gathered firewood, and prepared meals for him. I even allowed my body to be his seat. I never felt tired in body and mind. I served him for a thousand years. In order to hear the Dharma from him, I served him so strenuously that I did not cause him to be short of anything."

Thereupon the World-Honored One, wishing to repeat what he had said, sang in gāthās:

I remember that I became a king in a kalpa of the past.
Although I was a king,
I did not indulge in the pleasures of the five desires
Because I was seeking the Great Dharma.

I tolled a bell, and said loudly in all directions;
"Who knows the Great Dharma?
If anyone expounds the Dharma to me,
I will become his servant."

There was a seer called Asita.
He came to [me, who was] the great king, and said:
"I know the Wonderful Dharma.
It is rare in the world.
If you serve me well,
I will expound the Dharma to you."

Hearing this, I had great joy.
I became his servant at once.
I offered him
Anything he wanted.

I collected firewood and the fruits of trees and grasses,
And offered these things to him respectfully
from time to time.
I never felt tired in body and mind
Because I was thinking of the Wonderful Dharma.

I sought the Great Dharma strenuously
Because I wished to save all living beings.
I did not wish to benefit myself
Or to have the pleasures of the five desires.

Although I was the king of a great country,
I sought the Dharma strenuously.
I finally obtained the Dharma and became a Buddha.
Therefore, I now expound it to you.

The Buddha said to the bhikṣus:

"The king at that time was a previous life of myself.[2] The seer at that time was a previous life of Devadatta. Devadatta was my teacher. He caused me to complete the six pāramitās. He caused me to have loving-kindness, compassion, joy and impartiality. He caused me to have the thirty-two major marks and the eighty minor marks [of the Buddha]. He caused me to have my body purely gilt. He caused me to have the ten powers and the four kinds of fearlessness. He caused me to know the four ways to attract others. He caused me to have the eighteen properties and supernatural powers [of the Buddha]. He caused me to have the power of giving discourses. I attained perfect enlightenment and now save all living beings because Devadatta was my teacher."

He said to the four kinds of devotees:

"Devadatta will become a Buddha after innumerable kalpas.[3] He will be called Heavenly-King, the Tathāgata, the Deserver of Offerings, the Perfectly Enlightened One, the Man of Wisdom and Practice, the Well-Gone, the Knower of the World, the Unsurpassed Man, the Controller of Men, the Teacher of Gods and Men, the Buddha, the World-Honored One. The world of that Buddha will be called Heavenly-Way. That Buddha will live for twenty intermediate kalpas. He will expound the Wonderful Dharma to all living beings. [Hearing the Dharma from him,] as

2 This redundant statement may have been put here according to the regular proceedings after the narration of a jātaka in which the Bodhisattva is usually expressed in the third person.

3 This expresses a finite length of time.

many living beings as there are sands in the River Ganges will obtain Arhatship; another group of innumerable living beings will aspire for the enlightenment of cause-knowers; and another group of living beings as many as there are sands in the River Ganges will aspire for unsurpassed enlightenment, obtain the truth of birthlessness, and reach the stage of irrevocability. After the Parinirvāṇa of Heavenly-King Buddha, his right teachings will be preserved in that world for twenty intermediate kalpas. During that time a stūpa of the seven treasures sixty yojanas tall and forty yojanas wide and deep will be erected to enshrine the śarīras of his perfect body. Gods and men will bow to the wonderful stūpa of the seven treasures and offer various flowers, incense powder, incense to burn, incense applicable to the skin, garments, necklaces, banners, streamers, jeweled canopies, music and songs of praise [to the stūpa]. [By doing all this,] innumerable living beings will attain Arhatship; another group of innumerable living beings will attain Pratyekabuddhahood; and another group of inconceivably numerous living beings will aspire for Bodhi and reach the stage of irrevocability."

He said to the bhikṣus:

"Good men or women in the future who hear this chapter of Devadatta of the Sūtra of the Lotus Flower of the Wonderful Dharma with faithful respect caused by their pure minds, and have no doubts [about this chapter], will not fall into hell or the region of hungry spirits or the region of animals. They will be reborn before the Buddhas of the worlds of the ten quarters. They will always hear this sūtra at the places of their rebirth. Even when they are reborn among men or gods, they will be given wonderful pleasures. When they are reborn before the Buddhas, they will appear in lotus-flowers."

At that time Many-Treasures, the World-Honored One, who had come from the nadir,[4] was accompanied by a Bodhisattva called Accumulated-Wisdom. The Bodhisattva said to Many-Treasures Buddha, "Shall we go back to our home world?"

Śākyamuni Buddha said to Accumulated-Wisdom:

---

4 It is held here that Many-Treasures Buddha came from the nadir, not from the east.

"Good man, wait for a while! A Bodhisattva called Mañjuśrī is coming.[5] See him, talk about the Wonderful Dharma with him, and then go back to your home world!"

Thereupon Mañjuśrī came sitting on a one-thousand-petaled lotus-flower as large as the wheel of a chariot. He was accompanied by other Bodhisattvas who were also sitting on jeweled lotus-flowers. Mañjuśrī had sprung up from the palace of Dragon-King Sāgara in the great ocean, gone up to the sky[, and traveled through the sky towards Mt. Sacred Eagle]. Having reached Mt. Sacred Eagle, he descended from the lotus-flower, came to the two World-Honored Ones,[6] and worshipped their feet with his head. Having completed the worship, he came to Accumulated-Wisdom, exchanged greetings with him, retired and sat to one side.

Accumulated-Wisdom Bodhisattva asked Mañjuśrī, "You went to the palace of the dragon-king. How many living beings did you lead into the Way to Bodhi there?"

Mañjuśrī answered, "Their number is immeasurable, incalculable, inexplicable, unthinkable. Wait for a while! You will be able to see them."

No sooner had he said this than innumerable Bodhisattvas, who were sitting on jeweled lotus-flowers, sprang up from the sea, came to Mt. Sacred Eagle, went up to the sky, and stayed there. All these Bodhisattvas had been led [into the Way to Bodhi] by Mañjuśrī. They had already performed the Bodhisattva practices. [Up in the sky] they [began to] expound the six pāramitās. Some of them were formerly Śrāvakas. When they were Śrāvakas, they expounded the Śrāvaka practices in the sky. Now they were acting according to the truth of the Void of the Great Vehicle.

Mañjuśrī said to Accumulated-Wisdom, "Now you see the living beings whom I taught in the sea."

Thereupon Accumulated-Wisdom Bodhisattva praised him with gāthās:

---

5 It is not given when Mañjuśrī went to the palace of the Dragon-King Sāgara in the ocean.

6 Here the two Buddhas are on Mt. Sacred Eagle, not in the stūpa hanging in the sky.

Possessor of Great Wisdom and Virtue!
You were brave in saving innumerable living beings.
This great congregation and I understand
That you expounded
The truth of the reality of all things,
Revealed the teaching of the One Vehicle,
And led those innumerable living beings
[Into the Way] to Bodhi quickly.

Mañjuśrī said, "In the sea I expounded only the Sūtra of the Lotus Flower of the Wonderful Dharma."

Accumulated-Wisdom asked Mañjuśrī:

"The sūtra is exceedingly profound and wonderful. This is the treasure of all the sūtras. It is rare in the world. Do you know anyone who acted according to this sūtra so strenuously that he has already been qualified to become a Buddha quickly?"

Mañjuśrī answered:

"Yes. There is a daughter of Dragon-King Sāgara [among those whom I taught]. She is eight years old. She is clever. She knows the karmas of all living beings. She obtained dhāraṇīs. She keeps all the treasury of the profound and hidden core expounded by the Buddhas. She entered deep into dhyāna-concentration, and understood all teachings. She aspired for Bodhi in a kṣana, and reached the stage of irrevocability. She is eloquent without hindrance. She is compassionate towards all living beings just as a mother is towards her babe. She obtained all merits. Her thoughts and words are wonderful and great. She is compassionate, humble, gentle and graceful. She [has already been qualified to] attain Bodhi[, and to become a Buddha quickly]."

Accumulated-Wisdom Bodhisattva said:

"As far as I know, [when he was a Bodhisattva,] Śākyamuni Buddha sought Bodhi, that is, enlightenment incessantly for innumerable kalpas. He accumulated merits by practicing austerities. Even the smallest part, even the part as large as a poppy-seed of this world—this world being composed of one thousand million Sumeru-worlds—is not outside the places where the Bodhisattva made efforts to save all living beings at the cost of his life. It was after doing all this that he attained Bodhi, that is, enlightenment. I do not believe that this girl will be able to attain perfect enlightenment[, that is, to become a Buddha] in a moment."

No sooner had he said this than the daughter of the dragon-king came to [Śākyamuni] Buddha.[7] She worshipped [his feet] with her head, retired, stood to one side, and praised him with gāthās:

You know the sins and merits
Of all living beings.
You illumine the worlds of the ten quarters.
Your wonderful, pure and sacred body
Is adorned with the thirty-two major marks
And with the eighty minor marks.

Gods and men are looking up at you.
Dragons also respect you.
None of the living beings
Sees you without adoration.

Only[8] you know that I [am qualified to] attain Bodhi
Because I heard [the Dharma].
I will expound the teachings of the Great Vehicle
And save all living beings from suffering.

Thereupon Śāriputra said to the daughter of the dragon-king:
"You think that you will be able to attain unsurpassed enlightenment [and become a Buddha] before long. This is difficult to believe because the body of a woman is too defiled to be a recipient of the teachings of the Buddha. How can you attain unsurpassed Bodhi? The enlightenment of the Buddha is far off. It can be attained only by those who perform the [Bodhisattva] practices with strenuous efforts for innumerable

7 The presence of Many-Treasures Buddha is ignored.
8 But in reality, Mañjuśrī knew this.

kalpas. A woman has five impossibilities. She cannot become 1. the Brahman-Heavenly-King, 2. King Śakra, 3. King Māra, 4. a wheel-turning-holy-king, and 5. a Buddha. How can it be that you, being a woman, will become a Buddha, quickly [or not]?"

At that time the daughter of the dragon-king had a gem. The gem was worth one thousand million Sumeru-worlds. She offered it to the Buddha. The Buddha received it immediately. She asked both Accumulated-Wisdom Bodhisattva and Venerable Śāriputra, "I offered a gem to the World-Honored One. Did he receive it quickly or not?"

Both of them answered, "Very quickly."

She said, "Look at me with your supernatural powers! I will become a Buddha more quickly."

Thereupon the congregation saw that the daughter of the dragon-king changed into a man all of a sudden, performed the Bodhisattva practices, went to the Spotless World in the south, sat on a jeweled lotus-flower, attained perfect enlightenment, obtained the thirty-two major marks and the eighty minor marks [of the Buddha], and [began to] expound the Wonderful Dharma to the living beings of the worlds of the ten quarters. Having seen from afar that [the man who had been] the daughter of the dragon-king had become a Buddha and [begun to] expound the Dharma to the men and gods in his congregation, all the living beings of the Sahā-World, including Bodhisattvas, Śrāvakas, gods, dragons, the [six other kinds, that is, in total] eight kinds of supernatural beings, men, and nonhuman beings, bowed [to that Buddha] with great joy. Having heard the Dharma [from that Buddha], [a group of] innumerable living beings [of that world] understood the Dharma, and reached the stage of irrevocability, and [another group of] innumerable living beings [of that world] obtained the assurance of their future attainment of enlightenment. At that time the Spotless World quaked in the six ways. Three thousand living beings of the Sahā-World reached the stage of irrevocability, and another group of three thousand living beings [of the Sahā-World] aspired for Bodhi, and obtained the assurance of their future attainment of enlightenment. The Accumulated-Wisdom Bodhisattva, Śāriputra, and all the other living beings in the congregation received the Dharma faithfully and in silence.

CHAPTER XIII

ENCOURAGEMENT FOR KEEPING THIS SŪTRA[1]

Thereupon Medicine-King Bodhisattva-mahāsattva and Great-Eloquence Bodhisattva-mahāsattva, together with their twenty thousand attendants who were also Bodhisattvas, vowed to the Buddha:

"World-Honored One, do not worry! We will keep, read, recite and expound this sūtra after your extinction. The living beings in the evil world after [your extinction] will have less roots of good, more arrogance, more greed for offerings of worldly things, and more roots of evil. It will be difficult to teach them because they will go away from emancipation. But we will patiently read, recite, keep, expound and copy this sūtra, and make various offerings to it. We will not spare even our lives [in doing all this]."

At that time there were five hundred Arhats[2] in this congregation. They had already been assured of their future attainment [of Anuttara-samyak-saṃbodhi]. They said to the Buddha, "World-Honored One! We also vow to expound this sūtra[, but we will expound it] in some other worlds [rather than in this Sahā-World]."

There were also eight thousand Śrāvakas[3] some of whom had something more to learn while others had nothing more to learn. They had already been assured of their future attainment [of Anuttara-samyak-saṃbodhi]. They rose from their seats, joined their hands together towards the Buddha and vowed:

---

1 This chapter is a continuation of Chapter XI. 勸持 Literally means "to encourage keeping."

2 These five hundred Arhats may be identified with the five hundred Arhats given in Chapter VI and VII.

3 Eight thousand Śrāvakas are not given as a group in the foregoing chapters.

"World-Honored One! We also will expound this sūtra in some other worlds because the people of this Sahā-World have many evils. They are arrogant. They have few merits. They are angry, defiled, ready to flatter others, and insincere."

There were Mahā-Prajāpatī Bhikṣuṇī, the sister of the mother of the Buddha, and six thousand bhikṣuṇīs, some of whom had something more to learn while others had nothing more to learn. They rose from their seats, joined their hands together with all their hearts, and looked up at the honorable face with unblenching eyes.

Thereupon the World-Honored One said to Gautamī:

"Why do you look at me so anxiously? You do not think that I assured you of your future attainment of Anuttara-samyak-saṃbodhi because I did not mention you by name, do you? Gautamī! I have already said that I assured all the Śrāvakas of their future attainment [of Anuttara-samyak-saṃbodhi]. Now you wish to know my assurance of your future attainment [of Anuttara-samyak-saṃbodhi]. You will become a great teacher of the Dharma under six billion and eight hundred thousand million Buddhas in the future. The six thousand bhikṣuṇīs, some of whom have something more to learn while others have nothing more to learn, also will become teachers of the Dharma. [By becoming a great teacher of the Dharma,] you will complete the Way of Bodhisattvas in the course of time, and become a Buddha called Gladly-Seen-By-All-Beings, the Tathāgata, the Deserver of Offerings, the Perfectly Enlightened One, the Man[4] of Wisdom and Practice, the Well-Gone, the Knower of the World, the Unsurpassed Man, the Controller of Men, the Teacher of Gods and Men, the Buddha, the World-Honored One. Gautamī! That Gladly-Seen-By-All-Beings Buddha will assure the six thousand [bhikṣuṇīs, that is,] Bodhisattvas[5] of their future attainment of Anuttara-samyak-saṃbodhi one after another."

Thereupon Yaśodharā Bhikṣuṇī, the mother of Rāhula, thought, "I am not among the persons whom the World-Honored One

4 A woman must change herself into a man in order to become a Buddha because a Buddha is a man.

5 The six thousand bhikṣuṇīs will be Bodhisattvas when they become teachers of the Dharma.

mentioned by name and assured of their future attainment of [Anuttara-samyak-saṃbodhi]."

The Buddha said to Yaśodharā:

"You will perform the Bodhisattva practices under hundreds of thousands of billions of Buddhas in the future. You will become a great teacher of the Dharma under those Buddhas. You will walk the Way to Buddhahood step by step, and finally become a Buddha in a good world. The name of that Buddha will be Emitting-Ten-Million-Rays-Of-Light, the Tathāgata, the Deserver of Offerings, the Perfectly Enlightened One, the Man of Wisdom and Practice, the Well-Gone, the Knower of the World, the Unsurpassed Man, the Controller of Men, the Teacher of Gods and Men, the Buddha, the World-Honored One. The duration of the life of that Buddha will be many asaṃkhyas of kalpas."

Thereupon Maha-Prajāpatī Bhikṣuṇī, Yaśodharā Bhikṣuṇī, and their attendants had the greatest joy that they had ever had. They sang in a gāthā before the Buddha:

> You, the World-Honored One, are our leader.
> You give peace to gods and men.
> Hearing that you assured us of our future Buddhahood,
> We are relieved and satisfied.

Having sung this gāthā, the bhikṣuṇīs said to the Buddha, "World-Honored One! We also will expound this sūtra in other worlds."

Thereupon the World-Honored One looked at the eighty billion nayuta[6] Bodhisattva-mahāsattvas. These Bodhisattvas had already reached the stage of avaivartika, turned the irrevocable wheel of the Dharma, and obtained dhāraṇīs. They rose from their seats, came to the Buddha, joined their hands together [towards him] with all their hearts, and thought, "If the World-Honored One commands us to keep and expound this sūtra, we will expound the Dharma just as the Buddha teaches."

6 "Eighty billion nayuta" may be a variation of "eighty thousand," given on p. 1.

They also thought, "The Buddha keeps silence.[7] He does not command us. What shall we do?"

In order to follow the wish of the Buddha respectfully, and also to fulfill their original vow, they vowed to the Buddha with a loud voice like the roar of a lion:

"World-Honored One! After your extinction, we will go to any place [not only of this Sahā-World but also] of the worlds of the ten quarters, as often as required, and cause all living beings to copy, keep, read and recite this sūtra, to expound the meanings of it, to act according to the Dharma, and to memorize this sūtra correctly. We shall be able to do all this only by your powers. World-Honored One! Protect us from afar even when you are in another world!"

Thereupon the Bodhisattvas sang in gāthās with one voice:

Do not worry!
We will expound this sūtra
In the dreadful, evil world
After your extinction.

Ignorant people will speak ill of us,
Abuse us, and threaten us
With swords or sticks.
But we will endure all this.

Some bhikṣus in the evil world will be cunning.
They will be ready to flatter others.
Thinking that they have obtained what they have not,
Their minds will be filled with arrogance.

Some bhikṣus will live in araṇyas or retired places,
And wear patched pieces of cloth.
Thinking that they are practicing the true Way,
They will despise others.

---

7 The silence of the Buddha on this occasion is interpreted as an implication that the Buddha did not encourage the Bodhisattvas to keep this sūtra.

Being attached to worldly profits,
They will expound the Dharma to men in white robes.[8]
They will be respected by the people of the world
As the Arhats who have the six supernatural powers.

They will have evil thoughts.
They will always think of worldly things.
Even when they live in araṇyas,
They will take pleasure in saying that we have faults.

They will say of us,
"Those bhikṣus[9] are greedy for worldly profits.
Therefore, they are expounding
The teachings of heretics.
They made that sūtra by themselves
In order to deceive the people of the world.
They are expounding that sūtra
Because they wish to make a name for themselves."

In order to speak ill of us, in order to slander us
In the midst of the great multitude,
In order to say that we are evil,
They will say to kings, ministers and brāhmaṇas,
And also to householders and other bhikṣus,
"They have wrong views.
They are expounding
The teachings of heretics."
But we will endure all this
Because we respect you.

They will despise us,
Saying to us [ironically],
"You are Buddhas."
But we will endure all these despising words.

---

8 A person in white robes means a layman.

9 Here we see that the Bodhisattvas took the form of bhikṣus and expounded the Dharma.

There will be many dreadful things
In the evil world of the kalpa of defilements.
Devils will enter the bodies [of those bhikṣus]
And cause them to abuse and insult us.

We will wear the armor of endurance
Because we respect and believe you.
We will endure all these difficulties
In order to expound this sūtra.

We will not spare even our lives.
We treasure only unsurpassed enlightenment.
We will protect and keep the Dharma in the future
If you transmit it to us.

World-Honored One, know this!
Evil bhikṣus in the defiled world will not know
The teachings that you expounded with expedients
According to the capacities of all living beings.

They will speak ill of us,
Or frown at us,
Or drive us out of our monasteries
From time to time.
But we will endure all these evils
Because we are thinking of your command.

When we hear of a person who seeks the Dharma
In any village or city,
We will visit him and expound the Dharma [to him]
If you transmit it to us.

Because we are your messengers,
We are fearless before multitudes.
We will expound the Dharma.
Buddha, do not worry!

We vow all this to you
And also to the Buddhas who have come
From the worlds of the ten quarters.[10]
Buddha, know what we have in our minds!

10 The presence of Many-Treasures Buddha is not referred to in this chapter.

CHAPTER XIV

PEACEFUL PRACTICES

Thereupon Mañjuśrī Bodhisattva-mahāsattva, the Son of the King of the Dharma, said to the Buddha:

"World-Honored One! These Bodhisattvas are extraordinarily rare. They made a great vow to protect, keep, read, recite and expound this Sūtra of the Lotus Flower of the Wonderful Dharma in the evil world after your extinction because they are following you respectfully. World-Honored One! How should an [ordinary] Bodhisattva-mahāsattva expound this sūtra in the evil world after [your extinction]?"

The Buddha said to him:

"A Bodhisattva-mahāsattva who wishes to expound this sūtra in the evil world after [my extinction] should practice four sets of things.

"First, he should perform proper practices, approach proper things, and then expound this sūtra to all living beings.

"Mañjuśrī! What are the proper practices the Bodhisattva-mahāsattva should perform? He should be patient, mild and meek. He should not be rash, timorous, or attached to anything. He should see things as they are. He should not be attached to his non-attachment to anything. Nor should he be attached to his seeing things as they are. These are the proper practices the Bodhisattva-mahāsattva should perform.

"What are the proper things the Bodhisattva-mahāsattva should approach? He should not approach kings, princes, ministers or other government directors. He should not approach heretics, aspirants for the teaching of Brahman, Nirgraṇṭhas, writers of worldly literature, writers of non-Buddhist songs of praise, Lokāyatas or Anti-Lokāyatas. He should not approach players of dangerous sports such as boxers or wrestlers. He should not approach naṭas or other various amusement-makers. He should not approach caṇḍālas, boar-keepers, shepherds, poulterers, dog-keepers, hunters, fishermen, or other people who do evils for their livelihood. When they come to him, he should expound the Dharma to them, but should not wish [to receive anything from them]. He should not approach those who seek Śrāvakahood, be they bhikṣus, bhikṣuṇīs, upāsakas or upāsikās. He should not exchange greetings with them. He should not stay with them in the same monastery, promenade or lecture-hall. When they come to him, he should expound the Dharma to them according to their capacities, but should not wish [to receive anything from them]. Mañjuśrī! The Bodhisattva-mahāsattva should not expound the Dharma to a woman with a desire for her. He should not wish to look at her. When he enters the house of others, he should not talk with a little girl, an unmarried woman or a widow. He should not approach or make friends with anyone of the five kinds of eunuchs. He should not enter the house of others alone. If he must enter it alone for some reason, he should think of the Buddha with all his heart. When he expounds the Dharma to a woman, he should not laugh with his teeth visible to her. He should not expose his breast to her. He should not be friendly with her even for the purpose of expounding the Dharma to her. Needless to say, he should not be so for other purposes. He should not wish to keep young disciples, śrāmaṇeras or children. He should not wish to have the same teacher with them.

"He should always make it a pleasure to sit in dhyāna. He should live in a retired place and concentrate his mind. Mañjuśrī! [A retired place] is the first thing he should approach.

"The Bodhisattva-mahāsattva also should know the following truth. All things are insubstantial. They are as they are. Things are not perverted. They do not move. They do not go. They do not turn. They have nothing substantial just as the sky has not. They are inexplicable. They are not born. They do not appear. They do not rise. They are nameless. They are formless. They have no property. They are immeasurable and limitless. They have no obstacle or hindrance. He should see all this. Things can exist only by dependent origination. Only perverted people say, 'Things are permanent and pleasant.' This truth is the second thing he should approach."

Thereupon the World-Honored One, wishing to repeat what he had said, sang in gāthās:

A Bodhisattva who wishes
To expound this sūtra without fear
In the evil world
After [my extinction]
Should perform proper practices
And approach proper things.

He should keep away
From kings, princes and ministers,
From other government officials,
From players of dangerous sports,
From caṇḍālas, from heretics,
And from aspirants for the teaching of Brahman.

He should not approach arrogant people,
Or the scholars who are deeply attached
To the Three Stores of the Lesser Vehicle,
Or the bhikṣus
Who violate the precepts,
Or self-appointed Arhats,
Or the bhikṣuṇīs
Who like to laugh playfully.

He should not approach the upāsikās
Who are attached to the five desires
Or who seek in their present life
The extinction[-without-remainder].[1]

1 This stands for Nirvāṇa-Without-Remainder, that is Parinirvāṇa.

When they come to him
With good intent
In order to hear
About the enlightenment of the Buddha,
He should expound the Dharma to them
Without fear,
But should not wish to receive
Anything from them.

He should not approach
Or make friends with a widow
Or with an unmarried woman
Or with a eunuch.

He should not approach
Slaughterers or cooks
Or those who kill for profit,
Such as hunters or fishermen.

He should not approach
Butchers
Or procurers
Of prostitutes.

He should not approach
Dangerous wrestlers
Or makers of various amusements
Or immoral women.

He should not expound the Dharma
To a woman in an enclosed place.
When he expounds the Dharma to her,
He should not laugh playfully.

When he goes to a village to beg for food,
He should take a bhikṣu with him.

If he cannot find a bhikṣu [to take with him],
He should think of the Buddha with all his heart.

These are the proper practices he should perform
And the proper things he should approach.
He should expound the Dharma peacefully
Only after doing all this![2]

He should disregard the differences
Between the superior, mean, and inferior vehicles,
Between the things free from causality
and those subject to it,
And between the real and the unreal.
He should not say:
"This is a man," or "This is a woman."
He should not obtain anything
Or know anything or see anything.
All these are the proper practices
That the Bodhisattva should perform.

Things are insubstantial.
They have no property.
They are not permanent.
They do not rise or perish.
This is the Dharma to be approached
By a man of wisdom.

Only perverted people say:
"All things exist," or "Nothing exists,"
Or "All things are real," or "Nothing is real,"
Or "All things are born," or "Nothing is born."

The Bodhisattva should live in a retired place,
And concentrate his mind.

2 This stanza should come after the stanza referring to proper practices and proper things on p. 221 because the proper practices and the proper things to approach are not yet explained.

He should be as peaceful
And as immovable as Mt. Sumeru.
Things have no property
Just as the sky has not.
They are not solid.
They are not born.
They do not appear or move or go.
They are permanently of one form.[3]
This truth is the proper thing
The Bodhisattva should approach.

A bhikṣu who lives after my extinction
Will be free from timidity
If he performs these proper practices,
And approaches these proper things
As previously stated,
And then expounds this sūtra.

A Bodhisattva will be peaceful,
And free from timidity
If he stays in a quiet room
For some time,
Recollects the Dharma correctly,
Understands the Dharma
According to the meanings of it,
And then emerges
From his dhyāna-concentration,
And leads kings, princes,
Common people and brāhmaṇas
By expounding this sūtra to them.

Mañjuśrī, all this is the first set of things
That the Bodhisattva should do
Before he expounds the Sūtra
Of the Lotus Flower of the Wonderful Dharma
In the world after [my extinction].

---

3 This is inconsistent with the statement, "They are not permanent," on p. 220.

"Second, Mañjuśrī! A Bodhisattva-mahāsattva who wishes to expound this sūtra in the age of the decline of the teachings after my extinction should perform the following peaceful practices. When he expounds or reads this sūtra, he should not point out the faults of other persons or sūtras. He should not despise other teachers of the Dharma. He should not speak of the good points or bad points or the merits or demerits of others. He should not mention Śrāvakas by name when he blames them. Nor should he do so when he praises them. He should not have hostile feelings against them or dislike them. He should have this peace of mind so that he may not act against the wishes of the hearers. When he is asked questions, he should not answer by the teachings of the Lesser Vehicle, but expound the Dharma only by the teachings of the Great Vehicle so that the questioners may be able to obtain the knowledge of the equality and differences of all things."

Thereupon the World-Honored One, wishing to repeat what he had said, sang in gāthās:

The Bodhisattva should wish
To make all living beings peaceful,
And then expound the Dharma to them.
He should make a seat in a pure place,
Apply ointment to his skin,
Wash dirt and dust off himself,
Wear a new and undefiled robe,
Clean himself within and without,
Sit on the seat of the Dharma peacefully,
And then expound the Dharma in answer to questions.

He should expound with a smile
The wonderful meaning of the Dharma
To bhikṣus and bhikṣuṇīs,
To upāsakas and upāsikās,
To kings and princes,
To government officials,
And to common people.

When he is asked questions,
He should answer
According to the meaning of the Dharma.

He should expound the Dharma to them
With stories of previous lives, parables and similes.
With these expedients he should cause them
To aspire for enlightenment,
To promote their understanding step by step,
And finally to enter into the Way to Buddhahood.

He should give up indolence,
Negligence, grief and sorrow.
He should expound the Dharma to them
Out of his compassion towards them.

He should expound to them
The teaching of unsurpassed enlightenment
With stories of previous lives
And with innumerable parables and similes
Day and night,
And cause them to rejoice.

He should not wish to receive
Garments or bedding,
Food and drink, or medicine
From them.

He should expound the Dharma to them,
Wishing only two things:
To attain the enlightenment of the Buddha
And also to cause them to do the same.
This is a peaceful offering to them.
This offering will bring them a great benefit.

A bhikṣu who expounds this Sūtra
Of the Lotus Flower of the Wonderful Dharma

With patience
After my extinction,
Will be emancipated
From jealousy, anger, and other illusions,
  That is to say, from all obstacles.
He will have no sorrow.
He will not be spoken ill of.
He will not be in fear.
He will not be threatened with swords or sticks,
Or driven out [of his monastery].

A man of wisdom
Who controls his mind
As previously stated
Will be peaceful.

His merits will be innumerable.
You would not be able to tell the number of them
By any parable or simile even if you tried to do so
For thousands of billions of kalpas.

"Again, Mañjuśrī! A Bodhisattva-mahāsattva who wishes to keep, read and recite this sūtra in the latter days after [my extinction] when the teachings are about to be destroyed, should not nurse jealousy against others, or flatter or deceive them. He should not despise those who study the Way to Buddhahood in any way. He should not speak ill of them or try to point out their faults. Some bhikṣus, bhikṣuṇīs, upāsakas or upāsikās will seek Śrāvakahood or Pratyekabuddhahood or the Way of Bodhisattvas. He should not disturb or perplex them by saying to them, 'You are far from enlightenment. You cannot obtain the knowledge of the equality and differences of all things because you are licentious and lazy in seeking enlightenment.' He should not have fruitless disputes or quarrels about the teachings with others. He should have great compassion towards all living beings. He should look upon all the Tathāgatas as his loving fathers, and upon all the Bodhisattvas as his great teachers. He should bow to all the great Bodhisattvas of the worlds of the ten quarters respectfully and from the bottom of his heart. He should expound the Dharma to all living beings without partiality. He should be obedient to the Dharma. He should not add anything to the Dharma or take away anything from the Dharma. He should not expound more teachings to those who love the Dharma more [than others do].

"Mañjuśrī! A Bodhisattva-mahāsattva who performs this third set of peaceful practices in the latter days after [my extinction] when the teachings are about to be destroyed, will be able to expound the Dharma without disturbance. He will be able to have good friends when he reads and recites this sūtra. A great multitude will come to him, hear and receive this sūtra from him, keep it after hearing it, recite it after keeping it, expound it after reciting it, copy it or cause others to copy it after expounding it, make offerings to the copy of this sūtra, honor it, respect it, and praise it."

Thereupon the World-Honored One, wishing to repeat what he had said, sang in gāthās:

Anyone who wishes to expound this sūtra
Should give up jealousy, anger, arrogance,
Flattery, deception and dishonesty.
He should always be upright.

He should not despise others,
Or have fruitless disputes about the teachings.
He should not perplex others by saying to them:
"You will not be able to attain Buddhahood."

Any son of mine who expounds the Dharma
Should be gentle, patient and compassionate
Towards all living beings.
He should not be lazy.

In the worlds of the ten quarters,
The great Bodhisattvas are practicing the Way
Out of their compassion towards all living beings.
He should respect them as his great teachers.

He should respect the Buddhas, the World-Honored Ones,
As his unsurpassed fathers.
He should give up arrogance
So that he may expound the Dharma without hindrance.

This is the third set of peaceful practices.
A man of wisdom should perform all this.
Anyone who performs these peaceful practices
Will be respected by innumerable living beings.

"Again, Mañjuśrī! A Bodhisattva-mahāsattva who keeps this Sūtra of the Lotus Flower of the Wonderful Dharma in the latter days after [my extinction] when the teachings are about to be destroyed, should have great loving-kindness towards laymen and monks, and great compassion towards those who are not Bodhisattvas. He should think: 'They do not know that the Tathāgata expounded expedient teachings according to the capacities of all living beings. They do not hear, know or notice it, or ask a question about it or believe or understand it. Although they do not ask a question about this sūtra, or believe or understand it, I will lead them and cause them, wherever they may be, to understand the Dharma by my supernatural powers and by the power of my wisdom when I attain Anuttara-samyak-saṃbodhi.'

"Mañjuśrī! A Bodhisattva-mahāsattva who performs this fourth set of [peaceful] practices after my extinction, will be able to expound the Dharma flawlessly. Bhikṣus, bhikṣuṇīs, upāsakas, upāsikās, kings, princes, ministers, common people, brāhmaṇas and householders will make offerings to him, honor him, respect him, and praise him. The gods in the sky will always serve him in order to hear the Dharma from him. When someone comes to his abode located in a village, in a city, in a retired place or in a forest, and wishes to ask him a question, the gods will protect him day and night for the sake of the Dharma so that the hearer may rejoice because this sūtra was, is, and will be protected by the supernatural powers of the past, present and future Buddhas.

"Mañjuśrī! It is difficult to hear even the title of this Sūtra of the Lotus Flower of the Wonderful Dharma [even if you try to do so, walking about] innumerable worlds. Needless to say, it is more difficult to see, keep, read and recite this sūtra.

"Mañjuśrī! I will tell you a parable. Suppose a powerful wheel-turning-holy-king demanded surrender of the kings of smaller countries by threat of force. They did not obey his demand. He led soldiers, and went and suppressed them. He was very glad to see that some soldiers distinguished themselves in war. According to their merits, he gave them paddyfields, houses, villages, cities, garments or ornaments; or various treasures such as gold, silver, lapis lazuli, shell, agate, coral or amber; or elephants, horses, vehicles, menservants, maidservants or subjects. But he did not give a brilliant gem which he was keeping in his top-knot to anyone because the gem on the head of the king was the only one [in the world]. If he had given it to anyone, the followers of the king would have been much surprised.

"Mañjuśrī! I am like the king. I obtained the world of the Dharma by my powers of dhyāna-concentration and of wisdom, and became the king of the triple world. But the kings of the Māras did not assent to my demand for surrender to me. Therefore, my army led by generals, that is, by sages and saints, fought with them. I was glad to see that some distinguished themselves [in war]. In order to cause them to rejoice, I expounded many sūtras to the four kinds of devotees. I gave them the treasures of the Dharma such as dhyāna-concentrations, emancipations, the roots without āsravas, and the powers without āsravas, and also the city of Nirvāṇa, telling them that they had already attained extinction. Although I led them [by giving these things to them] and caused them to rejoice, I did not expound to them the Sūtra of the Lotus Flower of the Wonderful Dharma.

"Mañjuśrī! When he saw a soldier of extraordinary merit, the wheel-turning-holy-king joyfully gave that soldier the unbelievably precious gem, which he had kept in his top-knot for a long time and had not given to anyone. I am like the king. I am the great king of the Dharma in the triple world. I expound the Dharma and teach all living beings. Because I see that my soldiers led by generals, that is, by sages and saints, have already obtained extraordinary merits in their fight with the Māra of the five aggregates, with the Māra of illusions, and with the Māra of death, and that they have already eliminated the three poisons, left the triple world, and destroyed the nets of the Māras, I now expound this Sūtra of the Lotus Flower of the Wonderful Dharma with great joy. This sūtra leads all living beings to the knowledge of all things. I did not expound it before because, if I had done so, many people in the world would have hated it and few would have believed it.

"Mañjuśrī! This Sūtra of the Lotus Flower of the Wonderful Dharma is the most excellent and profound teaching of all the Tathāgatas. Therefore, I expound it lastly just as the powerful king gave the brilliant gem lastly, the one which he had kept [in his topknot] for a long time.

"Mañjuśrī! This Sūtra of the Lotus Flower of the Wonderful Dharma is the treasury of the hidden core of the Buddhas, of the Tathāgatas. It is superior to all the other sūtras. I kept it [in secret] and refrained from expounding it for the long night. Now I expound it to you today for the first time."

Thereupon the World-Honored One, wishing to repeat what he had said, sang in gāthās:

Be patient, and compassionate
Towards all living beings,
And then expound this sūtra
Praised by the Buddhas!

Anyone who keeps this sūtra
In the latter days after my extinction
Should have compassion towards laymen and monks
And towards those who are not Bodhisattvas.
He should think:
'They do not hear this sūtra.
They do not believe it.
This is their great fault.
When I attain the enlightenment of the Buddha,
I will expound the Dharma to them
With expedients
And cause them to dwell in it.'

I will tell you a parable.
A wheel-turning-holy-king was powerful.
Some of his soldiers
Distinguished themselves in war.
He was glad to honor them.
He gave them elephants or horses,
Vehicles or ornaments,
Paddyfields or houses,
Villages or cities,
Garments or various treasures,
Menservants or maidservants,
Or other valuables.

He took a brilliant gem
Out of his top-knot
And gave it to the bravest man
Who had done the most difficult feats.

I am like the king.
I am the King of the Dharma.
I have the great power of patience
And the treasury of wisdom.
I save all living beings in the world by the Dharma
Out of my great compassion towards them.

The people were under the pressure
Of various sufferings.
They were fighting with the Māras
In order to emancipate themselves
From suffering.
Because I saw all this,
I expounded various teachings to them.
I expounded many sūtras with skillful expedients.

Now I know that they can understand the Sūtra
Of the Lotus Flower of the Wonderful Dharma.
Therefore, I expound it to them lastly

Just as the king took the brilliant gem
Out of his top-knot
And gave it [to the bravest man lastly].

This is the most honorable sūtra.
It is superior to all the other sūtras.
I kept it [in secret]
And refrained from expounding it.
Now is the time to do so.
Therefore, I expound it to you now.

Anyone who seeks
The enlightenment of the Buddha
And wishes to expound this sūtra
In peaceful ways after my extinction,
Should practice
These four sets of things.

Anyone who reads this sūtra
Will be free from grief,
Sorrow, disease or pain.
His complexion will be fair.
He will not be poor,
Humble or ugly.

All living beings
Will wish to see him
Just as they wish to see sages and saints.
Celestial pages will serve him.

He will not be struck with swords or sticks.
He will not be poisoned.
If anyone speaks ill of him,
The speaker's mouth will be shut.
He will be able to go anywhere
As fearless as the lion king.

The light of his wisdom will be
As bright as that of the sun.

He will see only wonderful things in his dream.
He will dream:
'Surrounded by bhikṣus,
The Tathāgatas are sitting
On the lion-like seats,
And expounding the Dharma.'

He also will dream:
'As many living beings, including dragons
and asuras,
As there are sands in the River Ganges,
Are joining their hands together
Towards me respectfully,
And I am expounding the Dharma to them.'

He also will dream:
'The bodies of the Buddhas are golden-colored.
They are emitting innumerable rays of light,
And illumining all things.
The Buddhas are expounding all teachings
With their brahma voices.
I am among the four kinds of devotees
To whom a Buddha is expounding
The unsurpassed Dharma.
I praised the Buddha
With my hands joined together.
I heard the Dharma from him with joy.
I made offerings to him, and obtained dhāraṇīs.
I also obtained irrevocable wisdom.
The Buddha knew
That I entered deep into the Way to Buddhahood.
So he assured me of my future attainment
Of perfect enlightenment, saying:

'Good man, in your future life,
You will be able to attain immeasurable wisdom,
That is, the great enlightenment of the Buddha.
Your world will be pure and large
Without a parallel.
There will be the four kinds of devotees there.
They will hear the Dharma from you
With their hands joined together.'

He also will dream:
'I am now in the forest of a mountain.
I studied and practiced good teachings.
I attained the truth of the reality of all things.
I am now in deep dhyāna-concentration.
I see the Buddhas of the worlds of the ten quarters.'

He also will have a good dream:
'The bodies of the Buddhas are golden-colored.
They are adorned with a hundred marks of merits.
Having heard the Dharma from them,
I am now expounding it to others.'

He also will dream:
'Although I was a king, I gave up the five desires
And the most wonderful pleasures.
I left my palace and attendants,
And reached the place of enlightenment.
I sat on the lion-like seat under the Bodhi-tree,
And sought enlightenment.
After seven days, I obtained the wisdom of the Buddhas
And attained unsurpassed enlightenment.
I emerged [from dhyāna] and turned the wheel of the Dharma.
I expounded the Dharma to the four kinds of devotees
For a thousand billion kalpas.

I expounded the Wonderful Dharma-without-āsravas
And saved innumerable living beings.
Then I entered into Nirvāṇa
Just as a flame dies when smoke is gone.'

Anyone who expounds
This supreme teaching
In the evil world after [my extinction]
Will obtain great benefits as previously stated.

CHAPTER XV

THE APPEARANCE OF BODHISATTVAS FROM UNDERGROUND[1]

Thereupon the Bodhisattva-mahāsattvas, more than eight times the number of the sands of the River Ganges, who had come from the other worlds,[2] rose from among the great multitude, joined their hands together towards the Buddha, bowed to him, and said:

"World-Honored One! If you permit us to protect, keep, read, recite and copy this sūtra, and make offerings to it strenuously in this Sahā-World after your extinction, we will [do so, and] expound it in this world."

Thereupon the Buddha said to those Bodhisattva-mahāsattvas:

"No, good men! I do not want you to protect or keep this sūtra because there are Bodhisattva-mahāsattvas sixty thousand times as many as the sands of the River Ganges in this Sahā-World. They are each accompanied by attendants also numbering sixty thousand times as many as the sands of the River Ganges. They will protect, keep, read, recite and expound this sūtra after my extinction."

When he had said this, the ground of the Sahā-World, which was composed of one thousand million Sumeru-worlds, quaked and cracked, and many thousands of billions of Bodhisattva-mahāsattvas sprang up from underground simultaneously. Their bodies were golden-colored, and adorned with the thirty-two marks and with innumerable rays of light. They had lived in the sky below this Sahā-World. They came up here because they heard these words of Śākyamuni Buddha. Each of them was the leader of a great multitude. The Bodhisattvas included those who were

1 從地涌出 Literally means, "to spring up from underground."

2 It is not stated when these Bodhisattvas came from the other worlds. They are not the attendants of the Buddhas sitting under the trees.

each accompanied by attendants as many as sixty thousand times the number of the sands of the River Ganges. Needless to say, [they included those who were each accompanied by less attendants, for instance,] fifty thousand times, forty thousand times, thirty thousand times, twenty thousand times or ten thousand times the number of the sands of the River Ganges, or by attendants just as many of the sands of the River Ganges, or by attendants as many as a half, or a quarter of the number of the sands of the River Ganges, or by attendants as many as the sands of the River Ganges divided by a thousand billion nayuta, a billion, ten million, a million, ten thousand, a thousand, a hundred, ten, five, four, three or two attendants, or only by one attendant. [The Bodhisattvas] who preferred a solitary life came alone. The total number of the Bodhisattvas was innumerable, limitless, beyond calculation, inexplicable by any parable or simile.

Those Bodhisattvas who appeared from underground, came to Many-Treasures Tathāgata and Śākyamuni Buddha both of whom were in the wonderful stūpa of the seven treasures hanging in the sky. They [joined their hands together] towards the two World-Honored Ones, and worshipped their feet with their heads. Then they [descended onto the ground and] came to the Buddhas sitting on the lion-like seats under the jeweled trees, bowed to them, walked around them from left to right three times, joined their hands together respectfully, and praised them by the various ways by which Bodhisattvas should praise Buddhas. Then they [returned to the sky,] stood to one side, and looked up at the two World-Honored ones with joy. A period of fifty small kalpas elapsed from the Bodhisattva-mahāsattvas' springing up from underground till the finishing of the praising of the Buddhas by the various ways by which Bodhisattvas should praise Buddhas. All this while Śākyamuni Buddha sat in silence. The four kinds of devotees also kept silence for the fifty small kalpas. By his supernatural powers, however, the Buddha caused the great multitude to think that they kept silence for only half a day. Also by the supernatural powers of the Buddha, the four kinds of devotees were able to see that the skies of many hundreds of thousands of billions of worlds were filled with those Bodhisattvas.

Those Bodhisattvas had four leaders: 1. Superior-Practice, 2. Limitless-Practice, 3. Pure-Practice, and 4. Steadily-Established-Practice. These four [great] Bodhisattvas were the highest leaders [of those Bodhisattvas]. In the presence of the great multitude, they joined their hands together towards Śākyamuni Buddha, looked up at him, and inquired after him saying:

"World-Honored One! Are you in good health? Are you peaceful or not? Are the living beings, whom you are to save, ready to receive your teachings or not? Do they not fatigue you?'

Thereupon the four great Bodhisattvas sang in gāthās:

World-Honored One, are you peaceful?
Are you in good health?
Are you not tired
With teaching the living beings?
Are they ready
To receive your teaching,
Or are they not?
Do they not fatigue you?

Thereupon the World-Honored One said to them in the presence of the great multitude of Bodhisattvas:

"Truly, truly good men! I am peaceful. I am in good health. The living beings are ready to be saved. They do not fatigue me because I already taught them in their consecutive previous existences, and also because they have already honored the past Buddhas respectfully and planted the roots of good. As soon as they saw me and heard my teachings, they received my teachings by faith and entered into the wisdom of the Tathāgata, except those who had previously studied and practiced the teachings of the Lesser Vehicle. Now I am causing [the followers of the Lesser Vehicle] to hear this sūtra and to enter into the wisdom of the Buddha."

Thereupon the [four] great Bodhisattvas sang in gāthās:

Excellent, excellent, Great Hero!
World-Honored One!

The living beings are ready to be saved
Because in their previous existence
They already asked the [past] Buddhas
About their profound wisdom,
And having heard about it, understood it by faith.
We rejoice at seeing you.

Thereupon the World-Honored One praised the leading great Bodhisattvas, saying, "Excellent, excellent, good men! [I am glad that] you rejoice at seeing me."

Thereupon Maitreya Bodhisattva and the [other] Bodhisattvas [who had already been present in the congregation before the arrival of the Bodhisattvas from underground], eight thousand times as many as the sands of the River Ganges[3] in number, thought:

'We have never before seen these great Bodhisattva-mahāsattvas who sprang up from underground, stood before [Śākyamuni,] the World-Honored One, joined their hands together towards him, and made offerings to him. [Now we see that their leaders] inquire after him.'

Thereupon Maitreya Bodhisattva-mahāsattva, seeing what the Bodhisattvas numbering eight thousand times as many as the sands of the River Ganges had in their minds, and also wishing to remove his own doubts, joined his hands together towards the Buddha, and asked him in gāthās:

We have never seen
These many thousands of billions
Of Bodhisattvas.
Tell me, Most Honorable Biped!
Where did they come from?
They have gigantic bodies,[4]
Great supernatural powers, and inconceivable wisdom.
They are resolute in mind.

---

3 This number may be a variation of eighty thousand, given in Chapter I.

4 Because they are gigantic, the Bodhisattvas who sprang up from underground are sometimes modified by the adjective "great" while the other Bodhisattvas are never modified by that adjective in this chapter.

They have a great power of patience.
All living beings are glad to see them.
Where did they come from?

They are each accompanied
By as many attendants
As there are sands
In the River Ganges.

Some great Bodhisattvas are each accompanied
by attendants
Sixty thousand times as many as the sands
of the River Ganges.
They are seeking the enlightenment of the Buddha
With all their hearts.

The number of these great teachers is sixty thousand times
The number of the sands of the River Ganges.
They came together and made offerings to you.
Now they protect and keep this sūtra.

The attendants or disciples accompanying
Each [of the other great Bodhisattvas] number
Fifty thousand times or forty thousand times
Or thirty thousand times or twenty thousand times
Or ten thousand times or a thousand times
Or a hundred times as many as the sands
of the River Ganges,
Or a half, a third, or a quarter
Of the number of the sands of the River Ganges,
Or as many as the sands of the River Ganges
Divided by a billion;
Or ten million nayuta, a billion or fifty million,
Or a million, ten thousand, a thousand or a hundred,
Or fifty, ten, three, two or one.
[The great Bodhisattvas] who are accompanied
By less attendants are even more numerous.

Some [great Bodhisattvas] have no attendants
Because they prefer a solitary life.
They are the most numerous.
They came together to you.

No one will be able to count
All [these great Bodhisattvas] even if he uses
A counting wand for more kalpas
Then the number of the sands of the River Ganges.

These Bodhisattvas have
Great powers, virtues and energy.
Who expounded the Dharma to them?
  Who taught them?
Who qualified them to attain [perfect enlightenment]?

Under whom did they begin to aspire for enlightenment?
What teaching of the Buddha did they extol?
What sūtra did they keep and practice?
What teaching of the Buddha did they study?

These Bodhisattvas have supernatural powers
And the great power of wisdom.
The ground of this world quaked and cracked.
They sprang up from under the four quarters of this world.

World-Honored One!
I have never seen them before.
I do not know
Any of them.

They appeared suddenly from underground.
Tell me why!
Many thousands of myriads
Of millions of Bodhisattvas
In this great congregation
Also want to know this.

There must be some reason.
Possessor of Immeasurable Virtues!
World-Honored One!
Remove our doubts!

At that time the Buddhas, who had come from many thousands of billions of worlds outside [this world], were sitting cross-legged on the lion-like seats under the jeweled trees in [this world and] the neighboring worlds of the eight quarters.[5] Those Buddhas were the replicas of Śākyamuni Buddha. The attendant[6] of each of those Buddhas saw that many Bodhisattvas had sprung up from under the four quarters of the [Sahā-World which was composed of] one thousand million Sumeru-worlds and stayed in the sky. He said to the Buddha whom he was accompanying, "World-Honored One! Where did these innumerable, asaṃkhya Bodhisattvas come from?"

That Buddha said to his attendant:

"Good Man! Wait for a while! There is a Bodhisattva-mahāsattva called Maitreya [in this congregation]. Śākyamuni Buddha assured him of his future attainment of Buddhahood, saying, 'You will become a Buddha immediately after me.' Maitreya has already asked [Śākyamuni Buddha] about this matter. [Śākyamuni] Buddha will answer him. You will be able to hear his answer."

Thereupon Śākyamuni Buddha said to Maitreya Bodhisattva:

"Excellent, excellent, Ajita! You asked me a very important question. All of you should concentrate your minds, wear the armor of endeavors, and be resolute. Now I will reveal, I will show, the wisdom of the Buddhas, their supernatural powers without hindrance, their dauntless powers like a lion's, and their great power of bravery."

Thereupon the World-Honored One, wishing to repeat what he said, sang in gāthās:

---

5 The worlds in which the Buddhas were sitting were many but not all the worlds of the eight quarters. See Chapter XI.

6 Each Buddha was accompanied by a Bodhisattva.

Exert yourselves and concentrate your minds!
Now I will tell you about this matter.
Do not doubt me!
My wisdom is difficult to understand.

Arouse your power of faith,
And do good patiently!
You will be able to hear the Dharma
That you have never heard before.

Now I will relieve you.
Do not doubt me! Do not be afraid!
I do not tell a lie.
My wisdom is immeasurable.
The highest Dharma that I attained
Is profound and difficult to understand.
Now I will expound it.
Listen to me with all your hearts!

Thereupon the World-Honored One, having sung these gāthās, said to Maitreya Bodhisattva:

"Now I will tell all of you in this great multitude, Ajita! [I know that] you have never seen these great, innumerable, asaṃkhya Bodhisattva-mahāsattvas who sprang up from underground. After I attained Anuttara-samyak-saṃbodhi in this Sahā-World, I taught these Bodhisattvas, led them, trained them, and caused them to aspire for enlightenment. They lived in the sky below this Sahā-World. When they were there, they read many sūtras, recited them, understood them, thought them over, evaluated them, and remembered them correctly. Ajita! These good men did not wish to talk much with others [about things other than the Dharma] but to live in a quiet place. They practiced the way strenuously without a rest. They did not live among gods and men. They had no hindrance in seeking profound wisdom. They always sought the teaching of the Buddha. They sought unsurpassed wisdom strenuously with all their hearts."

Thereupon the World-Honored One, wishing to repeat what he had said, sang in gāthās:

Ajita, know this, these great Bodhisattvas
Have studied and practiced
The wisdom of the Buddha
For the past innumerable kalpas.

They are my sons because I taught them
And caused them to aspire for great enlightenment.
They have been living in this world
[For the past innumerable kalpas].

They always practiced the dhūta.
They wished to live in a quiet place.
They kept away from bustling crowds.
They did not wish to talk much.

These sons of mine studied my teachings
Strenuously day and night
In order to attain
The enlightenment of the Buddha.
They lived in the sky
Below this Sahā-World.

Resolute in mind,
They always sought wisdom,
And expounded
Various wonderful teachings without fear.

I once sat under the Bodhi-tree
In the City of Gayā,
Attained perfect enlightenment,
And turned the wheel of the unsurpassed Dharma.

Then I taught them,
And caused them to aspire for enlightenment.

Now they do not falter [in seeking enlightenment].
They will be able to become Buddhas.

My words are true.
Believe me with all your hearts!
I have been teaching them
Since the remotest past.

Thereupon Maitreya Bodhisattva-mahāsattva and the innumerable Bodhisattvas in the congregation doubted the Buddha's words which they had never heard before. They thought: 'How did the World-Honored One teach these great, innumerable, asaṃkhya Bodhisattvas, and qualify them to attain Anuttara-samyak-saṃbodhi in such a short time?'

[Maitreya Bodhisattva] said to the Buddha:

"World-Honored One! When you, the Tathāgata, were a crown prince, you left the palace of the Śākyas, sat at the place of enlightenment not far from the City of Gayā, and attained Anuttara-samyak-saṃbodhi. It is only forty and odd years since then.

"World-Honored One! How did you do these great deeds of the Buddha in such a short time? Did you teach these great, innumerable Bodhisattvas, and qualify them to attain Anuttara-samyak-saṃbodhi by your powers or by your merits?

"World-Honored One! No one can count the number of these great Bodhisattvas even if he goes on counting them for thousands of billions of kalpas. They have already planted roots of good, practiced the way, and performed brahma practices under innumerable Buddhas from the remotest past.

"World-Honored One! It is difficult for anyone in the world to believe this. It is as difficult as to believe a handsome, black-haired man twenty-five years old who points to men a hundred years old and says, 'They are my sons,' or as to believe men a hundred years old who point to a young man and say, 'This is our father. He brought us up.' You are like the young man. It is not long since you attained enlightenment. But it is many thousands of billions of kalpas since the great multitude of these Bodhisattvas began to practice the Way strenuously in order to attain the enlightenment of the Buddha. During that time they entered into, stayed in, and came out of many hundreds of thousands of billions of samādhis, and obtained great supernatural powers. They performed brahma practices for a long time. They learned good teachings one by one, and obtained the ability to answer questions skillfully. They are regarded as the treasures of the world of men by all the people of the world because they are rare. Today you say that, after you attained the enlightenment of the Buddha, you caused them to aspire for enlightenment, taught them, and led them into the Way to Anuttara-samyak-saṃbodhi.

"World-Honored One! You did these deeds of great merit although it is not long since you attained Buddhahood. We believe that your words given according to the capacities of all living beings are infallible, and that we understand all that you know. But the beginners in Bodhisattvahood after your extinction, if they hear these words of yours, will not receive them by faith but commit the sin of violating the Dharma. Therefore, World-Honored One! Explain all this so that we may be able to remove our doubts and that the good men in the future may have no doubts when they hear these words of yours!"

Thereupon Maitreya Bodhisattva, wishing to repeat what he had said, sang in gāthās:

It is not long
Since you renounced the family of the Śākyas
And sat under the Bodhi-tree
Near Gayā.

These sons of yours are innumerable.
They have practiced
The way to Buddhahood for a long time.
They have supernatural powers and the power of wisdom.

They have studied the Way of Bodhisattvas well.
They are not defiled by worldliness
Just as the lotus-flower
Is not defiled by water.

They sprang up from underground,
And are now standing before you respectfully.
This is difficult to understand.
How can we believe this?

You attained enlightenment quite recently.
But you have done so many things.
Remove our doubts!
Explain all this as it is!

Suppose a man twenty-five years old
Points to grey-haired and wrinkle-faced men
A hundred years old,
And says, "They are my sons."
Suppose old men point to a young man
And say, "He is our father."
No one in the world will believe
That a father is younger than his sons.

You are like the father.
You attained enlightenment quite recently.
These Bodhisattvas are resolute in mind.
They are not timid.
They have practiced the Way of Bodhisattvas
For the past innumerable kalpas.

They are good at answering difficult questions.
They are fearless and patient.
They are handsome, powerful and virtuous.
They are praised by the Buddhas
Of the worlds of the ten quarters.
They expound [the Dharma] clearly.

They did not wish to live among men.
They preferred dwelling in dhyāna-concentration.
They lived in the sky below
In order to attain the enlightenment of the Buddha.

We do not doubt your words
Because we heard them direct from you.
Explain all this so that the living beings in the future
May be able to understand your words, Buddha!

Those who doubt this sūtra
And do not believe it
Will fall into the evil regions.
Explain all this to us now!

How did you teach these innumerable Bodhisattvas
In such a short time,
And cause them to aspire for enlightenment
And not falter in seeking enlightenment?

[Here ends] the Fifth Volume of the Sūtra of the Lotus Flower of the Wonderful Dharma.

CHAPTER XVI

THE DURATION OF THE LIFE OF THE TATHĀGATA

Thereupon the Buddha said to the great multitude including Bodhisattvas and others, "Good men! Understand my sincere and infallible words by faith!"

He said to the great multitude again, "Understand my sincere and infallible words by faith!"

He said to them once again, "Understand my sincere and infallible words by faith!"

Thereupon the great multitude of Bodhisattvas, headed by Maitreya, joined their hands together and said to the Buddha, "World-Honored one, tell us! We will receive your words by faith."

They said this three times. Then they said once again, "Tell us! We will receive your words by faith."

Thereupon the World-Honored One, seeing that they repeated their appeal even after they repeated it three times, said to them:

"Listen to me attentively! I will tell you about my hidden core and supernatural powers. The gods, men and asuras in the world think that I, Śākyamuni Buddha, left the palace of the Śākyas, sat at the place of enlightenment not far from the City of Gayā, and attained Anuttara-samyak-saṃbodhi [forty and odd years ago]. To tell the truth, good men, it is many hundreds of thousands of billions of nayutas of kalpas since I became the Buddha. Suppose someone smashed into dust five hundred thousand billion nayuta asaṃkhya worlds, which were each composed of one thousand million Sumeru-worlds, and went to the east [carrying the dust with him]. When he reached a world at a distance of five hundred thousand billion nayuta asaṃkhya worlds [from this world], he put a particle of dust on that world. Then he went on again to the east, and repeated the putting of a particle of the dust [on the world at every distance of five hundred thousand billion nayuta asaṃkhya worlds] until the particles of the dust were exhausted. Good men! What do you think of this? Do you think that the number of the worlds he went through is conceivable, countable, or not?"

Maitreya Bodhisattva and others said to the Buddha:

"World-Honored One! Those worlds are innumerable, uncountable, inconceivable. No Śrāvaka or Pratyekabuddha could count them even by his wisdom-without-āsravas. We are now in the state of avaivartika, but cannot, either. World-Honoured One! Those worlds are innumerable."

Thereupon the Buddha said to the great multitude of Bodhisattvas:

"Good Men! Now I will tell you clearly. Suppose those worlds, whether they were marked with the particles of the dust or not, were smashed into dust. The number of the kalpas which have elapsed since I became the Buddha is one hundred thousand billion nayuta asaṃkhyas larger than the number of the particles of the dust thus produced. All this time I have been living in this Sahā-World, and teaching [the living beings of this world] by expounding the Dharma to them. I also have been leading and benefiting the living beings of one hundred thousand billion nayuta asaṃkhya worlds outside this world.

"Good men! During this time I gave various names to myself, for instance, the Burning-Light Buddha. I also said, 'That Buddha entered into Nirvāṇa.'[1] I did all these things only as expedients.

"Good men! When some people came to me, I saw the strength of the power of their faith and of the other faculties of theirs with the eyes of the Buddha. Then I named myself differently, and told them of the duration of my life differently, according to their capacities. I also said to them, 'I shall enter into Nirvāṇa.'[2] I expounded the Wonderful Dharma with these various expedients, and caused the living beings to rejoice.

---

1 This stands for Parinirvāṇa.

2 See footnote 1 above.

"Good men! When I saw that some people of little virtue and of much defilement were seeking the teachings of the Lesser Vehicle, I told them, 'I renounced my family when I was young, and attained Anuttara-samyak-saṃbodhi [forty and odd years ago].' In reality I became the Buddha in the remotest past as I previously stated. I told them this as an expedient to teach them, to lead them into the Way to Buddhahood.

"Good men! All the sūtras that I expounded [hitherto] were for the purpose of saving all living beings. I told the stories of my previous lives [in some sūtras,] and the stories of the previous lives of other Buddhas [in other sūtras]. I showed my replicas [in some sūtras,] and my transformations[3] [in other sūtras]. I described my deeds [in some sūtras,] and the deeds of others [in other sūtras].[4] All that I say is true, not false, because I see the triple world as it is. I see that the triple world is the world in which the living beings have neither birth nor death, that is to say, do not appear or disappear, that it is the world in which I do not appear or from which I do not disappear, that it is not real or unreal, and that it is not as it seems or as it does not seem. I do not see the triple world in the same way as [the living beings of] the triple world do. I see all this clearly and infallibly. The living beings are various in their natures, desires, deeds, thoughts and opinions. Therefore, I expounded the dharma with various stories of previous lives, with various parables, similes and discourses, in order to cause all living beings to plant the roots of good. I have never stopped doing what I should do. As I said before, it is very long since I became the Buddha. The duration of my life is innumerable, asaṃkhya kalpas. I am always here. I shall never pass away.

"Good men! The duration of my life, which I obtained by the practice of the way of Bodhisattvas, has not yet expired. It is twice as long as the length of time as previously stated. Although

---

3 The replicas of Śākyamuni Buddha coexist with Śākyamuni Buddha, but his transformations cannot coexist with him because he disappears when he transforms himself into another living being.

4 或說己身或說他身或示己身或示他身或示己事或示他事 Literally means, "I explain myself or others. I show myself or others. I show my things or the things of others."

I shall never enter into Nirvāṇa,[5] I say to men of little virtue, 'I shall pass away.' I teach them with this expedient. Why is that? It is because, if they see me for a long time, they will not plant the roots of good, but become poor and base, and cling to the five desires so much that they will be caught in the nets of wrong views. If they think that I am always here, and do not think that I will pass away, they will become too arrogant and lazy to realize the difficulty of seeing me, and they will not respect me. Therefore I say [to them] expediently, 'Bhikṣus, know this! It is difficult to see a Buddha who appears in [this] world.' Why is that? It is because some men of little virtue cannot see me even during many hundreds of thousands of billions of kalpas while the others can. Therefore, I say [to them], 'Bhikṣus! It is difficult to see a Tathāgata.' Those who hear this and know that it is difficult to see me, will adore me, admire me, and plant the roots of good. Therefore I say [to them], 'I shall pass away,' although I shall not.

"Good men! All the Buddhas, all the Tathāgatas, do the same as I do. [They expound their teachings] for the purpose of saving all living beings. Therefore, [their teachings] are true, not false.

"I will tell you a parable. There was once an excellent and wise physician. He was good at dispensing medicines and curing diseases. He had many sons, numbering ten, twenty, or a hundred. [One day] he went to a remote country on business. After he left home, the sons took poison. The poison passed into their bodies, and the sons writhed in agony, rolling on the ground. At that time the father returned home. Some sons had already lost their right minds while the others still had not. All the sons saw their father in the distance and had great joy. They begged him on their knees, saying, 'You came back safely. We were ignorant. We took poison by mistake. Cure us, and give us back our lives!'

"Seeing his sons suffering so much, the father consulted books of prescriptions, and collected good herbs having a good color, smell and taste. He compounded a medicine by pounding and sieving the herbs, and gave it to them, saying, 'This is a very

5 This stands for Parinirvāṇa.

good medicine. It has good color, smell and taste. Take it! It will remove the pain at once and you will not suffer any more.'

"The sons who had not lost their right minds saw that this good medicine had a good color and smell, took it at once, and were cured completely. But the sons who had already lost their right minds did not consent to take the medicine given to them, although they rejoiced at seeing their father come home and asked him to cure them, because they were so perverted that they did not believe that this medicine having a good color and smell had a good taste.

"The father thought, 'These sons are pitiful. They are so poisoned that they are perverted. Although they rejoice at seeing me and ask me to cure them, they do not consent to take this good medicine. Now I will have them take it with an expedient.'

"He said to them, 'Know this! Now I am old and decrepit. I shall die soon. I am leaving this good medicine here. Take it! Do not be afraid that you will not be cured!' Having thus advised them, he went to a [remote] country again. Then he sent home a messenger to tell them, 'Your father has just died.'

"Having heard that their father had passed away from this world, leaving them behind, they felt extremely sorry. They thought, 'If our father were alive, he would love and protect us. Now he has deserted us and died in a remote country.'

"They felt lonely and helpless because they thought that they were parentless and shelterless. Their constant sadness finally caused them to recover their right minds.[6] They realized that the medicine had a good color, smell and taste. They took it and were completely cured of the poison. On hearing that they had recovered their health, the father returned home, and showed himself to them.

"Good men! What do you think of this? Do you think that anyone can accuse this excellent physician of falsehood?"

"No, World-Honored One!"

---

6 The statement that the perverted sons recovered their right minds when they heard of the death of their father is inconsistent with the statement earlier that the perverted people will plant the roots of good when they hear that the Buddha will pass away, not that the Buddha has passed away.

The Buddha said:

"I am like the father. It is many hundreds of thousands of billions of nayutas of asaṃkhyas of kalpas since I became the Buddha. In order to save the [perverted] people, I say expediently, 'I shall pass away.' No one will accuse me of falsehood by the [common] law."[7]

Thereupon the World-Honored One, wishing to repeat what he had said, sang in gāthās:

It is many hundreds of thousands
Of billions of trillions
Of asaṃkhyas of kalpas
Since I became the Buddha.

For the past innumerable kalpas
I have always been expounding the Dharma
To many hundreds of millions of living beings
In order to lead them into the Way to Buddhahood.

In order to save the [perverted] people,
I expediently show my Nirvāṇa[8] to them.
In reality I shall never pass away.
I always live here and expound the Dharma.

Although I always live here
With the perverted people
I disappear from their eyes
By my supernatural powers.

When they see me seemingly pass away,
And make offerings to my śarīras,[9]
And adore me, admire me,
And become devout, upright and gentle,

---

7 法 Law in this sentence is the common and formal law, not the Dharma philosophically established by the Buddha.

8 This stands for Parinirvāṇa.

9 The śarīras of the Buddha are not referred to in the prose section of this chapter.

And wish to see me
With all their hearts
At the cost of their lives,
I reappear on Mt. Sacred Eagle
With my Saṃgha,
And say to them:
"I always live here.
I shall never be extinct.
I show my extinction to you expediently
Although I never pass away.
I also expound the unsurpassed Dharma
To the living beings of the other worlds
If they respect me, believe me,
And wish to see me.
You have never heard this;
Therefore, you thought that I pass away."

I see the [perverted] people sinking
In an ocean of suffering.
Therefore, I disappear from their eyes
And cause them to admire me.
When they adore me,
I appear and expound the Dharma to them.

I can do all this by my supernatural powers.
I live on Mt. Sacred Eagle
And also in the other abodes
For asaṃkhya kalpas.[10]

The [perverted] people think:
"This world is in a great fire.
The end of the kalpa [of destruction][11] is coming."
In reality this world of mine is peaceful.
It is filled with gods and men.

10 See *Kalpa* in the English/Sanskrit Glossary.

11 See footnote 10 above.

The gardens, forests and stately buildings
Are adorned with various treasures;
The jeweled trees have many flowers and fruits;
The living beings are enjoying themselves;
And the gods are beating heavenly drums,
Making various kinds of music,
And raining mandārava-flowers
  on the great multitude and me.

[This] pure world of mine is indestructible.
But the [perverted] people think:
"It is full of sorrow, fear, and other sufferings.
It will soon burn away."

Because of their evil karmas,
These sinful people will not be able
To hear even the names of the Three Treasures
During asaṃkhya kalpas.

To those who have accumulated merits,
And who are gentle and upright,
And who see me living here,
Expounding the Dharma,
I say:
"The duration of my life is immeasurable."
To those who see me after a long time,
I say, "It is difficult to see a Buddha."

I can do all this by the power of my wisdom.
The light of my wisdom knows no bound.
The duration of my life is innumerable kalpas.
I obtained this longevity by ages of practices.

All of you, wise men!
Have no doubts about this!
Remove your doubts, have no more!
My words are true, not false.

The physician, who sent a man expediently
To tell his perverted sons
Of the death of their father in order to cure them,
Was not accused of falsehood although he was still alive.

In the same manner, I am the father of the world.
I am saving all living beings from suffering.
Because they are perverted,
I say that I pass away even though I shall not.
If they always see me,
They will become arrogant and licentious,
And cling to the five desires
So much that they will fall into the evil regions.

I know who is practicing the Way and who is not.
Therefore I expound various teachings
To all living beings
According to their capacities.

I am always thinking:
"How shall I cause all living beings
To enter into the unsurpassed Way
And quickly become Buddhas?"

CHAPTER XVII

THE VARIETY OF MERITS

Thereupon the innumerable, asaṃkhya living beings in the great congregation, who had heard from the Buddha that the duration of his life was so many kalpas as previously stated, obtained great benefits.

At that time the World-Honored One said to Maitreya Bodhisattva-mahāsattva:

"Ajita! When I said that the duration of my life was so long, six hundred and eighty billion nayuta living beings, that is, the living beings as many as there are sands in the River Ganges, obtained the truth of birthlessness. Bodhisattva-mahāsattvas numbering one thousand times the number of these living beings obtained the dhāraṇīs by which they could memorize all that they had heard. Bodhisattva-mahāsattvas as many as the particles of earth of a Sumeru-world obtained eloquence without hindrance. Another group of Bodhisattva-mahāsattvas as many as the particles of earth of a Sumeru world obtained the dhāraṇīs by which they could memorize many hundreds of thousands of billions of repetitions of teachings. Bodhisattva-mahāsattvas as many as the particles of earth of one thousand million Sumeru-worlds obtained the faculty of turning the irrevocable wheel of the Dharma. Bodhisattva-mahāsattvas as many as the particles of earth of one million Sumeru-worlds obtained the faculty of turning the wheel of the pure Dharma. Bodhisattva-mahāsattvas as many as the particles of earth of one thousand Sumeru-worlds obtained the faculty of attaining Anuttara-samyak-saṃbodhi after eight rebirths. Bodhisattva-mahāsattvas four times the number of the particles of earth of the four continents obtained the faculty of attaining

Anuttara-samyak-saṃbodhi after four rebirths. Bodhisattva-mahāsattvas three times the number of the particles of earth of the four continents obtained the faculty of attaining Anuttara-samyak-saṃbodhi after three rebirths. Bodhisattva-mahāsattvas twice the number of the particles of earth of the four continents obtained the faculty of attaining Anuttara-samyak-saṃbodhi after two rebirths. Bodhisattva-mahāsattvas as many as the particles of earth of the four continents obtained the faculty of attaining Anuttara-samyak-saṃbodhi immediately after this life. Living beings as many as the particles of earth of eight Sumeru-worlds aspired for Anuttara-samyak-saṃbodhi."

When the Buddha said that these Bodhisattva-mahāsattvas had obtained the great benefits of the Dharma, [the gods] in heaven rained mandārava-flowers and mahā-mandārava-flowers on the many hundreds of thousands of billions of Buddhas sitting on the lion-like seats under the jeweled trees. They also rained those flowers on [the two Buddhas:] Many-Treasures Tathāgata, who had passed away a long time ago, and Śākyamuni Buddha, both of whom were sitting on the lion-like seat in the stūpa of the seven treasures. They also rained those flowers on the great Bodhisattvas[1] and the four kinds of devotees. They also rained the fine powder of the incense of candana and aloes [on them]. Heavenly drums automatically sounded wonderful and deep in the sky. [The gods] also rained thousands of heavenly garments and hung many necklaces made of pearls, maṇi gems or free-at-will gems over the nine quarters.[2] They also burned priceless incense which was put in incense-burners of many treasures. The incense-burners automatically went around the great congregation, and the odor of the incense was offered to all the members of the congregation. Above each of the Buddhas [sitting under the trees], Bodhisattvas lined up vertically one upon another to the Heaven of Brahman, holding canopies and streamers. They praised the Buddhas, singing innumerable verses with their wonderful voices.

---

1 They are not the Bodhisattvas who sprang up from underground. There is no distinction between the great Bodhisattvas and the Bodhisattvas not modified by the adjective "great" in this chapter.

2 The eight quarters and the stūpa in the sky. The stūpa was hanging in the sky below the heavens of the gods.

Thereupon Maitreya Bodhisattva rose from his seat, bared his right shoulder, joined his hands together towards the Buddha, and sang in gāthās:

You expounded a rare teaching.
I have never heard it before.
You have great powers.
The duration of your life is immeasurable.

Having heard from you that they were given
The various benefits of the Dharma,
The innumerable sons of yours
Were filled with joy.

Some of them reached the stage of irrevocability.
Some obtained dhāraṇīs, or eloquence without hindrance,
Or the all-holding formulas
For memorizing billions of repetitions of teachings.

Bodhisattvas as many as the particles of earth
Of one thousand million Sumeru-worlds obtained
The faculty of turning
The irrevocable wheel of the Dharma.

Bodhisattvas as many as the particles of earth
Of one million Sumeru-worlds obtained
The faculty of turning
The wheel of the pure Dharma.

Bodhisattvas as many as the particles of earth
Of one thousand Sumeru-worlds obtained
The faculty of attaining the enlightenment of the Buddha
After eight rebirths.

Bodhisattvas numbering four times or three times or twice
The number of the particles of earth of the four continents

Obtained the faculty of becoming Buddhas
After four, three or two rebirths respectfully.

Bodhisattvas as many as the particles of earth
Of the four continents obtained
The faculty of attaining the knowledge of all things
Immediately after this life.

Having heard of your longevity,
They obtained these effects and rewards,
Pure, immeasurable, and without āsravas.
Having heard from you
Of the duration of your life,
Living beings as many as the particles of earth
Of eight Sumeru-worlds
Aspired for unsurpassed [enlightenment].

You expounded the teachings
Immeasurable and inconceivable,
And benefited living beings
As limitless as the sky.

[The gods] rained down mandārava-flowers,
And mahā-mandārava-flowers of heaven.
Śakras and Brahmans came from the [other] Buddha-worlds
As many as there are sands in the River Ganges.

[The gods] rained down candana and aloes [powder],
And offered it to the Buddhas.
The powder came down fluttering
Just as birds fly down from the sky.

Heavenly drums automatically sounded
Wonderful in the sky.
Thousands of billions of heavenly garments
Whirled down.

[The gods] burned priceless incense which was put
In wonderful incense-burners of many treasures.
The incense-burners automatically went around,
And the odor was offered to the World-Honored Ones.[3]

The great Bodhisattvas lined up vertically one upon another
To the Heaven of Brahman, holding
Billions of lofty and wonderful canopies and streamers
Made of the seven treasures.

[The great Bodhisattvas] hoisted before the Buddhas
Jeweled banners adorned with excellent streamers.
They also praised the Tathāgatas
With tens of millions of gāthās.

I have never seen these things before.
All living beings
Rejoice at hearing
That the duration of your life is immeasurable.

Your fame is extended over the worlds of the ten quarters.
You benefit all living beings.
The roots of good which they have planted
Will help them aspire for unsurpassed [enlightenment].

Thereupon the Buddha said to Maitreya Bodhisattva-mahāsattva: "Ajita! Anyone who hears that my life is so long, and understands it by faith even at a moment's thought, will be able to obtain innumerable merits. Suppose good men or women practiced [the six pāramitās] except the prajñā-pāramitā, that is, the five pāramitās: the dāna-pāramitā, the śīla-pāramitā, the kṣānti-pāramitā, the vīrya-pāramitā, and the dhyāna-pāramitā, for eighty billion nayuta kalpas in order to attain Anuttara-samyak-saṃbodhi. These merits of the good men or women are far less than one hundredth or one thousandth of the merits of the person [who understands my

3 The odor of the incense was offered to all the members of the congregation on p. 257.

longevity by faith even at a moment's thought], or less than his merits divided by one hundred thousand billion. [The superiority of his merits to theirs] cannot be explained by any calculation or parable or simile.

It cannot be that the good man who obtained merits [by understanding my longevity by faith even at a moment's thought] falters in walking the Way to Anuttara-samyak-saṃbodhi."

Thereupon the World-Honored One, wishing to repeat what he had said, sang in gāthās:

Suppose someone practiced
The five pāramitās
For eighty billion nayuta kalpas
In order to attain the wisdom of the Buddha.

Throughout these kalpas he offered
Wonderful food and drink,
Excellent garments and bedding,
And monasteries made of candana
And adorned with gardens and forests
To the Buddhas,
To the cause-knowers, to the disciples,[4]
And to the Bodhisattvas.

Throughout these kalpas he made
These various and wonderful offerings
In order to attain
The enlightenment of the Buddha.

He also observed the precepts,
Kept purity and faultlessness,
And sought the unsurpassed enlightenment
Extolled by the Buddhas.

He was patient, gentle,
And friendly with others.

---

4 "Disciples" stands for Śrāvakas.

Even when many evils troubled him,
His mind was not moved.

He endured all insults and disturbances
Inflicted upon him by arrogant people who thought
That they had already obtained the Dharma.

He was strenuous and resolute in mind.
He concentrated his mind,
And refrained from indolence
For many hundreds of millions of kalpas.

He lived in a retired place
For innumerable kalpas.
He sat or walked to avoid drowsiness
And to concentrate his mind.

By doing so, he became able to practice
Many dhyāna-concentrations.
His mind was peaceful, not distracted
For eighty billion kalpas.

With these merits of concentration of his mind,
He sought unsurpassed enlightenment, saying:
"I will complete all these dhyāna-concentrations,
And obtain the knowledge of all things."

He performed
The meritorious practices
As previously stated
For hundreds of thousands of billions of kalpas.

The good men or women who believe my longevity,
Of which I told you,
Even at a moment's thought
Will be able to obtain more merits than he.

Those who firmly believe [my longevity],
And have no doubts about it
Even for a moment,
Will be able to obtain more merits [than he].

The Bodhisattvas who have practiced the Way
For the past innumerable kalpas,
Will believe my longevity
When they hear of it.

They will receive this sūtra on their heads,
And wish:
"May we live long and save all living beings
Just as the World-Honored One of today,
Who is the King of the Śākyas, [saves them]
By expounding the Dharma without fear
At the place of enlightenment
With [a voice like] a lion's roar!
When we sit at the place of enlightenment,
Respected by all living beings,
May we preach that we also shall live
As long [as the World-Honored One of today]!"

Those who have firm faith,
And who are pure and upright,
And who hear much and memorize all teachings,
And who understand my words
According to their meaning,
Will have no doubts [about my longevity].

"Furthermore, Ajita! Those who hear of my longevity of which I told you, and understand the meaning of my words, will be able to obtain innumerable merits, which will help them attain the unsurpassed wisdom of the Tathāgata. Needless to say, those who hear this sūtra, cause others to hear it, keep it, cause others to keep it, copy it, cause others to copy it, or offer flowers, incense, necklaces, banners, streamers, canopies, perfumed oil, and lamps of butter oil to a copy of it, will be able to obtain immeasurable merits. These merits will help them obtain the knowledge of the equality and differences of all things.

"Ajita! The good men or women who hear of my longevity of which I told you, and understand it by firm faith, will be able to see that I am expounding the Dharma on Mt. Gṛdhrakūṭa, surrounded by great Bodhisattvas and Śrāvakas. They also will be able to see that the ground of this Sahā-World is made of lapis lazuli, that the ground is even, that the eight roads are marked off by ropes of jāmbūnada gold, that the jeweled trees are standing in lines, and that the magnificent buildings are made of treasures. They also will be able to see that the Bodhisattvas are living in those buildings. They will be able to see all this because, know this, they have already understood [my longevity] by firm faith.

"Furthermore, the good men or women who do not speak ill of this sūtra but rejoice at hearing it after my extinction, should be considered, know this, to have already understood my longevity by firm faith. It is needless to say this of those who [not only rejoice at hearing this sūtra but also] read, recite and keep it. They also should be considered to be carrying me on their heads. Ajita! They need not build a stūpa or a monastery in my honor, or make the four kinds of offerings[5] to the Saṃgha because those who keep, read and recite this sūtra should be considered to have already built a stūpa or a monastery or made offerings to the Saṃgha. They should be considered to have already erected a stūpa of the seven treasures tall enough to reach the Heaven of Brahman, the upper part of the stūpa being the smaller. They should be considered to have already equipped the stūpa with streamers, canopies and jeweled bells, and enshrined my śarīras therein. They also should be considered to have already offered flowers, incense, necklaces, incense powder, incense applicable to the skin, incense to burn, drums, music, reed pipes, flutes, harps, various kinds of dances, and songs of praise sung with wonderful voices [to the stūpa] continuously for many thousands of billions of kalpas.

5 Clothing, bedding, food, drink, and medicine.

"Ajita! Anyone who, after hearing this sūtra, keeps or copies it or causes others to copy it after my extinction, should be considered to have already built many hundreds of thousands of billions of monasteries, that is to say, innumerable monasteries, each of which was installed with thirty-two beautiful halls made of red candana, eight times as tall as the tāla-tree, and spacious enough to accommodate one hundred thousand bhikṣus. He also should be considered to have already furnished [those monasteries] with gardens, forests, pools for bathing, promenades, and caves for the practice of dhyāna, and filled [those monasteries] with clothing, food, drink, bedding, medicine, and things for amusements, and offered [those monasteries] to me and to the Saṃgha of bhikṣus in my presence. Therefore, I say, 'Anyone who keeps, reads or recites this sūtra, expounds it to others, copies it, causes others to copy it, or makes offerings to a copy of it after my extinction, need not build a stūpa or a monastery, or make offerings to the Saṃgha.' Needless to say, anyone who not only keeps this sūtra but also gives alms, observes the precepts, practices patience, makes endeavors, concentrates his mind, and seeks wisdom, will be able to obtain the most excellent and innumerable merits. His merits will be as limitless as the sky is in the east, west, south, north, the four intermediate quarters, the zenith, and the nadir. These innumerable merits of his will help him obtain the knowledge of the equality and differences of all things.

"Anyone who reads, recites or keeps this sūtra, expounds it to others, copies it, or causes others to copy it [in my lifetime,] should be considered to have already built stūpas and monasteries, made offerings to the Saṃgha of Śrāvakas, praised them, praised Bodhisattvas for their merits by hundreds of thousands of billions of ways of praising, expounded this Sūtra of the Lotus Flower of the Wonderful Dharma to others with various stories of previous lives according to the meanings of it, observed the precepts without fallacy, lived with gentle persons, practiced patience, refrained from anger, become resolute in mind, preferred sitting in dhyāna, practiced deep concentrations of mind, become strenuous and brave, practiced good teachings, become clever and wise, and answered questions satisfactorily.

Ajita! Any good man or woman who keeps, reads, or recites this sūtra after my extinction, also will be able to obtain these merits. Know this! He or she should be considered to have already reached the place of enlightenment, approached Anuttara-samyak-saṃbodhi, and sat under the tree of enlightenment. Ajita! Erect a stūpa in the place where he or she sat, stood or walked! All gods and men should make offerings to that stūpa just as they do to the stūpa of a Buddha."

Thereupon the World-Honored One, wishing to repeat what he had said, sang in gāthās:

Anyone who keeps this sūtra
After my extinction
Will be able to obtain
Innumerable merits as previously stated.

He should be considered
To have already made various offerings.
He should be considered
To have already built a stūpa
With a yaṣṭi soaring up to the Heaven of Brahman,
The upper part of it being the smaller,
A stūpa which was adorned with the seven treasures,
And with thousands of billions of jeweled bells
Sounding wonderful when fanned by the wind.
He should be considered to have already enshrined
My śarīras in this stūpa,
And offered flowers, incense, necklaces,
heavenly garments,
And various kinds of music to it,
And lit lamps of perfumed oil around it
for innumerable kalpas.

Anyone who keeps this sūtra in the evil world
In the age of the decline of my teachings
Should be considered
To have already made these offerings.

Anyone who keeps this sūtra should be considered
To have already built a monastery
Made of the cow-head candana,
Installed with thirty-two beautiful halls,
Eight times as tall as the tāla-tree,
Provided with delicious food and drink,
With wonderful garments and bedding,
With accommodations for one hundred thousand people,
With gardens, forests, and pools for bathing,
And with promenades and caves for the practice
of dhyāna.
He should be considered to have already offered
That monastery to me in my presence.

Anyone who not only understands
This sūtra by faith
But also keeps, reads and recites it,
And copies it, or causes others to copy it,
And strews flowers, incense,
And incense powder to a copy of it,
And lights lamps of the perfumed oil
Of sumanas, campaka, and atimuktaka
Around the copy of this sūtra
And offers the light thus produced to it,
Will be able to obtain innumerable merits.
His merits will be as limitless as the sky.

Needless to say, so will be the merits of the person
Who keeps this sūtra, gives alms, observes the precepts,
Practices patience, prefers dhyāna-concentrations,
And does not get angry or speak ill of others.

Anyone who respects the stūpa-mausoleum,
Who is modest before bhikṣus,
Who gives up self-conceit,
Who always thinks of wisdom,

Who does not get angry when asked questions,
And who expounds the Dharma
According to the capacities of the questioners,
Will be able to obtain innumerable merits.

When you see any teacher of the Dharma
Who has obtained these merits,
You should strew heavenly flowers to him,
Dress him in a heavenly garment,
Worship his feet with your head,
And think that he will become a Buddha.

You should think
"He will go to the place of enlightenment before long.
He will be free from āsravas and free from causality.
He will benefit all gods and men."

Erect a stūpa in the place
Where he expounded even a gāthā of this sūtra
While he was standing,
Walking, sitting or reclining!
Adorn the stūpa beautifully,
And make various offerings to it!

He is my son.
I will accept his place as mine.
I will be there.
I will walk, sit or recline there.

CHAPTER XVIII

THE MERITS OF A PERSON WHO REJOICES AT HEARING THIS SŪTRA[1]

Thereupon Maitreya Bodhisattva-mahāsattva said to the Buddha: "World-Honored One! How many merits will be given to a good man or woman who rejoices at hearing this Sūtra of the Lotus Flower of the Wonderful Dharma?" He sang in a gāthā:

How many merits will be given
To a person who rejoices
At hearing this sūtra
After your extinction?

Thereupon the Buddha said to Maitreya Bodhisattva-mahāsattva: "Ajita! Suppose a bhikṣu, a bhikṣuṇī, an upāsaka, an upāsikā, or some other wise person, whether young or old, rejoices at hearing this sūtra in a congregation after my extinction. After leaving the congregation, he or she goes to some other place, for instance, to a monastery, a retired place, a city, a street, a town, or a village. There he or she expounds this sūtra, as he or she has heard it, to his or her father, mother, relative, friend or acquaintance as far as he or she can. Another person who has heard [this sūtra from him or her], rejoices, goes [to some other place] and expounds it to a third person. The third person also rejoices at hearing it and expounds it to a fourth person. In this way this sūtra is heard by a fiftieth person. Ajita! Now I will tell you the merits of the fiftieth good man or woman who rejoices at hearing [this sūtra]. Listen attentively!

---

1 随喜功徳 Literally means "the merits of rejoicing."

"Suppose the Jambudvīpa was filled with wonderful treasures such as gold, silver, lapis lazuli, shell, agate, coral and amber; elephant-carts and horse-carts; and palaces and stately buildings made of the seven treasures. Suppose a man who was seeking merits gave all those pleasing things [filling the Jambudvīpa] to the living beings of four hundred billion asaṃkhya worlds according to their wishes. A world consists of the six regions. The living beings [of the six regions] are of one or another of the four kinds of births: oviparous, viviparous, from moisture, or without any medium.[2] Some of them have forms while others do not. Some have desires while others do not. Some have no feet while others have two feet or four or more. Having continued giving those alms to them for eighty years, this great almsgiver thought, 'I gave those pleasing things to them according to their wishes. Now they are old and decrepit. They are more than eighty years old. Their hair is grey; and their faces, wrinkled. They will die before long. I will lead them by the Dharma of the Buddha.'

"Then he collected them. He propagated the Dharma to them, led them by the Dharma, showed them the Dharma, taught them, benefited them, and caused them to rejoice. He caused them to attain in a moment the enlightenment of the Srota-āpanna, of the Sakṛdāgāmin, of the Anāgāmin or of the Arhat, eliminate all āsravas, practice deep dhyāna-concentration without hindrance, and obtain the eight emancipations. What do you think of this? Do you think that the merits obtained by this great almsgiver were many or not?"

Maitreya said to the Buddha:

"World-Honored One! I think that his merits were many, immeasurable and limitless. His merits were already immeasurable when he gave all those pleasing things to them. Needless to say, so were his merits when he caused them to attain Arhatship."

The Buddha said to Maitreya:

"Now I will tell you clearly. The merits of the person who gave all those pleasing things to the living beings of the six regions of four hundred billion asaṃkhya worlds, and caused them to attain Arhatship are less than the merits of the fiftieth person who rejoices

---

2 See p. 159, footnote 3.

at hearing even a gāthā of this Sūtra of the Lotus Flower of the Wonderful Dharma. The merits of the former person are less than a hundredth or a thousandth of the merits of the latter person, or less than the merits of the latter person divided by a hundred thousand billion. [The superiority of the merits of the latter person to those of the former person] cannot be explained by any calculation, parable or simile.

"Ajita! The merits of the fiftieth person who rejoices at hearing this Sūtra of the Lotus Flower of the Wonderful Dharma are immeasurable, limitless, asaṃkhya. Needless to say, so are the merits of the first person who rejoices at hearing [this sūtra] in the congregation. His merits are immeasurable, limitless, asaṃkhya and incomparable.

"Furthermore, Ajita! Anyone who goes to a monastery in order to hear this sūtra and hears it even for a moment while he is sitting or standing, in his next life will be able to go up to the palace of heaven, riding in a beautiful and wonderful elephant-cart or horsecart or in a palanquin of wonderful treasures by his merits. Anyone who, while sitting in the place of the expounding of the Dharma, persuades another person to sit down or shares his seat with him to hear [the Dharma] when he sees him coming to the place, in his next life by his merits, will be able to obtain the seat of King Śakra, of the Brahman Heavenly-King or of a wheel-turning-holy-king.

"Ajita! Anyone who[, while he is staying outside the place of the expounding of the Dharma,] says to another person, 'Let us go and hear the sūtra called the Lotus Flower of the Wonderful Dharma which is being expounded [in that place],' and causes him to hear it even for a moment, in his next life by his merits, will be able to live with the Bodhisattvas who obtain dhāraṇīs. He will be clever and wise. He will not be dumb throughout thousands of millions of his future existences. His breath will not be foul. He will have no disease of the tongue or the mouth. His teeth will not be defiled, black, yellow, few, fallen out, uneven or crooked. His lips will not be pendulous, shrunk, chapped, cracked, broken, distorted, thick, large, yellow-black or loathsome. His nose will not be flat or awry. His face will not be black, long, distorted or displeasing. His lips, tongue and teeth will be well-shaped; his nose, long, high and straight. His face will be full; his eyebrows, thick and long; and his forehead, broad and even. In a word, he will have all the good features of a man. He will be able to see the Buddhas, hear the Dharma from them, and receive their teachings by faith throughout his future existences.

"Ajita, look! The merits of the person who causes even a single man to go and hear the Dharma are so many. It is needless to speak of the merits of the person who hears [this sūtra] with all his heart, reads it, recites it, expounds it to the great multitude, and acts according to its teachings.

Thereupon the World-Honored One, wishing to repeat what he had said, sang in gāthās:

Suppose a man rejoices at hearing this sūtra
Or at hearing even a gāthā of it
In a congregation,
And expounds it to a second person.

The second person expounds it to a third person.
In this way it is heard by a fiftieth person.
Now I will tell you of the merits
Of the fiftieth person.

Suppose there was a great almsgiver.
He continued giving alms
To innumerable living beings
For eighty years according to their wishes.

Those living beings became old and decrepit.
Their hair became grey; their faces, wrinkled;
And their teeth, fewer and deformed.
Seeing this, he thought:

"I will teach them because they will die before long.
I will cause them to obtain the fruit of enlightenment."

Then he expounded the truth of Nirvāṇa to them
As an expedient, saying:
"This world is as unstable
As a spray of water,
Or as a foam, or as a filament of air.
Hate it, and leave it quickly!"

Hearing this teaching, they attained Arhatship,
And obtained the six supernatural powers,
Including the three major supernatural powers,
And the eight emancipations.

The superiority of the merits of the fiftieth person
Who rejoices at hearing even a gāthā [of this sūtra]
To the merits of this [great almsgiver]
Cannot be explained by any parable or simile.

The merits of the [fiftieth] person
[Who hears this sūtra] are immeasurable.
Needless to say, so are the merits of the first person
Who rejoices at hearing it in the congregation.

Anyone who persuades even a single person
To hear the Sūtra of the Lotus Flower
Of the Wonderful Dharma, saying:
"This sūtra is profound and wonderful.
It is difficult to meet it
Even during ten million kalpas,"
And causes him to go and hear it even for a moment,
Will be able to obtain the following merits:

In his future lives, he will have no disease of the mouth.
His teeth will not be few, yellow or black.

His lips will not be thick, shrunk or broken.
There will be nothing loathsome [on his lips].
His tongue will not be dry, black or short.
His nose will be high, long and straight.
His forehead will be broad and even.
His face will be handsome.
All people will wish to see him.
His breath will not be foul.
The fragrance of the utpala-flowers
Will always be emitted from his mouth.

Anyone who visits a monastery to hear
The Sūtra of the Lotus Flower of the Wonderful Dharma
And rejoices at hearing it even for a moment,
Will be able to obtain the following merits:

He will be reborn among gods and men.
He will be able to go up to the palace of heaven,
Riding in a wonderful elephant-cart or horse-cart,
Or in a palanquin of wonderful treasures.

Anyone who persuades others to sit and hear this sūtra
In the place where the Dharma is expounded,
Will be able to obtain the seat of Śakra or of Brahman
Or of a wheel-turning-holy-king by his merits.

Needless to say, boundless will be the merits
Of the person who hears this sūtra with all his heart,
And expounds its meanings,
And acts according to its teachings.

CHAPTER XIX

THE MERITS OF THE TEACHER OF THE DHARMA

Thereupon the Buddha said to Constant-Endeavor Bodhisattva-Mahāsattva:

"The good men or women who keep, read, recite, expound or copy this Sūtra of the Lotus Flower of the Wonderful Dharma, will be able to obtain eight hundred merits of the eye, twelve hundred merits of the ear, eight hundred merits of the nose, twelve hundred merits of the tongue, eight hundred merits of the body, and twelve hundred merits of the mind. They will be able to adorn and purify their six sense-organs with these merits. With their pure eyes given by their parents, these good men or women will be able to see all the mountains, forests, rivers and oceans inside and outside the one thousand million Sumeru-worlds, [each of which is composed of six regions] down to the Avīci Hell and up to the Highest Heaven. They also will be able to see the living beings of those worlds, to know the karmas which those living beings are now doing and the region to which each of those living beings is destined to go by his karmas."

Thereupon the World-Honored One, wishing to repeat what he had said, sang in gāthās:

Listen! I will tell you of the merits
Of those who fearlessly expound
To the great multitude
This Sūtra of the Lotus Flower of the Wonderful Dharma.

They will be able to obtain the excellent eyes
Adorned with eight hundred merits.

Their eyes will be pure
Because of this adornment.

With their eyes given by their parents,
They will be able to see Mt. Meru, Mt. Sumeru,
The Surrounding Iron Mountains,
And the other mountains,
And the forests, oceans and rivers
Inside and outside the one thousand million
Sumeru-worlds.

They will be able to see the living beings
Of those worlds [each being composed of the six regions]
Down to the Avīci Hell and up to the Highest Heaven.
Although they have not yet obtained heavenly eyes,
They will be able to see all this
With their natural eyes.

"Furthermore, Constant-Endeavor! The good men or women who keep, read, recite, expound or copy this sūtra, will be able to obtain twelve hundred merits of the ear. With their pure ears, they will be able to recognize all the various sounds and voices inside and outside the one thousand million Sumeru-worlds, [each of which is composed of the six regions] down to the Avīci Hell and up to the Highest Heaven. They will be able to recognize the voices of elephants, horses and cows; the sounds of carts; cryings and sighings; the sounds of conch-shell horns, drums, gongs and bells; laughter and speech; the voices of men, women, boys and girls; meaningful voices, meaningless voices; painful voices, delightful voices; the voices of the unenlightened ones, the voices of the enlightened ones; joyful voices, joyless voices; the voices of gods, dragons, yakṣas, gandharvas, asuras, garuḍas, kiṃnaras and mahoragas; the sounds of fire, water and wind; the voices of hellish denizens, animals and hungry spirits; and the voices of bhikṣus, bhikṣuṇīs, Śrāvakas, Pratyekabuddhas, Bodhisattvas and Buddhas. In a word, with their pure and natural ears given by their parents, they will be able to recognize all the sounds and voices inside and outside the one thousand million Sumeru-worlds, although they have not yet obtained heavenly ears. Even when they recognize all these various sounds and voices, their organ of hearing will not be destroyed."

Thereupon the World-Honored One, wishing to repeat what he had said, sang in gāthās:

Their ears given by their parents will be purified,
  not defiled.
With their natural ears,
They will be able to recognize the sounds of voices
Of the one thousand million Sumeru-worlds.

They will be able to recognize
The voices of elephants, horses and cows;
The sounds of carts, gongs, bells, conch-shell horns,
And of drums, lyres, harps, reed-pipes and flutes.
Although they recognize pure and sweet songs,
They will not be attached to them.
They also will be able to recognize
The countless kinds of voices of men.

They will be able to recognize
The voices of gods,
The wonderful songs [of gods],
And the voices of men, women, boys and girls.

They will be able to recognize
The songs of kalaviṅkas, of jīvakajīvakas,
And of the other birds in mountains,
And on rivers and ravines.

The expounder of the Dharma
Will be able to recognize from afar,
While he is staying in the world [of men],
The cryings and shriekings
Of the denizens in hell,

The shoutings of hungry and thirsty spirits
Who are seeking food and drink,
And the voices of asuras
Bellowing to each other
[As they pound] on the seacoasts.
Even when he recognizes all this by hearing,
His organ of hearing will not be destroyed.

The expounder of the Dharma will be able to recognize,
While he is staying [in this world],
The voices of birds and animals calling each other
In the worlds of the ten quarters.

The teacher of the Dharma will be able to recognize,
While he is staying [in the world of men],
The voices of the gods of the heavens
Above the Heaven of Brahman,
[That is,] of the Light-Sound Heaven,
Of the Universal-Pure Heaven, and of the Highest Heaven.

The teacher of the Dharma
Will be able to recognize,
Without moving about,
The voices of the bhikṣus and bhikṣuṇīs
Who read or recite sūtras
Or expound them to others.

He will be able to recognize
The voices of the Bodhisattvas
Who read or recite sūtras
Or expound the meanings
Of quotations from them
To others.

Anyone who keeps this Sūtra
Of the Lotus Flower of the Wonderful Dharma
Will be able to recognize the voices of the Buddhas,

That is, the voices of the Great Honorable Saints
Who teach all living beings,
And who expound the Wonderful Dharma
in great congregations.

He will be able to recognize
All the sounds and voices
Inside and outside the one thousand million
Sumeru-worlds,
[Each being composed of the six regions]
Down to the Avīci Hell and up to the Highest Heaven.
And yet his organ of hearing will not be destroyed.
He will be able to recognize everything by hearing
Because his ears are sharp.

Anyone who keeps
This Sūtra of the Lotus Flower of the Wonderful Dharma
Will be able to obtain these merits with his natural ears
Although he has not yet obtained heavenly ears.

"Furthermore, Constant-Endeavor! The good men or women who keep, read, recite, expound or copy this sūtra, will be able to obtain eight hundred merits of the nose. With their pure noses, they will be able to recognize all the various things above, below, within and without the one thousand million Sumeru-worlds.

"Those who keep this sūtra will be able to recognize, without moving about, the scents of the sumanas-flowers, jātika-flowers, mallikā-flowers, campaka-flowers, pāṭala-flowers, red lotus flowers, blue lotus flowers, white lotus flowers, flower-trees and fruit-trees. They also will be able to recognize the scents of candana, aloes, tamālapattra and tagara, and the scents of tens of millions of kinds of mixed incense which are either powdered or made in lumps or made applicable to the skin. They also will be able to recognize the living beings including elephants, horses, cows, sheep, men, women, boys and girls by smell. They also will be able to recognize without fallacy grasses, trees, thickets and forests by smell, be they nearby or at a distance.

"Those who keep this sūtra also will be able to recognize the gods [and things] in heaven by smell while they are staying [in the world of men]. They will be able to recognize the scents of the pārijātaka-trees, kovidāra-trees, mandārava-flowers, mahā-mandārava-flowers, mañjūṣaka-flowers, mahā-mañjūṣaka-flowers [in heaven]; the powdered incense of candana and aloes, the scents of other flowers, and the mixture of these scents in heaven without fail.[1] They will be able to recognize the gods by smell. They will be able to recognize from afar the scent that Śakra-Devānām-Indra gives forth when he satisfies his five desires and enjoys himself in his excellent palace, or when he expounds the Dharma to the Trāyastriṃśa Gods at the wonderful hall of the Dharma, or when he plays in the gardens. They also will be able to recognize by smell from afar the gods and goddesses of the other heavens, including the Heaven of Brahman and the Highest Heaven. They also will be able to recognize the incense burned by the gods in those heavens. They also will be able to locate the Śrāvakas, Pratyekabuddhas, Bodhisattvas, and Buddhas by smelling their bodies from afar. Even when they recognize all this by smell, their organ of smell will not be destroyed or put out of order. If they wish, they will be able to tell others of the differences [of those scents] because they remember them without fallacy."

Thereupon the World-Honored One, wishing to repeat what he had said, sang in gāthās:

Their noses will be purified.
They will be able to know
The smells of all things,
Be they good or bad.

They will be able to recognize by smell
The sumanas-flowers and jātika-flowers;
Tamalā[pattra] and candana;
Aloes and sappanwood;
Various flowers and fruits;
And all living beings including men and women.

---

1 The upper part of Mt. Sumeru is regarded as part of heaven.

Anyone who expounds the Dharma will be able to locate
All living beings from afar by smell.
He will be able to locate by smell
The wheel-turning-kings of great [countries],
The wheel-turning-kings of small [countries],
And their sons, ministers and attendants.

He will be able to locate by smell
The wonderful treasures of personal ornaments,
The underground stores of treasures,
And the ladies of the wheel-turning-kings.

He will be able to recognize persons
By smelling their ornaments or garments
Or by smelling their necklaces
Or by smelling the incense applied to their skin.

Anyone who keeps
This Sūtra of the Lotus Flower of the Wonderful Dharma
Will be able to know by smell
Whether the gods are walking, sitting, playing or
performing wonders.

Anyone who keeps this sūtra
Will be able to locate by smell, without moving about,
The flowers and fruits of trees,
And the oil taken from sumanas-flowers.

He will be able to recognize by smell
The flowers of the candana-trees
Blooming in steep mountains,
And the living beings in those mountains.

Anyone who keeps this sūtra
Will be able to locate by smell
The living beings in the Surrounding Iron Mountains,
In the oceans, and underground.

He will be able to know by smell
Whether asuras and their daughters
And their attendants are fighting
Or playing with each other.

He will be able to locate by smell
Lions, elephants, tigers,
Wolves, wild oxen and buffalos
In the wilderness and in steep places.

He will be able to know by smell
Whether an unborn child is a boy or a girl,
Or a child of ambiguous sex,
Or the embryo of a nonhuman being.

He will be able to know by smell
Whether a woman is an expectant mother,
Or whether she will give an easy birth
To a happy child or not.

He will be able to know by smell
What a man or a woman is thinking of,
Or whether he or she is greedy, ignorant or angry,
Or whether he or she is doing good.

He will be able to recognize by smell
The gold, silver, and other treasures
Deposited underground,
And the things enclosed in a copper box.

He will be able to know by smell
The values of various necklaces,
And the deposits of their materials,
And also to locate the necklaces [when they are lost].

He will be able to recognize by smell
The mandārava-flowers,
And the mañjūṣaka-flowers,
And the pārijātaka-trees in heaven.

He will be able to know by smell
Whether a heavenly palace
Adorned with jeweled flowers
Is superior, mean or inferior.

He will be able to recognize by smell
Gardens, forests, excellent palaces,
And the wonderful hall of the Dharma in heaven,
And other stately buildings where [the gods]
    enjoy themselves.

He will be able to know by smell
Whether the gods are hearing the Dharma
Or satisfying their five desires,
Or coming, going, walking, sitting or reclining.

He will be able to know by smell
Whether the goddesses, clad in the garments
Adorned with fragrant flowers,
Are playing as they are moving about.

He will be able to know by smell
Who has reached the Heaven of Brahman,
Who has entered into dhyāna,
And who has come out of it.

He will be able to know by smell
The person who has appeared for the first time
    in the Light-Sound Heaven
Or in the Universal-Pure Heaven or in the
    Highest Heaven,
And who has disappeared from there.

Anyone who keeps this sūtra
Will be able to locate by smell
The bhikṣus who are sitting or walking about
In seeking the Dharma strenuously,
And the bhikṣus who are reading or reciting [this] sūtra
Or devoting themselves
To sitting in dhyāna
Under the trees of forests.

He will be able to know by smell
The Bodhisattvas who are resolute in mind,
And who are sitting in dhyāna or reading [this] sūtra
Or reciting it or expounding it to others.

He will be able to locate by smell
The World-Honored One who is expounding
the Dharma
Out of his compassion
Towards all living beings who respect him.

He will he able to know by smell
Those who rejoice at hearing [this] sūtra
From the Buddha,
And act according to the Dharma.

Anyone who keeps this sūtra
Will be able to have these merits of the nose
Although he has not yet obtained the nose
Of the Bodhisattva [who attained] the
Dharma-without-āsravas.

"Furthermore, Constant-Endeavor! The good men or women who keep, read, recite, expound or copy this sūtra, will be able to obtain twelve hundred merits of the tongue. Anything which tastes good, bad, delicious, distasteful, bitter or astringent, will become as delicious as the nectar of heaven and not distasteful when it is put on their tongues. When they expound the Dharma to the great multitude with their tongues, they will be able to raise deep and wonderful voices, to cause their voices to reach the hearts of the great multitude so that the great multitude may be joyful and cheerful. Hearing their speeches given in good order by their deep and wonderful voices, Śakra, Brahman, and the other gods and goddesses will come and listen to them. In order to hear the Dharma, dragons, dragons' daughters, yakṣas, yakṣas' daughters, gandharvas, gandharvas' daughters, asuras, asuras' daughters, garuḍas, garuḍas' daughters, kiṃnaras, kiṃnaras' daughters, mahoragas, and mahoragas' daughters also will come to them, respect them, and make offerings to them. Bhikṣus, bhikṣuṇīs, upāsakas, and upāsikās; and kings, princes, ministers, and their attendants [also will come and hear the Dharma]. The wheel-turning-[holy-]kings of small [countries], and the wheel-turning-[holy-]kings of great [countries, each of whom has the] seven treasures[2] and one thousand children, also will come with their [treasures, children and] internal and external retinues, riding in their [movable] palaces, and hear the Dharma. These [good men or women, that is,] Bodhisattvas will expound the Dharma so well that the brāhmanas, householders, and people of their country will, throughout their lives, attend on them, and make offerings to them. The Śrāvakas, Pratyekabuddhas, Bodhisattvas, and Buddhas also will wish to see them. [These good men or women] will expound the Dharma in the places which the Buddhas will face. They will keep all the teachings of the Buddhas and raise deep and wonderful voices of the Dharma."

Thereupon the World-Honored One, wishing to repeat what he had said, sang in gāthās:

Their tongues will be purified.
Their tongues will not receive anything bad.
Anything they eat will become
As delicious as nectar.

When they expound the Dharma to the great multitude
And lead them

2 The seven treasures of a king are different from the seven treasures denoting the seven kinds of jewels. See *Seven Treasures* in the English/Sanskrit Glossary.

By telling them the stories of previous lives,
 parables, and similes
With their deep, pure and wonderful voices,
The hearers will rejoice
And make excellent offerings to them.

All gods, dragons,
Yakṣas and asuras
Will come together
And hear the Dharma respectfully.

Anyone who expounds the Dharma, if he wishes,
Will be able to cause the living beings
Of the one thousand million Sumeru-worlds
To hear his wonderful voice.

The wheel-turning-kings of great and small [countries],
Who have each one thousand children,
Will come with their children and attendants,
And join their hands together respectfully to hear
 the Dharma.

Gods, dragons, yakṣas,
Rākṣasas and piśācakas
Also will come joyfully,
And make offerings to him.

The Brahman-Heavenly-King,
King Māra, Freedom [God],
Great-Freedom [God],
And the other gods also will come to him.

The Buddhas and their disciples who hear
The voice of the expounder of the Dharma,
Will think of him, protect him,
And sometimes appear before him.

"Furthermore, Constant-Endeavor! The good men or women who keep, read, recite, expound or copy this sūtra, will be able to obtain eight hundred merits of the body. Their bodies will become as pure as lapis lazuli. All living beings will wish to see them. Some of the living beings in the one thousand million Sumeru-worlds are just born or have just died. All living beings are either noble or humble. They are either handsome or ugly. They are destined to be reborn either in a better region or in a worse region. All of them will be reflected on the pure bodies [of the good men or women]. The Surrounding Iron Mountains, the Great Surrounding Iron Mountains, Mt. Meru, Mt. Mahā-Meru, and the other great mountains, and the living beings in those mountains also will be reflected on their bodies. [All the six regions] down to the Avīci Hell and up to the Highest Heaven and the living beings therein also will be reflected on their bodies. The Śrāvakas, Pratyekabuddhas, and Bodhisattvas as well as the Buddhas who are expounding the Dharma, also will show their reflections on their bodies."

Thereupon the World-Honored One, wishing to repeat what he had said, sang in gāthās:

Anyone who keeps
This Sūtra of the Lotus Flower of the Wonderful Dharma
Will be able to have his body purified like lapis lazuli.
All living beings will wish to see him.

Just as a reflection is seen
In a clear mirror,
All things in the world will be reflected
On the pure body of this [person, that is, of this]
Bodhisattva.
No one but he
Will be able to see all things clearly.

The gods, men, asuras,
Hellish denizens,
Hungry spirits and animals,
That is, all living beings

Of the one thousand million Sumeru-worlds
Will be reflected on his body.

The palaces of the gods in the heavens
Up to the Highest Heaven,
The Surrounding Iron Mountains,
Mt. Meru, Mt. Mahā-Meru,
And the great oceans also
Will be reflected on his body.

The Buddhas, Śrāvakas, Bodhisattvas who are sons
of the Buddhas,
[That is, the saints] of whom some live a solitary life
While others are expounding the Dharma to the multitude,
Also will be reflected on his body.

Although he has not yet obtained the wonderful body
[Of the Bodhisattva who knows] the nature of
the Dharma-without-āsravas,
He will be able to have all these things
Reflected on his pure and natural body.

"Furthermore, Constant-Endeavor! The good men or women who keep, read, recite, expound or copy this sūtra after my extinction, will be able to obtain twelve hundred merits of the mind. When they hear even a gāthā or a phrase [of this sūtra] with their pure minds, they will be able to understand the innumerable meanings [of this sūtra]. When they understand the meanings [of this sūtra] and expound even a phrase or a gāthā [of this sūtra] for a month, four months, or a year, their teachings will be consistent with the meanings [of this sūtra], and not against the reality of all things. When they expound the scriptures of non-Buddhist schools, or give advice to the government, or teach the way to earn a livelihood, they will be able to be in accord with the right teachings of the Buddha. They will be able to know all the thoughts, deeds, and words, however meaningless, of the living beings of the one thousand million Sumeru-worlds each of which is composed of the six regions.

Although they have not yet obtained the wisdom-without-āsravas, they will be able to have their minds purified as previously stated. Whatever they think, measure or say will be all true, and consistent not only with my teachings but also with the teachings that the past Buddhas have already expounded in their sūtras."

Thereupon the World-Honored One, wishing to repeat what he had said, sang in gāthās:

Their minds will become pure, clear, keen and undefiled.
They will be able to recognize with their wonderful minds
The superior, mean and inferior teachings.
When they hear even a gāthā [of this sūtra],
They will be able to understand
The innumerable meanings of [this sūtra].

When they expound [this sūtra]
In good order according to the Dharma
For a month, four months or a year,
They will be able to understand at once
The thoughts of gods, dragons, men, yakṣas, demigods,
And of all the other living beings
Inside and outside this world
Composed of the six regions
Because they keep
The Sūtra of the Lotus Flower of the Wonderful Dharma.

They also will be able to hear and keep
The Dharma expounded to all living beings
By the innumerable Buddhas of the worlds
of the ten quarters
Who are adorned with the marks of one hundred merits.

When they think over the innumerable meanings
[of this sūtra],
And endlessly repeat the expounding of those meanings,
They will not forget or mistake the beginnings
and ends [of quotations]

Because they keep the Sūtra of the Lotus Flower
of the Wonderful Dharma.

They will see the reality of all things.
Knowing the position [of this sūtra in the series of sūtras],
And the names and words [of this sūtra],
according to the meanings of it,
They will expound [this sūtra] as they understand it.

They will expound the Dharma
Already taught by the past Buddhas.
Therefore, they will be fearless
Before the multitude.

Anyone who keeps the Sūtra of the Lotus Flower
of the Wonderful Dharma
Will have his mind purified as previously stated.
Although he has not yet obtained the [wisdom-]
without-āsravas,
He will be able to obtain [these merits of the mind].

When he keeps this sūtra,
He will be able to reach a rare stage.[3]
He will be joyfully loved and respected
By all living beings.

He will be able to expound the Dharma
With tens of millions of skillful words
Because he keeps
The Sūtra of the Lotus Flower of the Wonderful Dharma.

[Here ends] the Sixth Volume of the Sūtra of the Lotus Flower of the Wonderful Dharma.

3 This implies that he will be able to become a teacher of the Dharma.

CHAPTER XX

NEVER-DESPISING BODHISATTVA

Thereupon the Buddha said to Great-Power-Obtainer Bodhisattva-mahāsattva:

"Know this! Anyone who speaks ill of or abuses or slanders the bhikṣus, bhikṣuṇis, upāsakas or upāsikās who keep the Sūtra of the Lotus Flower of the Wonderful Dharma, will incur the retributions previously stated.[1] Anyone [who keeps this sūtra] will he able to have his eyes, ears, nose, tongue, body and mind purified, that is to say, to obtain the merits as stated in the previous chapter.

"Great-Power-Obtainer! Innumerable, limitless, inconceivable, asaṃkhya kalpas ago, there lived a Buddha called Powerful-Voice-King, the Tathāgata, the Deserver of Offerings, the Perfectly Enlightened One, the Man of Wisdom and Practice, the Well-Gone, the Knower of the World, the Unsurpassed Man, the Controller of Men, the Teacher of Gods and Men, the Buddha, the World-Honored One. The kalpa in which he lived was called Free-From-Decay; and his world, Great-Achievement. Powerful-Voice-King Buddha expounded the Dharma to the gods, men and asuras of his world. To those who were seeking Śrāvakahood, he expounded the teaching suitable for them, that is, the teaching of the four truths, saved them from birth, old age, disease and death, and caused them to attain Nirvāṇa. To those who were seeking Pratyekabuddhahood, he expounded the teaching suitable for them, that is, the teaching of the twelve causes. To the Bodhisattvas who were seeking Anuttara-samyak-saṃbodhi, he expounded the teaching suitable for them, that is, the teaching of the six pāramitās, and caused them to obtain the wisdom of the Buddha.

---

1 See p. 179.

"Great-Power-Obtainer! The duration of the life of Powerful-Voice-King Buddha was forty billion nayuta kalpas, that is, as many kalpas as there are sands in the River Ganges. His right teachings were preserved for as many kalpas as the particles of dust of the Jambudvīpa. The counterfeit of his right teachings was preserved for as many kalpas as the particles of dust of the four continents, The Buddha benefited all living beings and then passed away. After [the two ages:] the age of his right teachings and the age of their counterfeit, there appeared in that world another Buddha also called Powerful-Voice-King, the Tathāgata, the Deserver of Offerings, the Perfectly Enlightened One, the Man of Wisdom and Practice, the Well-Gone, the Knower of the World, the Unsurpassed Man, the Controller of Men, the Teacher of Gods and Men, the Buddha, the World-Honored One. After him, the Buddhas of the same name appeared one after another, two billion altogether.

"There lived arrogant bhikṣus in the age of the counterfeit of the right teachings of the first Powerful-Voice-King Tathāgata, that is, after the end of the age of his right teachings which had come immediately after his extinction. [Those arrogant bhikṣus] were powerful. At that time there lived a Bodhisattva called Never-Despising.[2] He took the form of a bhikṣu.

"Great-Power-Obtainer! Why was this bhikṣu called Never-Despising? It was because, every time he saw bhikṣus, bhikṣuṇis, upāsakas or upāsikās, he bowed to them and praised them, saying, 'I respect you deeply. I do not despise you. Why is that? It is because you will be able to practice the Way of Bodhisattvas and become Buddhas.'

"He did not read or recite sūtras. He only bowed to the four kinds of devotees. When he saw them in the distance, he went to them on purpose, bowed to them, and praised them, saying, 'I do not despise you because you can become Buddhas.'

"Some of the four kinds of devotees had impure minds. They got angry, spoke ill of him and abused him, saying, 'Where did this ignorant bhikṣu come from? He says that he does not despise us, and assures us that we will become Buddhas. We do not need such a false assurance of our future Buddhahood.' Although he was

2 The Sanskrit word for this is Sadāparibhūta, which means, "always despised."

abused like this for many years, he did not get angry. He always said to them, 'You will become Buddhas.'

"When he said this, people would strike him with a stick, a piece of wood, a piece of tile or a stone. He would run away to a distance, and say in a loud voice from afar, 'I do not despise you. You will become Buddhas.' Because he always said this, he was called Never-Despising by the arrogant bhikṣus, bhikṣuṇis, upāsakas and upāsikās. When he was about to pass away, he heard [from a voice] in the sky the twenty thousand billion gāthās of the Sūtra of the Lotus Flower of the Wonderful Dharma, which had been expounded by the Powerful-Voice-King Buddha. Having kept all these gāthās, he was able to have his eyes, ears, nose, tongue, body and mind purified as previously stated. Having his six sense-organs purified, he was able to prolong his life for two hundred billion nayuta more years. He expounded this Sūtra of the Lotus Flower of the Wonderful Dharma to many people [in his prolonged life]. The arrogant bhikṣus, bhikṣuṇis, upāsakas and upāsikās, that is, the four kinds of devotees who had abused him and caused him to be called Never-Despising, saw that he had obtained great supernatural powers, the power of eloquence, and the great power of good tranquility. Having seen all this, and having heard the Dharma from him, they took faith in him, and followed him.

"This Bodhisattva also taught thousands of billions of living beings, and led them into the Way to Anuttara-samyak-saṃbodhi. After the end of his prolonged life, he was able to meet two hundred thousand million Buddhas, all of them being called Sun-Moon-Light. He also expounded the Sūtra of the Lotus Flower of the Wonderful Dharma under them. After that, he was able to meet two hundred thousand million Buddhas, all of them being called Cloud-Freedom-Light-King. He also kept, read and recited this sūtra, and expounded it to the four kinds of devotees under those Buddhas so that he was able to have his natural eyes, ears, nose, tongue, body and mind purified and to become fearless in expounding the Dharma to the four kinds of devotees.

"Great-Power-Obtainer! This Never-Despising Bodhisattva-mahāsattva made offerings to those Buddhas, respected them, honored them, praised them, and planted the roots of good. After that, he was able to meet thousands of billions of Buddhas. He also expounded this sūtra under those Buddhas. By the merits he had accumulated in this way, he was able to become a Buddha.

"Great-Power-Obtainer! What do you think of this? The Never-Despising Bodhisattva at that time was no one but myself. If I had not kept, read or recited this sūtra or expounded it to others in my previous existence, I should not have been able to attain Anuttara-samyak-saṃbodhi so quickly. Because I kept, read and recited this sūtra, and expounded it to others under those past Buddhas, I attained Anuttara-samyak-saṃbodhi quickly.

"Great-Power-Obtainer! The four kinds of devotees: the bhikṣus, bhikṣuṇis, upāsakas, and upāsikās at that time failed to meet the Buddha, hear the Dharma, and see the Saṃgha for twenty thousand million kalpas because they abused me with anger. They suffered much in the Avīci Hell for one thousand kalpas. Having expiated their sin in this way, they met [me, who was] Never-Despising Bodhisattva again, and were led into the Way to Anuttara-samyak-saṃbodhi.

"Great-Power-Obtainer! What do you think of this? The four kinds of devotees who always abused [me, who was] that Bodhisattva at that time are now present here in this congregation in the persons of the five hundred Bodhisattvas including Bhadrapāla, the five hundred bhikṣuṇīs including Lion-Moon, and the five hundred upāsakas including Thinking-Of-Buddha. Now they do not falter in seeking Anuttara-samyak-saṃbodhi.

"Great-Power-Obtainer, know this! This Sūtra of the Lotus Flower of the Wonderful Dharma benefits[3] Bodhisattva-mahāsattvas, and causes them to attain Anuttara-samyak-saṃbodhi. Therefore, they should keep, read, recite, expound and copy this sūtra after my extinction."

Thereupon the World-Honored One, wishing to repeat what he had said, sang in gāthās:

There was once a Buddha
Called Powerful-Voice-King.

---

3 Here the sūtra is personified.

His supernatural powers and wisdom
Were immeasurable.
Leading all living beings, he is honored
By gods, men and dragons with offerings.

Some time after the extinction of that Buddha,
His teachings had almost died out.
At that time there lived a Bodhisattva
Called Never-Despising.
The four kinds of devotees at that time
Were attached to [wrong] views.

Never-Despising Bodhisattva
Went to them,
And said,
"I do not despise you
Because you will practice the Way
And become Buddhas."

When they heard this,
They spoke ill of him and abused him.
But Never-Despising Bodhisattva
Endured all this.

Thus he expiated his sin.[4]
When he was about to pass away,
He heard this sūtra,
And had his six sense-organs purified.
He prolonged his life
By his supernatural powers,
And expounded this sūtra
To many people.

Those who were attached to [wrong] views
Were led into the Way

4 The expiation of sin is referred to in connection with those who abused the Bodhisattva, not with the Bodhisattva, on p. 294.

To the enlightenment of the Buddha
By this Bodhisattva.

Never-Despising [Bodhisattva] met
Innumerable Buddhas after the end of his life.
He expounded this sūtra,
And obtained innumerable merits,
He quickly attained the enlightenment of the Buddha
By these accumulated merits.

Never-Despising [Bodhisattva] at that time
Was myself.
The four kinds of devotees,
Who were attached to [wrong] views at that time,
Were able to meet innumerable Buddhas
After they heard
The words of Never-Despising [Bodhisattva]:
"You will become Buddhas."
They are now present here
In this congregation.

They are the five hundred Bodhisattvas
And the four kinds of devotees
Including men and women of pure faith,
Who are now hearing the Dharma from me.

In my previous existence
I encouraged them
To hear this sūtra,
That is, the most excellent Dharma.
In all my previous existences
I taught them the Way to Nirvāṇa.
But really this is the sūtra
I taught them to keep.

This Sūtra of the Lotus Flower of the Wonderful Dharma
Can be heard only once

In hundreds of millions of billions of kalpas,
That is, in an inconceivable number of kalpas.

The Buddhas, the World-Honored Ones,
Expound this sūtra only once
In hundreds of millions of billions of kalpas,
That is, in an inconceivable number of kalpas.

Therefore, anyone who hears this sūtra
And practices the Way
After my extinction,
Should have no doubts about [this sūtra].

He should expound this sūtra with all his heart;
Then he will be able to meet Buddhas
Throughout all his existences,
And quickly attain the enlightenment of the Buddha.

CHAPTER XXI

THE SUPERNATURAL POWERS OF THE TATHĀGATAS

Thereupon the Bodhisattva-mahāsattvas as many as the particles of dust of one thousand worlds, who had sprung up from underground, joined their hands together towards the Buddha with all their hearts, looked up at his honorable face, and said to him:

"World-Honored One! After your extinction, we will expound this sūtra in the worlds of the Buddhas of your replicas and also in the place from which you will pass away. Why is that? It is because we also wish to obtain this true, pure and great Dharma, to keep, read, recite, expound and copy [this sūtra], and to make offerings to it."

Thereupon the World-Honored One displayed his great supernatural powers in the presence of the multitude, which included not only the many hundreds of thousands of billions of Bodhisattva-mahāsattvas who had already lived in this Sahā-World [before the arrival of the Bodhisattvas from underground], headed by Mañjuśrī,[1] but also bhikṣus, bhikṣuṇis, upāsakas, upāsikās, gods, dragons, yakṣas, gandharvas, asuras, garuḍas, kiṃnaras, mahoragas, men and nonhuman beings. He stretched out his broad and long tongue upwards until the tip of it reached the World of Brahman. Then he emitted rays of light with an immeasurable variety of colors from his pores. The light illumined all the worlds of the ten quarters. The Buddhas who were sitting on the lion-like seats under the jeweled trees also stretched out their broad and long tongues and emitted innumerable rays of light. Śākyamuni Buddha and the Buddhas under the jeweled trees displayed these supernatural powers of theirs for one hundred thousand years.

1 The presence of the Bodhisattvas who came from other worlds is not referred to.

Then they pulled back their tongues, coughed at the same time, and snapped their fingers. These two sounds [of coughing and snapping] reverberated over the Buddha-worlds of the ten quarters, and the ground of those worlds quaked in the six ways. By the supernatural powers of the Buddhas, the living beings of those worlds, including gods, dragons, yakṣas, gandharvas, asuras, garuḍas, kiṃnaras, and mahoragas, men and nonhuman beings, saw the many hundreds of thousands of billions of Buddhas sitting on the lion-like seats under the jeweled trees in this Sahā-World.[2] They also saw Śākyamuni Buddha sitting by the side of Many-Treasures Tathāgata on the lion-like seat in the stūpa of treasures. They also saw that the many hundreds of thousands of billions of Bodhisattva-mahāsattvas and the four kinds of devotees were surrounding Śākyamuni Buddha respectfully, Having seen all this, they had the greatest joy that they had ever had.

At that time the gods in the skies [of the worlds of the ten quarters] said loudly:

"There is a world called Sahā beyond a distance of many hundreds of thousands of billions of asaṃkhyas of worlds.[3] In that world lives a Buddha called Śākyamuni. He is now expounding to Bodhisattva-mahāsattvas a sūtra of the Great Vehicle, called the 'Lotus Flower of the Wonderful Dharma, the Dharma for Bodhisattvas, the Dharma Upheld by the Buddhas.' Rejoice from the bottom of your hearts! Bow and make offerings to Śākyamuni Buddha!"

Having heard their voices from the skies, the living beings of those worlds joined their hands together towards the Sahā-World, and said, "Namaḥ Śākyamunaye Buddhāya,[4] namaḥ Śākyamunaye Buddhāya." Then they strewed various flowers, various kinds of incense, various necklaces, streamers, canopies, personal ornaments, treasures, and other wonderful things to the Sahā-World from afar.

---

2 According to Chapter XI, these Buddhas are some of the replicas of Śākyamuni Buddha. The Buddhas of his replicas sitting in the four hundred billion worlds of each of the eight quarters are not referred to. See Chapter XI, p. 190.

3 This may be the distance from the remotest worlds.

4 It means, "Namas to Śākyamuni Buddha," See *Namas* in the English/Sanskrit Glossary.

The strewn things came from the worlds of the ten quarters like gathering clouds and changed into a jeweled awning over the Sahā-World. The awning extended over the Buddhas staying in this world. At that time the worlds of the ten quarters became passable through each other without hindrance as if they had been a single Buddha-world.

Thereupon the Buddha said to the great Bodhisattvas headed by Superior-Practice:

"The supernatural powers of the Buddhas are as immeasurable, limitless, and inconceivable as previously stated. But I shall not be able to tell all the merits of this sūtra to those to whom this sūtra is to be transmitted even if I continue telling them by my supernatural powers for many hundreds of thousands of billions of asaṃkhyas of kalpas. To sum up, all the teachings of the Tathāgata, all the unhindered, supernatural powers of the Tathāgata, all the treasury of the hidden core of the Tathāgata, and all the profound achievements of the Tathāgata are revealed and expounded explicitly in this sūtra. Therefore, keep, read, recite, expound and copy this sūtra, and act according to the teachings of it with all your hearts after my extinction! In any world where anyone keeps, reads, recites, expounds or copies this sūtra, or acts according to its teachings, or in any place where a copy of this sūtra is put, be it in a garden, in a forest, under a tree, in a monastery, in the house of a person in white robes, in a hall, in a mountain, in a valley, or in the wilderness, there should a stūpa be erected and offerings be made to it because, know this, the place [where the stūpa is erected] is the place of enlightenment. Here the Buddhas attained Anuttara-samyak-saṃbodhi. Here the Buddhas turned the wheel of the Dharma. Here the Buddhas entered into Parinirvāṇa."

Thereupon the World-Honored One, wishing to repeat what he had said, sang in gāthās:

> The Buddhas, the World-Saviors, have
> Great supernatural powers.
> They display their immeasurable, supernatural powers
> In order to cause all living beings to rejoice.

The tips of their tongues reach the Heaven of Brahman.
Innumerable rays of light are emitted from their bodies.
For those who are seeking the enlightenment of the Buddha
The Buddhas do these things rarely to be seen.

The sound of coughing of the Buddhas
And the sound of their finger-snapping
Reverberate over the worlds of the ten quarters,
And the ground [of those worlds] quakes in the six ways.

The Buddhas joyfully display
Their immeasurable, supernatural powers
Because [the Bodhisattvas from underground]
[Vow to] keep this sūtra after my extinction.

Even if I praise for innumerable kalpas
The keeper of this sūtra,
To whom it is to be transmitted,
I cannot praise him highly enough.

His merits are as limitless,
As infinite, as boundless
As the skies of the worlds
Of the ten quarters.

Anyone who keeps this sūtra
Will be able to see me. He also will be able to see
Many-Treasures Buddha,
[The Buddhas of] my replicas,
And the Bodhisattvas whom I have taught today.

Anyone who keeps this sūtra will be able
to cause me to rejoice.
He also will be able to bring joy
To [the Buddhas of] my replicas
And also to Many-Treasures Buddha
who once passed away.

He also will be able to see
The present, past and future Buddhas
Of the worlds of the ten quarters,
Make offerings to them, and cause them to rejoice.

The Buddhas sat at the place of enlightenment,
And obtained the hidden core.
Anyone who keeps this sūtra will be able
To obtain the same before long.

Anyone who keeps this sūtra
Will be able to expound
The meanings of the teachings,
And the names and words [of this sūtra].
Their eloquence will be as boundless
And as unhindered as the wind in the sky.

Anyone who understands why the Buddhas
  expound [many] sūtras,
Who knows the position [of this sūtra
  in the series of sūtras],
And who expounds it after my extinction
According to its true meaning,
Will be able to eliminate the darkness.
Of the living beings of the world where he walks about,
Just as the light of the sun and the moon
Eliminates all darkness.
He will be able to cause innumerable Bodhisattvas
To dwell finally in the One Vehicle.

Therefore, the man of wisdom
Who hears the benefits of these merits
And who keeps this sūtra after my extinction,
Will be able to attain
The enlightenment of the Buddha
Definitely and doubtlessly.

CHAPTER XXII

TRANSMISSION

Thereupon Śākyamuni Buddha rose from the seat of the Dharma, and by his great supernatural powers, put his right hand on the heads of the innumerable Bodhisattva-mahāsattvas, and said:

"For many hundreds of thousands of billions of asaṃkhyas of kalpas, I studied and practiced the Dharma difficult to obtain, and [finally attained] Anuttara-samyak-saṃbodhi. Now I will transmit the Dharma to you. Propagate it with all your hearts, and make it known far and wide!"

He put his [right] hand on their heads twice more, and said:

"For many hundreds of thousands of billions of asaṃkhyas of kalpas, I studied and practiced the Dharma difficult to obtain, and [finally attained] Anuttara-samyak-saṃbodhi. Now I will transmit [the Dharma] to you. Keep, read, recite and expound [this sūtra in which the Dharma is given], and cause all living beings to hear it and know it! Why is that? It is because I have great compassion. I do not begrudge anything. I am fearless. I wish to give the wisdom of the Buddha, the wisdom of the Tathāgata, the wisdom of the Self-Existing One, to all living beings. I am the great almsgiver to all living beings. Follow me, and study my teachings without begrudging efforts! In the future, when you see good men or women who believe in the wisdom of the Tathāgata, you should expound this Sūtra of the Lotus Flower of the Wonderful Dharma to them, and cause them to hear and know [this sūtra] so that they may he able to obtain the wisdom of the Buddha. When you see anyone who does not receive [this sūtra] by faith, you should show him some other profound teachings of mine, teach him, benefit him, and cause him to rejoice. When you do all this, you will be able to repay the favors given to you by the Buddhas."

Having heard these words of the Buddha, the Bodhisattva-mahāsattvas were filled with great joy. With more respect than ever, they bent forward, bowed, joined their hands together towards him, and said simultaneously. "We will do as you command. Certainly, World-Honored One! Do not worry!"

The Bodhisattva-mahāsattvas said simultaneously twice more, "We will do as you command. Certainly, World-Honored One! Do not worry!"

Thereupon Śākyamuni Buddha, wishing to send back to their home worlds [Many-Treasures Buddha and] the Buddhas of his replicas, who had come from the worlds of the ten quarters, said, "May the Buddhas be where they wish to be! May the stūpa of Many-Treasures Buddha be where it was!"[1]

Having heard these words of the Buddha, not only the innumerable Buddhas of his replicas,[2] who had come from the worlds of the ten quarters and were sitting on the lion-like seats under the jeweled trees, Many-Treasures Buddha, and the great multitude of the innumerable, asaṃkhya Bodhisattvas, including Superior-Practice, but also the four kinds of devotees including Śāriputra and other Śrāvakas, and the gods, men and asuras of the world, had great joy.

---

1 It is understood that Śākyamuni Buddha had already left the stūpa and descended onto the ground at the beginning of this chapter.

2 The Buddhas of the replicas of Śākyamuni Buddha never appear in the following chapters. It should be considered that they went back to their home worlds at the end of this chapter.

CHAPTER XXIII

THE PREVIOUS LIFE OF MEDICINE-KING BODHISATTVA

Thereupon Star-King-Flower Bodhisattva said to the Buddha:

"World-Honored One! Why does Medicine-King Bodhisattva walk about this Sahā-World? World-Honored One! This Medicine-King Bodhisattva will have to practice hundreds of thousands of billions of nayutas of austerities in this world. World-Honored One! Tell me why! Not only the gods, dragons, yakṣas, gandharvas, asuras, garuḍas, kiṃnaras, mahoragas, men and nonhuman beings but also the Bodhisattvas who have come from the other worlds[1] and the Śrāvakas present here will be glad to hear the reason."

Thereupon the Buddha said to Star-King-Flower Bodhisattva:

"Innumerable kalpas ago, that is, as many kalpas as there are sands in the River Ganges ago, there lived a Buddha called Sun-Moon-Pure-Bright-Virtue, the Tathāgata, the Deserver of Offerings, the Perfectly Enlightened One, the Man of Wisdom and Practice, the Well-Gone, the Knower of the World, the Unsurpassed Man, the Controller of Men, the Teacher of Gods and Men, the Buddha, the World-Honored One. He was accompanied by eight thousand million great Bodhisattva-mahāsattvas and also by great Śrāvakas numbering seventy-two times as many as there are sands in the River Ganges. The duration of his life was forty-two thousand kalpas. So were the durations of the lives of the Bodhisattvas. His world was devoid of women, hellish denizens, hungry spirits, animals and asuras. There was no calamity in his world. The ground of his world was as even as the palm of the hand. It was

1 These Bodhisattvas are not referred to in the following chapters.
The Bodhisattvas who sprang up from underground are not referred to in this and the following chapters.

made of lapis lazuli, adorned with jeweled trees, and covered with a jeweled awning from which the streamers of jeweled flowers were hanging down. Jeweled vases and incense-burners were seen everywhere in that world. There was a platform of the seven treasures at the distance of a bowshot from each of the jeweled trees under which the Bodhisattvas and Śrāvakas were sitting. On each of the platforms of treasures, myriads of millions of gods were making heavenly music, singing songs of praise of the Buddha, and offering the music and songs to the Buddha.

"Thereupon [Sun-Moon-Pure-Bright-Virtue] Buddha expounded the Sūtra of the Lotus Flower of the Wonderful Dharma to Gladly-Seen-By-All-Beings Bodhisattva, to the other Bodhisattvas, and also to the Śrāvakas. Gladly-Seen-By-All-Beings Bodhisattva willingly practiced austerities under Sun-Moon-Pure-Bright-Virtue Buddha. He walked about the world, seeking Buddhahood strenuously with all his heart for twelve thousand years until at last he obtained the samādhi by which he could transform himself into any other living being.[2] Having obtained this samādhi, he had great joy.

"He thought, 'I have obtained the samādhi by which I can transform myself into any other living being because I heard the Sūtra of the Lotus Flower of the Wonderful Dharma. Now I will make offerings to Sun-Moon-Pure-Bright-Virtue Buddha and also to the Sūtra of the Lotus Flower of the Wonderful Dharma.'

"He entered into this samādhi at once. He filled the sky with the clouds of mandārava-flowers, mahā-mandārava-flowers and the powdered incense of hard and black candana, and rained down those flowers and incense. He also rained down the powdered incense of the candana grown on this shore of the sea [between Mt. Sumeru and the Jambudvīpa]. Six *shu* of this incense was worth the Sahā-World. He offered all these things to the Buddha.

"Having made these offerings [to the Buddha], he emerged from the samādhi, and thought, 'I have now made offerings to the Buddha by my supernatural powers. But these offerings are less valuable than the offering of my own body.'

2 But he never transformed himself.

"Then he ate various kinds of incense taken from candana, kunduruka, turuṣka, pṛkkā, aloes and sumac, and drank perfumed oil taken from the flowers of campaka and other flowers[. He continued doing all this] for twelve hundred years. Then he applied perfumed oil to his skin, put on a heavenly garment of treasures in the presence of Sun-Moon-Pure-Bright-Virtue Buddha, sprinkled various kinds of perfumed oil on the garment, and set fire to his body, making a vow by his supernatural powers. The light of the flame illumined the worlds numbering eight thousands of millions of times the number of the sands of the River Ganges.

"The Buddhas of those worlds praised him, saying simultaneously, 'Excellent, excellent, good man! All you did was a true endeavor. You made an offering to us according to the true Dharma. This offering excels the offerings of flowers, incense, necklaces, incense to burn, powdered incense, incense applicable to the skin, streamers and canopies of heavenly cloth, and the incense of the candana grown on this shore of the sea. It also excels the offerings of countries, cities, wives and children. Good man! This is the most excellent and honorable offering because you made it to us according to the Dharma.'

"Having said this, they became silent. The body of the Bodhisattva kept burning for twelve hundred years, and then was consumed. Having made this offering according to the Dharma, Gladly-Seen-By-All-Beings Bodhisattva passed away. In his next life, he appeared again in the world of Sun-Moon-Pure-Bright-Virtue Buddha. It was in the house of King Pure-Virtue [in that world] that he suddenly appeared with his legs crossed [in the person of the son of the king]. He said to his father in a gāthā:

Great King, know this, [in my previous existence]
I walked about this world, and at once obtained
The samādhi by which I can transform myself
Into any other living being. With a great endeavor,
I gave up my own dear body.

"Having sung this gāthā, he said to his father, 'Sun-Moon-Pure-Bright-Virtue Buddha is still alive. [In my previous existence]

I made offerings to him, and obtained the dhāraṇīs by which I can understand the words of all living beings. I also heard from him the eight hundred thousands of billions of nayutas of kaṅkaras of biṃbaras of akṣobhyas of gāthās of this Sūtra of the Lotus Flower of the Wonderful Dharma. Great King! Now I will make another offering to the Buddha.'

"Having said this, he sat on a platform of the seven treasures. The platform went up to the sky seven times as high as the tāla-tree. He came to the Buddha [who was staying in the sky], worshipped the feet of the Buddha with his head, joined his ten fingers [and palms] together, and praised the Buddha in a gāthā:

> Your face is most wonderful.
> Your light illumines the worlds of the ten quarters.
> I once made offerings to you.
> Now I have come to see you again.

"Having sung this gāthā, Gladly-Seen-By-All-Beings Bodhisattva said to the Buddha, 'World-Honored One! You do not change, do you?'

"Sun-Moon-Pure-Bright-Virtue Buddha said to Gladly-Seen-By-All-Beings Bodhisattva, 'Good man! The time of my Nirvāṇa[3] is near at hand. The time of my extinction is coming. Prepare me a comfortable couch! I shall enter into Parinirvāṇa tonight.'

"Then he instructed Gladly-Seen-By-All-Beings Bodhisattva, saying, 'Good man! I will transmit all my teachings to you. [I also will transmit] to you all the Bodhisattvas and all my great disciples.[4] [I also will transmit] to you my teachings for Anuttara-samyak-saṃbodhi. I also will transmit to you the one thousand Sumeru worlds made of the seven treasures, the jeweled trees, the jeweled platforms, and the gods attending on me. I also will transmit to you the śarīras to be left after my extinction. Distribute my śarīras far and wide and make offerings to them! Erect thousands of stūpas [to enshrine them]!'

---

3 This stands for Parinirvāṇa.

4 "Disciples" stands for Śrāvakas.

"Having given these instructions to Gladly-Seen-By-All-Beings Bodhisattva, Sun-Moon-Pure-Bright-Virtue Buddha entered into Nirvāṇa in the last watch of that night. Having seen the extinction of the Buddha, Gladly-Seen-By-All-Beings Bodhisattva was overcome with sorrow. He adored the Buddha all the more. He made a pyre of the candana grown on this shore of the sea, offered it to the body of the Buddha, and burned it. After it burned up, he collected the śarīras. He made eighty-four thousand urns of treasures[, and put the śarīras therein]. He erected eighty-four thousand stūpas[, and enshrined the urns therein]. The stūpas were higher than the Third Dhyana-Heaven. They were adorned with yaṣṭis. Many streamers and canopies were hanging down [from the stūpas]. Many jeweled bells also were fixed [on the stūpas].

"Thereupon Gladly-Seen-By-All-Beings Bodhisattva thought again, 'I have now made these offerings, yet I do not think that they are enough. I will make another offering to the śarīras.'

"He said to the Bodhisattvas, to the great disciples,[5] and also to all the other living beings in the great multitude including gods, dragons and yakṣas, 'Look with one mind! Now I will make another offering to the śarīras of Sun-Moon-Pure-Bright-Virtue Buddha.'

"Having said this, he burned his arms adorned with the marks of one hundred merits, and offered the light of the flame to the eighty-four thousand stūpas for seventy-two thousand years. [By doing so,] he caused innumerable seekers of Śrāvakahood and many other asaṃkhyas of people to aspire for Anuttara-samyak-saṃbodhi, and obtain the samādhi by which they could transform themselves into the other living beings.

"Having seen him deprived of his arms, the Bodhisattvas, gods, men, asuras and others were overcome with sorrow. They said, 'This Gladly-Seen-By-All-Beings Bodhisattva is our teacher. He is leading us. Now he has burned off his arms. He is deformed.'

"Thereupon Gladly-Seen-By-All-Beings Bodhisattva vowed to the great multitude, saying, 'I shall be able to obtain the golden body of the Buddha because I gave up my arms. If my words are true and not false, I shall be able to have my arms restored.'

5 "Disciples" stands for Śrāvakas.

"When he had made this vow, his arms were restored because his merits, virtues and wisdom were abundant. Thereupon the one thousand million Sumeru-worlds quaked in the six ways, and the gods rained down jeweled flowers. All the gods and men had the greatest joy that they had ever had."

The Buddha said to Star-King-Flower Bodhisattva:

"What do you think of this? Gladly-Seen-By-All-Beings Bodhisattva was no one but Medicine-King Bodhisattva of today. He gave up his body in this way, offered it [to the Buddha], and repeated this offering many hundreds of thousands of billions of nayutas of times [in his previous existence]. [He knows that he can practice any austerity in this Sahā-World. Therefore, he does not mind walking about this world.]

"Star-King-Flower! Anyone who aspires for, and wishes to attain Anuttara-samyak-saṃbodhi, should offer a light to the stūpa of the Buddha by burning a finger or a toe. Then he will be given more merits than the person who offers not only countries, cities, wives and children, but also the mountains, forests, rivers and ponds of the one thousand million Sumeru-worlds, and various kinds of treasures. But the merits to be given to the person who fills the one thousand million Sumeru-worlds with the seven treasures and offers that amount of the seven treasures to the Buddhas, to the Great Bodhisattvas, to the Pratyekabuddhas, and to the Arhats, are less than the merits to be given to the person who keeps even a single gāthā of four lines of this Sūtra of the Lotus Flower of the Wonderful Dharma.

"Star-King-Flower! Just as the sea is larger than the rivers, this Sūtra of the Lotus Flower of the Wonderful Dharma is more profound than any of the other sūtras expounded by the Tathāgatas. Just as Mt. Sumeru is the largest of all the mountains including earth mountains, black mountains, the Small Surrounding Iron Mountains, the Great Surrounding Iron Mountains, and the Ten Treasure Mountains, this Sūtra of the Lotus Flower of the Wonderful Dharma is above all the other sūtras. Just as the Moon God is brighter than the stars, this Sūtra of the Lotus Flower of the Wonderful Dharma gives us more light than any of the other sūtras numbering thousands of billions. Just as the Sun God dispels all darkness, this sūtra drives away all the darkness of evils. Just as the wheel-turning-holy-king is superior to the kings of small countries, this sūtra is more honorable than the other sūtras. Just as King Śakra is the king of the thirty-three gods, this sūtra is the king of all the sūtras. Just as the Great Brahman Heavenly-King is the father of all living beings, this sūtra is the father of all the sages and saints, of the Śrāvakas who have something more to learn, of the Śrāvakas who have nothing more to learn, and of those who aspire for Bodhisattvahood. Just as Srota-āpannas, Sakṛdāgāmins, Anāgāmins, Arhats, and Pratyekabuddhas are superior to ordinary men, this sūtra is superior to any of the other sūtras expounded either by Tathāgatas or by Bodhisattvas or by Śrāvakas. The person who keeps this sūtra is superior to any other living being. Just as Bodhisattvas are superior to Śrāvakas or to Pratyekabuddhas, this sūtra is superior to any other sūtra. Just as the Buddha is the king of the Dharma, this sūtra is the king of all the sūtras.

"Star-King-Flower! This sūtra saves all living beings.[6] This sūtra saves them from all sufferings, and gives them great benefits. All living beings will be able to fulfill their wishes by this sūtra just as a man who reaches a pond of fresh water when he is thirsty, just as a man who gets fire when he suffers from cold, just as a man who is given a garment when he is naked, just as a party of merchants who find a leader, just as a child who meets its mother, just as a man who gets a ship when he wants to cross [a river], just as a patient who finds a physician, just as a man who is given a light in the darkness, just as a poor man who gets a treasure, just as the people of a nation who see a new king enthroned, just as a trader who reaches the seacoast. Just as a torch dispels darkness, this Sūtra of the Lotus Flower of the Wonderful Dharma saves all living beings from all sufferings, from all diseases, and from all the bonds of birth and death. The merits to be given to the person who, after hearing this Sūtra of the Lotus Flower of the Wonderful Dharma, copies it, or causes others to copy it, cannot be measured even by the wisdom of the

6 Here the sūtra is personified.

Buddha. Neither can the merits to be given to the person who copies this sūtra and offers flowers, incense, necklaces, incense to burn, powdered incense, incense applicable to the skin, streamers, canopies, garments, and various kinds of lamps such as lamps of butter oil, oil lamps, lamps of perfumed oil, lamps of campaka oil, lamps of sumanas oil, lamps of pāṭala oil, lamps of vārṣika oil, and lamps of navamālikā oil [to the copy of this sūtra].

"Star-King-Flower! Anyone who hears [especially] this chapter of the Previous Life of Medicine-King Bodhisattva also will be able to obtain innumerable merits. The woman who hears and keeps this chapter of the Previous Life of Medicine-King Bodhisattva will not be a woman in her next life. The woman who hears this sūtra and acts according to the teachings of it in the later[7] five hundred years after my extinction, will be able to be reborn, after her life in this world, [as a man sitting] on the jeweled seat in the lotus flower blooming in the World of Happiness where Amitāyus Buddha lives surrounded by great Bodhisattvas. He [no more she] will not be troubled by greed, anger, ignorance, arrogance, jealousy, or any other impurity. He will be able to obtain the supernatural powers of a Bodhisattva and the truth of birthlessness. When he obtains this truth, his eyes will be purified. With his purified eyes, he will be able to see seven billion and two hundred thousand million nayuta Buddhas or Tathāgatas, that is, as many Buddhas as there are sands in the River Ganges. At that time those Buddhas will praise him, saying simultaneously from afar, 'Excellent, excellent, good man! You kept, read and recited this sūtra, thought it over, and expounded it to others under Śākyamuni Buddha. Now you have obtained innumerable merits and virtues, which cannot be burned by fire or washed away by water. Your merits cannot be described even by the combined efforts of one thousand Buddhas. Now you have defeated the army of Māra, beaten the forces of birth and death, and annihilated all your enemies. Good man! Hundreds of thousands of Buddhas are now protecting you by their supernatural powers. None of the gods or men in the world surpasses you. None but the Tathāgatas, none of the Śrāvakas or Pratyekabuddhas or

---

7 後五百歳 K'ui-chi interprets it as the fourth or fifth five hundred years. This explanation is found in *Iwanami Bunko, Hokekyō, Ge,* p. 368.

Bodhisattvas surpasses you in wisdom and dhyāna-concentration.' Star-King-Flower! [He is a Bodhisattva.] This Bodhisattva will obtain these merits and the power of wisdom.

"Anyone who rejoices at hearing this chapter of the Previous Life of Medicine-King Bodhisattva and praises [this chapter], saying, 'Excellent,' will be able to emit the fragrance of the blue lotus flower from his mouth and the fragrance of the candana of Mt. Ox-Head from his pores, and obtain these merits in his present life.

"Therefore, Star-King-Flower! I will transmit this chapter of the Previous Life of Medicine-King Bodhisattva to you. Propagate this chapter throughout the Jambudvīpa in the later five hundred years after my extinction lest it should be lost, and lest Māra the Evil One, the followers of Māra, gods,[8] dragons, yakṣas, and kumbhāṇḍas should take advantage [of the weak points of the people of the Jambudvīpa].

"Star-King-Flower! Protect this sūtra by your supernatural powers! Why is that? It is because this sūtra is a good medicine for the diseases of the people of the Jambudvīpa. The patient who hears this sūtra will be cured of his disease at once. He will not grow old or die.

"Star-King-Flower! Strew blue lotus flowers and a bowlful of powdered incense to the person who keeps this sūtra when you see him! After strewing these things [to him], you should think, 'Before long he will collect grass [for his seat], sit at the place of enlightenment, and defeat the army of Māra. He will blow the conch-shell horn of the Dharma, beat the drum of the great Dharma, and save all living beings from the ocean of old age, disease and death.'

"In this way, those who seek the enlightenment of the Buddha should respect the keeper of this sūtra whenever they see him."

When the Buddha expounded this chapter of the Previous Life of Medicine-King Bodhisattva, eighty-four thousand Bodhisattvas obtained the dhāraṇīs by which they could understand the words of all living beings. Many-Treasures Tathāgata in the stūpa of treasures praised Star-King-Flower Bodhisattva, saying:

---

8 Here gods are treated as devils.

"Excellent, excellent, Star-King-Flower! You obtained inconceivable merits. You asked this question to Śākyamuni Buddha, and benefited innumerable living beings."

CHAPTER XXIV

WONDERFUL-VOICE BODHISATTVA

Thereupon Śākyamuni Buddha [faced the east and] emitted rays of light from the fleshy tuft on his head, that is, from one of the marks of a great man, and also from the white curls between his eyebrows. The light illumined one hundred and eight billion nayuta Buddha-worlds, that is, as many worlds in the east as there are sands in the River Ganges. There was a world called [All-] Pure-Light-Adornment [in the east] beyond those worlds. In that world was a Buddha called Pure-Flower-Star-King-Wisdom, the Tathāgata, the Deserver of Offerings, the Perfectly Enlightened One, the Man of Wisdom and Practice, the Well-Gone, the Knower of the World, the Unsurpassed Man, the Controller of Men, the Teacher of Gods and Men, the Buddha, the World-Honored One. He expounded the Dharma to a great multitude of innumerable Bodhisattvas who were surrounding him respectfully. The ray of light, which was emitted from the white curls [between the eyebrows] of Śākyamuni Buddha, also illumined that world.

At that time there was a Bodhisattva called Wonderful-Voice in the All-Pure-Light-Adornment World. He had already planted roots of virtue a long time ago. He had already made offerings to many hundreds of thousands of billions of Buddhas, and attended on them. He had already obtained profound wisdom. He had already obtained hundreds of thousands of billions of great samādhis, that is, as many great samādhis as there are sands in the River Ganges, such as the samādhi as wonderful as the banner of a general, the samādhi for the traveling of the king of the stars, the samādhi for freedom from causality, the samādhi for the seal of wisdom, the samādhi by which one could understand the words of all living beings, the samādhi by which one could collect all merits, the samādhi for purity, the samādhi for exhibiting supernatural powers, the samādhi for the torch of wisdom, the samādhi for the Adornment-King, the samādhi for pure light, the samādhi for pure store, the samādhi for special teachings, and the samādhi for the revolution of the sun.

When he was illumined by the light of Śākyamuni Buddha, he said to the Pure-Flower-Star-King-Wisdom Buddha:

"World-Honored One! I wish to visit the Sahā-World, bow to Śākyamuni Buddha, attend on him, and make offerings to him. I also wish to see Mañjuśrī Bodhisattva, who is the Son of the King of the Dharma. [I also wish to see] Medicine-King Bodhisattva, Brave-In-Giving Bodhisattva, Star-King-Flower Bodhisattva, Superior-Practice-Intent Bodhisattva, Adornment-King Bodhisattva, and Medicine-Superior Bodhisattva."

Thereupon Pure-Flower-Star-King-Wisdom Buddha said to Wonderful-Voice Bodhisattva:

"Do not despise that world! Do not consider it to be inferior [to our world]! Good Man! The Sahā-World is not even. It is full of mud, stones, mountains[1] and impurities. The Buddha [of that world] is short in stature.[2] So are the Bodhisattvas [of that world]. You are forty-two thousand yojanas tall. I am six million and eight hundred thousand yojanas tall. You are the most handsome. You have thousands of millions of marks of merits, and your light is wonderful. Do not despise that world when you go there! Do not consider that the Buddha and Bodhisattvas of that world are inferior [to us]! Do not consider that that world is inferior [to ours]!"

Wonderful-Voice Bodhisattva said to the Buddha "World-Honored One! I can go to the Sahā-World by your powers, by your supernatural powers of traveling, and by your merits and wisdom which adorn me."

Thereupon Wonderful-Voice Bodhisattva entered into a samādhi. He did not rise from his seat or make any other movement. By

---

1 Judging from this, there is no mountain in the All-Pure-Light-Adornment World.

2 Judging from the statement that a Buddha in the east is superior to Śākyamuni Buddha, we see that the conception of the Buddhas of the worlds of the ten quarters as the replicas of Sakyamuni Buddha is absent from this chapter. It is also absent from the following chapters.

the power of this samādhi, he caused eighty-four thousand lotus-flowers of treasures to appear in a place not far from the seat of the Dharma situated on Mt. Gṛdhrakūṭa. Those flowers had stalks of jāmbūnada gold, leaves of silver, stamens of diamond, and calyxes of kiṃśuka treasures.

Thereupon Mañjuśrī, the Son of the King of the Dharma, having seen these lotus-flowers, said to Śākyamuni Buddha:

"World-Honored One! What does this omen mean? Tens of millions of lotus-flowers have appeared. They have stalks of jāmbūnada gold, leaves of silver, stamens of diamond, and calyxes of kiṃśuka treasures."

Thereupon Śākyamuni Buddha said to Mañjuśrī:

"This means that Wonderful-Voice Bodhisattva-mahāsattva, surrounded by eighty-four thousand Bodhisattvas, is coming from the World of Pure-Flower-Star-King-Wisdom Buddha to this Sahā-World in order to make offerings to me, attend on me, bow to me, make offerings to the Sūtra of the Lotus Flower of the Wonderful Dharma, and hear it."

Mañjuśrī said to the Buddha:

"World-Honored One! What root of good did he plant and what kind of meritorious deed did he do in order to obtain this great supernatural power? What samādhi did he practice? Tell us the name of the samādhi! We also wish to practice it strenuously so that we may be able to see how tall he is and how he behaves himself. World-Honored One! Cause me to see him by your supernatural powers when he comes!"

Thereupon Śākyamuni Buddha said to Mañjuśrī, "This Many-Treasures Tathāgata, who passed away a long time ago, will cause him to appear before you all."

Thereupon Many-Treasures Buddha called [loudly] to [Wonderful-Voice] Bodhisattva [from afar], "Good man! Come! Mañjuśrī, the Son of the King of the Dharma, wishes to see you."

Thereupon Wonderful-Voice Bodhisattva, accompanied by eighty-four thousand Bodhisattvas, left his world [for the Sahā-World]. As they passed through the [one hundred and eight billion nayuta] worlds, the ground of those worlds quaked in the six ways; lotus flowers of the seven treasures rained [on those worlds], and hundreds of thousands of heavenly drums sounded [over those worlds] although no one beat them. The eyes of [Wonderful-Voice] Bodhisattva were as large as the leaves of the blue lotus. His face was more handsome than the combination of thousands of millions of moons. His body was golden-colored, and adorned with many hundreds of thousands of marks of merits. His power and virtue were great. His light was brilliant. His body had all the characteristics of the muscular body of Nārāyaṇa.

[Before he started,] he stepped on a platform of the seven treasures. The platform went up to the sky seven times as high as the tāla[-tree, and moved through the sky, carrying him]. Together with the Bodhisattvas surrounding him respectfully, he came to Mt. Gṛdhrakūṭa of this Sahā-World, and descended from the platform of the seven treasures. He came to Śākyamuni Buddha, carrying with him a necklace worth hundreds of thousands. He worshipped the feet of the Buddha with his head, offered the necklace to the Buddha, and said to him:

"World-Honored One! I bring you a message from Pure-Flower-Star-King-Wisdom Buddha. [He wishes to say this.] Are you in good health? Are you happy and peaceful or not? Are the four elements of your body working in harmony or not? Are the worldly affairs bearable or not? Are the living beings easy to save or not? Do they not have much greed, anger, ignorance, jealousy, stinginess and arrogance, or do they? Are they not undutiful to their parents, or are they? Are they not disrespectful to śramaṇas, or are they? Do they not have wrong views, or do they? Are they not evil, or are they? Do they not fail to control their five desires, or do they? World-Honored One! Did they defeat the Māras, who are their enemies, or not? Is Many-Treasures Tathāgata, who passed away a long time ago and has now come here riding in the stūpa of the seven treasures, hearing the Dharma or not? [Pure-Flower-Star-King-Wisdom Buddha] also wishes to know whether Many-Treasures Tathāgata is peaceful and healthy, and able to stay long or not. World-Honored One! Now I wish to see Many-Treasures Buddha. World-Honored One! Show him to me!"

Thereupon Śākyamuni Buddha said to Many-Treasures Buddha, "This Wonderful-Voice Bodhisattva wishes to see you."

Thereupon Many-Treasures Buddha said to Wonderful-Voice Bodhisattva:

"Excellent, excellent! You have come here to make offerings to Śākyamuni Buddha, hear the Sūtra of the Lotus Flower of the Wonderful Dharma, and see Mañjuśrī and others."

Thereupon Flower-Virtue Bodhisattva said to Śākyamuni Buddha:

"World-Honoured One! What root of good did this Wonderful-Voice Bodhisattva plant and what kind of meritorious deeds did he do in order to obtain this supernatural power?"

Śākyamuni Buddha said to Flower-Virtue Bodhisattva:

"There was once a Buddha called Cloud-Thunder-Sound-King, the Tathāgata, the Arhat, the Samyak-saṃbuddha. His world was called Appearance-Of-All-Worlds; and the kalpa in which he lived, Gladly-Seen. [There lived] a Bodhisattva called Wonderful-Voice [under that Buddha. The Bodhisattva] offered hundreds of thousands of kinds of music and eighty-four thousand pātras of the seven treasures to Cloud-Thunder-Sound-King Buddha for twelve thousand years. Because of this, he was able to appear in the world of Pure-Flower-Star-King-Wisdom Buddha, and obtain supernatural power such as this.

"Flower-Virtue! What do you think of this? Wonderful-Voice Bodhisattva who had offered the music and the jeweled bowls to Cloud-Thunder-Sound-King Buddha [at that time] was no one but this Wonderful-Virtue Bodhisattva-mahāsattva [whom you see here now].

"Flower-Virtue! This Wonderful-Voice Bodhisattva already made offerings to innumerable Buddhas, attended on them, and planted the roots of virtue a long time ago. He also already saw hundreds of thousands of billions of nayutas of Buddhas, that is, as many Buddhas as there are sands in the River Ganges.

"Flower-Virtue! Now you see Wonderful-Voice Bodhisattva here and nowhere else. But formerly he transformed himself into various living beings and expounded this sūtra to others in various places. He became King Brahman, King Śakra, Freedom

God, Great-Freedom God, a great general in heaven, Vaiśravaṇa Heavenly-King, a wheel-turning-holy-king, the king of a small country, a rich man, a householder, a prime minister, a brāhmaṇa, a bhikṣu, a bhikṣuṇī, an upāsaka, an upāsikā, the wife of a rich man, that of a householder, that of a prime minister, that of a brāhmaṇa, a boy, a girl, a god, a dragon, a yakṣa, a gandharva, an asura, a garuḍa, a kiṃnara, a mahoraga, a human being or a nonhuman being. [After he transformed himself into one or another of these living beings,] he expounded this sūtra, and saved the hellish denizens, hungry spirits, animals, and all the other living beings in the places of difficulties. When he entered an imperial harem, he became a woman and expounded this sūtra.

"Flower-Virtue! This Wonderful-Voice Bodhisattva protects all living beings in this Sahā-World. He transforms himself into one or another of these various living beings in this Sahā-World and expounds this sūtra to all living beings without reducing his supernatural powers, [his power of] transformation, and his wisdom. He illumines this Sahā-World with the many [rays of light] of his wisdom, and causes all living beings to know what they should know. He also does the same in the innumerable worlds of the ten quarters, that is, in as many worlds as there are sands in the River Ganges. He takes the shape of a Śrāvaka and expounds the Dharma to those who are to be saved by a Śrāvaka. He takes the shape of a Pratyekabuddha and expounds the Dharma to those who are to be saved by a Pratyekabuddha. He takes the shape of another Bodhisattva and expounds the Dharma to those who are to be saved by that Bodhisattva. He takes the shape of a Buddha and expounds the Dharma to those who are to be saved by a Buddha. He takes these various shapes according to the capacities of those who are to be saved. He shows his extinction to those who are to be saved by his extinction. Flower-Virtue! Such are the great supernatural powers and the power of wisdom obtained by Wonderful-Voice Bodhisattva-mahāsattva."

Thereupon Flower-Virtue Bodhisattva said to the Buddha:

"World-Honored One! This Wonderful-Voice Bodhisattva planted deeply the roots of good. World-Honored One! What is the name of the samādhi by which he can transform himself into various living beings and appear in various places to save all living beings?"

The Buddha said to Flower-Virtue Bodhisattva:

"Good man! This is called the 'samādhi by which one can transform oneself into any other living being.' Wonderful-Voice Bodhisattva entered into this samādhi and benefited innumerable living beings as previously stated."

When the Buddha expounded this chapter of Wonderful-Voice Bodhisattva, the eighty-four thousand people, who had come accompanying Wonderful-Voice Bodhisattva, obtained the ability to practice the samādhi by which they could transform themselves into other living beings. Innumerable Bodhisattvas of this Sahā-World also obtained the ability to practice this samādhi. They also obtained dhāraṇīs.

Thereupon Wonderful-Voice Bodhisattva-mahāsattva made offerings to Śākyamuni Buddha and to the stūpa of Many-Treasures Buddha, [benefited the living beings of the Sahā-World,] and left for his home world[, accompanied by the eighty-four thousand Bodhisattvas]. As they passed through the [one hundred and eight billion nayuta] worlds, the ground of those worlds quaked in the six ways; lotus-flowers of treasures rained down; and hundreds of thousands of billions of kinds of music were made. Having reached his home world, accompanied by the eighty-four thousand Bodhisattvas who surrounded him, he came to Pure-Flower-Star-King-Wisdom Buddha. He said to the Buddha:

"World-Honored One! I went to the Sahā-World and benefited the living beings there. I saw Śākyamuni Buddha and the stūpa of Many-Treasures Buddha.[3] I bowed and made offerings to them. I also saw Mañjuśrī Bodhisattva, the Son of the King of the Dharma. [I also saw] Medicine-King Bodhisattva, Endeavor-Power-Obtainer Bodhisattva, Brave-In-Giving Bodhisattva, and others. I also caused

3 He saw only the stūpa, not Many-Treasures Buddha. From this we see that the door of the stūpa was shut at the end of Chapter XXII. See p. 304.

these eighty-four thousand Bodhisattvas to obtain the ability to practice the samādhi by which they could transform themselves into any other living being."

When [Śākyamuni Buddha] expounded this chapter of the Coming and Going of Wonderful-Voice Bodhisattva, forty-two thousand gods obtained the truth of birthlessness, and Flower-Virtue Bodhisattva obtained the ability to practice the samādhi for the Lotus Flower of the Wonderful Dharma.

[Here ends] the Seventh Volume of the Sūtra of the Lotus Flower of the Wonderful Dharma.

CHAPTER XXV

THE UNIVERSAL GATE OF WORLD-VOICE-PERCEIVER BODHISATTVA

Thereupon Endless-Intent Bodhisattva rose from his seat, bared his right shoulder, joined his hands together towards the Buddha, and said, "World-Honored One! Why is World-Voice-Perceiver Bodhisattva called World-Voice-Perceiver?"

The Buddha said to Endless-Intent Bodhisattva:

"Good man! If many hundreds of thousands of billions of living beings hear [the name of] World-Voice-Perceiver Bodhisattva and call his name with all their hearts when they are under various sufferings, World-Voice-Perceiver Bodhisattva will immediately perceive their voices, and cause them to emancipate themselves [from the sufferings]. Those who keep the name of this World-Voice-Perceiver Bodhisattva will not be burned when they are put into a conflagration [because they are protected] by the supernatural powers of this Bodhisattva. Those who call his name will be able to take ground when they are washed by an inundation. Suppose hundreds of thousands of billions of living beings are crossing an ocean in order to obtain gold, silver, lapis lazuli, shell, agate, coral, amber, pearl, and other treasures, and suppose the ship carrying them is blown to the country of rākṣasa-devils by a storm. If one of the crew calls the name of World-Voice-Perceiver Bodhisattva, all the crew will be saved from the attacks of the rākṣasas. Because of this, [this Bodhisattva] is called World-Voice-Perceiver.

"If anyone calls the name of World-Voice-Perceiver Bodhisattva when he is about to be killed, the sword or stick raised against him will suddenly break asunder, and he will be saved. If as many yakṣas and rākṣasas as to fill one thousand million Sumeru-worlds hear a person call the name of World-Voice-Perceiver

Bodhisattva when they come to him with the intention of killing him, those devils will not be able even to see him with their malicious eyes, and needless to say, kill him. If anyone, guilty or not, calls the name of World-Voice-Perceiver Bodhisattva when he is bound up in manacles, fetters, pillories or chains, those things [in which he is bound up] will break asunder, and he will be saved. Suppose the chief of a party of merchants is leading his party carrying invaluable treasures along a dangerous road haunted by as many bandits as to fill one thousand million Sumeru-worlds, and suppose one of the members of the party says [to others], 'Good men! Do not be afraid! Call the name of World-Voice-Perceiver Bodhisattva with all your hearts! This Bodhisattva gives fearlessness to all living beings. If you call his name, you will be saved from [the attacks of] these bandits.' If the other members of the party hear this and say simultaneously, 'Namas to World-Voice-Perceiver Bodhisattva,' all of them will be saved because of their calling of his name. Endless-Intent! The supernatural powers of World-Voice-Perceiver Bodhisattva-mahāsattva are as great as previously stated.

"Those who have much lust will be saved from lust if they constantly think of World-Voice-Perceiver Bodhisattva and respect him. Those who have much anger will be saved from anger if they constantly think of World-Voice-Perceiver Bodhisattva and respect him. Those who have much stupidity will be saved from stupidity if they constantly think of World-Voice-Perceiver Bodhisattva and respect him. Endless-Intent! World-Voice-Perceiver Bodhisattva has these great supernatural powers. He gives many benefits to all living beings. Therefore, they should constantly think of him.

"A woman who, wishing to have a boy, bows and makes offerings to World-Voice-Perceiver Bodhisattva, will be able to give birth to a boy endowed with merits, virtues and wisdom. [A woman] who, wishing to have a girl, [does the same,] will be able to give birth to a beautiful girl who will be loved and respected by many people because of the roots of virtue which the [newly-born] girl planted in her previous existence. Endless-Intent! Because World-Voice-Perceiver Bodhisattva has these powers, the merits of those who respect him and bow to him will not be fruitless.

Therefore, all living beings should keep the name of World-Voice-Perceiver Bodhisattva.

"Endless-Intent! Suppose a good man or woman keeps the names of six thousand and two hundred million Bodhisattvas, that is, of as many Bodhisattvas as there are sands in the River Ganges, and offers drink, food, clothing, bedding and medicine to them throughout his or her life. What do you think of this? Are his or her merits many or not?"

Endless-Intent said, "Very many. World-Honored One!"

The Buddha said:

"Anyone who keeps the name of World-Voice-Perceiver Bodhisattva and bows and makes offerings to him even for a moment, will be given as many merits as to be given to the good man or woman as previously stated. The merits will not be exhausted even after hundreds of thousands of billions of kalpas. Endless-Intent! Anyone who keeps the name of World-Voice-Perceiver Bodhisattva will be given these benefits of innumerable merits and virtues."

Endless-Intent Bodhisattva said to the Buddha:

"World-Honored One! How does World-Voice-Perceiver Bodhisattva go about this Sāha-World? How does he expound the Dharma to the living beings? What expedients does he employ?"

The Buddha said to Endless-Intent Bodhisattva:

"Good man! In a certain world, World-Voice-Perceiver Bodhisattva takes the shape of a Buddha and expounds the Dharma to those who are to be saved by a Buddha. He takes the shape of a Pratyekabuddha and expounds the Dharma to those who are to be saved by a Pratyekabuddha. He takes the shape of a Śrāvaka and expounds the Dharma to those who are to be saved by a Śrāvaka. He takes the shape of King Brahman and expounds the Dharma to those who are to be saved by King Brahman. He takes the shape of King Śakra and expounds the Dharma to those who are to be saved by King Śakra. He takes the shape of Freedom God and expounds the Dharma to those who are to be saved by Freedom God. He takes the shape of Great-Freedom God and expounds the Dharma to those who are to be saved by Great-Freedom God. He takes the shape of a great general in heaven and expounds the Dharma to those who are to be saved by a great general in heaven. He takes the shape of Vaiśravaṇa and expounds the Dharma to those who are to be saved by Vaiśravaṇa. He takes the shape of the king of a small country and expounds the Dharma to those who are to be saved by the king of a small country. He takes the shape of a rich man and expounds the Dharma to those who are to be saved by a rich man. He takes the shape of a householder and expounds the Dharma to those who are to be saved by a householder. He takes the shape of a prime minister and expounds the Dharma to those who are to be saved by a prime minister. He takes the shape of a brāhmaṇa and expounds the Dharma to those who are to be saved by a brāhmaṇa. He takes the shape of a bhikṣu, a bhikṣuṇī, an upāsaka or an upāsikā and expounds the Dharma to those who are to be saved by a bhikṣu, a bhikṣuṇī, an upāsaka or an upāsikā. He takes the shape of a wife and expounds the Dharma to those who are to be saved by the wife of a rich man, of a householder, of a prime minister, or of a brāhmaṇa. He takes the shape of a boy or a girl and expounds the Dharma to those who are to be saved by a boy or a girl. He takes the shape of a god, a dragon, a yakṣa, a gandharva, an asura, a garuḍa, a kiṃnara, a mahoraga, a human being or a nonhuman being and expounds the Dharma to those who are to be saved by one or another of these living beings. He takes the shape of Vajra-Holding God and expounds the Dharma to those who are to be saved by Vajra-Holding God.

"Endless-Intent! This World-Voice-Perceiver Bodhisattva does these meritorious deeds. He takes various shapes, walks about many worlds, and saves the living beings [of those worlds]. Make offerings to World-Voice-Perceiver Bodhisattva with all your hearts! This World-Voice-Perceiver Bodhisattva-mahāsattva gives fearlessness [to those who are] in fearful emergencies. Therefore, he is called the 'Giver of Fearlessness' in this Sahā-World."

The Endless-Intent Bodhisattva said to the Buddha, "World-Honored One! Now I will make an offering to World-Voice-Perceiver Bodhisattva." From around his neck, he took a necklace of many gems worth hundreds of thousands of ryō of gold, and offered it [to the Bodhisattva], saying, "Man of Virtue! Receive this necklace of wonderful treasures! I offer this to you according to the Dharma!"

World-Voice-Perceiver Bodhisattva did not consent to receive it. Endless-Intent said to World-Voice-Perceiver Bodhisattva again, "Man of Virtue! Receive this necklace out of your compassion towards us!"

Thereupon the Buddha said to World-Voice-Perceiver Bodhisattva:

"Receive it out of your compassion towards this Endless-Intent Bodhisattva, towards the four kinds of devotees, and towards the other living beings including gods, dragons, yakṣas, gandharvas, asuras, garuḍas, kiṃnaras, mahoragas, men and nonhuman beings!"

Thereupon World-Voice-Perceiver Bodhisattva received the necklace out of his compassion towards the four kinds of devotees, and towards the other living beings including gods, dragons, men and nonhuman beings. He divided [the necklace] into two parts, and offered one part of it to Śākyamuni Buddha and the other to the stūpa of Many-Treasures Buddha.[1]

[The Buddha said to Endless-Intent Bodhisattva,] "Endless-Intent! World-Voice-Perceiver Bodhisattva goes about the Sahā-World, employing these supernatural powers without hindrance."

Thereupon Endless-Intent Bodhisattva asked the Buddha in gāthās:[2]

> World-Honored One with the wonderful marks
> I ask you about this again.
> Why is the son of the Buddha
> Called World-Voice-Perceiver?

The Honorable One with the wonderful marks answered Endless-Intent in gāthās:[3]

---

1 The stūpa of Many-Treasures Buddha is not referred to in the following chapters.

2 These gāthās and the prose section following them up to the end of this chapter were not translated by Kumārajīva. See Introduction.

3 These two lines were primarily prose, and not included in the gāthās.

Listen! World-Voice-Perceiver practiced
According to the conditions of the places [of salvation].
His vow to save [people] is as deep as the sea.
You cannot fathom it even for kalpas.

On many hundreds of thousands of millions of Buddhas
He attended and made a great and pure vow.
I will tell you about his vow in brief.
If you hear his name, and see him,
And think of him constantly,
You will be able to eliminate all sufferings.

Suppose you are thrown into a large pit of fire
By someone who has an intention of killing you.
If you think of the power of World-Voice-Perceiver,
The pit of fire will change into a pond of water.

Suppose you are in a ship drifting on a great ocean
Where dragons, fish and devils are rampant.
If you think of the power of World-Voice-Perceiver,
The ship will not be sunk by the waves.

Suppose you are pushed
Off the top of Mt. Sumeru by someone.
If you think of the power of World-Voice-Perceiver,
You will be able to stay in the air like the sun.

Suppose you are chased by an evil man,
And pushed off [the top of] a mountain made of diamond.
If you think of the power of World-Voice-Perceiver,
You will not lose even a hair.

Suppose bandits are surrounding you,
And attempting to kill you with swords.
If you think of the power of World-Voice-Perceiver,
The bandits will become compassionate towards you.

Suppose you are sentenced to death,
And the sword is drawn to behead you.
If you think of the power of World-Voice-Perceiver,
The sword will suddenly break asunder.

Suppose you are bound up
In pillories, chains, manacles or fetters.
If you think of the power of World-Voice-Perceiver,
You will be released from them.

Suppose someone curses you to death,
Or attempts to kill you by various poisons.
If you think of the power of World-Voice-Perceiver,
Death will be brought to that person, instead.

Suppose you meet rākṣasas
Or poisonous dragons or other devils.
If you think of the power of World-Voice-Perceiver,
They will not kill you.

Suppose you are surrounded by wild animals
Which have sharp, fearful tusks and claws.
If you think of the power of World-Voice-Perceiver,
They will flee away to distant places.

Suppose you meet lizards, snakes, vipers or scorpions
Emitting poisonous vapor like flames.
If you think of the power of World-Voice-Perceiver,
They will go away as you call his name.[4]

Suppose clouds arise, lightning flashes, thunder peals,
Hail falls, and a heavy rain comes down.
If you think of the power of World-Voice-Perceiver,
The thunderstorm will stop at once.

---

4 Here we notice that "to think of the power of World-Voice-Perceiver" means "to call his name."

World-Voice-Perceiver will save
All living beings from misfortunes
And from innumerable sufferings of the world
By the wonderful power of his wisdom.

He has these supernatural powers.
He employs various expedients with his wisdom.
In the ten quarters there is no kṣetra
In which he does not appear at all.

Hell, the region of hungry spirits, and the region of animals,
That is, the [three] evil regions will be eliminated.
The sufferings of birth, old age, disease and death
Will gradually be eliminated.

He sees the truth of all things and their purity.
He sees all things with his great wisdom.
He sees all things with loving-kindness and compassion.
Think of him constantly! Look up at him constantly!

All darkness is dispelled by the light of his wisdom
As spotless and as pure as the light of the sun.
The light destroys the dangers of wind and fire,
And illumines the whole world brightly.

His precepts out of his loving-kindness
brace us up as thunderbolts.
His wishes out of his compassion are as wonderful
as large clouds.
He pours the rain of the Dharma as sweet as nectar,
And extinguishes the fire of illusions.

Suppose you are in a law-court for a suit,
Or on a battlefield, and are seized with fear.
If you think of the power of World-Voice-Perceiver,
All your enemies will flee away.

His wonderful voice [comes from] his perceiving
the voice of the world.
It is like the voice of Brahman, like the sound
of a tidal wave.
It excels all the other voices of the world.
Therefore, think of him constantly!

Do not doubt him even at a moment's thought!
The Pure Saint World-Voice-Perceiver is reliable
When you suffer, and when you are confronted
With the calamity of death.

By all these merits, he sees
All living beings with his compassionate eyes.
The ocean of his accumulated merits is boundless.
Therefore, bow before him!

Thereupon Earth-Holding Bodhisattva rose from his seat, proceeded to the Buddha, and said to him:

"World-Honored One! Those who hear of his supernatural powers by which he opened the universal gate without hindrance, and which are expounded in this chapter of World-Voice-Perceiver Bodhisattva, know this, will be able to obtain not a few merits."

When the Buddha expounded this chapter of the Universal Gate, the eighty-four thousand living beings in the congregation began to aspire for the unparalleled Anuttara-samyak-saṃbodhi.

CHAPTER XXVI

DHĀRAṆĪS

Thereupon Medicine-King Bodhisattva rose from his seat, bared his right shoulder, joined his hands together towards the Buddha, and said to him:

"World-Honored One! How many merits will be given to the good men or women who keep, read, recite, understand or copy the Sūtra of the Lotus Flower of the Wonderful Dharma?"

The Buddha said to him:

"Suppose some good men or women make offerings to eight hundred billion nayuta Buddhas, that is, as many Buddhas as there are sands in the River Ganges. What do you think of this? Are the merits given to them many or not?"

"Very many, World-Honored One!" The Buddha said: "More merits will be given to the good men or women who keep, read or recite even a single gāthā of four lines of this sūtra, understand the meanings of it or act according to it."

Thereupon Medicine-King Bodhisattva said to the Buddha, "World-Honored One! Now I will give dhāraṇī-spells to the expounder of the Dharma[1] in order to protect him."

Then he uttered spells:[2]

"Ani (1), mani (2), manei (3), mamanei (4), shirei (5), sharitei (6), shamya (7), shabi-tai (8), sentei (9), mokutei (10), mokutabi (11), shabi (12), aishabi (13), sōbi (14), shabi (15), shaei (16), ashaei (17), agini (18), sentei (19), shabi (20), darani (21), arokya-basai-hashabi-

1 "The Dharma" means the Sūtra of the Lotus Flower of the Wonderful Dharma.

2 The Japanese pronunciation of the dhāraṇīs given in this chapter and in Chapter XXVIII is quoted from the Nissōbon Edition of the Myōhōrengekyō published about the beginning of the eighteenth century.

shani (22), neibitei (23), abentaraneibitei (24), atantahareishudai (25), ukurei (26), mukurei (27), ararei (28), hararei (29), shukyashi (30), asammasambi (31), botsudabikirijittei (32), darumaharishitei (33), sōgyanekkushanei (34), bashabashashudai(35), mantara (36), mantarashayata (37), urotaurota (38), kyōsharya(39), ashara (40), ashayataya (41), abaro (42), amanyanataya (43)."[3]

[He said to the Buddha:]

"World-Honored One! These dhāraṇīs, these divine spells, have already been uttered by six thousand and two hundred million Buddhas, that is, as many Buddhas as there are sands in the River Ganges. Those who attack and abuse this teacher of the Dharma should be considered to have attacked and abused those Buddhas."

Thereupon Śākyamuni Buddha praised Medicine-King Bodhisattva, saying:

"Excellent, excellent, Medicine-King! You uttered these dhāraṇīs in order to protect this teacher of the Dharma out of your compassion towards him. You will be able to give many benefits to all living beings."

Thereupon Brave-In-Giving Bodhisattva said to the Buddha:

"World-Honored One! I also will utter dhāraṇīs in order to protect the person who reads, recites and keeps the Sūtra of the Lotus Flower of the Wonderful Dharma. If he keeps these dhāraṇīs, this teacher of the Dharma will not have his weak points taken advantage of by any yakṣa, rākṣasa, pūtana, kṛtya, kumbhāṇḍa or hungry spirit."

Then he uttered spells before the Buddha:

---

3 In Wogihara's text, it reads, "Anye manye mane mamane citte carite same samitā viśānte mukte muktatame same aviṣame samasame jaye kṣaye akṣaye akṣiṇe śānte samite dhāraṇi āloka-bhāṣe pratyavekṣaṇi nidhiru abhyantara-niviṣṭe abhyantara-pāriśuddhi mutkule mutkule araḍe paraḍe sukāṅkṣi asamasame buddhavilokite dharma-parīkṣite saṃgha-nirghoṣaṇi nirghoṇi bhayābhaya-viśodhani mantre mantrākṣayate rute ruta-kauśalye akṣaye akṣaya-vanatāye vakkule valoḍa amanyanatāye svāhā." In Kern's translation, it runs, "Anye manye mane mamane citte carite same, samitāvi, sānte, mukte, muktatame, same aviṣame, samasame, jaye, kṣaye, akṣīṇe, sānte sani, dhāraṇi ālokabhāṣe, pratyavekṣaṇi, nidhini, abhyantaravisiṣṭe, utkule mutkule, asaḍe, paraḍe, sukāṅkṣī, asamasame, buddhavilokite, dharmaparīkṣite, saṅghanirghoṣaṇi, nirgoṣaṇī bhayābhayasodhanī, mantre mantrākṣayate, rutakauśalye, akṣaye, akṣavanatāya, vakule valoḍa, amanyatāya."

"Zarei (1), makazarei (2), ukki (3), mokki (4), arei (5), arahatei (6), netsureitei (7), netsureitahatei (8), ichini (9), ichini (10), shichini (11), netsureichini (12), netsurichihachi (13)."[4]

[He said to the Buddha:]

"World-Honored One! These dhāraṇīs, these divine spells, have already been uttered by as many Buddhas as there are sands in the River Ganges. Those Buddhas uttered them with joy. Those who attack and abuse this teacher of the Dharma should be considered to have attacked and abused those Buddhas."

Thereupon Vaiśravaṇa Heavenly-King, the Protector of the World, said to the Buddha, "World-Honored One! I also will utter dhāraṇīs in order to protect this teacher of the Dharma out of my compassion towards all living beings."

Then he uttered spells, "Ari (1), nari (2), tonari (3), anaro (4), nabi (5), kunabi (6)."[5]

[He said to the Buddha:]

"World-Honored One! I will protect this teacher of the Dharma with these divine spells. I also will protect the person who keeps this sūtra so that he may have no trouble within a hundred yojanas' distance [from here]."

Thereupon World-Holding Heavenly-King, accompanied by thousands of billions of nayutas of gandharvas who were surrounding him respectfully, came to the Buddha, joined his hands together, and said to him, "World-Honored One! I also will protect the keeper of the Sūtra of the Lotus Flower of the Wonderful Dharma with dhāraṇīs, with divine spells."

Then he uttered spells, "Akyanei (1), kyanei (2), kuri (3), kendari (4), sendari (5), matōgi (6), jōguri (7), furoshani (8), atchi (9)."[6]

[He said to the Buddha:]

---

4 In Wogihara's text, it reads, "Jvale mahā-jvale ukke tukke mukke aḍe aḍāvati nṛtye nṛtyāvati iṭṭini viṭṭini ciṭṭini nṛtyani nṛtyāvati svāhā." In Kern's translation, it reads, "Jvale mahājvale, ukke mukke, aḍe aḍāvati, tṛtye tṛtyāvati, iṭini viṭini ciṭini tṛṭṭi tṛṭyāvati svāhā."

5 In Wogihara's text, it reads, "Aṭṭe taṭṭe naṭṭe vanaṭṭe anaḍe nāḍi kunaḍi svāhā." In Kern's translation, "taṭṭe" is omitted.

6 In Wogihara's text, it runs, "Agaṇe gaṇe gauri gandhāri caṇḍāli mātaṅgi pukkasi saṃkule vrūsali sisi svāhā." In Kern's translation, "sisi" is omitted.

"World-Honored One! These dhāraṇīs, these divine spells, have already been uttered by four thousand and two hundred million Buddhas. Those who attack and abuse this teacher of the Dharma should be considered to have attacked and abused those Buddhas."

There are rākṣasīs called 1. Lambā, 2. Vilambā, 3. Crooked-Teeth, 4. Flower-Teeth, 5. Black-Teeth, 6. Many-Hairs, 7. Insatiable, 8. Necklace-Holding, 9. Kuntī, and 10. Plunderer-Of-Energy-Of-All-Beings. These ten rākṣasīs [and their attendants] came to the Buddha, together with Mother-Of-Devils and her children and attendants. They said to the Buddha simultaneously:

"World-Honored One! We also will protect the person who reads, recites and keeps the Sūtra of the Lotus Flower of the Wonderful Dharma so that he may have no trouble. No one shall take advantage of the weak points of this teacher of the Dharma."

Then they uttered spells before the Buddha:

"Ideibi (1), ideibin (2), ideibi (3), adeibi (4), ideibi (5), deibi (6), deibi (7), deibi (8), deibi (9), deibi (10), rokei (11), rokei (12), rokei (13), rokei (14), takei (15), takei (16), takei (17), tokei (18), tokei (19)."[7]

[They said to the Buddha:]

"Anyone may step on our heads, but shall not trouble this teacher of the Dharma. Neither shall any yakṣa, rākṣasa, hungry spirit, pūtana, kṛtya, vetāḍa, kumbhāṇḍa, umāraka, apasmāraka, yakṣa-kṛtya or human kṛtya. Neither shall anyone who causes others to suffer from a fever for a day, two days, three days, four days, seven days or forever. Neither shall anyone who takes the shape of a man, a woman, a boy or a girl and appears in his dream."

Then they sang in gāthās before the Buddha:

Anyone who does not keep our spells
But troubles the expounder of the Dharma
Shall have his head split into seven pieces
Just as the branches of the arjaka-tree [are split].

---

7 In Wogihara's text, it reads, "Iti me iti me iti me iti me iti me, nime nime nime nime nime, ruhe ruhe ruhe ruhe ruhe, stuhe stuhe stuhe stuhe stuhe svāhā." In Kern's translation, it reads the same.

Anyone who attacks this teacher of the Dharma
Will receive the same retribution
As to be received by the person who kills his parents,
Or who makes [sesame] oil without taking out worms
  [from the sesame],
Or who deceives others by using wrong measures
  and scales,
Or by Devadatta who split the Saṃgha.

Having sung these gāthās, the rākṣasīs said to the Buddha:

"World-Honored One! We also will protect the person who keeps, reads and recites this sūtra, and acts according to it so that he may be peaceful, that he may have no trouble, and that poison taken by him may be neutralized."

The Buddha said to the rākṣasīs:

"Excellent, excellent! Your merits will be immeasurable even when you protect the person who keeps only the name of the Sūtra of the Lotus Flower of the Wonderful Dharma. Needless to say, so will be your merits when you protect the person who keeps the sūtra itself, and makes to a copy of this sūtra hundreds of thousands of offerings such as flowers, incense, necklaces, powdered incense, incense applicable to the skin, incense to burn, streamers, canopies, music, and various lamps like lamps of butter oil, oil lamps, lamps of perfumed oil, lamps of sumanas-flower oil, lamps of campaka flower oil, lamps of vārṣika-flower oil, and lamps of utpala-flower oil. Kuntī! You [rākṣasīs] and your attendants should protect this teacher of the Dharma."

When the Buddha expounded this chapter of Dhāraṇīs, sixty eight thousand people obtained the truth of birthlessness.

CHAPTER XXVII

KING WONDERFUL-ADORNMENT AS THE PREVIOUS LIFE OF A BODHISATTVA

Thereupon the Buddha said to the great multitude:

"Innumerable, inconceivable, asaṃkhya kalpas ago, there lived a Buddha called Cloud-Thunderpeal-Star-King-Flower-Wisdom, the Tathāgata, the Arhat, the Samyak-saṃbuddha. His world was called Light-Adornment; the kalpa in which he lived, Gladly-Seen. Under that Buddha lived a king called Wonderful-Adornment. His wife was called Pure-Virtue. They had two sons, Pure-Store and Pure-Eyes by name. The two sons had great supernatural powers, merits, virtues and wisdom. A long time ago, they had already practiced the Way which Bodhisattvas should practice. They had already practiced the dāna-pāramitā, the śīla-pāramitā, the kṣānti-pāramitā, the virya-pāramitā, the dhyāna-pāramitā, the prajñā-pāramitā, and the pāramitā of expediency. They also had already obtained [the four states of mind towards all living beings:] compassion, loving-kindness, joy and impartiality. They also had already practiced the thirty-seven ways to enlightenment. They had done all this perfectly and clearly. They also had already obtained the samādhis of Bodhisattvas: that is, the samādhi for purity, the samādhi for the sun and the stars, the samādhi for pure light, the samādhi for pure form, the samādhi for pure brightness, the samādhi for permanent adornment, and the samādhi for the great treasury of powers and virtues. They had already practiced all these samādhis.

"Thereupon that Buddha expounded the Sūtra of the Lotus Flower of the Wonderful Dharma, wishing to lead King Wonderful-Adornment also out of his compassion towards all living beings. The two sons, Pure-Store and Pure-Eyes, came to their mother, joined their ten fingers and palms together, and said, 'Mother! Go to Cloud-Thunderpeal-Star-King-Flower-Wisdom Buddha! We also will go to attend on him, approach him, make offerings to him, and bow to him because he is expounding the Sūtra of the Lotus Flower of the Wonderful Dharma to all gods and men. Hear and receive [the sūtra]!'

"The mother said to them, '[Yes, I will. But] your father believes in heresy. He is deeply attached to the teachings of brāhmaṇas. Go and tell him to allow us to go [to that Buddha]!'

"Pure-Store and Pure-Eyes joined their ten fingers and palms together, and said to their mother, 'We were born in this family attached to wrong views although we are sons of the King of the Dharma.'

"The mother said to them, 'Show some wonders to your father out of your compassion towards him! If he sees [the wonders], he will have his mind purified and allow us to go to that Buddha.'

"Thereupon the two sons went up to the sky seven times as high as the tāla-tree, and displayed various wonders because they were thinking of their father. They walked, stood, sat, and reclined in the sky. Then they issued water from the upper parts of their bodies, and fire from the lower parts. Then they issued water from the lower parts of their bodies, and fire from the upper parts. Then they became giants large enough to fill the sky, became dwarfs, and became giants again. Then they disappeared from the sky and suddenly appeared on the earth. Then they dived into the earth just as into water, and stepped on the surface of water just as on the earth. [Then they went up to the sky and stayed there.] By displaying these various wonders, they purified the mind of their father, that is, of the king, and caused him to understand the Dharma by faith.

"Seeing [these wonders displayed by] the supernatural powers of his sons, the father had the greatest joy that he had ever had. He joined his hands together towards his sons [staying in the sky], and said, 'Who is your teacher? Whose disciples are you?'

"The two sons said, 'Great King! Cloud-Thunderpeal-Star-King-Flower-Wisdom Buddha, who is now sitting on the seat of the Dharma under the Bodhi-tree of the seven treasures, is expounding the Sūtra of the Lotus Flower of the Wonderful Dharma to all the gods and men of the world. He is our teacher. We are his disciples.'

"The father said to them, 'I also wish to see your teacher. I will go with you.'

"Thereupon the two sons descended from the sky, came to their mother, joined their hands together, and said to her, 'Our father, the king, has now understood the Dharma by faith. He is now able to aspire for Anuttara-samyak-saṃbodhi. We did the work of the Buddha for the sake of our father. Mother! Allow us to renounce the world and practice the Way under that Buddha!'

"Thereupon the two sons, wishing to repeat what they had said, said to their mother in gāthās:

Mother! Allow us to renounce the world
And become śramaṇas!
It is difficult to see a Buddha.
We will follow that Buddha and study.

To see a Buddha is as difficult
As to see an udumbara[-flower].
To avert a misfortune is also difficult.
Allow us to renounce the world!

"The mother said, 'I allow you to renounce the world because it is difficult to see a Buddha.'

"Thereupon the [father came to them. The] two sons said to their parents, 'Excellent, Father and Mother! Go to Cloud-Thunderpeal-Star-King-Flower-Wisdom Buddha, see him, and make offerings to him because to see a Buddha is as difficult as to see an udumbara-flower or as for a one-eyed tortoise to find a hole in a floating piece of wood! We accumulated so many merits in our previous existence that we are now able to meet the teachings of the Buddha in this life of ours. Allow us to renounce the world because it is difficult to see a Buddha, and also because it is difficult to have such a good opportunity as this to see him.'

"Thereupon the eighty-four thousand people in the harem of King Wonderful-Adornment became able to keep the Sūtra of the Lotus Flower of the Wonderful Dharma.

"Pure-Eyes Bodhisattva had already practiced the samādhi for the Lotus Flower of the Wonderful Dharma for a long time. Pure-Store Bodhisattva had already practiced the samādhi for the release from evil regions in order to release all living beings from evil regions for many hundreds of thousands of billions of kalpas.

"Now the queen practiced the samādhi for the assembly of Buddhas, and understood the treasury of their hidden core. The two sons led their father by these expedients and caused him to understand the teachings of the Buddha by faith and to wish [to act according to those teachings].

"Thereupon King Wonderful-Adornment, Queen Pure-Virtue, and their two sons came to that Buddha. The king was accompanied by his ministers and attendants; the queen, by her ladies and attendants; and their two sons, by forty-two thousand men. They worshiped the feet of that Buddha with their heads, walked around the Buddha three times, retired, and stood to one side.

"Thereupon the Buddha expounded the Dharma to the king, showed him the Way, taught him, benefited him, and caused him to rejoice. The king had great joy. The king and queen took off their necklaces of pearls worth hundreds of thousands, and strewed the necklaces to the Buddha. The necklaces flew up to the sky [seven times as high as the tāla-tree], and changed into a jeweled platform equipped with four pillars. On the platform was a couch of great treasures, and thousands of millions of heavenly garments were spread [on the couch]. The Buddha [went up,] sat cross-legged [on the couch], and emitted great rays of light. King Wonderful-Adornment thought, 'The Buddha is exceptional. He is exceedingly handsome. He has the most wonderful form.'

"Thereupon Cloud-Thunderpeal-Star-King-Flower-Wisdom Buddha said to the four kinds of devotees, 'Do you see this King Wonderful-Adornment standing before me with his hands joined together, or not? This king will become a bhikṣu under me, strenuously study and practice the various ways to the enlightenment of the Buddha, and then become a Buddha called

Śāla-Tree-King in a world called Great-Light in a kalpa called Great-Height-King. Śāla-Tree-King Buddha will be accompanied by innumerable Bodhisattvas and Śrāvakas. The ground of his world will be even. [King Wonderful-Adornment] will have these merits.'

"Thereupon the king abdicated from the throne in favor of his younger brother, renounced the world, and with his wife, two sons, and attendants, practiced the Way under that Buddha. After he renounced the world, the king acted according to the Sūtra of the Lotus Flower of the Wonderful Dharma constantly and strenuously for eighty-four thousand years. Then he practiced the samādhi for the adornment of all pure merits. Then he went up to the sky seven times as high as the tāla-tree, and said to that Buddha, 'World-Honored One! These two sons of mine did the work of the Buddha. They converted me from wrong views by displaying wonders. They caused me to dwell peacefully in your teachings. They caused me to see you. These two sons of mine are my teachers. They appeared in my family in order to benefit me. They inspired the roots of good which I had planted in my previous existence.'

"Thereupon Cloud-Thunderpeal-Star-King-Flower-Wisdom Buddha said to King Wonderful-Adornment, 'So it is, so it is. It is just as you say. The good men or women who plant the roots of good will obtain teachers in their successive lives. The teachers will do the work of the Buddha, show the Way [to them], teach them, benefit them, cause them to rejoice, and cause them to enter into the Way to Anuttara-samyak-saṃbodhi. Great King, know this! A teacher is a great cause [of your enlightenment] because he leads you, and causes you to see a Buddha and aspire for Anuttara-samyak-saṃbodhi. Great King! Do you see these two sons of yours, or not? They made offerings to six trillion and five hundred thousand billion Buddhas, that is, as many Buddhas as there are sands in the River Ganges, in their previous existence. They attended on those Buddhas respectfully. They kept the Sūtra of the Lotus Flower of the Wonderful Dharma under those Buddhas, and caused the people of wrong views to have right views out of their compassion towards them.'

"King Wonderful-Adornment came down from the sky and said to that Buddha [staying in the sky], 'World-Honored One! You are exceedingly exceptional. You have merits and wisdom. Therefore, the fleshy tuft on your head shines bright. Your eyes are long, wide, and deep blue in color. The curls between your eyebrows are as white as a bright moon. Your teeth are white, regular and bright. Your lips are as red and as beautiful as the fruits of a bimba-tree.'

"Thereupon King Wonderful-Adornment, having praised the Buddha for his many hundreds of thousands of billions of merits including those previously stated, joined his hands together towards the Tathāgata, and with all his heart, said to that Buddha again, 'World-Honored One! I have never seen anyone like you before. Your teachings have these inconceivable, wonderful merits. The practices performed according to your teachings and precepts are peaceful and pleasant. From today on, I will not act according to my own mind. I will not have wrong views, arrogance, anger or any other evil thought.' Having said this, he bowed to that Buddha and retired."

The Buddha said to the great multitude:

"What do you think of this? King Wonderful-Adornment was no one but Flower-Virtue Bodhisattva of today. Queen Pure-Virtue was no one but the Light-Adornment-Appearance Bodhisattva who is now before me. She appeared in that world out of her compassion towards King Wonderful-Adornment and his attendants. The two sons were Medicine-King Bodhisattva and Medicine-Superior Bodhisattva of today. Medicine-King Bodhisattva and Medicine-Superior Bodhisattva have already obtained those great merits. Because they planted the roots of virtue under many hundreds of thousands of billions of Buddhas [in their previous existence], they obtained those inconceivable merits. All gods and men in the world should bow to those who know the names of these two Bodhisattvas."

When the Buddha expounded this chapter of King Wonderful-Adornment as the Previous Life of a Bodhisattva, eighty-four thousand people released themselves from the dust and dirt of illusions, and had their eyes purified enough to see all teachings.

CHAPTER XXVIII

THE ENCOURAGEMENT OF UNIVERSAL-SAGE BODHISATTVA

Thereupon Universal-Sage Bodhisattva, who was famous for his virtues and supernatural powers without hindrance, came from a world [in the distance of many worlds] to the east [of this Sahā-World]. He was accompanied by innumerable, uncountable great Bodhisattvas. All the worlds quaked as he passed through. [The gods] rained down jeweled lotus-flowers, and made many hundreds of thousands of billions of kinds of music. He was also surrounded by a great multitude of innumerable gods, dragons, yakṣas, gandharvas, asuras, garuḍas, kiṃnaras, mahoragas, men and nonhuman beings. They reached Mt. Gṛdhrakūṭa of the Sahā-World by their virtues and supernatural powers. [Universal-Sage Bodhisattva] worshiped [the feet of] Śākyamuni Buddha with his head, walked around the Buddha [from left] to right seven times, and said to the Buddha:

"World-Honored One! I heard the Sūtra of the Lotus Flower of the Wonderful Dharma, which you expounded in this Sahā World, from a remote world in which lives Treasure-Power-Virtue-Superior-King Buddha. I came here with many hundreds of thousands of billions of Bodhisattvas in order to hear and receive [this Sūtra]. World-Honored One! Tell me how the good men or women who live after your extinction will be able to obtain this Sūtra of the Lotus Flower of the Wonderful Dharma!"

The Buddha said to Universal-Sage Bodhisattva:

"The good men or women will be able to obtain this Sūtra of the Lotus Flower of the Wonderful Dharma after my extinction if they do the following four things: 1. secure the protection of the Buddhas, 2. plant the roots of virtue, 3. reach the stage of steadiness [in proceeding to enlightenment], and 4. resolve to save all living beings. The good men or women will be able to obtain this sūtra after my extinction if they do these four things."

Thereupon Universal-Sage Bodhisattva said to the Buddha:

"World-Honored One! If anyone keeps this sūtra in the defiled world in the later five hundred years after [your extinction], I will protect him so that he may be free from any trouble, that he may be peaceful, and that no one may take advantage [of his weak points]. Māra, his sons, his daughters, his subjects, his attendants, yakṣas, rākṣasas, kumbhāṇḍas, piśācakas, kṛtyas, pūtanas, vetāḍas or other living beings who trouble men shall not take advantage [of his weak points]. If anyone keeps, reads and recites this sūtra while he walks or stands, I will mount a kingly white elephant with six tusks, go to him together with great Bodhisattvas, show myself to him, make offerings to him, protect him, and comfort him, because I wish to make offerings to the Sūtra of the Lotus Flower of the Wonderful Dharma. If he sits and thinks over this sūtra, I also will mount a kingly white elephant and appear before him. If he forgets a phrase or a gāthā of the Sūtra of the Lotus Flower of the Wonderful Dharma, I will remind him of it, and read and recite it with him so that he may be able to understand it. Anyone who keeps, reads and recites the Sūtra of the Lotus Flower of the Wonderful Dharma [after your extinction], will be able to see me with such joy that he will make more efforts. Because he sees me, he will he able to obtain samādhis and a set of dhāraṇīs. The set of dhāraṇīs will be the dhāraṇīs by which he can memorize repetitions of teachings, the dhāraṇīs by which he can memorize hundreds of thousands of billions of repetitions of teachings, and the dhāraṇīs by which he can understand the expediency of the voice of the Dharma.

"World-Honored One! The bhikṣus, bhikṣunīs, upāsakās or upāsikās who seek, keep, read, recite and copy this Sūtra of the Lotus Flower of the Wonderful Dharma in the defiled world in the later five hundred years after [your extinction], if they wish to study and practice this sūtra, should concentrate their minds [on study and practice] strenuously for three weeks. When they complete [the study and practice of] three weeks, I will mount a white elephant with six tusks, and appear before them with my body which all living beings wish to see, together with innumerable Bodhisattvas surrounding me. I will expound the Dharma to them, show them the Way, teach them, benefit them, and cause them to rejoice. I also will give them dhāraṇī-spells. If they obtain these dhāraṇīs, they will not be killed by nonhuman beings or captivated by women. Also I myself will always protect them. World-Honored One! Allow me to utter these dhāraṇī-spells!"

Thereupon he uttered spells before the Buddha:

"Atandai (1), tandahatai (2), tandahatei (3), tandakusharei (4), tandashudarei (5), shudarei (6), shudarahachi (7), botsudahasennei (8), sarubadarani-abatani (9), sarubabasha-abatani (10), shu-abatani (11), sōgyahabishani (12), sōgyaneku-kyadani (13), asōgi (14), sōgyahagyadai (15), teirei-ada-sōgyatorya-aratei-haratei (16), sarubasōgya-sammaji-kyarandai (17), sarubadaruma-shuharisettei (18), saru-basatta-rodakyōsharya-atogyadai (19), shin-abikiridaitei (20)."[1]

[He said to the Buddha:]

"World-Honored One! It is by my supernatural powers, know this, that a Bodhisattva can hear these dhāraṇīs. Anyone who keeps the Sūtra of the Lotus Flower of the Wonderful Dharma [while it is] propagated in the Jambudvīpa, should think, 'I can keep [this sūtra] only by the supernatural powers of Universal-Sage.' Anyone who keeps, reads and recites this sūtra, memorizes it correctly, understands the meanings of it, and acts according to it, know this, does the same practices that I do. He should be considered to have already planted deeply the roots of good under innumerable Buddhas [in his previous existence]. He will be caressed on the head by the hands of the Tathāgatas. Anyone who copies this sūtra will be reborn in the Heaven of the Trāyastriṃśa Gods immediately after his present life. On that

1 In Wogihara's text, it reads, "Adaṇḍe daṇḍa-pati daṇḍ'āvartāni daṇḍa-kuśale daṇḍa-sudhāri sudhāri sudhāra-pati buddha-paśyane sarva-dhāraṇi āvartani saṃvartani saṃgha-parikṣite saṃgha-nirghātani dharma-parikṣite sarva-ruta-kauśalyānugate siṃha-vikrīḍite anuvarte vartani vartāli svāhā." In Kern's translation, it reads, "Adaṇḍe daṇḍapati, daṇḍāvartani daṇḍakuśale daṇḍasudhāri dhāri sudhārapati, buddhapaśyani dhāraṇi āvartani saṃvartani saṃghaparīkṣite saṃghanirghātani dharmaparīkṣite sarvasattvarutakauśalyānugate siṃhavikrīḍite."

occasion, eighty-four thousand goddesses will come and receive him, making many kinds of music. A crown of the seven treasures will be put on his head, and he will enjoy himself among the ladies in waiting. Needless to say, [more merits will be given to] the person who [not only copies this sūtra but also] keeps, reads and recites it, memorizes it correctly, understands the meanings of it, and acts according to it. Anyone who keeps, reads and recites this sūtra, and understands the meanings of it, will be given helping hands by one thousand Buddhas immediately after his present life. He will be fearless. He will not fall into any evil region. He will be reborn in the Tuṣita Heaven. There he will go to Maitreya Bodhisattva who, adorned with the thirty-two marks, will be surrounded by great Bodhisattvas, and attended on by hundreds of thousands of billions of goddesses.[2] He will be given the benefits of these merits. Therefore, anyone who has wisdom should copy this sūtra with all his heart, cause others to copy it, and also keep, read and recite it, memorize it correctly, and act according to it.

"World-Honored One! I will protect this sūtra with my supernatural powers so that it may be propagated and not be destroyed in the Jambudvīpa after your extinction."

Thereupon Śākyamuni Buddha praised him, saying:

"Excellent, excellent, Universal-Sage! You will protect this sūtra so that many living beings may obtain peace and benefits. You have already obtained inconceivable merits and great compassion. You aspired for Anuttara-samyak-saṃbodhi and vowed [to protect this sūtra] by your supernatural powers in the remotest past, and have been protecting this sūtra since then. By my supernatural powers, I will protect anyone who keeps your name.

"Universal-Sage! Anyone who keeps, reads and recites this Sūtra of the Lotus Flower of the Wonderful Dharma, memorizes it correctly, studies it, practices it, and copies it, should be considered to see me, and hear this sūtra from my mouth. He should be considered to be making offerings to me. He should be considered to be praised by me with the word 'Excellent!' He

2 In this chapter Maitreya Bodhisattva lives in the Tuṣita Heaven. He was active in the presence of the Buddha in the four chapters from XV to XVIII.

should be considered to be caressed by me on the head. He should be considered to be covered with my robe. He will not be attached to worldly pleasures. He will not like to read heretical scriptures or any other writings of heretics. He will not be intimate with heretics, slaughterers, boar-breeders, sheep-breeders, fowl-breeders, dog-breeders, hunters, prostitutes, or any other evil people. He will be upright. He will have correct memory and the powers of merits and virtues. He will not be troubled by the three poisons. He will not be troubled by jealousy, arrogance from selfishness, arrogance from self-assumed attainment of enlightenment, or arrogance from self-assumed acquisition of virtues. He will want little, know contentment, and practice just as you do.

"Universal-Sage! If you see anyone who keeps, reads and recites the Sūtra of the Lotus Flower of the Wonderful Dharma in the later five hundred years after my extinction, you should think, 'Before long he will go to the place of enlightenment, defeat Māra and his followers, attain Anuttara-samyak-saṃbodhi, turn the wheel of the Dharma, beat the drum of the Dharma, blow the conch-shell horn of the Dharma, send the rain of the Dharma, and sit on the lion-like seat of the Dharma in the midst of the great multitude of gods and men.'

"Universal-Sage! Anyone who keeps, reads and recites this sūtra [in the later five hundred years] after [my extinction], will not be attached to clothing, bedding, food or drink, or any other thing for living. What he wishes will not remain unfulfilled. He will be able to obtain the rewards of his merits in his present life. Those who abuse him, saying, 'You are perverted. You are doing this for nothing,' will be reborn blind in their successive lives in retribution for their sin. Those who make offerings to him and praise him, will be able to obtain rewards in their present life. Those who, upon seeing the keeper of this sūtra, blame him justly or unjustly, will suffer from white leprosy in their present life. Those who laugh at him will have few teeth, ugly lips, flat noses, contorted limbs, squint eyes, and foul and filthy bodies, and suffer from bloody pus of scabs, abdominal dropsy, tuberculosis, and other serious diseases in their successive lives. Therefore, Universal-Sage! When you see the keeper of this sūtra in the distance, you should rise from your seat, go to him, receive him, and respect him just as you respect me.

When the Buddha expounded this chapter of the Encouragement of Universal-Sage, as many Bodhisattvas as there are sands in the River Ganges obtained the dhāraṇīs by which they could memorize hundreds of thousands of billions of repetitions of teachings, and as many Bodhisattvas as the particles of dust of one thousand million Sumeru-worlds [understood how to] practice the Way of Universal-Sage.

When the Buddha expounded this sūtra, the great congregation including the Bodhisattvas headed by Universal-Sage, the Śrāvakas headed by Śāriputra, and the other living beings such as gods, dragons, men and nonhuman beings, had great joy, kept the words of the Buddha, bowed [to him], and retired.

[Here ends] the Eighth Volume of the Sūtra of the Lotus Flower of the Wonderful Dharma.

ENGLISH/SANSKRIT GLOSSARY

SANSKRIT WORDS, ENGLISH BUDDHIST TERMS AND TRANSLATED PROPER NAMES GIVEN IN THIS TRANSLATION

Note: For the policy of the translator, see Translator's Note (p. xvii).

1. Corresponding Japanese pronunciation of Chinese Buddhist terms are given in brackets following the English/Sanskrit term. Please refer to the Chinese/Japanese Glossary for more information on these terms.
2. The Roman numeral shows the chapter in which the term appears for the first time with the particular meaning indicated.

A

Abhirati (World) [Kangi] VII: The World of Joy.
Abhyudgatarāja (Kalpa) [Daikō-ō] XXVII: Great-Height-King Kalpa.
Acalā (Rākṣasī) [Muenzoku] XXVI: Insatiable.
Accumulated-Treasure (Bodhisattva) [Hōshaku] I: Ratnākara.
Accumulated-Wisdom (Bodhisattva) [Chishaku] XII: Prajñakūṭa.
Accumulated-Wisdom (Prince) [Chishaku] VII: Jñānākara.
Adbhuta [Mizōu] II: miracles. See *Nine Elements of Sūtras.*
Adhimātrakāruṇika (Brahman) [Daihi] VII: Great-Compassion.
Adornment-King (Bodhisattva) [Shōgonnō] XXIV: Śubhavyūharāja.
Ajātaśatru [Ajase] I: a king. See *Śākyamuni.*
Ajita [Aitta] XVII: an epithet of Maitreya.
Ājñāta-Kauṇḍinya [Anyakkyōjinnyo] I: a disciple of the Buddha. Also Kauṇḍinya. See *Śākyamuni.*
Akaniṣṭha (Heaven) [Akanita] I: The Highest Heaven. See *Sumeru-World.*
Ākāśapratiṣṭhita (Buddha) [Kokūjū] VII: Sky-Dwelling.
Akṣayamati (Bodhisattva) [Mujinni] XXV: Endless-Intent.
Akṣobhya [Ashukuba] XXIII: the twentieth power of ten.
Akṣobhya (Buddha) [Ashuku] VII.
All-Pure-Light-Adornment (World) [Issai-jōkō-shōgon] XXIV: Vairocanaraśmipratimaṇḍitā.

All-Saving (Brahman) [Ku-issai] VII: Sarvasattvatrātar.
Always-Raising-Banner-of-Victory (World) [Jōrisshōban] IX: Anavanāmitavaijayantī.
Amitāyus [Amida] VII: Amida.
Anāgāmin [Anagon] XVIII: one of the four types of Śrāvaka. See *Śrāvaka.*
Ānanda [Anan] I: a disciple of the Buddha. See *Śākyamuni.*
Anantacāritra (Bodhisattva) [Muhengyō] XV: Limitless-Practice.
Anantamati (Prince) [Muryō-i] I: Infinite-Intention.
Anantavikrāmin (Bodhisattva) [Muryōriki] I: Immeasurable-Power.
Anavanāmitavaijayantī (World) [Jōrisshōban] IX: Always-Raising-Banner-of-Victory.
Anavatapta (Dragon-King) [Anabadatta] I.
Anikṣiptadhura (Bodhisattva) [Fukusoku] I: Never-Resting.
Aniruddha [Anuruda] I: a disciple of the Buddha. See *Śākyamuni.*
Anti-Lokāyatas [Gyaku-rokayada] XIV: anti-materialists. See *Lokāyatas.*
Anuttara-samyak-saṃbodhi [Anokutara-sammyaku-sambodai] I: Perfect Enlightenment.
Apasmāraka [Abatsumara] XXVI: a devil.
Appearance-of-All-Worlds (World) [Gen-issai-seken] XXIV: Sarvarūpasaṃdarśanā.
Araṇya [Arennya] XIII: a retired place. Originally, a forest.
Arhat [Araka] I: one of the four types of Śrāvaka. See *Śrāvaka.*
Arjaka [Ariju] XXVI: a tree. *Ocimum Gratissimum.*
Aśaikṣa [Mugaku] I: the Śrāvakas who have nothing more to learn. See *Śrāvaka.*
Asaṃkhya [Asōgi] I: innumerable. It sometimes means the fifty-second power of ten.
Asita [Ashi] XII: a seer.
Āsrava [Ro, Uro] I: leakings. Illusions are so called because impure things leak out of the body of the person who has illusions.
Asura [Ashura] I: a demon. He fights with Śakra.
Atimuktaka [Adaimokutaka] XVII: a plant. *Premna Spinosa.*
Aupamya [Hiyu] II: parables and similes.
Avabhāsaprāptā (World) [Kōtoku] VI: Light-Virtue.
Avaivartika [Abeibatchi, Abibatchi, Ayui-otchi] III: the stage of irrevocability; XIII: irrevocability.
Avalokitasvara (Bodhisattva) [Kanzeon] I: World-Voice-Perceiver.
Avalokiteśvara (Bodhisattva) [Kanzeon] I: World-Voice-Perceiver.
Avīci [Abigoku, Abijigoku] I: The Hell of Incessant Suffering. See *Sumeru-World.*

B

Bakkula [Hakura] I: a disciple of the Buddha. See *Śākyamuni.*
Balin (Asura-King) [Baji] I.
Beautiful (Gandharva-King) [Mi] I: Madhura.
Beautiful-Form (Buddha) [Myōsō] VI: Śaśiketu.
Beautiful-Moon (God) [Myōgatsu] I: Candra.
Beautiful-Voice (Gandharva-King) [Mion] I: Madhurasvara.

Bhadra (Kalpa) [Gengō] VIII: the Kalpa of Sages.
Bhadrapāla (Bodhisattva) [Batsudabara] I.
Bhaiṣajyarāja (Bodhisattva) [Yakuō] I: Medicine-King.
Bhaiṣajyasamudgata (Bodhisattva) [Yakujō] XXVII: Medicine-Superior.
Bharadvāja [Harada] I: the name of a family.
Bhikṣu [Biku] I: a monk.
Bhikṣuṇī [Bikuni] I: a nun.
Bhīṣmagarjitasvararāja (Buddha) [Ionnō] XX: Powerful-Voice-King.
Bimba [Bimba] XXVII: a tree. *Momordica Monadelpha.*
Biṃbara [Bimbara] XXIII: the eighteenth power of ten.
Birth Without Any Medium [Keshō] VIII, XII, XXIII: birth not through the medium of a mother or an egg or moisture but by one's own karmas. It is held that those who are born without any medium appear in a moment in their adult forms.
Black-Teeth (Rākṣasī) [Kokushi (variant 2)] XXVI: Makuṭadanti.
Bodhi [Bodai] XII: enlightenment.
Bodhi-Tree [Dōju] XVII: the tree of enlightenment.
Bodhisattva [Bosatsu] I: one who seeks Buddhahood.
Brahma [Bon] I: pure.
Brahmadvaja (Buddha) [Bonsō] VII: Brahma-Form.
Brahman [Bon] VII. See *Sumeru-World.*
Brāhmaṇa [Baramon] I: a priest of Brahmanism.
Brave-In-Giving (Bodhisattva) [Yuze] I: Pradānaśūra.
Buddha [Butsu] I: The Enlightened One. See *Ten Epithets of the Buddha.*
Burning-Light (Buddha) [Nentō] I: Dīpaṃkara.

C

Cakravartin [Tenrinjō-ō] I: wheel-turning-holy-king. See *Wheel-Turning-Holy-King.*
Campaka [Semboku] XVII: a tree.
Caṇḍāla [Sendara] XIV: the lowest caste. The half-blood of śūdra and brāhmaṇī.
Candana [Sendan] I: Sandalwood.
Candra (God) [Myōgatsu] I: Beautiful-Moon.
Candrasūryapradīpa (Buddha) [Nichigattōmyō] I: Sun-Moon-Light.
Candrasvararāja (Buddha) [Nichigattōmyō] XX: Sun-Moon-Light.
Candravimalasūryaprabhāsaśrī (Buddha) [Nichigatsujōmyōtoku] XXIII: Sun-Moon-Pure-Bright-Virtue.
Cause-Knower [Engaku] I: Pratyekabuddha. More properly, Pratyayabuddha. One who realizes the truth of the twelve causes.
Cloud-Freedom (Buddha) [Unjizai] VII: Meghasvarapradīpa.
Cloud-Freedom-King (Buddha) [Unjizai-ō] VII: Meghasvararāja.
Cloud-Freedom-Light-King (Buddha) [Unjizaitō-ō] XX: Meghasvararāja.
Cloud-Thunder-Sound-King (Buddha) [Unrai-onnō] XXIV: Meghadundubhisvararāja.
Cloud-Thunderpeal-Star-King-Flower-Wisdom (Buddha) [Unrai-onshuku-ōkechi] XXVII: Jaladharagarjitaghoṣasusvaranakṣatrarājasaṃkusumitābhijña.

Constant-Endeavor (Bodhisattva) [Jōshōjin] I: Nityodyukta.

Cow-Head Candana [Gozusendan] IV: Gośīrṣacandana. Some say that Gośīrṣa is the name of a mountain.

Crooked-Teeth (Rākṣasī) [Kokushi (variant 1)] XXVI: Kūṭadanti.

Cunda [Shuda] VIII: a disciple of the Buddha. See *Śākyamuni.*

D

Dāna-Pāramitā [Dambaramitsu] XVII: the Bodhisattva practice of Almsgiving. See *Six Bodhisattva Practices.*

Devadatta [Daibadatta, Jōdatsu] XII, XXVI: a cousin and disciple of the Buddha. See *Śākyamuni.*

Devarāja (Buddha) [Tennō] XII: Heavenly-King.

Devasopāna (World) [Tendō] XII: Heavenly-Way.

Dhāraṇī [Darani] I: a formula to memorize teachings.

Dharaṇiṃdhara [Jiji] XXV: Earth-Holding.

Dharma (Kiṃnara-King) [Hō] I: Druma, which literally means "tree."

Dharma-Brightness (Buddha) [Hōmyō] VIII: Dharmaprabhāsa.

Dharma-Intention (Prince) [Hō-i (variant 1)] I: Dharmamati.

Dharma-Keeping (Kiṃnara-King) [Jihō] I: Dharmadhara.

Dharmadhara (Kiṃnara-King) [Jihō] I: Dharma-Keeping.

Dharmagaganābhyudgatarāja (Buddha) [Kū-ō] IX: Void-King.

Dharmamati (Prince) [Hō-i (variant 1)] I: Dharma-Intention.

Dharmaprabhāsa (Buddha) [Hōmyō] VIII: Dharma-Brightness.

Dhṛtiparipūrṇa (Bodhisattva) [Kemman] III: Resolution-Fulfillment.

Dhūta [Zuda] XI: also dhuta. Discipline to release from ties to clothing, food, and dwelling.

Dhyāna [Zen] I: meditation.

Dhyāna-Pāramitā [Zembaramitsu] XVII: the Bodhisattva practice of Meditation. See *Six Bodhisattva Practices.*

Diamond (Mountain) [Kongōsen] XXV: a mountain made of diamond.

Dīpaṃkara (Buddha) [Nentō] I: Burning-Light.

Doubts-Removing-Intention (Prince) [Jogi-i] I: Vimatisamudghātin.

E

Earth-Holding (Bodhisattva) [Jiji] XXV: Dharaṇiṃdhara.

Eight Emancipations [Hachigedatsu] VI. Emancipation (1) from the view that the body is pure, (2) from the view that the outside world is pure, (3) from illusions, (4) from the view that matter exists, (5) from the view that consciousness has limit, (6) from the view that a thing has its own property, (7) from the view that thought exists or that thought does not exist, and (8) from the view that mentality exists in any sense.

Eight Kinds of Supernatural Beings [Hachibu] XII: gods, dragons, yakṣas, gandharvas, asuras, garuḍas, kiṃnaras, and mahoragas.

Eight Right Ways [Hasshōdō] VII: the eightfold path: right views, thoughts, words, deeds, livelihood, endeavor, memory, and concentration of mind.

Eighteen Unique Properties of the Buddha [Jūhappuguhō] III: (1) freedom from illusions, (2) eloquence, (3) absence of attachments, (4) impartiality, (5) constant concentration of mind, (6) the knowledge of all things, (7) untiring intention of salvation, (8) incessant endeavor, (9) consistence of his teachings with those of the other Buddhas, (10) perfect wisdom, (11) perfect emancipation, (12) perfect insight, (13) consistence of his deeds with his wisdom, (14) consistence of his words with his wisdom, (15) consistence of his thought with his wisdom, (16) the knowledge of the past, (17) the knowledge of the future, and (18) the knowledge of the present.

Eliminating-Fear-of-All-Worlds (Buddha) [E-issai-seken-fui] VII: Sarvalokabhayacchambhitatvavidhvaṃsanakara.

Emitting-Ten-Million-Rays-of-Light (Buddha) [Gusoku-semman-kōsō] XIII: Raśmiśatasahasraparipūrṇadhvaja.

Emperor-Form (Buddha) [Taisō] VII: Indradhvaja.

Endeavor-Power-Obtainer (Bodhisattva) [Tokugonshōjinriki] XXIV.

Endless-Intent (Bodhisattva) [Mujinni] XXV: Akṣayamati.

Eternal-Extinction (Buddha) [Jōmetsu] VII: Nityaparinirvṛta.

Evil Karmas [Akugō] XVI. See *Karma.*

Evil Regions [Akudō] II. See *Sumeru-World.*

F

Fame-Seeking (Bodhisattva) [Gumyō] I: Yaśaskāma.

Five Aggregates [Go-on] XIV: matter, perception, conception, volition, and consciousness.

Five Bhikṣus [Gobiku] II: the five monks. See *Śākyamuni.*

Five Defilements [Gojoku] II: (1) by the decay of the kalpa, (2) by illusions, (3) by the deterioration of the living beings, (4) by wrong views, and (5) by the shortening of lives.

Five Desires [Goyoku] II: the desires to have the pleasures of the five senses.

Five Pāramitās [Goharamitsu] XVII: the six pāramitās except the wisdom practice. See *Six Bodhisattva Practices.*

Five Supernatural Powers [Gojinzū] I: the six supernatural powers except the sixth: to eliminate illusions. See *Six Supernatural Powers.*

Flower-Foot-Easy-Walking (Buddha) [Kesoku-angyō] III: Padmavṛṣabhavikrāmin.

Flower-Light (Buddha) [Kekō] III: Padmaprabha.

Flower-Teeth (Rākṣasī) [Keshi] XXVI: Puṣpadantī.

Flower-Virtue (Bodhisattva) [Ketoku] XXIV: Padmaśrī.

Four Continents [Shitenge] XVIII: Pūrvavideha, Jambudvīpa, Aparagodānīya and Uttarakuru. See *Sumeru-World.*

Four Elements [Shidai] XXIV: the four elements of the body: earth, water, fire and air, composing the physical body.

Four Evil Regions [Shi-akudō] VI: Hell, the region of hungry spirts, the region of animals and the region of Asuras. See *Sumeru-World.*

Four Great Heavenly-Kings [Shidaitennō] I: the four quarter kings: Dhṛtarāṣṭra, Virūḍhaka, Virūpākṣa and Vaiśravaṇa. See *Sumeru-World.*

Four Heavenly World-Guardian Kings [Gose-shitennō] II: the four great heavenly-kings. See *Sumeru-World.*

Four Intermediate Quarters [Shiyui] VII: southeast, southwest, northwest, and northeast.

Four Kinds of Birth [Shishō] XVIII: oviparous birth, viviparous birth, birth from moisture, and birth without any medium.

Four Kinds of Devotees [Shishu, Shibushu] I: bhikṣus, bhikṣuṇīs, upāsakas, and upāsikās. See *Bhikṣu, Bhikṣuṇī, Upāsaka,* and *Upāsikā.*

Four Kinds of Fearlessness [Shimushoi] XII: the Buddha is fearless (1) because he knows all, (2) because he eliminated illusions, (3) when he expounds that illusions are the obstacles to enlightenment, and (4) when he expounds the Way to eliminate sufferings.

Four Kinds of Unhindered Eloquence [Shimugechi, Shimuge-e] VIII: (1) eloquence over the words of the teachings, (2) eloquence over the meanings of the teachings, (3) eloquence over the meanings of dialects, and (4) eloquence enough to cause the hearers to rejoice.

Four States of Mind [Shimuryōshin] II: compassion, loving-kindness, joy and impartiality.

Four Truths [Shitai] I: the Four Noble Truths: (1) All is suffering; (2) The cause of suffering is illusions; (3) Extinction of illusions is Nirvāṇa; and (4) the Way to Nirvāṇa is the eight right ways. See *Eight Right Ways.*

Four Ways to Attract Others [Shishōbō] XII: (1) to give alms and expound the Dharma, (2) to speak affectionately, (3) to benefit others, and (4) to cooperate with them.

Free-At-Will (Garuḍa-King) [Nyoi] I: Maharddhiprāpta.

Free-From-Decay (Kalpa) [Risui] XX: Vinirbhoga.

Free-From-Taint (World) [Riku] III: Viraja.

Freedom (God) [Jizai] I: Īśvara. See *Sumeru-World.*

Full-Moon (Bodhisattva) [Mangachi] I: Pūrṇacandra.

G

Gadgadasvara (Bodhisattva) [Myō-on] XXIV: Wonderful-Voice.

Gandharva [Kendatsuba] I: a heavenly musician.

Garuḍa [Karura] I: a golden-winged bird.

Gāthā [Ge, Kada] I, II: a verse. As one of the nine elements of sūtras, it means a set of verses in which the contents of the preceding prose are not repeated.

Gautamī [Kyōdommi] XIII: the Buddha's Aunt. See *Śākyamuni.*

Gavāṃpati [Kyōbon-handai] I: a disciple of the Buddha. See *Śākyamuni.*

Gayā (City) [Gaya] XV. See *Śākyamuni.*

Gayā-Kāśyapa [Gaya-kashō] I: a disciple of the Buddha. See *Śākyamuni.*

Geya [Giya] II: a set of verses in which the contents of the preceding prose are repeated. See *Nine Elements of Sūtras.*

Ghoṣamati (Prince) [Kō-i] I: Resounding-Intention.

Gladly-Seen (Kalpa) [Kiken] XXIV, XXVII: Priyadarśana.

Gladly-Seen-By-All-Beings (Bodhisattva) [Issaishujōkiken] XXIII: Sarvasattvapriyadarśana.

Gladly-Seen-By-All-Beings (Buddha) [Issaishujōkiken] XIII: Sarvasattvapriyadarśana.

Golden Mountains [Konzen] I. See *Sumeru-World.*

Good-Intention (Prince) [Zenni] I: Sumati.

Good-Purity (World) [Zenjō] VIII: Suviśuddha.

Gośīrṣacandana. [Gozusendan] IV: the cow-head candana. Some say that Gośīrṣa is the name of a mountain.

Gṛdhrakūṭa (Mountain) [Gishakutsu, Ryōju] I: Sacred Eagle. See *Śākyamuni.*

Great Surrounding Iron Mountains [Daitetchisen] XV. See *One Thousand Million Sumeru-Worlds.*

Great-Achievement (World) [Daijō] XX: Mahāsaṃbhavā.

Great-Body (Garuḍa-King) [Daishin] I: Mahākāya.

Great-Compassion (Brahman) [Daihi] VII: Adhimātrakāruṇika.

Great-Dharma (Kiṃnara-King) [Daihō] I: Mahādharma.

Great-Eloquence (Bodhisattva) [Daigyōsetsu] XI: Mahā-Pratibhāna.

Great-Form (Kalpa) [Daisō] VII: Mahārūpa.

Great-Freedom (God) [Daijizai] I: Maheśvara. See *Sumeru-World.*

Great-Fulfillment (Garuḍa-King) [Daiman] I: Mahāpūrṇa.

Great-Height-King (Kalpa) [Daikō-ō] XXVII: Abhyudgatarāja.

Great-Light (World) [Daikō] XXVII: The Vistīrṇavati.

Great-Power (Bodhisattva) [Dairiki] I: Mahāvikrāmin.

Great-Power-Obtainer (Bodhisattva) [Tokudaisei] I: Mahāsthāmaprāpta.

Great-Power-Virtue (Garuḍa-King) [Dai-itoku] I: Mahātejas.

Great-Treasure-Adornment (Kalpa) [Daihō-shōgon] III: Mahāratnapratimaṇḍita.

Great-Universal-Wisdom-Excellence (Buddha) [Daitsūchishō] VII: Mahābhijñājñānābhibhū.

H

Hārītī (Rākṣasī) [Kishimo] XXVI: the Mother-of-Devils.

Having-Intention (Prince) [Ui] I: Mati.

Having-Treasures (Kalpa) [Uhō] VI: Ratnaprabhāsa.

Heavenly-King (Buddha) [Tennō] XII: Devarāja.

Heavenly-Way (World) [Tendō] XII: Devasopāna.

Hīnayāna [Shōjō] II: the Lesser Vehicle.

I

Immeasurable-Power (Bodhisattva) [Muryōriki] I: Anantavikrāmin.

Increasing-Intention (Prince) [Zō-i] I: Viśeṣamati.

Indradhvaja (Buddha) [Taisō] VII: Emperor-Form.

Infinite-Intention (Prince) [Muryō-i] I: Anantamati.

Insatiable (Rākṣasī) [Muenzoku] XXVI: Acalā.

Īśvara (God) [Jizai] I: Freedom.

Itivṛttaka. [Honji] II: the story of the previous life of the disciple of a Buddha. See *Nine Elements of Sūtras.*

J

Jaladharagarjitaghoṣasusvaranakṣatrarājasaṃkusumitābhijña (Buddha) [Unrai-onshuku-ōkechi] XXVII: Cloud-Thunderpeal-Star-King-Flower-Wisdom.

Jambudvīpa [Embudai, lchiembudai] XX: one of the four continents. See *Sumeru-World.*

Jāmbūnada Gold [Embudan-gon] XVII: the gold found in the river running through the forest of the jāmbū trees.

Jāmbūnada-Gold-Light (Buddha) [Embunadaikonkō] VI: Jāmbūnadaprabhāsa.

Jāmbūnadaprabhāsa (Buddha) [Embunadaikonkō] VI: Jāmbūnada-Gold-Light.

Jātaka [Honjō] II: the story of the previous life of the Buddha.

Jātika [Shadai] XIX: a plant.

Jīvakajīvaka [Myōmyō] XIX: a bird.

Jñānākara (Prince) [Chishaku] VII: Accumulated-Wisdom.

Joy (World) [Kangi] VII: Abhirati.

Joyfulness (Kalpa) [Kiman] VI: Ratiprapūrṇa.

Jyotiṣprabha (Brahman) [Kōmyō] I: Light.

K

Kalaviṅka [Karyōbinga] VII: a bird.

Kālodāyin [Karudai] VIII: a disciple of the Buddha. See *Śākyamuni.*

Kalpa [Kō] I: a period of as many years as to be spent for the composition of a world. It is held that the world is maintained also for a kalpa, that the world is destroyed also in a kalpa, and that the world remains in the state of the Void also for a kalpa until another world begins to be composed. Innumerable worlds appear and disappear one after another in this cycle of the four kalpas: the kalpas of composition, of maintenance, of destruction and of the Void. The duration of a kalpa can be measured by the duration of the kalpa of maintenance. The kalpa of maintenance has twenty periods each of which has the same duration. In the first period the average age of men decreases one year every century down to ten years. In the second period the age increases one year every century up to 80,000 years and decreases in the same way down to ten years. This is repeated eighteen times up to the nineteenth period. In the last period the age increases in the same way, and does not decrease. Each period is called an antara-kalpa or a small kalpa. In Chapter XII, this is rendered as an intermediate kalpa. Now we are in the kalpa of maintenance of the Sahā-World. This is called Bhadra Kalpa or the Kalpa of Sages.

Kalpa of Sages [Gengō] VIII: Bhadra Kalpa.

Kamaladalavimalanakṣatrarājasaṃkusumitābhijña (Buddha) [Jōkeshukuōchi] XXIV: Pure-Flower-Star-King-Wisdom.

Kaṅkara [Kengara] XXIII: the sixteenth power of ten.

Kapphina [Kōhinna] I: a disciple of the Buddha. Also Kapphiṇa. See *Śākyamuni.*

Karma [Gō] II: anything which is thought, said, or done; XVI: practice.

Kāśyapa [Kashō] V: a disciple of the Buddha. Also Mahā-Kāśyapa.

Kauṇḍinya [Kyōjinnyo] I: a disciple of the Buddha. Also Ājñāta-Kauṇḍinya. See *Śākyamuni.*

Keśini (Rakṣasī) [Tahotsu] XXVI: Many-Hairs.
Kharaskandha (Asura-King) [Karakenda] I.
Kiṃnara [Kinnara] I: a heavenly musician.
Kiṃśuka [Kenshukuka] XXIV: a tree. The flower is red; hence, red.
King-House (City) [Ōsha] I: Rājagṛha. See *Śākyamuni.*
Kovidāra [Kubeidara, Kubidara] XIX: a tree. *Bauhinia Variegata.*
Kṛtya [Kissha] XXVI: a devil.
Kṣaṇa [Setsuna] XII: a moment.
Kṣānti [Sendai] XVII: patience.
Kṣānti-Pāramitā [Sendai-haramitsu] XVII: the Bodhisattva practice of Patience. See *Six Bodhisattva Practices.*
Kṣatriya [Setsuri] IV: Warriors.
Kṣetra [Setsu] II: a world.
Kumbhānda [Kenda, Kuhanda] III, XXVI: a devil.
Kunduruka [Kunroku] XXIII: a tree.
Kuntī (Rākṣasī) [Kōtai] XXVI: Mother-of-Devils.
Kūṭadanti (Rākṣasī) [Kokushi (variant 1)] XXVI: Crooked-Teeth.

L

Lambā (Rākṣasī) [Ramba] XXVI.
Leading-Teacher (Bodhisattva) [Dōshi] I.
Light (Brahman) [Kōmyō] I: Jyotiṣprabha.
Light (Buddha) [Kōmyō] VI: Raśmiprabhāsa.
Light-Adornment (World) [Kōmyō-shōgon] XXVII: Vairocanaraśmipratimaṇḍitā.
Light-Adornment-Appearance (Bodhisattva) [Kōshō-shōgonsō] XXVII: Vairocanaraśmipratimaṇḍitadhvajarāja.
Light-Sound (Heaven) [Kō-on] XIX. See *Sumeru-World.*
Light-Virtue (World) [Kōtoku] VI: Avabhāsaprāptā.
Limitless-Practice (Bodhisattva) [Muhengyō] XV: Anantacāritra.
Lion-Form (Buddha) [Shishisō] VII: Siṃhadhvaja.
Lion-Moon (Bhikṣunī) [Shishigatsu] XX: Siṃhacandra.
Lion-Voice (Buddha) [Shishi-on] VII: Siṃhaghoṣa.
Lokāyatas [Rokayada] XIV: the materialists of the time of the Buddha.

M

Madhura (Gandharva-King) [Mi] I: Beautiful.
Madhurasvara (Gandharva-King) [Mion] I: Beautiful-Voice.
Mahā-Kāśyapa [Makakashō] I: a disciple of the Buddha. See *Śākyamuni.*
Mahā-Kātyāyana [Daikasennen, Makakasennen] I: a disciple of the Buddha. See *Śākyamuni.*
Mahā-Kauṣṭhila [Makakuchira] I: a disciple of the Buddha. See *Śākyamuni.*
Mahā-Mandārava [Makamandarake] I: great mandārava-flowers.
Mahā-Mañjūṣaka [Makamanjushake] I: great mañjūṣaka-flowers.

Mahā-Maudgalyāyana [Daimokkenren] I: a disciple of the Buddha. See *Śākyamuni.*

Mahā-Meru (Mountain) [Makamiru] XIX: Mahā-Meru. See *Sumeru-World.*

Mahā-Mucilinda (Mountain) [Makamokushinrinda] XI: Mahā-Mucilinda. See *Śākyamuni.*

Mahā-Prajāpati [Makahajahadai] I: the Buddha's Aunt. See *Śākyamuni.*

Mahā-Pratibhāna (Bodhisattva) [Daigyōsetsu] XI: Great-Eloquence.

Mahābhijñājñānābhibhū (Buddha) [Daitsūchishō] VII: Great-Universal-Wisdom-Excellence.

Mahādharma (Kiṃnara-King) [Daihō] I: Great-Dharma.

Mahākāya (Garuḍa-King) [Daishin] I: Great-Body

Mahāpūrṇa (Garuḍa-King) [Daiman] I: Great-Fulfillment.

Mahāratnapratimaṇḍita (Kalpa) [Daihō-Shōgon] III: Great-Treasure-Adornment.

Maharddhiprāpta (Garuḍa-King) [Nyoi] I: Free-At-Will.

Mahārūpa (Kalpa) [Daisō] VII: Great-Form.

Mahāsaṃbhavā (World) [Daijō] XX: Great-Achievement.

Mahāsattva [Makasatsu] III: great being.

Mahāsattva [Daiji] I: a great man. A man of the Great Vehicle.

Mahāsthāmaprāpta (Bodhisattva) [Tokudaisei] I: Great-Power-Obtainer.

Mahātejas (Garuḍa-King) [Dai-itoku] I: Great-Power-Virtue.

Mahāvikrāmin (Bodhisattva) [Dairiki] I: Great-Power.

Mahāyāna [Daijo] I: the Great Vehicle.

Maheśvara (God) [Daijizai] I: Great-Freedom. See *Sumeru-World.*

Mahoraga [Magoraga] I: a boa.

Maitrāyaṇī [Mitarani] I: a lady of the Maitrāyaṇa family. See *Śākyamuni.*

Maitreya (Bodhisattva) [Miroku] I.

Makuṭadanti (Rākṣasī) [Kokushi (variant 2)] XXVI: Black-Teeth.

Mālādhārī (Rākṣasī) [Jiyōraku] XXVI: Necklace-Holding.

Mallikā [Matsuri] XIX: a plant. *Jasminum Sambac.*

Manasvin (Dragon-King) [Manashi] I.

Mandārava [Manda, Mandarake] I, XIX: flowers. They are white. Also māndārava, mandāra.

Maṇi [Mani] I: a gem.

Mañjūṣaka [Manjushake] I: Red flowers.

Mañjuśrī (Bodhisattva) [Monjushiri] I.

Manobhirāma (World) [Iraku] VI: Mind-Happiness.

Manojña (Gandharva-King) [Gaku] I: Musical. The Chinese symbol for this was once pronounced Gyō, meaning "to wish."

Manojñaśabdābhigarjita (Kalpa) [Myō-on-hemman] X: Wonderful-Voice-Resounding-Everywhere.

Manojñasvara (Gandharva-King) [Gakuon] I: Musical-Voice. The Chinese symbol for this was once pronounced Gyō-on.

Many-Hairs (Rakṣasī) [Tahotsu] XXVI: Keśini.

Many-Treasures (Buddha) [Tahō] XIX: Prabhūtaratna.

Māra [Ma] I: the Evil One; XIV: an evil. See *Sumeru-World.*

Mati (Prince) [Ui] I: Having-Intention.

Medicine-King (Bodhisattva) [Yakuō] I: Bhaiṣajyarāja.

Medicine-Superior (Bodhisattva) [Yakujō] XXVII: Bhaiṣajyasamudgata.

Meghadundubhisvararāja (Buddha) [Unrai-Onnō] XXIV: Cloud-Thunder-Sound-King.

Meghasvarapradīpa (Buddha) [Unjizai] VII: Cloud-Freedom.

Meghasvararāja (Buddha) [Unjizai-ō] VII: Cloud-Freedom-King.

Meghasvararāja (Buddha) [Unjizaitō-ō] XX: Cloud-Freedom-Light-King.

Men in White Robes [Byakue] XIII: laymen.

Meru (Mountain) [Miru] XIX. See *Sumeru-World.*

Merukalpa (Buddha) [Shumisō] VII: Sumeru-Form.

Merukūṭa (Buddha) [Shumichō] VII: Sumeru-Peak.

Mind-Happiness (World) [Iraku] VI: Manobhirāma.

Moon-Light (Bodhisattva) [Gakkō] I: Ratnaprabha.

Mother-of-Devils (Rākṣasī) [Kishimo] XXVI: the Mother-of-Devils. Hārītī.

Mountain-Sea-Wisdom-Supernatural-Power-King (Buddha) [Sengaie-jizaitsū-ō] IX: Sāgaravaradharabuddhivikrīḍitābhijña.

Mucilinda (Mountain) [Mokushinrinda] XI. See *Śākyamuni.*

Musical (Gandharva-King) [Gaku] I: Manojña. The Chinese symbol for this was once pronounced Gyō, meaning "to wish."

Musical-Voice (Gandharva-King) [Gakuon] I: Manojñasvara. The Chinese symbol for this was once pronounced Gyō-on.

N

Nadi-Kāśyapa [Nadaikashō] I: a disciple of the Buddha. See *Śākyamuni.*

Nāga [Ryū] I: a dragon.

Nakṣatrarājasaṃkusumitābhijña (Bodhisattva) [Shukuōke] XXIII: Star-King-Flower.

Namaḥ Śākyamunaye Buddhāya [Namu-shakamunibutsu] XXI: Honor to Śākyamunl Buddha.

Namas [Namu] XXV: Honor to.

Namo Buddhāya [Namubutsu] II: Honor to the Buddha.

Nanda [Nanda] I: a disciple of the Buddha. See *Śākyamuni.*

Nanda (Dragon-King) [Nanda] I.

Nārāyaṇa [Naraen] XXIV: a wrestler in the time of the Buddha.

Naṭa [Nara] XIV: a dancer.

Navamālikā [Nabamari] XXIII: a plant. *Jasminum Sambac.*

Nayuta [Nayuta] VI: Hundred thousand million.

Necklace-Holding (Rākṣasī) [Jiyōraku] XXVI: Mālādhārī.

Never-Despising (Bodhisattva) [Jōfukyō] XX: Sadāparibhūta. Literally, "Always Despised."

Never-Faltering (Bodhisattva) [Futai-bosatsu] III.

Never-Resting (Bodhisattva) [Fukusoku] I: Aniksiptadhura.

Nidāna [Innen] II: purpose; the reason why a sūtra was expounded. See *Nine Elements of Sutras.*

Nine Elements of Sūtras [Kubuhō] II: (1) collection of the Buddha's teachings *(sūtra)*, (2) verse *(gāthā)*, (3) stories of the previous life of the disciple of a Buddha *(itivṛttaka)*, (4) stories of the previous life of the Buddha *(jātaka)*, (5) miracles *(adbhuta)*, (6) why a sūtra was expounded *(nidāna)*, (7) parables and similes *(aupamya)*, (8) verses in which the contents of the preceding prose are repeated *(geya)*, and (9) discourse *(upadeśa)*.

Nirgranthas [Nikenshi] XIV: the followers of Nirgrantha Jñātiputra. The Jains.

Nirvāṇa [Nehan] I: extinction.

Nityaparinirvṛta (Buddha) [Jōmetsu] VII: Eternal-Extinction.

Nityodyukta (Bodhisattva) [Jōshōjin] I: Constant-Endeavor.

O

One Million Sumeru-Worlds [Chūsengai] XVII. See *One Thousand Million Sumeru-Worlds.*

One Thousand Million Sumeru-Worlds [Sanzendaisensekai, Sanzendaisenzekai] V: a set of worlds of which the living beings are to be saved by one Buddha. The one thousand million Sumeru-worlds are considered to be arranged horizontally in the form of a disc, disregarding geometrical impossibility. The clustering of one thousand Sumeru-worlds is called Shōsengai or Shōsenkokudo. The clustering of one million Sumeru-worlds is called Chūsengai or Nisenchūkokudo. The Sanzendaisensekai is also called Daisengai. Sanzendaisengai. Sanzengai or Sanzensekai. It is held that a sanzendaisensekai is surrounded by the Daitetchisen or Great Surrounding Iron Mountains. See *Sumeru-World.*

One Thousand Sumeru-Worlds [Shōsengai, Shōsenkokudo] XVIII. See *Sumeru-World.*

Other Shore [Higan] I: Nirvāṇa, as contrasted with this shore, which is the world of birth and death.

P

Padmaprabha (Buddha) [Kekō] III: Flower-Light.

Padmaśrī (Bodhisattva) [Ketoku] XXIV: Flower-Virtue.

Padmavṛṣabhavikrāmin (Buddha) [Kesoku-angyō] III: Flower-Foot-Easy-Walking.

Pāpīyas [Hajun] III: another name of Māra.

Pāramitā [Haramitsu] I: a Bodhisattva practice. A practice required for crossing over to the Other Shore or Nirvāṇa. See *Other Shore.*

Pārijātaka [Harishitta] XIX: a tree which grows in the garden of Śakra.

Parinirvāṇa [Hatsunehan, Muyonehan] I: complete extinction; the death of the Buddha; the Nirvāṇa-without-remainder.

Pāṭala [Harara] XIX: a plant.

Pātra [Hatsu] XXIV: an alms bowl.

Peaceful Practices [Anrakugyō] XIV.

Pilindavatsa [Hitsuryōgabasha] I: a disciple of the Buddha. See *Śākyamuni.*

Piśācaka [Bishaja] XIX: a devil.

Plunderer-of-Energy-of-All-Beings (Rākṣasī) [Datsu-issai-shujō-shōke] XXVI: Sarvasattvojohārī.

Powerful-Voice-King (Buddha) [Ionnō] XX: Bhīṣmagarjitasvararāja.

Prabhūtaratna (Buddha) [Tahō] XIX: Many-Treasures.

Pradānaśūra (Bodhisattva) [Yuze] I: Brave-In-Giving.

Prajñā [Hannya] XVII: attainment of wisdom.

Prajñā-pāramitā [Hannya-haramitsu] XVII: the Bodhisattva practice of Wisdom. See *Six Bodhisattva Practices.*

Prajñakūṭa (Bodhisattva) [Chishaku] XII: Accumulated-Wisdom.

Pratyekabuddha [Byakushibutsu, Hyakushibutsu] I: one who has learned the causes of all things.

Priyadarśana (Kalpa) [Kiken] XXIV: Gladly-Seen.

Pṛkkā [Hitsurikika] XXIII: a plant.

Pure-Body (Buddha) [Jōshin] I: Vimalanetra.

Pure-Eyes (Prince) [Jōgen] XXVII: Vimalanetra.

Pure-Flower-Star-King-Wisdom (Buddha) [Jōkeshukuōchi] XXIV: Kamaladalavimalanakṣatrarājasaṃkusumitābhijña.

Pure-Practice (Bodhisattva) [Jōgyō (variant 1)] XV: Viśuddhacāritra.

Pure-Store (Prince) [Jōzō] XXVII: Vimalagarbha.

Pure-Virtue (King) [Jōtoku] XXIII: Vimaladatta.

Pure-Virtue (Queen) [Jōtoku] XXVII: Vimaladattā.

Pūrṇa [Furuna] I: a disciple of the Buddha. See *Śākyamuni.*

Pūrṇacandra (Bodhisattva) [Mangachi] I: Full-Moon.

Puṣpadantī (Rākṣasī) [Keshi] XXVI: Flower-Teeth.

Pūtana [Futanna] XXVI: a devil.

R

Rāhu (Asura-King) [Rago] I.

Rāhula [Ragora] I: the son of the Buddha. See *Śākyamuni.*

Rājagṛha (City) [Ōsha] I: King-House. See *Śākyamuni.*

Rākṣasa [Rasetsu, Akurasetsu] XXV: a devil.

Rākṣasī [Rasetsunyo] XXVI: a female rākṣasa devil.

Raśmiprabhāsa (Buddha) [Kōmyō] VI: Light.

Raśmiśatasahasraparipūrṇadhvaja (Buddha) [Gusoku-semman-kōsō] XIII: Emitting-Ten-Million-Rays-of-Light.

Ratiprapūrṇa (Kalpa) [Kiman] VI: Joyfulness.

Ratnacandra (Bodhisattva) [Hōgachi] I: Treasure-Moon.

Ratnākara (Bodhisattva) [Hōshaku] I: Accumulated-Treasure.

Ratnaketurāja (Buddha) [Hōsō] XI: Treasure-Form.

Ratnamati (Prince) [Hō-i (variant 2)] I: Treasure-Intention.

Ratnapāṇi (Bodhisattva) [Hōshō] I: Treasure-Palm.

Ratnaprabha (Bodhisattva) [Gakkō] I: Moon-Light.

Ratnaprabha (God) [Hōkō] I: Treasure-Light.

Ratnaprabhāsa (Kalpa) [Uhō] VI: Having-Treasures.

Ratnasaṃbhava (World) [Hōshō] VI: Treasure-Born.

Ratnatejobhyudgatarāja (Buddha) [Hō-itoku-jō-ō] XXVIII: Treasure-Power-Virtue-Superior-King.

Ratnāvabhāsa (Kalpa) [Hōmyō] VIII: Treasure-Brightness.

Ratnaviśuddha (World) [Hōjō] XI: Treasure-Purity.

Resolution-Fulfillment (Bodhisattva) [Kemman] III: Dhṛtiparipūrṇa.

Resounding-Intention (Prince) [Kō-i] I: Ghoṣamati.

Revata [Rihata] I: a disciple of the Buddha. See *Śākyamuni.*

S

Sacred Eagle (Mountain) [Gishakku, Ryōju] XII: Gṛdhrakūṭa. See *Śākyamuni.*

Sadāparibhūta (Bodhisattva) [Jōfukyō] XX: Never-Despising. Literally, "Always Despised."

Sāgara (Dragon-King) [Shakara] I, XII.

Sāgaravaradharabuddhivikrīḍitābhijña (Buddha) [Sengaie-jizaitsū-ō] IX: Mountain-Sea-Wisdom-Supernatural-Power-King.

Sahā (World) [Shaba] I: the earth. The world inhabited by men.

Śakra (God) [Taishaku, Tentaishaku] II: the King of the Gods. See *Sumeru-World.*

Śakra-Devānām-Indra (God) [Shakudaikannin, Tentaishaku, Taishaku] I: King of Gods Śakra. See *Sumeru-World.*

Sakṛdāgāmin [Shidagon] XXIII: one of the four types of Śrāvaka. See *Śrāvaka.*

Śākya [Shakushi, Shakushu] XV, XVI: the clan into which the Buddha was born. See *Śākyamuni.*

Śākyamuni (Buddha) [Shakamuni] VII: The Sage of the Śākyas. Born of the Gautama family of the Śākyas. His father was Śuddhodana, the king of Kapilavastu. His mother was Māyā. He was named Siddhārtha. Seven days after his birth, Māyā died, and he was brought up by Mahā-Prajāpatī, the younger sister of his mother and second wife of his father. She was also called Gautamī or the Lady of the Gautama family. Mahā-Prajāpatī became the mother of Nanda. Nanda was also called Sundarananda. When Siddhārtha grew up, the king sought a wife for his son. A message was sent to Suprabuddha of Koli asking for his daughter Yaśodharā. The answer came that daughters of the family were given only to those who excelled in various arts and martial exercises. Siddhārtha proved himself the superior of all. Among the defeated Śākyas were two cousins of his, Ānanda and Devadatta. He married Yaśodharā, and became the father of Rāhula. When he renounced the world, five of his attendants also became bhikṣus and followed him by the order of the king. The five bhikṣus were Ājñāta-Kauṇḍinya, Aśvajit, Bhadrika, Daśabala-Kāśyapa, and Mahānāman. Gautama and the five bhikṣus went to the village of Uruvilvā near the City of Gayā in the Kingdom of Magadha. Mt. Mucilinda or Mt. Mahā-Mucilinda was near the village. In this village they practiced asceticism under three fire-worshippers. The fire-worshippers were brothers: Uruvilvā-Kāśyapa, Gayā-Kāśyapa, and Nadī-Kāśyapa. After six years Gautama gave up asceticism. The five bhikṣus left him and went to Vārāṇasī of Kāśi. Gautama attained enlightenment and became the Buddha. The Buddha went to Vārāṇasī. The five bhikṣus heard the Dharma from him and became his disciples. The Buddha came back to Uruvilvā and expounded the Dharma to the three brothers. They and their 1,000 followers became disciples of the Buddha. He went to Rajāgṛha or the City of King-House, the capital city of Magadha. He expounded the Dharma on Mt. Gṛdhrakūṭa or Sacred Eagle and at other places in the city. King Bimbisāra and Queen Vaidehī followed him. Śāriputra and Mahā-Maudgalyāyana, who were prominent ascetics living near Rajāgṛha, also followed the Buddha together with their 250 disciples. King Śuddhodana sent his minister Kālodāyin to invite the Buddha. Kālodāyin was another name of Udāyin. Kālodāyin became a disciple of the Buddha. The Buddha visited Kapilavastu. On this occasion or soon after this, Rāhula, Ānanda, Nanda, Devadatta, Mahā-Prajāipatī, Yaśodharā, and others joined the Order. Devadatta proposed to the Buddha that, because of the Buddha's advanced age, the leadership of the Order should be vested in himself. The suggestion was refused. At the instigation of Devadatta, Ajātaśatru, the son of Bimbisāra, killed his father and usurped the throne. Devadatta vainly attempted to kill the Buddha. It is said that Devadatta went alive to hell. Ajātaśatru followed the Buddha on the advice of his physician Jīvaka. The Buddha had many disciples. Ten of them: Śāriputra, Mahā-Maudgalyāyana, Mahā-Kāśyapa, Aniruddha, Subhūti, Pūrṇa, Mahā-Katyāyana, Upāli, Rāhula, and Ānanda were called the ten great disciples. Śāriputra was the wisest. Aniruddha was a cousin of the Buddha. Pūrṇa was famous for his eloquence. His mother was Maitrāyanī. Upāli was a slave. Ānanda accompanied the Buddha as his personal attendant. The names of the other disciples mentioned in this sūtra are Kapphina, Gavāṃpati, Revata, Pilindavatsa. Bakkula, Mahā-Kauṣṭhila, Cunda, and Svāgata. Gavāṃpati was once a disciple of Śāriputra. Mahā-Kauṣṭhila was an uncle of Śāriputra. The duration of the period from the enlightenment of the Buddha to some day of his teaching was forty and odd years. The end of his life came when he took the meal offered by Cunda. He died at midnight that night.

Sāla-Tree-King (Buddha) [Sharaju-ō] XXVII: Śālendrarāja.

Śālendrarāja (Buddha) [Sharaju-ō] XXVII: Śāla-Tree-King.

Samādhi [Sammai] I: concentration of mind.

Samantabhadra (Bodhisattva) [Fugen] XXVIII: Universal-Sage.

Samantagandha (God) [Fukō] I: Universal-Fragrance.

Samantaprabhāsa (Buddha) [Fumyō] VIII: Universal-Brightness.

Saṃbhavā (World) [Kōjō] VII: Well-Composed.

Saṃgha [Sō] I: the Buddhist community.

Samyak-Saṃbuddha [Sammyaku-sambutsuda] I: The Perfectly Enlightened One. See *Ten Epithets of the Buddha.*

Saptaratnapadmavikrāntagāmin (Buddha) [Tōshippōke] IX: Stepping-On-Flower-of-Seven-Treasures.

Śāriputra [Sharihotsu] I: a disciple of the Buddha. See *Śākyamuni.*

Śarīra [Shari] I: the relics; especially, those of the Buddha.

Sarvalokabhayacchambhitatvavidhvaṃsanakara (Buddha) [E-issai-seken-fui] VII: Eliminating-Fear-of-All-Worlds.

Sarvalokadhātūpadravodvegapratyuttīrṇa (Buddha) [Do-issai-seken-kunō] VII: Saving-All-Worlds-From-Suffering.

Sarvarūpasaṃdarśanā (World) [Gen-issai-seken] XXIV: Appearance-of-All-Worlds.

Sarvasattvapriyadarśana (Bodhisattva) [Issaishujōkiken] XXIII: Gladly-Seen-By-All-Beings.

Sarvasattvapriyadarśana (Buddha) [Issaishujōkiken] XIII: Gladly-Seen-By-All-Beings.

Sarvasattvatrātar (Brahman) [Ku-issai] VII: All-Saving.

Sarvasattvojohārī (Rākṣasī) [Datsu-issai-shujō-shōke] XXVI: Plunderer-of-Energy-of-All-Beings.

Śaśiketu (Buddha) [Myōsō] VI: Beautiful-Form.

Saving-All-Worlds-From-Suffering (Buddha) [Do-issai-seken-kunō] VII: Sarvalokadhātūpadravodvegapratyuttīrṇa.

Seven Buddhas [Shichibutsu] VIII: the Buddhas who appeared in this world successively with Śākyamuni as the seventh: Vipaśyin, Śikhin, Viśvabhū, Krakucchanda, Kanakamuni, Kāśyapa, and Śākyamuni.

Seven Treasures [Shippō] I: gold, silver, pearl, mani, shell, agate, and diamond; II: gold, silver, crystal, shell, agate, ruby, and lapis lazuli; IX: gold, silver, lapis lazuli, shell, agate, pearl, and ruby; XIV: gold, silver, lapis lazuli, shell, agate, coral, and amber; XIX: the seven treasures of the wheel-turning-holy-king: wheels, elephants, horses, gems, ministers, women, and soldiers.

Śikhin (Brahman) [Shiki] I. See *Sumeru-World.*

Śīla [Shira] XVII: precepts.

Śīla-Pāramitā [Shira-haramitsu] XVII: the Bodhisattva practice of observing the precepts. See *Six Bodhisattva Practices.*

Siṃhacandra (Bhikṣuṇī) [Shishigatsu] XX: Lion-Moon.

Siṃhadhvaja (Buddha) [Shishisō] VII: Lion-Form.

Siṃhaghoṣa (Buddha) [Shishion] VII: Lion-Voice.

Six Bodhisattva Practices [Rokuharamitsu] I: generosity, observing the precepts, patience, endurance, meditation and wisdom. See *Dāna-Pāramitā, Śīla-Pāramitā, Kṣānti-Pāramitā, Vīrya-Pāramitā Dhyāna-Pāramitā,* and *Prajñā-Pāramitā.*

Six Regions [Rokudō] I: hell, the region of hungry spirits, the region of animals, the region of Asuras, the region of men and heaven. See *Sumeru-World.*

Six Sense-Organs [Rokkon] XIX: eye, ear, nose, tongue, body and mind.

Six Supernatural Powers [Rokujinzū, Rokutsū] III: (1) to see everything, (2) to hear everything, (3) to read the minds of others, (4) to go everywhere, (5) to know the previous lives of oneself and of others, and (6) to eliminate illusions. The first five are called the five supernatural powers (Gojinzū). The first, fifth, and sixth are called the three major supernatural powers (Sammyō).

Six Ways, to Quake in the [Rokushu-shindō, Roppen-shindō] I, XII: to shake, rise, reverberate, beat, roar, and crackle.

Sky-Dwelling (Buddha) [Kokūjū] VII: Ākāśapratiṣṭhita.

Small Surrounding Iron Mountains [Shōtetchisen] XXIII. See *Sumeru-World.*

Spotless (World) [Muku] XII: Vimalā.

Śramaṇa [Shamon] I: an ascetic, a monk.

Śrāmaṇera [Shami] VII: a novice.

Śrāvaka [Shōmon] I: originally, a hearer or a disciple of the Buddha. According to Mahāyāna Buddhism, Śrāvakas are those who attain enlightenment through the realization of the Four Noble Truths. There are four kinds of Śrāvaka: (1) the Srota-āpanna or the Śrāvaka who has entered the Way to enlightenment, (2) the Sakṛdāgāmin or the Śrāvaka who is to return to the world of men only once more, (3) the Anāgāmin or the Śrāvaka who does not have to return to the world of men any more, and (4) the Arhat or the Śrāvaka who deserves respect because he has attained enlightenment. The first three are called Śaikṣa or those who have something more to learn while the fourth is called Aśaikṣa or the person who has nothing more to learn. See *Four Noble Truths.*

Śrīgarbha (Bodhisattva) [Tokuzō] I: Virtue-Store.

Srota-Āpanna [Shudaon] XVIII: one of the four types of Śrāvaka. See *Śrāvaka*.
Star-King-Flower (Bodhisattva) [Shukuōke] XXIII: Nakṣatrarājasaṃkusumitābhijña.
Stepping-On-Flower-of-Seven-Treasures (Buddha) [Tōshippōke] IX: Saptaratnapadmavikrāntagāmin.
Stūpa [Tō] I: originally, a mound enshrining the relics of the Buddha.
Śubhavyūha (King) [Myōshōgon] XXVII: Wonderful-Adornment.
Śubhavyūharāja (Bodhisattva) [Shōgonnō] XXIV: Adornment-King.
Subhūti [Shubodai] I: a disciple of the Buddha. See *Śākyamuni*.
Sudharma (Brahman) [Myōhō] VII: Wonderful-Dharma.
Sudharma (Kiṃnara-King) [Myōhō] I: Wonderful-Dharma.
Sukhāvatī (World) [Anraku] XXIII: The World of Happiness.
Sumanas [Shumanna, Shuman] XIX: a plant.
Sumati (Prince) [Zenni] I: Good-Intention.
Sumeru (Mountain) [Shumi] VII: Sumeru. See *Sumeru-World*.
Sumeru-Form (Buddha) [Shumisō] VII: Merukalpa.
Sumeru-Peak (Buddha) [Shumichō] VII: Merukūṭa.
Sumeru-World [Sekai] I: a world of which Mt. Sumeru exists in the center. This was primarily a description of the world conceived by the Indians of those days, but it is later held that there are innumerable worlds of the same form in the universe. Mt. Sumeru is surrounded by golden mountain ranges (golden mountains) seven rounds deep between which there are seven fresh-water oceans. Outside the seventh mountain range is a salt-water ocean, in which are four continents: east Pūrvavideha, south Jambudvīpa, west Aparagodānīya, and north Uttarakuru. The salt-water ocean is surrounded by the Cakravāḍa-parvata or Surrounding Iron Mountains. These mountains are also called the Small Surrounding Iron Mountains when they are referred to in connection with the Great Surrounding Iron Mountains which surround a set of one thousand million Sumeru-worlds. Mt. Sumeru is also called Mt. Meru or Mt. Mahā-Meru. There are the Ten Treasure-Mountains, the tenth being Mt. Sumeru. There are many hells underground, the Avīci Hell or the Hell of Incessant Suffering being the lowest. Men live on the ground; animals, hungry spirits, and asuras, on the ground or in the ocean or underground. Hell, the region of hungry spirits, and the region of animals are called the three evil regions. Hell, the region of hungry spirits, the region of animals, and the region of asuras are called the four evil regions. The upper part of Mt. Sumeru is regarded as part of heaven. Halfway down the slope of Mt. Sumeru is the Heaven of the Four Great Heavenly-Kings: east Dhṛtarāṣṭra, south Virūḍhaka, west Virūpākṣa, and north Vaiśravaṇa. They are also called the four heavenly kings or the four heavenly world-guardian kings. The sun, the moon, and the stars exist in this heaven. The top of Mt. Sumeru is called the Heaven of the Trāyastriṃśa or Thirty-Three Gods, where King Śakra lives in the center and eight gods in each of the four quarters. Above this heaven is the Yama Heaven. Above the Yama Heaven is the Tuṣita Heaven. Above the Tuṣita Heaven is the Nirmāṇarati Heaven. Above the Nirmāṇarati Heaven is the Paranirmitavaśavartin Heaven. In this heaven lives Māra the Evil One and his followers. The realm including hell, the region of hungry spirits, the region of animals, the region of asuras, the world of men, and part of heaven up to the Paranirmitavaśavartin Heaven, is called the realm of desire because the living beings in this realm have desires. Above the Paranirmitavaśavartin Heaven is

the First Dhyāna-Heaven. This is also called the Heaven of Brahman or the World of Brahman because Brahman and his followers live in this heaven. Brahman is also called the Brahman Heavenly-King or King Brahman or Mahā-Brahman or the Great Brahman Heavenly-King. Above the First Dhyāna-Heaven is the Second Dhyāna-Heaven. The Second Dhyāna-Heaven is divided into three spheres, the highest sphere being the Ābhāsvara or Light-Sound Heaven. Above the Second Dhyāna-Heaven is the Third Dhyāna-Heaven, which is also divided into three spheres, the highest sphere being the Śubhakṛtsna or Universal-Pure Heaven. Above the Third Dhyāna-Heaven is the Fourth Dhyāna-Heaven, which is divided into nine spheres, the highest sphere being the Akaniṣṭha or Highest Heaven. In the Akaniṣṭha Heaven lives Īśvara or the Freedom God, who is also called Maheśvara or the Great-Freedom God. In this sūtra Maheśvara is treated as a god different from Īśvara. These four dhyāna-heavens are called the Realm of Form because the gods living there have forms and no desire. Above the Realm of Form is the Formless Realm, in which exists only mind, no form. The Akaniṣṭha Heaven is practically the highest heaven; therefore, it is also called Bhavāgra or the Heaven of the Top of the Realm of Existence. The Realm of Desire, the Realm of Form, and the Formless Realm are called Sangai or the triple world. Heaven, the world of men, the region of asuras, the region of animals, the region of hungry spirits, and hell are called the six regions. Below this world is the sky; that is to say, this world is hanging in the sky. See *One Thousand Million Sumeru-Worlds.*

Sun-Moon-Light (Buddha) [Nichigattōmyō] I: Candrasūryapradīpa; XX: Candrasvararāja.

Sun-Moon-Pure-Bright-Virtue (Buddha) [Nichigatsujōmyōtoku] XXIII: Candravimalasūryaprabhāsaśrī.

Sundarananda [Sondarananda] I: a disciple of the Buddha. See *Śākyamuni.*

Superior-Practice (Bodhisattva) [Jōgyō (variant 2)] XV: Viśiṣṭacāritra.

Superior-Practice-Intent (Bodhisattva) [Jōgyō-i] XXIV: Viśiṣṭacāritra.

Supratiṣṭhitacārita (Bodhisattva) [Anryūgyō] XV: Steadily-Established-Practice.

Surrounding Iron Mountains [Tetchisen] XI.

Sūtra [Kyō] I: a collection of the Buddha's teachings.

Suviśuddha (World) [Zenjō] VIII: Good-Purity.

Svāgata [Shakada] VIII: a disciple of the Buddha. See *Śākyamuni.*

T

Tagara [Takara] XIX: a tree.

Takṣaka (Dragon-King) [Tokushaka] I.

Tāla [Tara] XVII: a tree.

Tamālapattra [Tamaraba] XIX: a tree.

Tamālapattracandana-Fragrance (Buddha) [Tamaraba-sendankō] VI: Tamālapattracandanagandha.

Tamālapattracandana-Fragrance-Supernatural-Power (Buddha) [Tamaraba-sendankō-jinzū] VII: Tamālapattracandanagandhābhijña.

Tamālapattracandanagandha (Buddha) [Tamaraba-sendankō] VI: Tamālapattracandana-Fragrance.

Tamālapattracandanagandhabhijña (Buddha) [Tamaraba-sendankō-jinzū] VII: Tamālapattracandana-Fragrance-Supernatural-Power.

Tathāgata [Nyorai, Tada-akado] I: one who has come in this way. See *Ten Epithets of the Buddha.*

Ten Epithets of the Buddha [Jūgō] I: (1) the Deserver of Offerings, (2) the Perfectly-Enlightened One, (3) the Man of Wisdom and Practice, (4) the Well-Gone, (5) the Knower of the World, (6) the Unsurpassed Man, (7) the Controller of Men, (8) the Teacher of Gods and Men, (9) the Buddha, and (10) the World-Honored One.

Ten Powers of the Buddha [Jūriki] III: (1) to know right from wrong, (2) to know the effect inconsistent with the cause, (3) to know the variety of dhyāna-concentrations, (4) to know the capacities of all living beings, (5) to know the desires of all living beings, (6) to know the natures of all living beings, (7) to know the region each living being is destined to go to, (8) to recollect the past, (9) to foresee the future, and (10) to know the results of the elimination of illusions.

Ten Quarters [Jippō] II: east, southeast, south, southwest, west, northwest, north, northeast, zenith, and nadir.

Ten Treasure-Mountains [Jippōsen] XXIII. See *Sumeru-World.*

Thinking-of-Buddha (Upāsaka) [Shibutsu] XX.

Third Dhyāna-Heaven [Sansekai] XXIII. See *Sumeru-World.*

Thirty-Seven Ways to Enlightenment [Sanjūshichihon-jodōhō] XXVII: the totality of the four thoughts: (1) that the body is impure, (2) that perception is suffering, (3) that the mind is impermanent, and (4) that nothing has its own self; the four right endeavors: (1) to stop evils, (2) to prevent evils, (3) to do good, and (4) to promote good; the four steps to supernatural powers: (1) wish, (2) endeavor, (3) mindfulness, and (4) thinking over things; the five faculties: (1) belief, (2) endeavor, (3) memory, (4) concentration of mind, and (5) wisdom; the five powers of the five faculties; the seven ways to enlightenment: (1) discrimination of the true from the false, (2) endeavor, (3) joy, (4) repose, (5) indifference, (6) concentration of mind, and (7) memory; and the eight right ways. See *Eight Right Ways.*

Thirty-Three Gods [Sanjusanten] XI. See *Sumeru-World.*

Three Evil Regions [Sannakudō] II: Hell, the region of hungry spirits and the region of animals. See *Sumeru-World.*

Three Kinds of Suffering [Sanku] IV: the suffering produced (1) by direct causes, (2) by disappearance, and (3) by the impermanence of all things.

Three Major Supernatural Powers [Sammyō] III: (1) to see everything, (2) to know the previous lives of oneself and of others, and (3) to eliminate illusions. See *Six Supernatural Powers.*

Three Poisons [Sandoku] III: greed, anger, and stupidity.

Three Stores [Sanzō] XIX: the tripiṭaka: the sūtra-piṭaka, vinaya-piṭaka, and abhidharma-piṭaka.

Three Treasures [Sambō] XVI: the Buddha, Dharma, and Saṃgha.

Three Vehicles [Sanjō] I: The Śrāvaka-Vehicle, Pratyekabuddha-Vehicle, and Bodhisattva-Vehicle (or Buddha-Vehicle).

Trailokyavikrāmin (Bodhisattva) [Ossangai] I: Trancending-Triple-World.

Transcending-Triple-World (Bodhisattva) [Ossangai] I: Trailokyavikrāmin.

Trāyastriṃśa Gods [Tōri-shoten] VII: the thirty-three gods. See *Sumeru-World.*

Treasure-Born (World) [Hōshō] VI: Ratnasaṃbhava.

Treasure-Brightness (Kalpa) [Hōmyō] VIII: Ratnāvabhāsa.

Treasure-Form (Buddha) [Hōsō] XI: Ratnaketurāja.

Treasure-Intention (Prince) [Hō-i (variant 2)] I: Ratnamati.

Treasure-Light (God) [Hōkō] I: Ratnaprabha.

Treasure-Moon (Bodhisattva) [Hōgachi] I: Ratnachandra.

Treasure-Palm (Bodhisattva) [Hōshō] I: Ratnapāṇi.

Treasure-Power-Virtue-Superior-King (Buddha) [Hō-itoku-jō-ō] XXVIII: Ratnatejobhyudgatarāja.

Treasure-Purity (World) [Hōjō] XI: Ratnaviśuddha.

Triple World [Sangai] I: the world of form, formlessness and desire. See *Sumeru-World.*

Turuṣka [Toruba] XXIII: a plant.

Tuṣita [Tosotsu] XXVIII. See *Sumeru-World.*

Twelve Causes [Jūni-innen] I: (1) ignorance, (2) predisposition, (3) consciousness, (4) name-and-form, (5) the six sense-organs, (6) touch, (7) sensation, (8) craving, (9) grasping, (10) existence, (11) birth, and (12) aging-and-death.

Twelve Elements of Sūtras [Jūnibukyō] XI: the nine elements of sūtras and the following three: (1) expounding of the Dharma without being questioned *(udāna),* (2) elaborate explanation *(vaipulya),* and (3) assurance of future Buddhahood *(vyākaraṇa).* See *Nine Elements of Sūtras.*

U

Udāna [Mumon-jisetsu] XI: expounding of the Dharma without being questioned. See *Twelve Elements of Sutras.*

Udāyin [Udai] VIII: a disciple of the Buddha. See *Śākyamuni.*

Udumbara [Udombara] VII: also uḍumbara. A plant.

Umāraka [Umarogya] XXVI: a devil.

Universal-Brightness (Buddha) [Fumyō] VIII: Samantaprabhāsa.

Universal-Fragrance (God) [Fukō] I: Samantagandha.

Universal-Pure (Heaven) [Henjō] XIX. See *Sumeru-World.*

Universal-Sage (Bodhisattva) [Fugen] XXVII: Samantabhadra.

Upadeśa [Ubadaishakyō] II: a discourse. See *Nine Elements of Sūtras.*

Upananda (Dragon-King) [Batsunanda] I.

Upāsaka [Ubasoku] I: a male lay devotee.

Upāsikā [Ubai] I: a female lay devotee.

Uruvilvā-Kāśyapa [Urubinra-kashō] I: a disciple of the Buddha. See *Śākyamuni.*

Utpalaka (Dragon-King) [Uhatsura] I.

V

Vaidehī (Queen) [Idaike] I: mother of King Ajātaśatru. See *Śākyamuni.*

Vaipulya [Hōkō] XI: elaborate explanation. See *Twelve Elements of Sutras.*

Vairocanaraśmipratimaṇḍita (World) [Kōmyō-shōgon] XXVII: Light-Adornment.

Vairocanaraśmipratimaṇḍitā (World) [Issai-jōkō-shōgon] XXIV: All-Pure-Light-Adornment.

Vairocanaraśmipratimaṇḍitadhvajarāja (Bodhisattva) [Kōshō-shōgonsō] XXVII: Light-Adornment-Appearance.

Vaiśravaṇa (God) [Bishamon] XXIV: one of the world-guardian kings. See *Sumeru-World.*

Vajra [Kongō] XXV: a weapon.

Vajra-Holding God [Shūkongōjin] XXV: Vajrapāṇi. More properly, Vajradhara.

Vajrapāṇi (God) [Shūkongō] XXV: Vajra-Holding.

Vārāṇasī [Haranai] II: Benares. See *Śākyamuni.*

Varaprabha (Bodhisattva) [Myōkō] I: Wonderful-Light.

Vārṣika [Harishika] XXIII: a plant.

Vāsuki (Dragon-King) [Washukitsu] I.

Vemacitrin (Asura-King) [Bimashittara] I.

Vetāḍa [Bidara, Idara] XXVI: a devil; XXVIII: a demon.

Vilambā (Rākṣasī) [Biramba] XXVI.

Vimalā (World) [Muku] XII: the Spotless World.

Vimaladatta (King) [Jōtoku] XXIII: Pure-Virtue.

Vimaladattā (Queen) [Jōtoku] XXVII: Pure-Virtue.

Vimalagarbha (Prince) [Jōzō] XXVII: Pure-Store.

Vimalanetra (Buddha) [Jōshin] I: Pure-Body.

Vimalanetra (Prince) [Jōgen] XXVII: Pure-Eyes.

Vimatisamudghātin (Prince) [Jogi-i] I: Doubts-Removing-Intention.

Vinirbhoga (Kalpa) [Risui] XX: Free-From-Decay.

Viraja (World) [Riku] III: Free-From-Taint.

Virtue-Store (Bodhisattva) [Tokuzō] I: Śrīgarbha.

Virūḍhaka (God) [Jikoku] XXVI: World-Holding.

Vīrya-pāramitā [Biriya-haramitsu] XVII: the Bodhisattva practice of Endeavor. See *Six Bodhisattva Practices.*

Viśeṣamati (Prince) [Zō-i] I: Increasing-Intention.

Viśiṣṭacāritra (Bodhisattva) [Jōgyō (variant 2)] XV: Superior-Practice.

Viśiṣṭacāritra (Bodhisattva) [Jōgyō-i] XXIV: Superior-Practice-Intent.

Vistīrṇavati (World) [Daikō] XXVII: Great-Light.

Viśuddhacāritra (Bodhisattva) [Jōgyō (variant 1)] XV: Pure-Practice.

Void-King (Buddha) [Kū-ō] IX: Dharmagaganābhyudgatarāja.

Vyākaraṇa [Juki] I: to assure one of his future Buddhahood. See *Twelve Elements of Sutras.*

W

Well-Composed (World) [Kōjō] VII: Saṃbhavā.

Wheel-Turning-Holy-King [Tenrinjō-ō, Tenrinnō] I: Cakravartin. A king of whose chariot the wheels turn to any place without-hindrance. The king of one or two or three or all of the four continents. See *Sumeru-World.*

Wonderful-Adornment (King) [Myōshōgon] XXVII: Śubhavyūha.

Wonderful-Dharma (Brahman) [Myōhō] I: Sudharma.

Wonderful-Dharma (Kiṃnara-King) [Myōhō] I: Sudharma.

Wonderful-Light (Bodhisattva) [Myōkō] I: Varaprabha.

Wonderful-Voice (Bodhisattva) [Myō-on] XXIV: Gadgadasvara.

Wonderful-Voice-Resounding-Everywhere (Kalpa) [Myō-on-hemman] X: Manojñaśabdābhigarjita.

World-Holding (God) [Jikoku] XXVI: Virūḍhaka.

World-Voice-Perceiver (Bodhisattva) [Kanzeon] I: Avalokiteśvara. More properly, Avalokitasvara.

Worlds of the Ten Quarters [Jippōkai] II: east, southeast, south, southwest, west, northwest, north, northeast, zenith, and nadir. It is held that each world is a Buddha-world, which is composed of one thousand million Sumeru-worlds. Although the exact number of each of those worlds is not given, it is held that the worlds of each quarter are equal in number, and that, as far as the first eight quarters are concerned, they are adjacent to each other, passable through each other. It is also held that one can travel through the sky from and to any of the worlds of the ten quarters. See *One Thousand Million Sumeru-Worlds.*

Y

Yakṣa [Yasha] I: a devil.

Yaśaskāma (Bodhisattva) [Gumyō] I: Fame-Seeking.

Yaśodharā [Yashutara] I: the wife of the Buddha. See *Śākyamuni.*

Yaṣṭi [Setsu] XVII: a rod.

Yojana [Yujun] I: the distance of a day's journey by the chariot of a king.

CHINESE/JAPANESE GLOSSARY

IMPORTANT CHINESE BUDDHIST TERMS GIVEN IN THE LOTUS SUTRA

Notes:

1. The Chinese Buddhist terms are given in the Japanese pronunciation.
2. The Roman numeral shows the chapter in which the term appears for the first time with the particular meaning indicated.

A

Abatsumara 阿跋摩羅 XXVI: a devil. Apasmāraka.

Abeibatchi, Abibatchi 阿鞞跋致 III: the stage of irrevocability. See *Ayui-Otchi, Futai, Futaiten.*

Abigoku 阿鼻獄 I: the Avīci Hell. The Hell of Incessant Suffering. See *Abijigoku.* See *Sumeru World* in the English/Sanskrit Glossary.

Abijigoku 阿鼻地獄 I. See *Abigoku.* See *Sumeru World* in the English/Sanskrit Glossary.

Adaimokutaka 阿提目多伽 XVII: a plant. *Premna Spinosa.*

Ai 愛 VII: craving. One of the twelve causes. See *Jūni-innen.*

Aitta 阿逸多 XVII: Ajita – "Invincible." An epithet of Maitreya Bodhisattva.

Ajase (King) 阿闍世 I: Ajātaśatru. See *Śākyamuni* in the English/Sanskrit Glossary.

Akanita (Heaven) 阿迦尼吒 I: the Highest Heaven. Akaniṣṭha. See *Sumeru World* in the English/Sanskrit Glossary.

Akki 惡鬼 III: a devil, a demon.

Akudō 惡道 II: evil regions. See *Sumeru World* in the English/Sanskrit Glossary.

Akugō 惡業 XVI: evil karmas.

Akuma 惡魔 XXIII: Māra the Evil One. See *Sumeru World* in the English/Sanskrit Glossary.

Akurasetsu 惡羅刹 XXV: a devil. Rākṣasa.

Akuritsugi 惡律義 XVI: people who do evils for their livelihood.

Akuse 惡世 II: an evil world.

Akushu 惡趣 VII: the evil regions. See *Sumeru World* in the English/Sanskrit Glossary.

Amida (Buddha) 阿彌陀 VII: Amitāyus.

Anabadatta (Dragon-King) 阿那婆達多 I: Anavatapta.

Anagon 阿那含 XVIII: Anāgāmin. See *Shōmon*. See *Śrāvaka* in the English/Sanskrit Glossary.

Anagondō 阿那含道 XVII: the enlightenment of the Anāgāmin. See *Śrāvaka* in the English/Sanskrit Glossary.

Anan 阿難 I: Ānanda. See *Śākyamuni* in the English/Sanskrit Glossary.

Anjū 安住 III: with, to obtain; VII: to dwell peacefully in; X: to do; XIV: to practice; XVII: peaceful; XIX: without moving about, to reach; XXVII: to find peace in.

Annon 安穩 II: peace; VII: to have a good rest; VIII: to comfort.

Anokutara-sammyaku-sambodai 阿耨多羅三藐三菩提 I: perfect enlightenment. Anuttara-samyak-saṃbodhi. See *Tōshōgaku, Shōgaku.*

Anraku 安樂 VI: happy and peaceful, comfortable, easy; XXIII: the World of Happiness. Sukhāvatī.

Anrakugyō 安樂行 XIV: peaceful practices.

Anryūgyō (Bodhisattva) 安立行 XV: Steadily-Established-Practice. Supratiṣṭhitacārita.

Anuruda 阿㝹樓馱 I: Aniruddha. See *Śākyamuni* in the English/Sanskrit Glossary.

Anyakyōjinnyo 阿若憍陳如 I: Ājñāta-Kauṇḍinya. Also Kauṇḍinya. See *Śākyamuni* in the English/Sanskrit Glossary.

Araka 阿羅訶 I: Arhat. See *Ōgu.*

Arakan 阿羅漢 I: Arhat. Also Rakan. See *Shōmon*. See *Śrāvaka* in the English/Sanskrit Glossary.

Arakandō 阿羅漢道 VIII: Arhatship, the enlightenment of the Arhat. See *Śrāvaka* in the English/Sanskrit Glossary.

Arakanga 阿羅漢果 XII: Arhatship. See *Śrāvaka* in the English/Sanskrit Glossary.

Arennya 阿練若 XIII: a retired place. Originally, a forest. Aranya.

Ariju 阿梨樹 XXVI: a tree. *Ocimum Gratissimum.* Arjaka.

Ashi 阿私 XII: a seer. Asita.

Ashuku (Buddha) 阿閦 VII: Akṣobhya.

Ashukuba 阿閦婆 XXIII: akṣobhya, the twentieth power of ten.

Ashura 阿修羅 I: a demon. He fights with Śakra. Asura. See *Sumeru World* in the English/Sanskrit Glossary.

Ashura-ō 阿修羅王 I: an asura-king.

Ashuradō 阿修羅道 VI: the region of asuras. See *Sumeru World* in the English/Sanskrit Glossary.

Asōgi 阿僧祇 I: asaṃkhya. Innumerable. It sometimes means the fifty-second power of ten.

Ayui-otchi 阿惟越致 XIII: Irrevocability. See *Abeibatchi.*

B

Baji (Asura-King) 婆稚 I: Balin.

Bangai 旛蓋 II: streamers and canopies.

Baramon 婆羅門 I: brāhmaṇa. A priest of Brahmanism.

Batsudabara (Bodhisattva) 颰陀婆羅 I: Bhadrapāla.

Batsunanda (Dragon-King) 跋難陀 I: Upananda.

Benzai 辯才 I: eloquence.

Bidara 毗陀羅 XXVI: vetāḍa. Also vetāla. A devil.
Biku 比丘 I: bhikṣu, a monk.
Bikuni 比丘尼 I: bhikṣuṇī, a nun.
Bikusō 比丘僧 III: the Saṃgha of Bhikṣus.
Bimashittara (Asura-King) 毗摩質多羅 I: Vemacitrin.
Bimba 頻婆 XXVII: a tree. *Momordica Monadelpha.*
Bimbara 頻婆羅 XXIII: biṃbara. The eighteenth power of ten.
Biramba (Rākṣasī) 毗藍婆 XXVI: Vilambā.
Biriya-haramitsu 毘梨耶波羅蜜 XVII: the vīrya-pāramitā. Endeavor. See *Rokuharamitsu.*
Bishaja 毗舎闍 XIX: piśācaka. A devil.
Bishamon (God) 毗沙門 XXIV: Vaiśravaṇa. See *Sumeru World* in the English/Sanskrit Glossary.
Bodai 菩提 XII: Bodhi. Enlightenment.
Bodaiju 菩提樹 VII: the Bodhi tree.
Bombu 凡夫 III: men; IV: ordinary men; XVI: people; XIX: unenlightened ones.
Bon 梵 I: brahma, pure; VII: Brahman. See *Sumeru World* in the English/Sanskrit Glossary.
Bonden 梵天 VII: a brahman-heavenly(-king); XI: the Heaven of Brahman. See *Sumeru World* in the English/Sanskrit Glossary.
Bondennō 梵天王 I: the Brahman Heavenly-King. See *Sumeru World* in the English/Sanskrit Glossary.
Bongyō 梵行 I: brahma practices, Pure Practices.
Bonji 梵志 III: aspirants for the teaching of Brahman.
Bonju 梵衆 VII: the Brahmans. See *Sumeru World* in the English/Sanskrit Glossary.
Bonnō 梵王 II: a brahman; XXIV: King Brahman. See *Sumeru World* in the English/Sanskrit Glossary.
Bonnō 煩悩 I: illusions.
Bonnōjoku 煩悩濁 II: defilement by illusions. See *Gojoku.*
Bonnōma 煩悩魔 XIV: the māra of illusions. The evil that is illusions.
Bonnon 梵音 I: brahma voice, pure voice; XXV: the voice of Brahman.
Bonsō (Buddha) 梵相 VII: Brahma-Form. Brahmadvaja.
Bonze 梵世 XXI: the World of Brahman. See *Sumeru World* in the English/Sanskrit Glossary.
Bosatsu 菩薩 I: Bodhisattva. One who seeks Buddhahood.
Bosatsu-Makasatsu 菩薩摩訶薩 I: Bodhisattva-mahāsattva. See *Daiji.*
Bosatsudō 菩薩道 I: the way of Bodhisattvas.
Buppō 佛法 I: the teachings of the Buddha.
Busshari 佛舎利 I: the śarīras of the Buddha. The relics of the Buddha.
Busshu 佛種 II: the seed of Buddhahood.
Butsu 佛 I: the Buddha. The Enlightened One. One of the ten epithets of the Buddha. See *Jūgō.*
Butsudo 佛土 I: a Buddha world.
Butsudō 佛道 I: the enlightenment of the Buddha, the Way to Buddhahood; XV: the teachings of the Buddha.

Butsuji 佛事 VIII: the work of the Buddha, a deed of the Buddha; XVI: what a Buddha should do.
Butsujō 佛乘 II: the Buddha-Vehicle.
Butsuju 佛壽 XVI: the duration of the life of the Buddha.
Butsumyō 佛廟 II: a mausoleum of the Buddha.
Buttō 佛塔 II: a stūpa of the Buddha.
Byakue 白衣 XIII: men of white robes, laymen; XXI: a person in white robes.
Byakugon 白銀 XXIV: silver.
Byakuhotsu 白拂 IV: an insect-sweeper of white hairs.
Byakushibutsu 辟支佛 I: Pratyekabuddha. See *Engaku, Hyakushibutsu.*
Byakuzō-ō 白象王 XXVIII: a kingly white elephant.
Byōdō 平等 V: equally; XI: the teaching of equality; XIV: without partiality.

C

Chi 癡 I: stupidity.
Chie 智慧 I: wisdom.
Chigu, Chigū 值遇 II: to meet, to see.
Chiin-zammai 智印三昧 XXIV: the samādhi for the emblem of wisdom.
Chiken 知見 II: insight.
Chiken-haramitsu 知見波羅蜜 II: the pāramitā of insight.
Chikushō 畜生 III: animals.
Chisha 智者 I: men of wisdom; XVIII: a wise person.
Chishaku (Bodhisattva) 智積 XII: Accumulated-Wisdom. Prajñakūṭa.
Chishaku (Prince) 智積 VII: Accumulated-Wisdom. Jñānākara.
Chishiki 知識 I: known to; XVIII: an acquaintance.
Chishō 智性 III: intelligence.
Chōdai 頂戴 IV: to carry on one's head.
Chōju 長壽 XVII: to live long.
Chōju 頂受 III: to receive on one's head.
Chōko 聽許 VII: to concede.
Chōrai 頂禮 XXV: to bow.
Chōtan 長短 XIV: merits and demerits.
Chū 籌 XV: a counting wand.
Chūki 注記 IV: notes.
Chūkō 中劫 XII: an intermediate kalpa. See *Kō.*
Chūrin 稠林 II: thick forests.
Chūryō 籌量 III: to think over; IV: to see; VII: to consider; XIX: to measure.
Chūsengai 中千界 XVII: one million Sumeru-worlds. See *Sanzendaisensekai.*
Chūya 中夜 I: midnight.

D

Dai 臺 XXIII: a platform.
Dai-ichigi 第一義 II: the highest truth.
Dai-itoku (Garuḍa-King) 大威德 I: Great-Power-Virtue. Mahātejas.

Dai-ō 大雄 XV: the Great Hero. An epithet of the Buddha.
Dai-ō-myō 大雄猛 VI: the Great Hero. An epithet of the Buddha.
Daibadatta 提婆達多 XII: Devadatta. See *Śākyamuni* in the English/Sanskrit Glossary.
Daibon 大梵 I: the Great Brahman. See *Sumeru World* in the English/Sanskrit Glossary.
Daibondennō 大梵天王 VII: the Great Brahman-Heavenly-King.
Daichi 大智 III: a man of great wisdom; VIII: the wisdom of the Great Vehicle.
Daigyōsetsu (Bodhisattva) 大樂說 XI: Great-Eloquence. Mahā-Pratibhāna.
Daihi 大悲 III: great loving-kindness.
Daihi (Brahman) 大悲 VII: Great-Compassion. Adhimātrakāruṇika.
Daihō (Kiṃnara-King) 大法 I: Great-Dharma. Mahādharma.
Daihō-shōgon (Kalpa) 大寶莊嚴 III: Great-Treasure-Adornment. Mahāratnapratimaṇḍita.
Daiitokuzō-Sammai 大威德藏三昧 XXVII: the samādhi for the great store of powers and virtues.
Daiji 大慈 III: great compassion.
Daiji 大士 I: a great man. Mahāsattva. A man of the Great Vehicle.
Daijizai (God) 大自在 I: Great-Freedom. Maheśvara. See *Sumeru World* in the English/Sanskrit Glossary.
Daijō 大乘 I: the Great Vehicle. Mahāyāna.
Daijō (World) 大成 XX: Great-Achievement. Mahāsaṃbhavā.
Daijōkyō 大乘經 I: a sūtra of the Great Vehicle.
Daikan 臺觀 VIII: tall buildings.
Daikasennen 大迦旃延 VI: the Great Kātyāyana. Mahā-Kātyāyana. See *Śākyamuni* in the English/Sanskrit Glossary.
Daikō (World) 大光 XXVII: Great-Light. Vistīrṇavati.
Daikō-ō (Kalpa) 大高王 XXVII: Great-Height-King. Abhyudgatarāja.
Daiman (Garuḍa-King) 大滿 I: Great-Fulfillment. Mahāpūrṇa.
Daimokkenren 大目犍連 I: the Great-Maudgalyāyana. Mahā-Maudgalyāyana. See *Śākyamuni* in the English/Sanskrit Glossary.
Daininsō 大人相 XXIV: the marks of a great man.
Dairiki (Bodhisattva) 大力 I: Great-Power. Mahāvikrāmin.
Daisei 大勢 II: great power.
Daisengai 大千界 XI: one thousand million Sumeru-worlds. See *Sanzendaisensekai.*
Daishi 大師 XV: a great teacher.
Daishin (Garuḍa-King) 大身 I: Great-Body. Mahākāya.
Daishō 大聖 I: the Great Saint. An epithet of the Buddha.
Daishōshu 大聖主 II: the Great Saintly Master. An epithet of the Buddha.
Daishōson 大聖尊 II: The Great Honorable Saint. An epithet of the Buddha.
Daishu 大衆 I: the great multitude.
Daisō (Kalpa) 大相 VII: Great-Form. Mahārūpa.
Daitetchisen 大鐵圍山 XV: the Great Surrounding Iron Mountains. See *Sanzendaisensekai.*
Daitoku 逮得 I: to attain.
Daitsūchishō (Buddha) 大通智勝 VII: Great-Universal-Wisdom-Excellence. Mahābhijñājñānābhibhū.

Dambaramitsu 檀波羅蜜 XVII: the dāna-pāramitā. Almsgiving. See *Rokuharamitsu.*

Danzetsu 斷絕 XXIII: to be lost; XXVIII: to be destroyed.

Darani 陀羅尼 I: dhāraṇī. A formula to memorize teachings.

Darani-bosatsu 陀羅尼菩薩 XVIII: the Bodhisattvas who obtained dhāraṇīs.

Daranishu 陀羅尼咒 XXVI: dhāraṇī-spells. Dhāraṇīs used as spells.

Datsu-issai-shujō-shōke (Rākṣasī) 奪一切衆生精氣 XXVI: Plunderer-of-Energy-of-All-Beings. Sarvasattvojohārī.

Dendō 殿堂 XVII: a hall.

Deshi 弟子 I: a disciple.

Do-issai-seken-kunō (Buddha) 度一切世間苦惱 VII: Saving-All-Worlds-From-Suffering Sarvalokadhātūpadravodvegapratyuttīrṇa.

Dōban 幢旛 I: banners and streamers.

Dodatsu 度脫 I: to save.

Dōhō 道法 II: teachings.

Dōjō 道場 I: the place of enlightenment.

Dōju 道樹 XVII: the tree of enlightenment. The Bodhi-tree.

Dōka 道果 V: the fruit of enlightenment.

Dōkaku 堂閣 III: buildings; XVI: stately buildings; XVII: halls.

Dokuju 讀誦 I: to read and recite.

Dongon 鈍根 II: dull.

Dōri 導利 XVI: to lead and benefit.

Dōriki 道力 XII: the power of giving discourses.

Dōshi 導師 I: the Leading Teacher, an epithet of the Buddha; VII: a leader.

Dōshi (Bodhisattva) 導師 I: Leading-Teacher.

Dōtai 道諦 I: the truth that the Way to Nirvāṇa is the eight right ways. See *Hasshōdō, Shitai.*

E

E 會 I: a congregation.

E-issai-seken-fui (Buddha) 壞一切世間怖畏 VII: Eliminating-Fear-of-All-Worlds. Sarvalokabhayacchambhitatvavidhvaṃsanakara.

Egen-dai-ichijō 慧眼第一淨 VII: the purest eyes of wisdom.

Eigo 衛護 X: to protect.

Ejoku 穢濁 XIX: defiled.

Ekka 悅可 I: to delight; III: to approve.

Eko 依怙 III: to rely on.

Ekō 回向 VII: to distribute the merits.

Eko-sammai 慧炬三昧 XXIV: the samādhi for the torch of wisdom.

Ekoku 衣祴 III: a flower plate.

Embudai 閻浮提 XVIII: the Jambudvīpa. Also Ichiembudai. See *Sumeru World* in the English/Sanskrit Glossary.

Embudan-gon 閻浮檀金 XVII: Jāmbūnada Gold. The gold found in the river running through the forest of the jāmbū trees.

Embukonkō (Buddha) 閻浮金光 VI. See *Embunadaikonkō.*

Embunadaikonkō (Buddha) 閻浮那提金光 VI: Jāmbūnada-Gold-Light. Jāmbūnadaprabhāsa.

Emmoku 宴默 I: silent in peace.

Emyō 慧命 IV: men living the life of wisdom.

Enchō 演暢 III: to expound.

Engaku 縁覺 I: a cause-knower. Pratyekabuddha. More properly, Pratyayabuddha. One who realizes the truth of the twelve causes. See *Twelve Causes* in the English/Sanskrit Glossary.

Engakujō 縁覺乘 II: the Vehicle of cause-knowers.

Enichi 慧日 II: the Sun of Wisdom, an epithet of the Buddha; XXV: the light of wisdom as pure as that of the sun.

Enjaku 宴寂 VII: peaceful extinction.

Eshi 依止 II: to be attached to; XV: to live with, to live in.

Etsuyo 悅豫 V: to rejoice.

F

Fuchison 普智尊 III: the Honorable One of Universal Wisdom. An epithet of the Buddha.

Fuchitenninson 普智天人尊 VII: the All-Knower, the Most Honorable of Gods and Men. An epithet of the Buddha.

Fuen 敷演 I: to explain, to expound.

Fugen (Bodhisattva) 普賢 XXVIII: Universal-Sage. Samantabhadra.

Fugu-sammai 不共三昧 XXIV: the samādhi for special teachings.

Fui 怖畏 VII: fear.

Fujitsu 不實 II: insincere; XV: to tell a lie.

Fūju 諷誦 VII: to recite.

Fukashigi 不可思議 I: inconceivable.

Fukō (God) 普香 I: Universal-Fragrance. Samantagandha.

Fukue 福慧 II: merits and wisdom.

Fukugō 福業 III: good karmas.

Fukuhō 福報 XXVIII: the rewards of one's merits.

Fukuju 福聚 XXV: accumulated merits.

Fukusoku (Bodhisattva) 不休息 I: Never-Resting. Anikṣiptadhura.

Fukutoku 福德 II: merits and virtues.

Fumbetsu 分別 I: to explain clearly; II: to divide; X: to expound; XV: to evaluate; XVI: opinions; XVII: variety; XVIII: to tell of.

Fumbu 分布 I: to distribute.

Fumon 普門 XXV: the universal gate.

Fumyō (Buddha) 普明 VIII: Universal-Brightness. Samantaprabhāsa.

Funan 不男 XIV: eunuchs.

Funjin 分身 XI: the replicas of Śākyamuni Buddha.

Furōfushi 不老不死 XXIII: not to get older or die.

Furuna 富樓那 I: Pūrṇa. See *Śākyamuni* in the English/Sanskrit Glossary.

Fuse 布施 I: to give; II: almsgiving; XVII: to offer; XXIII: offerings.

Fushin 不信 II: unfaithful.

Futai 不退 II: never-faltering; VI: irrevocable; XII: the stage of irrevocability. See *Futaiten, Abeibatchi, Ayui-otchi.*

Futai-bosatsu 不退菩薩 III: Never-Faltering Bodhisattva.

Futaichi 不退智 XIV: irrevocable wisdom.

Futaiten 不退轉 I: the state of irrevocability. See *Futai, Abeibatchi, Ayui-otchi.*

Futanna 富單那 XXVI: Pūtana, A devil.

Fuzengon 不善根 II: roots of evil.

Fuzoku 付囑 XI: to transmit.

G

Gaki 餓鬼 III: hungry spirits.

Gakkō (Bodhisattva) 月光 I: Moon-Light. Ratnaprabha.

Gaku 學 I: the Śrāvakas who have something more to learn. Śaikṣa. See *Shōmon.* See *Śrāvaka* in the English/Sanskrit Glossary.

Gaku (Gandharva-King) 樂 I: Musical. Manojña. It was once pronounced Gyō, meaning "to wish."

Gakuon (Gandharva-King) 樂音 I: Musical-Voice. Manojñasvara. It was once pronounced Gyō-on.

Gakushū 學習 XV: to study.

Gaman 我慢 II: arrogant; XXVIII: arrogance from selfishness.

Ganriki 願力 XI: the power of one's vow.

Garyaku 瓦礫 VI: tile-pieces and rubble.

Gashaku 瓦石 III: tile-pieces and stones.

Gasshō 合掌 I: to join one's hands together.

Gattenji 月天子 XXIII: the Moon God.

Gaya (City) 伽耶 XV: Gayā. See *Śākyamuni* in the English/Sanskrit Glossary.

Gaya-kashō 伽耶迦葉 I: Gayā-Kāśyapa. See *Śākyamuni* in the English/Sanskrit Glossary.

Ge 偈 I: a verse. See *Gāthā* in the English/Sanskrit Glossary.

Ge-issaishujō-gogon-darani 解一切衆生語言陀羅尼 XXIII: the dhāraṇīs by which one can understand the words of all living beings.

Ge-issaishujō-gogon-zammai 解一切衆生語言三昧 XXIV: the samādhi by which one can understand the words of all living beings.

Gedatsu 解脫 II: emancipation; XXV: to be released.

Gedō 外道 III: heresy, heretics.

Gen-issai-seken (World) 現一切世間 XXIV: Appearance-of-All-Worlds. Sarvarūpasaṃdarśanā.

Gen-issai-shikishin-zammai 現一切色身三昧 XXIII: the samādhi by which one can transform oneself into any other living being. See *Issai-gen-shoshin-zammai.*

Genge 限礙 V: to hinder.

Gengō 賢劫 VIII: the Kalpa of Sages. Bhadra Kalpa. See *Kō.*

Genjō 賢聖 VIII: sages and saints.

Genjō 閑靜 I: a retired place.

Genke 現化 VIII: transformation.

Genko 閑居 III: to live in a retired place.

Genze 現世 V: the present life.

Geshi 牙齒 XXVIII: teeth.

Gesho 外書 XIV: non-Buddhist books.

Gi 義 I: teaching, meaning, truth.

Gigaku 伎樂 妓樂 I: music.

Gigi 巍巍 XXV: great.

Gike 疑悔 I: doubts; XIV: to be perplexed.

Giku 疑懼 VI: doubts and fears; XV: to doubt, to be afraid.

Gimō 疑網 II: the mesh of doubts.

Gishakutsu (Mountain) 耆闍崛 I: Gṛdhrakūṭa. Also Mt. Sacred Eagle. See *Ryōju*. See *Śākyamuni* in the English/Sanskrit Glossary.

Gishiki 儀式 II: manner.

Gishu 義趣 XI: meaning.

Giya 祇夜 II. See *Kubuhō*. See *Geya* in the English/Sanskrit Glossary.

Gō 業 II: karma, anything which is thought, said, or done; XVI: practice.

Go-on-ma 五陰魔 XIV: the māra of the five aggregates. The evil that is the five aggregates.

Go-on 五陰 XIV. See *Goshū*. See *Five Aggregates* in the English/Sanskrit Glossary.

Gobiku 五比丘 II: the five bhikṣus. See *Śākyamuni* in the English/Sanskrit Glossary.

Gobun 後分 XXIII: the last watch of a night.

Gōgashakō 恒河沙劫 II: as many kalpas as there are sands in the River Ganges.

Goharamitsu 五波羅蜜 XVII: the five pāramitās. The six pāramitās except the prajñā-pāramitā. See *Rokuharamitsu*.

Goji 護持 VIII: to protect, to keep.

Gojinzū 五神通 I: the five supernatural powers. The six supernatural powers except the sixth. See *Rokujinzū*.

Gojo 護助 XXVIII: to protect.

Gojō 五情 XXIV: the five desires. See *Goyoku*.

Gojoku 五濁 II. See *Kōjoku, Bonnōjoku, Shujōjoku, Kenjoku, Myōjoku*. See *Five Defilements* in the English/Sanskrit Glossary.

Gokon 五根 XXVII: the five faculties. See *Sanjūshichihon-jodōhō*. See *Thirty-Seven Ways to Enlightenment* in the English/Sanskrit Glossary.

Gonen 護念 I: to protect.

Gongu 勤求 I: to seek strenuously.

Gongyō 勤行 XII: to practice, to do.

Gonji 言辭 II: voices, discourses; XXI: words.

Gonjō 嚴淨 I: beautiful and pure.

Gonka 勤加 IV: strenuous, to make efforts.

Gonkō 嚴好 XVII: beautiful; XVIII: well-shaped.

Gonku 勤苦 VII: to make painstaking efforts; VIII: to work hard; XII: with strenuous efforts.

Gonsa 勤作 IV: to work hard.

Gonshu 勤修 III: to exert oneself; VIII: to practice strenuously.

Gonshu 言趣 XIX: the meaning of words.

Gonzetsu 言說 II: teachings; III: words, to expound, to say.

Goppōsho 業報處 I: the region in which a living beings is destined to be reborn by his karmas.

Goriki 五力 XXVII: the five powers. See *Sanjūshichihon-jodōhō.* See *Thirty-Seven Ways to Enlightenment* in the English/Sanskrit Glossary.

Gose 後世 V: the future life.

Gose-shitennō 護世四天王 II: the four heavenly world-guardian kings. The four great heavenly-kings. See *Sumeru World* in the English/Sanskrit Glossary.

Goseja 護世者 XXVI: the protector of the world.

Gōshiki 强識 III: to remember well; VII: to have a good memory.

Goshin 後身 VI: the final stage of one's physical existence.

Goshū 五衆 III: the five aggregates. See *Go-on.*

Goyoku 五欲 II: the desires to have the pleasures of the five senses.

Gozusendan 牛頭旃檀 IV: the cow-head candana. Gośīrṣacandana. Some say that Gośīrṣa is the name of a mountain.

Guchi 愚癡 III: stupidity.

Gummō, Gummyō 群萌 XIX: living beings.

Gumyō (Bodhisattva) 求名 I: Fame-Seeking. Yaśaskāma.

Gunjō 群生 VII: living beings.

Gusoku 具足 I: perfect; II: to have; X: to complete; XXV: with.

Gusoku-semman-kōsō (Buddha) 具足千萬光相 XIII: Emitting-Ten-Million-Rays-of-Light. Raśmiśatasahasraparipūrṇadhvaja.

Gusokudō 具足道 II: the Perfect Way.

Gyaku-rokayada 逆路伽耶陀 XIV: Anti-Lokāyatas. See *Rokayada.*

Gyō 行 I: practices; VII: predisposition.

Gyōja 行者 XX: one who practices the Way. See *Jūni-innen.*

Gyōjūzaga 行住坐臥 XXVII: to walk, stand, sit, and lie.

Gyōsetsu 樂說 X: to expound with joy; XXI: eloquence.

Gyōsho 行處 XIV: proper practices.

H

Hachibu 八部 XII. See *Eight Kinds of Supernatural Beings* in the English/Sanskrit Glossary.

Hachigedatsu 八解脫 VI. See *Eight Emancipations* in the English/Sanskrit Glossary.

Hachijisshu-myōkō 八十種妙好 III: the eighty wonderful physical marks. See *Hachijisshugō.*

Hachijisshugō 八十種好 XII: the eighty minor marks. A more detailed description of the body of the Buddha than thirty-two physical marks of the Buddha. See *Sanjūnisō.*

Hajun 波旬 III: Pāpīyas. Another name of Māra. See *Ma.*

Hakai 破戒 XIV: to violate the precepts.

Hakura 薄拘羅 I: Bakkula. See *Śākyamuni* in the English/Sanskrit Glossary.

Hannya 般若 XVII: the attainment of wisdom.

Hannya-haramitsu 般若波羅蜜 XVII: the Prajñā-pāramitā. Attainment of wisdom. See *Rokuharamitsu.*

Harada 頗羅墮 I: Bharadvāja. The name of a family.

Haramitsu 波羅蜜 I: pāramitā. A Bodhisattva practice. A practice required for crossing over to the Other Shore or Nirvāṇa.

Haranai 波羅奈 II: Vārāṇasī. Benares. See *Śākyamuni* in the English/Sanskrit Glossary.

Harara 波羅羅 XIX: pāṭala. A plant.

Hari 頗黎 I: crystal.

Harishika 婆利師迦 XXIII: vārṣika. A plant.

Harishitta 波利質多 XIX: pārijātaka. A tree which grows in the garden of Śakra. See *Harishittara.*

Harishittara 波利質多羅 XIX. See *Harishitta.*

Hashikake-yutō 婆師迦華油燈 XXVI: lamps of vārṣika-flower oil.

Hasshōdō 八正道 VII. See *Eight Right Ways* in the English/Sanskrit Glossary.

Hatsu 鉢 XXIV: pātra. An alms bowl.

Hatsunehan 般涅槃 I: complete extinction. Parinirvāṇa. The death of the Buddha.

Henge 變化 VI: to transform oneself; XXIV: the power of transformation.

Hengen 變現 XXIV: to transform oneself.

Hengenin 變化人 X: men produced by the supernatural powers of the Buddha.

Hengeshō 變化生 VIII: to be born without any medium. See *Keshō.*

Henjō (Heaven) 徧淨 XIX: Universal-Pure. See *Sumeru World* in the English/Sanskrit Glossary.

Hentō 偏黨 III: partiality.

Hiai 悲哀 XXIII: sorrow.

Hien 疲厭 V: to be tired of.

Higan 彼岸 I: the Other Shore, as contrasted with this shore, which is the world of birth and death. Nirvāṇa.

Hihō 誹謗 III: to slander.

Hikkyō 畢竟 XXI: finally.

Himitsu 秘密 XVI: the secret lore.

Hinin 非人 I: nonhuman beings.

Hinō 悲惱 I: sorrow.

Hinzui 擯出 XIII: to drive out.

Hippaku 逼迫 II: to trouble; IV: to force to.

Hitsurikika 畢力迦 XXIII: pṛkkā. A plant.

Hitsuryōgabasha 畢陵伽婆蹉 I: Pilindavatsa. See *Śākyamuni* in the English/Sanskrit Glossary.

Hiyō 秘要 II: the secret lore.

Hiyu 譬喩 II: parables and similes. Aupamya. See *Kubuhō.*

Hizō 秘藏 IV: the store of the secret lore.

Hō (Kiṃnara-King) 法 I: Dharma. Druma, which literally means "tree."

Hō-e 法會 XVIII: a congregation.

Hō-i 法位 II: the position of the Dharma.

Hō-i (Prince) (variant 1) 法意 I: Dharma-Intention. Dharmamati.

Hō-i (Prince) (variant 2) 寶意 I: Treasure-Intention. Ratnamati.

Hō-in 法印 III: the emblem of the Dharma.

Hō-itoku-jō-ō (Buddha) 寶威德上王 XXVIII: Treasure-Power-Virtue-Superior-King. Ratnatejobhyudgatarāja.

Hō-itsu 放逸 I: license.

Hō-ō 法王 I: the King of the Dharma. An epithet of the Buddha.

Hō-ō-ji 法王子 XIV: a son of the King of the Dharma. A Bodhisattva.

Hō-on 法音 III: the voice of the Dharma. The sacred voice.

Hō-on-hōben-darani 法音方便陀羅尼 XXVIII: the dhāraṇīs by which one can understand the expediency of the voice of the Dharma.

Hō-u 法雨 I: the rain of the Dharma.

Hōben 方便 I: an expedient.

Hōben-haramitsu 方便波羅蜜 XXVII: the pāramitā of expediency.

Hōbuku 法服 I: the robe of the Dharma. The sacred robe.

Hōbyō 寶瓶 XXIII: jeweled vases.

Hōchō 寶帳 IV: a jeweled awning.

Hōgachi (Bodhisattva) 寶月 I: Treasure-Moon. Ratnacandra.

Hōgai 寶蓋 XII: jeweled canopies.

Hōgenjō 法眼淨 XXVII: eyes purified enough to see all teachings.

Hōjakumessō 法寂滅相 I: tranquil extinction of all things.

Hōjō (World) 寶淨 XI: Treasure-Purity. Ratnaviśuddha.

Hōju 寶珠 I: a gem.

Hōjū 法住 II: the abode of the Dharma.

Hōke 法化 VII: to propagate the Dharma; XVIII: to lead others by the Dharma.

Hōki 法喜 XI: the delight in the Dharma.

Hōki 法器 XII: a recipient of the teachings of the Buddha.

Hokke-sammai 法華三昧 XXIV: the samādhi for the Lotus Flower of the Wonderful Dharma.

Hokki 發起 XXVII: to inspire.

Hokku 法鼓 I: the drum of the Dharma.

Hōkō (God) 寶光 I: Treasure-Light. Ratnaprabha.

Hōkō 方廣 IX: elaborate explanation. See *Jūnibukyō.*

Hōmon 法門 II: a teaching.

Hōmyō (Buddha) 法明 VIII: Dharma-Brightness. Dharmaprabhāsa.

Hōmyō (Kalpa) 寶明 VIII: Treasure-Brightness. Ratnāvabhāsa.

Hongan 本願 III: an original vow; VIII: a wish.

Honin 保任 III: to assure.

Honji 本事 II: the story of the previous life of the disciple of a Buddha. Itivṛttaka. See *Kubuhō.*

Honjō 本生 II: the story of the previous life of a Buddha. Jātaka. See *Kubuhō.*

Honseigan 本誓願 II: an original vow.

Honshin 本心 XVI: the right mind.

Hōnyo 寶女 XIX: the ladies of a king.

Hōri 法利 XVII: the benefits of the Dharma.

Hōrin 法輪 I: the wheel of the Dharma.

Hōse 法施 XXV: to offer according to the Dharma.

Hōshaku (Bodhisattva) 寶積 I: Accumulated-Treasure. Ratnākara.

Hōshō (Bodhisattva) 寶掌 I: Treasure-Palm. Ratnapāṇi.
Hōshō (World) 寶生 VI: Treasure-Born. Ratnasaṃbhava.
Hōsō (Buddha) 寶相 XI: Treasure-Form. Ratnaketurāja.
Hosshi 法師 I: the teacher of the Dharma.
Hosshi 法子 IX: the son of the Dharma.
Hosshin 法身 XII: the body of the Dharma. The sacred body.
Hosshin 發心 XIV: to aspire for enlightenment.
Hosshō 法性 III: the world of the Dharrna; XIX: the nature of the Dharma.
Hossō 法相 XIV: truth.
Hōtō 寶塔 I: a stūpa of treasures.
Hōza 法座 I: the seat of the Dharma.
Hōzō 法藏 I: the store of the Dharma; IX: the store of the teachings.
Hyakufuku-shōgonsō 百福莊嚴相 II: the physical marks each representing one hundred good karmas; XIX: adorned with the marks of one hundred merits.
Hyakufuku 百福 VII: the marks of one hundred merits.
Hyakumannoku 百萬億 XI: hundred million.
Hyakumannokugai 百萬億姟 VII: ten quadrillion.
Hyakuoku 百億 XXIII: myriad million.
Hyakusemman 百千萬 II: thousand million.
Hyakusemmannoku 百千萬億 I: hundred thousand billion.
Hyakusen 百千 I: hundred thousand.
Hyakusennoku 百千億 II: thousand myriad million.
Hyakushibutsu 辟支佛 I: Pratyekabuddha. See *Byakushibutsu, Engaku.*
Hyōsetsu 表剎 XVII: a yaṣṭi. A rod put on a stūpa.

I

Ichibutsujō 一佛乘 II: the One Buddha-Vehicle.
Ichiembudai 一閻浮提 XX: the Jambudvīpa. See *Sumeru World* in the English/Sanskrit Glossary.
Ichijō 一乘 II: the One Vehicle; XXI: the teaching of the One Vehicle.
Ichijōdō 一乘道 II: the teaching of the One Vehicle.
Ichijōhō 一乘法 II: the teaching of the One Vehicle.
Ichimi 一味 V: the same taste.
Ichinen 一念 IV: a moment's thought.
Idaike (Queen) 韋提希 I: Vaidehī. Mother of King Ajātaśatru. See *Śākyamuni* in the English/Sanskrit Glossary.
Idara 韋陀羅 XXVIII: vetāḍa. A demon.
Ifu 委付 IV: to transfer.
Igi 威儀 I: deportment; XXIV: to behave oneself.
Igi-gusoku 威儀具足 V: to live a monastic life.
Ijinriki 威神力 XXV: supernatural powers.
Imo 姨母 XIII: the sister of a mother.
Imyō-daisei 威猛大勢 XV: the great power of bravery.

Innen 因縁 I: reason, the stories of previous lives, the karmas which one did in one's previous existence; II: purpose; the reason why a sūtra was expounded; XIV: dependent origination. See *Kubuhō*. See *Nidāna* in the English/Sanskrit Glossary.

Inyō 圍繞 I: to surround.

Ionnō (Buddha) 威音王 XX: Powerful-Voice-King. Bhīṣmagarjitasvararāja.

Iraku (World) 意樂 VI: Mind-Happiness. Manobhirāma.

Ishin 異心 III: perfidy.

Ishu 意趣 II: purpose.

Issai-gen-shoshin-zammai 一切現諸身三昧 XXIII: the samādhi by which one can transform oneself into any other living being. See *Gen-issai-shikishin-zammai*.

Issai-jōkō-shōgon (World) 一切淨光莊嚴 XXIV: All-Pure-Light-Adornment. Also Jōkō-shōgon. Vairocanaraśmipratimaṇḍitā.

Issai-jōkudoku-shōgon-zammai 一切淨功德莊嚴三昧 XXVII: the samādhi for the adornment of all pure merits.

Issaichi 一切智 III: the knowledge of all things.

Issaichiji 一切智地 V: the stage of knowing all things.

Issaihōkū 一切法空 X: the voidness of all things.

Issaishuchi 一切種智 I: the knowledge of the equality and differences of all things.

Issaishujōkiken (Bodhisattva) 一切衆生憙見 XXIII: Gladly-Seen-By-All-Beings. Sarvasattvapriyadarśana.

Issaishujōkiken (Buddha) 一切衆生喜見 XIII: Gladly-Seen-By-All-Beings. Sarvasattvapriyadarśana.

Issendō 一箭道 XXIII: the distance of a bowshot.

Isshin 一心 I: with all one's heart; XV: to concentrate one's mind.

Isshu 一種 III: the same species.

Issō 一相 III: the same nature; V: the same content.

Itoku 威德 I: powers and virtues.

J

Jagi 邪僞 XIV: dishonesty.

Jaken 邪見 II: wrong views.

Jakumetsu 寂滅 I: tranquil extinction.

Jakusō 著相 II: attached to the appearances of things.

Jaman 邪慢 XXVIII: arrogance from self-assumed attainment of enlightenment.

Jigen 慈眼 XXV: compassionate eyes.

Jigoku 地獄 I: hell. See *Sumeru World* in the English/Sanskrit Glossary.

Jihikisha 慈悲喜捨 XII: the four states of mind: loving-kindness, compassion, joy, and impartiality. See *Shimuryōshin*.

Jihishin 慈悲心 X: compassion.

Jihō (Kiṃnara-King) 持法 I: Dharma-Keeping. Dharmadhara.

Jiji (Bodhisattva) 持地 XXV: Earth-Holding. Dharaṇiṃdhara.

Jikai 持戒 II: to observe the precepts.

Jikō 自高 XVII: self-conceit.

Jikoku (God) 持國 XXVI: World-Holding. Virūḍhaka. See *Sumeru World* in the English/Sanskrit Glossary.

Jikyōriki 示教利喜 VII: to show the Way to others, teach them, benefit them, and cause them to rejoice.

Jimben 神變 I: a wonder; XIX: to perform wonders.

Jinden 塵點 VII: a dot as large as a particle of dust.

Jinen 自然 I: naturally; IV: unexpectedly; XXII: the Self-Existing One.

Jinen-e 自然慧 III: the self-originating wisdom.

Jinenchi 自然智 III: the self-originating wisdom.

Jinjō 深定 XVII: to practice deep concentration of mind.

Jinriki 神力 I: supernatural powers.

Jinshin 深心 II: deep in one's mind; XIV: from the bottom of one's heart.

Jinshinge 深信解 XVII: to understand by firm faith.

Jinshu 神咒 XXVI: divine spells.

Jinzū 神通 I: a wonder; IV: supernatural powers.

Jinzū-henge 神通變化 VI: supernatural powers; XXVII: to display wonders.

Jinzū-yuke-sammai 神通遊戯三昧 XXIV: the samādhi for exhibiting supernatural powers.

Jinzui 沈水 II: aloes.

Jinzūriki 神通力 I: supernatural powers.

Jippō 十方 II. See *Ten Quarters* in the English/Sanskrit Glossary.

Jippōkai 十方界 II. See *Sanzendaisensekai.* See *Worlds of the Ten Quarters* in the English/Sanskrit Glossary.

Jippōsen 十寶山 XXIII: the Ten Treasure-Mountains. See *Sumeru World* in the English/Sanskrit Glossary.

Jishu 地種 VII: earth-particles.

Jissemmannoku 十千萬億 IX: ten thousand billion.

Jissō 實相 II: reality; XIX: the reality of all things.

Jissō-in 實相印 II: the emblem of truth, that is, the reality of all things.

Jittai 集諦 I: the truth that the cause of suffering is illusions. See *Shitai.*

Jiyōraku (Rākṣasī) 持瓔珞 XXVI: Necklace-Holding. Mālādhārī.

Jizai 自在 VIII: unhindered, without hindrance.

Jizai (God) 自在 I: Freedom. Īśvara. See *Sumeru World* in the English/Sanskrit Glossary.

Jōbu 丈夫 VIII: a man.

Jōbuku 調伏 IV: to recondition, to train.

Jōbutsu 成佛 I: to become a Buddha.

Jobutsudōhō 助佛道法 XXVII: the ways to the enlightenment of the Buddha.

Jōdatsu 調達 XXVI: Devadatta. See *Śākyamuni* in the English/Sanskrit Glossary.

Jōdo 淨土 XVI: the pure world.

Jōdō 成道 XI: to attain enlightenment.

Jōfukyō (Bodhisattva) 常不輕 XX: Never-Despising. Sadāparibhūta. Literally, "Always Despised."

Jōgen 常眼 XX: natural eyes.

Jōgen (Prince) 淨眼 XXVII: Pure-Eyes. Vimalanetra.

Jogi-i (Prince) 除疑意 I: Doubts-Removing-Intention. Vimatisamudghātin.

Jōgojōbu 調御丈夫 I: the Controller of Men. One of the ten epithets of the Buddha. See *Jūgō.*

Jōgyō (Bodhisattva) (variant 1) 淨行 XV: Pure-Practice. Viśuddhacāritra.

Jōgyō (Bodhisattva) (variant 2) 上行 XV: Superior-Practice. Viśiṣṭacāritra.

Jōgyō-i (Bodhisattva) 上行意 XXIV: Superior-Practice-Intent. Viśiṣṭacāritra.

Jōjakumessō 常寂滅相 V: eternal tranquility or extinction.

Jōjitsu 貞實 II: sincere.

Jōjū 常住 II: permanent.

Jōjuku 成熟 IV: to develop to the full.

Jōkengo 淨堅固 X: pure and indestructible.

Jōkeshukuōchi (Buddha) 淨華宿王智 XXIV: Pure-Flower-Star-King-Wisdom. Kamaladalavimalanakṣatrarājasaṃkusumitābhijña.

Jokkō 濁劫 XIII: the kalpa of defilements. See *Gojoku.*

Jōkō 淨光 I: a pure ray of light.

Jōkō-sammai 淨光三昧 XXVII: the samādhi for pure light.

Jōkō-shōgon (World) 淨光莊嚴 XXIV: All-Pure-Light-Adornment. See *Issai-jōkō-shōgon.*

Jōkōmyō-sammai 淨光明三昧 XXIV: the samādhi for pure light.

Jokuakuse 濁惡世 II: a defiled world.

Jōmetsu (Buddha) 常滅 VII: Eternal-Extinction. Nityaparinirvṛta.

Jōmyō 淨明 III: pure, clear.

Jōrisshōban (World) 常立勝旛 IX: Always-Raising-Banner-of-Victory. Anavanāmitavaijayantī.

Jōruri 淨瑠璃 I: pure lapis lazuli.

Jōsammai 淨三昧 XXVII: the samādhi for purity.

Jōshiki-sammai 淨色三昧 XXVII: the samādhi for pure form.

Jōshin 淨身 XIX: a pure body.

Jōshin (Buddha) 淨身 I: Pure-Body. Vimalanetra.

Jōshōgon-zammai 長莊嚴三昧 XXVII: the samādhi for permanent adornment.

Jōshōjin (Bodhisattva) 常精進 I: Constant-Endeavor. Nityodyukta.

Jōshōmyō-sammai 淨照明三昧 XXVII: the samādhi for pure brightness.

Jōtai 誠諦 XVI: sincere and infallible.

Jōtoku (King) 淨德 XXIII: Pure-Virtue. Vimaladatta.

Jōtoku (Queen) 淨德 XXVII: Pure-Virtue. Vimaladattā.

Jōtoku-sammai 淨德三昧 XXIV: the samādhi for pure virtue.

Jōzō (Prince) 淨藏 XXVII: Pure-Store. Vimalagarbha.

Jōzō-sammai 淨藏三昧 XXIV: the samādhi for pure store.

Ju 受 VII: sensation. One of the twelve causes. See *Jūni-innen.*

Ju 頌 XVII: verses.

Ju-ō 樹王 I: the kingly tree.

Jū-oku 十億 I: thousand million.

Jūgō 十號 I. See *Nyorai. Ōgu. Shōhenchi, Myōgyōsoku, Zenzei, Sekenge, Mujōji, Jōgojōbu, Tenninshi, Butsu, Seson.* See *Ten Epithets of the Buddha* in the English/Sanskrit Glossary.

Jūhappuguhō 十八不共法 III. See *Eighteen Unique Properties of the Buddha* in the English/Sanskrit Glossary.

Juji 受持 I: to keep.

Juki 受記 III: to be assured of future Buddhahood.

Juki 授記 I: to assure one of his future Buddhahood. Vyākaraṇa. See *Jūnibukyō.*

Jūmannoku 十萬億 XX: ten billion.

Jumbuku 順伏 XIV: to surrender.

Jūni-innen 十二因緣 I. See *Mumyō, Gyō, Shiki, Myōshiki, Rokunyū, Soku, Ju, Ai, Shu, U, Shō, Rōshi.* See *Twelve Causes* in the English/Sanskrit Glossary.

Jūnibukyō 十二部經 XI. See *Kubuhō.* See *Twelve Elements of Sūtras* in the English/Sanskrit Glossary.

Junkō 淳厚 XXIII: abundant.

Junzen 淳善 XI: purity and good.

Jūriki 十力 III. See *Ten Powers of the Buddha* in the English/Sanskrit Glossary.

K

Kada 伽陀 II: a verse. See *Kubuhō.* See *Gāthā* in the English/Sanskrit Glossary.

Kafu 跏趺 I: to sit cross-legged. See *Kekkafuza.*

Kagatsu 珂月 XXVII: a bright moon.

Kahō 果報 II: effects; rewards and retributions.

Kai 戒 I: the precepts.

Kaichō-on 海潮音 XXV: the sound of a tidal current.

Kainyō 憒閙 XV: bustling.

Kaisen 開闡 XII: to reveal.

Kaishigan-sendan 海此岸栴檀 XXIII: the candana grown on this shore of the sea between Mt. Sumeru and the Jambudvīpa.

Kaju 歌頌 X: songs of praise.

Kambotsu 勸發 XXVIII: encouragement.

Kangi 歡喜 I: glad, joy, to rejoice.

Kangi (World) 歡喜 VII: Joy. Abhirati.

Kanji 勸持 XIII: the encouragement of keeping [the sūtra].

Kanjin 勸進 IV: to persuade.

Kannin 堪忍 IV: capacity; XXIV: to be able to.

Kanro 甘露 V: nectar.

Kanshitsu 龕室 XI: chambers.

Kanzeon (Bodhisattva) 觀世音 I: World-Voice-Perceiver. Avalokiteśvara. More properly, Avalokitasvara.

Karakenda (Asura-King) 佉羅騫馱 I: Kharaskandha.

Karudai 迦留陀夷 VIII: Kālodāyin. See *Śākyamuni* in the English/Sanskrit Glossary.

Karura 迦漊羅 I: garuḍa, a golden-winged bird.

Karura-ō 迦漊羅王 I: a garuḍa-king.

Karyōbinga 迦陵頻伽 VII: kalaviṅka. A bird.

Kase 過世 III: previous existence.

Kashō 迦葉 V: Kāśyapa. Also Mahā-Kāśyapa.

Katan 歌歎 XXIII: songs of praise.

Katsubō 渴乏 X: thirsty.
Katsugō 渴仰 XVI: to admire.
Keban 華旛 IV: banners of flowers.
Kebutsu 化佛 XI: the Buddhas who are the replicas of Śākyamuni Buddha.
Kedo 化度 XII: to lead others to enlightenment; XV: to save.
Kegai 華蓋 I: flower-canopies.
Keige 罣礙 X: hindrance.
Keijaku 計著 XX: to be attached.
Keikō 桂香 XIX: sappanwood.
Keishu 稽首 VII: to bow.
Kejō 化城 VII: a magic city.
Kekkafuza 結跏趺坐 I: to sit cross-legged. See *Kafu.*
Kekkon 結恨 III: enmity.
Kekō 華香 II: flowers and incense; XIX: fragrant flowers.
Kekō (Buddha) 華光 III: Flower-Light. Padmaprabha.
Kekōyu 華香油 XXIII: perfumed oil taken from flowers.
Kembotsu 顯發 XV: to reveal.
Kemman (Bodhisattva) 堅滿 III: Resolution-Fulfillment. Dhṛtiparipūrṇa.
Ken-yaku 關鑰 XI: the bolt and lock.
Kenda 犍馱 XXVI: Kumbhāṇḍa. Also Kuhanda. A devil. See *Kuhanda.*
Kendatsu 乾闥 I: gandharva, a heavenly musician. See *Kendatsuba.*
Kendatsuba 乾闥婆 I. See *Kendatsu.*
Kendatsuba-ō 乾闥婆王 I: a gandharva-king.
Kengai 幰蓋 III: a canopy.
Kengara 甄迦羅 XXIII: kaṅkara. The sixteenth power of ten.
Kengo 堅固 II: strong; XIV: solid; XV: firmly.
Kenin 化人 X: people produced by the supernatural powers of the Buddha.
Kenjo 券疏 IV: bills, statements of money.
Kenjoku 見濁 II: defilement by wrong views. See *Gojoku.*
Kennon 懸遠 II: seldom.
Kenrin 慳悋 慳恪 XXII: to begrudge.
Kenshukuka 甄叔迦 XXIV: kiṃśuka. A tree. The flower is red; hence, red.
Kenzetsu 顯說 X: to expound [explicitly].
Kenzoku 眷屬 I: attendants.
Keraku 快樂 III: pleasure, peaceful; XXVIII: to enjoy oneself.
Keron 戲論 IV: fruitless discussions; XIX: meaningless words.
Kesa 化作 VII: to make by magic; XXIV: to cause others to appear.
Keshi (Rākṣasī) 華齒 XXVI: Flower-Teeth. Puṣpadantī.
Keshō 化生 VIII: to be born without any medium; XII: to be; XXIII: to appear. See *Shishō.* See *Birth Without Any Medium* in the English/Sanskrit Glossary.
Kesoku-angyō (Buddha) 華足安行 III: Flower-Foot-Easy-Walking. Padmavṛṣabhavikrāmin.
Ketoku (Bodhisattva) 華德 XXIV: Flower-Virtue. Padmaśrī.
Ketsujō 決定 II: definitely; III: resolute; X: convinced.

Ketsuryō 決了 II: to understand; X: to criticize.
Keyō 華瓔 III: garlands of flowers.
Ki 鬼 III: a demon, a devil.
Kihō 毀謗 III: to slander.
Kijin 鬼神 I: supernatural beings; III: demons; X: demigods.
Kikai 毀戒 V: to violate the precepts.
Kiken (Kalpa) 喜見 XXVII; 憙見 XXIV: Gladly-Seen. Priyadarśana.
Kiman (Kalpa) 喜滿 VI: Joyfulness. Ratiprapūrṇa.
Kime 毀罵 X: to speak ill of.
Kimi 鬼魅 III: a demon, a devil.
Kimyō 歸命 VII: to devote oneself.
Kiniku 毀辱 XIII: to insult.
Kinkai 禁戒 XVII: precepts.
Kinnara 緊那羅 I: kiṃnara. A heavenly musician.
Kinnara-ō 緊那羅王 I: a kiṃnara-king.
Kishi 毀訾 IV: to reproach, to speak ill of.
Kishimo (Rākṣasī) 鬼子母 XXVI: the Mother-of-Devils. Hārītī.
Kissha 吉蔗 XXVI: a kṛtya. A devil.
Kō 劫 I. See *Kalpa* in the English/Sanskrit Glossary.
Kō-i (Prince) 響意 I: Resounding-Intention. Ghoṣamati.
Kō-on (Heaven) 光音 XIX: Light-Sound. See *Sumeru World* in the English/Sanskrit Glossary.
Kōchōzetsu 廣長舌 XXI: a broad and long tongue. One of the thirty-two physical marks of the Buddha. See *Sanjūnisō.*
Kōge 香華 I: incense and flowers.
Kohaku 琥珀 IV: amber.
Kōhinna 劫賓那 I: Kapphina. Also Kapphiṇa. See *Śākyamuni* in the English/Sanskrit Glossary.
Koji 居士 IV: a householder.
Kōjō (World) 好成 VII: Well-Composed. Saṃbhavā.
Kōjoku 劫濁 II: defilement by the decay of the kalpa. As a kalpa decays, more calamities take place. See *Gojoku.*
Kokkai 國界 I: a world.
Kōkō 矜高 II: self-conceited.
Kokū 虛空 I: sky.
Kokudo 國土 I: a world.
Kokui 國位 XII: a throne.
Kokūjū (Buddha) 虛空住 VII: Sky-Dwelling. Ākāśapratiṣṭhita.
Kokushaku 剋責 III: to reproach oneself.
Kokushi (Rākṣasī) (variant 1) 曲齒 XXVI: Crooked-Teeth. Kūṭadanti.
Kokushi (Rākṣasī) (variant 2) 黑齒 XXVI: Black-Teeth. Makuṭadanti.
Komō 虛妄 II: false; III: unreal things.
Komōhō 虛妄法 II: unreal things.
Kōmyō (Brahman) 光明 I: Light. Jyotiṣprabha.
Kōmyō (Buddha) 光明 VI: Light. Raśmiprabhāsa.

Kōmyō-shōgon (World) 光明莊嚴 XXVII: Light-Adornment. Vairocanaraśmipratimaṇḍitā.

Kon-yaku 困厄 XXV: misfortunes.

Kongō 金剛 I: diamond; XXV: vajra, a weapon.

Kongōsen 金剛山 XXV: a mountain made of diamond.

Konjō 紺青 XXVII: deep blue.

Konrikikakudō 根力覺道 III: the [five] faculties, the [five] powers, the [seven] ways to enlightenment, and the [eight right] ways. See *Sanjūshichihon-jodōhō.* See *Thirty-Seven Ways to Enlightenment* in the English/Sanskrit Glossary.

Konsetsu 金刹 VI: a golden yaṣṭi. See *Hyōsetsu, Setsu.*

Konyaku 怯弱 VII: timid.

Konze 今世 V: present life.

Konzen 金山 I: the golden mountains. See *Sumeru World* in the English/Sanskrit Glossary.

Koro 孤露 XVI: lonely and helpless.

Kōro 香爐 XVII: an incense-burner.

Kōrōkaku 高樓閣 VII: tall buildings.

Kōshō 劫燒 XI: the fire at the end of the kalpa of destruction. See *Kō.*

Kōshō-shōgonsō (Bodhisattva) 光照莊嚴相 XXVII: Light-Adornment-Appearance. Vairocanaraśmipratimaṇḍitadhvajarāja.

Kōtai (Rākṣasī) 皐諦 XXVI: Kuntī.

Kōtoku (World) 光德 VI: Light-Virtue. Avabhāsaprāptā.

Kōya 曠野 II: the wilderness.

Kōyu 香油 XVII: perfumed oil.

Kōyutō 香油燈 XXVI: lamps of perfumed oil.

Ku 垢 II: illusions.

Kū 空 IV: the truth that nothing is substantial; XII: the Void.

Ku-issai (Brahman) 救一切 VII: All-Saving. Sarvasattvatrātar.

Kū-ō (Buddha) 空王 IX: Void-King. Dharmagaganābhyudgatarāja.

Kubaku 苦縛 II: the bonds of suffering.

Kubeidara, Kubidara 拘鞞陀羅 XIX: kovidāra. A tree. *Bauhinia Variegata.*

Kubuhō 九部法 II. See *Shutara, Kada, Honji, Honjō, Mizōu, Innen, Hiyu, Giya, Ubadaishakyō.* See *Nine Elements of Sūtras* in the English/Sanskrit Glossary.

Kudoku 功德 II: merits.

Kufu 恐怖 III: dreadful, scared, to be afraid.

Kūgen 空閑 I: a retired place.

Kugon 苦言 IV: to chide.

Kugyō 恭敬 I: to respect; respectfully.

Kugyō 苦行 XXIII: austerities.

Kuhanda 鳩槃荼 III: kumbhāṇḍa. A devil. See *Kenda.*

Kui 恐畏 III: dreadful.

Kūjaku 空寂 IV: void and tranquil.

Kujū 久住 XXIV: to stay long.

Kukai 苦海 XVI: the ocean of sufferings.

Kukyō 究竟 I: to attain; II: finally; IV: perfect.

Kun-yu 薫油 XVII: perfumed oil.

Kunroku 薰陸 XXIII: kunduruka. A tree.
Kuon 久遠 XV: the remotest past.
Kuongō 久遠劫 II: the past innumerable kalpas.
Kusesha 救世者 XXI: the World-Savior. An epithet of the Buddha.
Kūsho 空處 X: a retired place.
Kushū 苦集 VII: the cause of suffering.
Kutai 苦諦 III: the truth that all is suffering. See *Shitai.*
Kutō 句逗 X: a phrase.
Kuyō 供養 I: to make offerings.
Kyō 經 I: a sūtra.
Kyōbō 經法 I: the Dharma; III: a sūtra.
Kyōbon-handai 憍梵波提 I: Gavāṃpati. See *Śākyamuni* in the English/Sanskrit Glossary.
Kyōden 經典 I: a sūtra.
Kyōdommi 憍曇彌 XIII: Gautamī. See *Śākyamuni* in the English/Sanskrit Glossary.
Kyōgai 謦欬 XXI: to cough.
Kyōgan 經卷 X: the copy of a sūtra; XXIII: a sūtra.
Kyōgyō 經行 I: to walk about; XIV: a promenade.
Kyōjinnyo 憍陳如 I: Kauṇḍinya. Also Ājñāta-Kauṇḍinya. See *Anyakyōjinnyo.* See *Śākyamuni* in the English/Sanskrit Glossary.
Kyōjun 敬順 XIII: to follow respectfully.
Kyōke 教化 I: to teach, to save, to lead.
Kyōki 輕毀 XX: to abuse.
Kyōkō 膠香 XXIII: sumac-incense.
Kyōman 憍慢 II: arrogant.
Kyōman 輕慢 XIII: to despise.
Kyōmetsu 輕懱 XIV: to despise.
Kyōrai 敬禮 VII: to bow; XII: to worship.
Kyōshi 憍恣 XVI: arrogant.
Kyōsho 經書 XIX: scriptures.

M

Ma 魔 I: Māra; XIV: an evil. See *Sumeru World* in the English/Sanskrit Glossary.
Ma-ō 魔王 XII: King Māra. See *Ma.*
Magoraga 摩睺羅伽 I: mahoraga. A boa.
Magun 魔軍 VII: the army of Māra. See *Ma.*
Maie 玫瑰 II: ruby.
Makahajahadai 摩訶波闍波提 I: Mahā-Prajāpatī. See *Śākyamuni* in the English/Sanskrit Glossary.
Makakasennen 摩訶迦旃延 I: Mahā-Kātyāyana. See *Śākyamuni* in the English/Sanskrit Glossary.
Makakashō 摩訶迦葉 I: Mahā-Kāśyapa. See *Śākyamuni* in the English/Sanskrit Glossary.
Makakuchira 摩訶拘絺羅 I: Mahā-Kauṣṭhila. See *Śākyamuni* in the English/Sanskrit Glossary.

Makamandarake 摩訶曼陀羅華 I: mahā-mandārava-flowers. Great mandārava-flowers.

Makamanjushake 摩訶曼殊沙華 I: mahā-mañjūṣaka-flowers. Great mañjūṣaka-flowers.

Makamiru (Mountain) 摩訶彌樓 XIX: Mahā-Meru. See *Sumeru World* in the English/Sanskrit Glossary.

Makamokkenren 摩訶目犍連 IV: Mahā-Maudgalyāyana. See *Śākyamuni* in the English/Sanskrit Glossary.

Makamokushinrinda (Mountain) 摩訶目眞鄰陀 XI: Mahā-Mucilinda. See *Śākyamuni* in the English/Sanskrit Glossary.

Makasatsu 摩訶薩 III: Mahāsattva. See *Daiji.*

Makkō 抹香 VI: incense powder.

Mamin 魔民 VI: the followers of Māra. See *Ma.*

Mamō 魔網 XIV: the nets of Māra. See *Ma.*

Man 幔 I: curtains.

Manashi (Dragon-King) 摩那斯 I: Manasvin.

Manda 曼荼 XIX: mandārava. Also māndārava, mandāra.

Mandarake 曼陀羅華 I: mandārava-flowers. They are white.

Mangachi (Bodhisattva) 滿月 I: Full-Moon. Pūrṇacandra.

Mani 摩尼 I: maṇi. A gem.

Manjushake 曼殊沙華 I: Mañjūṣaka-flowers. They are red.

Mannoku 萬億 II: billion.

Manyo 魔女 XXVIII: the daughters of Māra. See *Ma.*

Maon 魔怨 XXIV: Māra the Enemy. See *Ma.*

Mappō 末法 XVII: the age of the decline of the teachings of the Buddha.

Mashi 魔子 XXVIII: the sons of Māra. See *Ma.*

Masse 末世 XIV: the latter days.

Matsuri 末利 XIX: mallikā. A plant. *Jasminum Sambac.*

Mazoku 魔賊 XXIII: the army of Māra. See *Ma.*

Menō 碼瑙 I: agate.

Meri 罵詈 XIII: to speak ill of.

Metsudo 滅度 I: extinction.

Mettai 滅諦 III: the truth of extinction. See *Shitai.*

Mi (Gaṇḍharva-King) 美 I: Beautiful. Madhura.

Mijin 微塵 VII: a particle of dust.

Miken-byakugō-sō 眉間白毫相 I: a ray of light emitted from the white curls between the eyebrows of the Buddha. One of the thirty-two physical marks of the Buddha. See *Sanjūnisō.*

Mimyō 微妙 I: wonderful.

Mion (Gandharva-King) 美音 I: Beautiful-Voice. Madhurasvara.

Miroku 彌勒 I: Maitreya.

Miru (Mountain) 彌樓 XIX: Meru. See *Sumeru World* in the English/Sanskrit Glossary.

Mitarani 彌多羅尼 I: Maitrāyaṇī. A lady of the Maitrāyaṇa family. See *Śākyamuni* in the English/Sanskrit Glossary.

Mitsugyō 密行 IX: secret practices.

Mizōu 未曾有 II: miracles. Adbhuta. See *Kubuhō.*

Mōken 妄見 XVI: wrong views.

Mokumitsu 木樒 II: agalloch.

Mokushinrinda (Mountain) 目眞隣陀 XI: Mucilinda. See *Śākyamuni* in the English/Sanskrit Glossary.

Monjidaranimon 聞持陀羅尼門 XVII: the dhāraṇīs by which one can memorize all that he hears.

Monjin 問訊 XI: to inquire; XIV: to exchange greetings; XV: to ask.

Monjushiri (Bodhisattva) 文殊師利 I: Mañjuśrī.

Monnan 問難 XVII: questions.

Motsuzai 沒在 II: to be enmeshed; XVI: to be sunk.

Muen-zammai 無緣三昧 XXIV: the samādhi for freedom from causality.

Muenzoku (Rākṣasī) 無厭足 XXVI: Insatiable. Acalā.

Mufumbeppō 無分別法 II: the Dharma beyond comprehension.

Mugaku 無學 I: the Śrāvakas who have nothing more to learn. Aśaikṣa. See *Shōmon*. See *Śrāvaka* in the English/Sanskrit Glossary.

Mugechi 無礙智 VII: unhindered wisdom.

Mugi 無僞 III: honest.

Muhengyō (Bodhisattva) 無邊行 XV: Limitless-Practice. Anantacāritra.

Mui 無爲 IV: things free from causality.

Mui 無畏 II: fearlessness.

Mujinni (Bodhisattva) 無盡意 XXV: Endless-Intent. Akṣayamati.

Mujō-e 無上慧 I: unsurpassed wisdom.

Mujōdō 無上道 I: unsurpassed enlightenment.

Mujōji 無上士 I: the Unsurpassed Man. One of the ten epithets of the Buddha. See *Jūgō*.

Mujōryōzokuson (Buddha) 無上兩足尊 II: the Most Honorable Biped. An epithet of the Buddha.

Mujōson 無上尊 II: the Most Honorable One. An epithet of the Buddha.

Muku (World) 無垢 XII: Spotless. Vimalā.

Mumon-jisetsu 無問自說 XI: expounding of the Dharma without being questioned. See *Jūnibukyō*.

Mumyō 無明 III: ignorance. One of the twelve causes. See *Jūni-innen*.

Muōshu 無央數 XI: innumerable.

Muro 無漏 II: without āsravas.

Murochi 無漏智 II: the wisdom-without-āsravas.

Murohō 無漏法 III: the Dharma-without-āsravas.

Muryō-i (Prince) 無量意 I: Infinite-Intention. Anantamati.

Muryōgi 無量義 I: innumerable teachings.

Muryōgishosammai 無量義處三昧 I: the samādhi for the purport of the innumerable teachings.

Muryōriki (Bodhisattva) 無量力 I: Immeasurable-Power. Anantavikrāmin.

Musa 無作 IV: the truth that nothing more is to be sought.

Mushichi 無師智 III: the wisdom to be obtained without teachers.

Mushiki 無識 IV: ignorant.

Mushōbōnin 無生法忍 XVII: the truth of birthlessness. See *Mushōnin*.

Mushoi 無所畏 II: fearlessness.

Mushōnin 無生忍 XII: the truth of birthlessness. See *Mushōbōnin.*

Muyonehan 無餘涅槃 I: the Nirvāṇa-without-remainder. Parinirvāṇa.

Myō-on 妙音 II: wonderful sound; V: wonderful voice.

Myō-on (Bodhisattva) 妙音 XXIV: Wonderful-Voice. Gadgadasvara.

Myō-on-hemman (Kalpa) 妙音徧滿 X: Wonderful-Voice-Resounding-Everywhere. Manojñaśabdābhigarjita.

Myōdōsōsammai 妙幢相三昧 XXIV: the samādhi as wonderful as the banner of a general.

Myōgatsu (God) 名月 I: Beautiful-Moon. Candra.

Myōgo 犛牛 II: a yak.

Myōgō 名號 IX: a name.

Myōgyōsoku 明行足 I: the Man of Wisdom and Practice. One of the ten epithets of the Buddha. See *Jūgō.*

Myōhō (Kiṃnara-King) 妙法 I: Wonderful-Dharma. Sudharma.

Myōhō (Brahman) 妙法 VII: Wonderful-Dharma. Sudharma.

Myōhōdō 妙法堂 XIX: the wonderful hall of the Dharma

Myōji 名字 II: a name; XIV: self-appointed.

Myōjoku 命濁 II: defilement by the shortening of lives. See *Gojoku.*

Myōke 名華 IV: beautiful flowers.

Myōkō (Bodhisattva) 妙光 I: Wonderful-Light. Varaprabha.

Myōmon 名聞 III: fame.

Myōmyō 命命 XIX: jīvakajīvaka. A bird.

Myōri 名利 I: fame and gain.

Myōrōkaku 妙樓閣 VIII: wonderful buildings.

Myōshiki 名色 V: name-and-form. One of the twelve causes. See *Jūni-innen.*

Myōshō 名稱 I: fame.

Myōshōgon (King) 妙莊嚴 XXVII: Wonderful-Adornment. Śubhavyūha.

Myōsō 妙相 XXV: wonderful marks.

Myōsō (Buddha) 名相 VI: Beautiful-Form. Śaśiketu.

N

Nabamari 那婆摩利 XXIII: navamālikā. A plant. *Jasminum Sambac.*

Nadaikashō 那提迦葉 I: Nadī-Kāśyapa. See *Śākyamuni* in the English/Sanskrit Glossary.

Nammon 難問 XIV: questions.

Namu 南無 XXV: namas. Honor to.

Namu-shakamunibutsu 南無釋迦牟尼佛 XXI: Namaḥ Śākyamunaye Buddhāya. Honor to Śākyamunl Buddha.

Namubutsu 南無佛 II: Namo Buddhāya. Honor to the Buddha.

Nan 難 XXIII: calamities; XXVII: misfortunes.

Nanda 難陀 I: Nanda. See *Śākyamuni* in the English/Sanskrit Glossary.

Nanda (Dragon-King) 難陀 I: Nanda.

Nangyōkugyō 難行苦行 XII: austerities.

Nanjo 難處 III: the places of difficulty in seeing the Buddha; XXIV: the places of difficulties.

Nara 那羅 XIV: naṭa, a dancer.

Naraen 那羅延 XXIV: Nārāyaṇa.

Nayuta 那由他 VI: nayuta. Hundred thousand million.

Nehan 涅槃 I: Nirvāṇa. Extinction.

Nembutsu 念佛 II: to think of the Buddha.

Nenki 年紀 XVI: the duration of a life.

Nentō (Buddha) 然燈 I: Burning-Light. Dīpaṃkara.

Nichigatsujōmyōtoku (Buddha) 日月淨明德 XXIII: Sun-Moon-Pure-Bright-Virtue. Candravimalasūryaprabhāsaśrī.

Nichigattōmyō (Buddha) 日月燈明 I: Sun-Moon-Light. Candrasūryapradīpa; XX: Candrasvararāja.

Nijō 二乘 II: a second vehicle, the two vehicles: the Śrāvaka-Vehicle and Pratyekabuddha-Vehicle.

Nikenshi 尼犍子 XIV: Nirgranthas. The followers of Nirgrantha Jñātiputra. The Jains.

Nikkei 肉髻 XXIV: fleshly excrescence. One of the thirty-two physical marks of the Buddha. See *Sanjūnisō.*

Ninchūson 人中尊 I: the Man of the Highest Honor. An epithet of the Buddha.

Ninden 人天 VIII: men and gods.

Ninja 仁者 XXV: a man of virtue.

Ninju 忍受 XX: to endure.

Ninkissha 人吉蔗 人吉遮 XXVI: a human-kṛtya. A devil.

Ninniku 忍辱 I: patience, endurance.

Ninzen 忍善 VII: to do good patiently.

Nisenchūkokudo 二千中國土 XVII: one million Sumeru-worlds. See *Sanzendaisensekai.*

Nisokuson 二足尊 VI: the Most Honorable Biped. An epithet of the Buddha.

Nissen-zammai 日旋三昧 XXIV: the samādhi for the race of the sun.

Nisshōshukusammai 日星宿三昧 XXVII: the samādhi for the sun and the stars.

Nittenji 日天子 XXIII: the Sun God.

Nō-e 納衣 XIII: to wear patched pieces of cloth.

Nyoi (Gandharva-King) 如意 I: Free-At-Will. Maharddhiprāpta.

Nyoishu 如意珠 XVII: free-at-will gems.

Nyorai 如來 I: Tathāgata. One who has come in this way. One of the ten epithets of the Buddha. See *Jūgō.*

Nyōyaku 饒益 I: to benefit.

O

Ōgu 應供 I: the Deserver of Offerings. One of the ten epithets of the Buddha. See *Jūgō.*

Ōji 狂子 XVI: perverted sons.

Oku 億 I: hundred million.

Okuhyakusen 億百千 III: thousand myriad million.

Okuman 億萬 I: billion.

Okunen 憶念 III: to remember, to recollect.

Okuokuman 億億萬 XX: hundred million billion.

Okusemman 億千萬 I: thousand billion.
Okusen 億千 III: hundred thousand million.
Ome 惡罵 I: to abuse.
On 恩 IV: favor.
Ongon 怨言 IV: to reproach.
Ongon 慇懃 II: enthusiastically, skillfully, deeply.
Ōnin 狂人 XXVIII: perverted people.
Onri 遠離 XIII: far from; XV: a solitary life; XVII: to give up.
Onrin 園林 I: gardens and forests.
Ōsha (City) 王舍 I: King-House. Rājagṛha. See *Śākyamuni* in the English/Sanskrit Glossary.
Ossangai (Bodhisattva) 越三界 I: Trancending-Triple-World. Trailokyavikrāmin.
Ōwaku 誑惑 XIII: to deceive.

R

Rago (Asura-King) 羅睺 I: Rāhu.
Ragora 羅睺羅 I: Rāhula. See *Śākyamuni* in the English/Sanskrit Glossary.
Raihai 禮拜 II: to bow, to pay homage.
Raikyō 禮敬 X: to bow, to worship.
Raise 來世 II: future life.
Rakan 羅漢 II: Arhat. See *Arakan.*
Ramba (Rākṣasī) 藍婆 XXVI: Lambā.
Ramō 羅網 III: nets.
Rasetsu 羅刹 XIX: a devil. Rākṣasa.
Rasetsunyo 羅刹女 XXVI: rākṣasī. A female rākṣasa.
Rembo 戀慕 XVI: to adore.
Ren-yo 輦輿 I: a palanquin.
Renjaku 戀著 III: to be attached.
Ri-shoakushu-sammai 離諸惡趣三昧 XXVII: the samādhi for the release from evil regions.
Richi 利智 II: wise.
Ridon 利鈍 II: keen or dull; clever or dull.
Rihata 離婆多 I: Revata. See *Śākyamuni* in the English/Sanskrit Glossary.
Riku (World) 離垢 III: Free-From-Taint. Viraja.
Rikuyō 利供養 XIII: the offerings of worldly things.
Rinjaku 悋惜 IV: to grudge.
Rinne 輪廻 II: to go to one from another of the six regions.
Risui (Kalpa) 離衰 XX: Free-From-Decay. Vinirbhoga.
Riyaku 利益 III: to benefit.
Riyō 利養 I: gain, worldly profits.
Ro 漏 I. See *Āsrava* in the English/Sanskrit Glossary.
Rō-i 良醫 XVI: an excellent physician.
Rōkan 樓觀 XVII: magnificent buildings.
Rokayada 路伽耶陀 XIV. See *Lokāyatas* in the English/Sanskrit Glossary.
Rokkon 六根 XIX. See *Six Sense-Organs* in the English/Sanskrit Glossary.

Rokudō 六道 I: the six regions. See *Sumeru World* in the English/Sanskrit Glossary.

Rokuge 六牙 XXVIII: six tusks.

Rokuharamitsu 六波羅蜜 I. See *Dambaramitsu, Shira-haramitsu. Sendai-haramitsu, Biriya-haramitsu. Zembaramitsu, Hannya-haramitsu.* See *Six Bodhisattva Practices* in the English/Sanskrit Glossary.

Rokujinzū 六神通 III. See *Rokutsū.* See *Six Supernatural Powers* in the English/Sanskrit Glossary.

Rokunyū 六入 VII: the six sense-organs. One of the twelve causes. See *Jūni-innen.*

Rokushu 六趣 I: the six regions. See *Sumeru World* in the English/Sanskrit Glossary.

Rokushu-shindō 六種震動 I. See *Roppen-shindō.* See *Six Ways, To Quake in the* in the English/Sanskrit Glossary.

Rokutsū 六通 VIII. See *Rokujinzū.* See *Six Supernatural Powers* in the English/Sanskrit Glossary.

Roppen-shindō 六反震動 XII. See *Rokushu-shindō.* See *Six Ways, To Quake in the* in the English/Sanskrit Glossary.

Rōshi 老死 VII: aging-and-death. One of the twelve causes. See *Jūni-innen.*

Rufu 流布 III: to distribute, to propagate.

Ruri 瑠璃 I: lapis lazuli.

Ryō 兩 XXV: a unit of the Chinese gold coinage.

Ryōju (Mountain) 靈鷲 XII: Sacred Eagle. Gṛdhrakūṭa. See *Gishakutsu, Shakyamuni.*

Ryōzokushōson (Buddha) 兩足聖尊 III: the Honorable Biped. An epithet of the Buddha. See *Ryōzokuson.*

Ryōzokuson (Buddha) 兩足尊 II: the Honorable Biped. An epithet of the Buddha. See *Ryōzokushōson.*

Ryū 龍 I: a dragon. A nāga.

Ryū-ō 龍王 I: a dragon-king.

Ryūgū 龍宮 XII: the palace of a dragon-king.

Ryūjin 龍神 I: a dragon.

Ryūnyo 龍女 XII: the daughter of a dragon-king.

S

Sabutsu 作佛 I: to become a Buddha.

Sai 載 XVI: trillion.

Saigoshin 最後身 II: the final stage of physical existence.

Saikan 宰官 XXIV: a prime minister.

Saishōgaku 最正覺 XIV: perfect enlightenment.

Sambō 三寶 XVI. See *Three Treasures* in the English/Sanskrit Glossary.

Sammai 三昧 I: samādhi. Concentration of mind.

Sammyaku-sambutsuda 三藐三佛陀 I: Samyak-saṃbuddha. The Perfectly Enlightened One. One of the ten epithets of the Buddha. See *Jūgō.*

Sammyō 三明 III. See *Rokujinzū, Rokutsū.* See *Three Major Supernatural Powers* in the English/Sanskrit Glossary.

Sandoku 三毒 III. See *Three Poisons* in the English/Sanskrit Glossary.

Sangai 三界 I. See *Triple World, Sumeru World* in the English/Sanskrit Glossary.

Sanjō 三乘 I. See *Three Vehicles* in the English/Sanskrit Glossary.

Sanjūnisō 三十二相 III: the thirty-two physical marks of the Buddha.

Sanjūsanten 三十三天 XI: the thirty-three gods. See *Sumeru World* in the English/Sanskrit Glossary.

Sanjūshichihon-jodōhō 三十七品助道法 XXVII. See *Hashōdō.* See *Thirty-seven Ways to Enlightenment* in the English/Sanskrit Glossary.

Sanku 三苦 IV. See *Three Kinds of Suffering* in the English/Sanskrit Glossary.

Sannakudō 三惡道 II: the three evil regions. See *Sumeru World* in the English/Sanskrit Glossary.

Sanran 散亂 II: distracted.

Sansekai 三世界 XXIII: the Third Dhyāna-Heaven. See *Sumeru World* in the English/Sanskrit Glossary.

Sanze 三世 II: the past, present, and future.

Sanzendaisengai 三千大千界 XIX: one thousand million Sumeru-worlds. See *Sanzendaisensekai.*

Sanzendaisensekai, Sanzendaisenzekai 三千大千世界 V: literally, three thousand great thousand worlds. The worlds numbering the third power of one thousand. See *One Thousand Million Sumeru-Worlds* in the English/Sanskrit Glossary.

Sanzengai 三千界 XIX: same as Sanzendaisensekai.

Sanzensekai 三千世界 XI: same as Sanzendaisensekai.

Sanzō 三藏 XIX. See *Three Stores* in the English/Sanskrit Glossary.

Se-ō 世雄 II: the World-Hero. An epithet of the Buddha.

Seigan 誓願 II: a vow.

Sekai 世界 I. See *Sumeru-World* in the English/Sanskrit Glossary.

Sekenge 世間解 I: the Knower of the World. One of the ten epithets of the Buddha. See *Jūgō.*

Sembokke-yutō 瞻蔔華油燈 XXVI: lamps of campaka-flower oil.

Semboku 瞻蔔 XVII: campaka. A tree.

Sembutsu 先佛 XIX: the past Buddhas.

Semman 千萬 I: ten million.

Semmannoku 千萬億 I: thousand billion.

Sempu 宣布 XVIII: to propagate.

Sen 仙 XII: a seer. See *Sennin.*

Sen-yō 宣揚 VII: to enhance.

Senchō 宣暢 VII: to expound.

Sendai 羼提 XVII: patience.

Sendai-haramitsu 羼提波羅蜜 XVII: the kṣānti-pāramitā. Patience. See *Rokuharamitsu.*

Sendan 栴檀 I: candana. Sandalwood.

Sendara 栴陀羅 XIV. See *Caṇḍāla* in the English/Sanskrit Glossary.

Sendarani 栴陀羅尼 XVII: the dhāraṇīs by which one can memorize many repetitions of teachings.

Senden 宣傳 III: to propagate.

Sengaie-jizaitsū-ō (Buddha) 山海慧自在通王 IX: Mountain-Sea-Wisdom-Supernatural-Power-King. Sāgaravaradharabuddhivikrīḍitābhijña.

Senjū 撰集 XIX: quotations.

Sennin 仙人 XII: a seer. See *Sen.*

Sennō 山王 XIX: great mountains.

Sennoku 千億 I: hundred thousand million.

Senshō 專精 XIX: to devote oneself.

Sensōji 旋總持 XVII: all-holding formulas of memorizing many repetitions of teachings.

Senze 先世 II: previous existence.

Seppō 説法 I: to expound the Dharma.

Seraku 世樂 III: the pleasures of the world, worldly pleasures.

Seshi 世師 II: the World-Teacher. An epithet of the Buddha.

Seshu 施主 XVIII: an almsgiver.

Seson 世尊 I: the World-Honored One. One of the ten epithets of the Buddha. See *Jūgō.*

Setsu 刹 II: kṣetra, a world; XVII: yaṣṭi, a rod. See *Hyōsetsu.*

Setsuna 刹那 XII: kṣaṇa. A moment.

Setsuri 刹利 IV: kṣatriya. Warriors.

Shaba (World) 娑婆 I: Sahā. The earth. The world inhabited by men.

Shadai 闍提 XIX: Jātika. A plant.

Shaka (Buddha) 釋迦 XII: Śākyamuni. See *Śākyamuni* in the English/Sanskrit Glossary.

Shakada 莎伽陀 VIII: Svāgata. See *Śākyamuni* in the English/Sanskrit Glossary.

Shakamon (Buddha) 釋迦文 II: Śākyamuni. See *Śākyamuni* in the English/Sanskrit Glossary.

Shakamuni (Buddha) 釋迦牟尼 VII. See *Śākyamuni* in the English/Sanskrit Glossary.

Shakara (Dragon-King) 娑伽羅 I; 娑竭羅 XII: Sāgara.

Shakara-ryūgū 娑竭羅龍宮 XII: the palace of the Sāgara Dragon-King.

Shako 硨磲 I: shell.

Shakubon 釋梵 V: Śakra and Brahman. See *Sumeru World* in the English/Sanskrit Glossary.

Shakudaikannin (God) 釋提桓因 I: Śakra-Devānām-Indra. King Śakra. See *Sumeru World* in the English/Sanskrit Glossary.

Shakushi 釋氏 XVI: the Śākyas. See *Śākyamuni* in the English/Sanskrit Glossary.

Shakushishi 釋師子 I: the Lion-Like One of the Śākyas. An epithet of the Buddha.

Shakushu 釋種 XV: the Śākyas.

Shami 沙彌 VII: śrāmaṇera. A novice.

Shamon 沙門 I: śramaṇa. An ascetic, a monk.

Sharaju-ō (Buddha) 娑羅樹王 XXVII: the Śāla-Tree-King. Śālendrarāja.

Shari 舍利 I: the relics, especially those of the Buddha. See *Śarīra* in the English/Sanskrit Glossary.

Sharihotsu 舍利弗 I: Śāriputra. See *Śākyamuni* in the English/Sanskrit Glossary.

Shi-akudō 四惡道 VI: the four evil regions. See *Sumeru World* in the English/Sanskrit Glossary.

Shibushu 四部衆 I: the four kinds of devotees. See *Shishu.*

Shibutsu (Upāsaka) 思佛 XX: Thinking-of-Buddha. In Wogihara's text, this is given as an upāsikā called Sugatacetanā.

Shichibutsu 七佛 VIII. See *Seven Buddhas* in the English/Sanskrit Glossary.

Shichijiki 質直 III: upright.

Shichikakushi 七覚支 XXVII: the seven ways to enlightenment. See *Sanjūshichihon-jodōhō.* See *Thirty-Seven Ways to Enlightenment* in the English/Sanskrit Glossary.

Shidagon 斯陀含 XXIII: Sakṛdāgāmin. See *Shōmon*. See *Śrāvaka* in the English/Sanskrit Glossary.

Shidagondō 斯陀含道 XVIII: the enlightenment of the Sakṛdāgāmin.

Shidai 四大 XXIV. See *Four Elements* in the English/Sanskrit Glossary.

Shidaitennō 四大天王 I. See *Four Great Heavenly-Kings* in the English/Sanskrit Glossary.

Shigan 志願 III: to aspire for.

Shijō 熾盛 III: violent, to prosper.

Shiki 識 VII: consciousness. One of the twelve causes. See *Jūni-innen.*

Shiki (Brahman) 尸棄 I: Śikhin. See *Sumeru World* in the English/Sanskrit Glossary.

Shikishōkōmisoku 色聲香味觸 III: forms, sounds, smells, tastes, and things tangible; X: things to see, hear, smell, taste, and touch.

Shikizō 色像 XIX: a reflection.

Shikuge 四句偈 XXIII: a gāthā of four lines.

Shima 死魔 XIV: the māra of death, the evil that is death.

Shima-konjiki 紫磨金色 XII: purely gilt.

Shimbotchi-bosatsu 新發意菩薩 II: a Bodhisattva who has just begun to aspire for enlightenment; IX: a Bodhisattva who has just resolved to aspire for Anuttara-samyak-saṃbodhi; X: beginners in Bodhisattvahood.

Shimuge-e 四無礙慧 VIII. See *Shimugechi.* See *Four Kinds of Unhindered Eloquence* in the English/Sanskrit Glossary.

Shimugechi 四無礙智 VIII. See *Shimuge-e.* See *Four Kinds of Unhindered Eloquence* in the English/Sanskrit Glossary.

Shimuryōshin 四無量心 II. See *Jihikisha.* See *Four States of Mind* in the English/Sanskrit Glossary.

Shimushoi 四無所畏 XII. See *Four Kinds of Fearlessness* in the English/Sanskrit Glossary.

Shinen-kengo 志念堅固 III: resolute in mind.

Shinenjo 四念処 四念處 XXVII: the four thoughts. See *Sanjūshichihon-jodōhō.* See *Thirty-Seven Ways to Enlightenment* in the English/Sanskrit Glossary.

Shinge 信解 I: to understand by faith.

Shingon 親近 I: to meet, to attend on, to approach, to see.

Shinyoisoku 四如意足 XXVII: the four steps to supernatural powers. See *Sanjūshichihon-jodōhō.* See *Thirty-Seven Ways to Enlightenment* in the English/Sanskrit Glossary.

Shiō-shoten 四王諸天 VII: the four heavenly kings. See *Sumeru World* in the English/Sanskrit Glossary.

Shippō 七寶 I. See *Seven Treasures* in the English/Sanskrit Glossary.

Shira 尸羅 XVII: precepts.

Shira-haramitsu 尸羅波羅蜜 XVII: the śīla-pāramitā. Observance of the precepts. See *Rokuharamitsu.*

Shishi 師子 I: the Lion-Like One. An epithet of the Buddha.

Shishi-on (Buddha) 師子音 VII: Lion-Voice. Siṃhaghoṣa.

Shishigatsu (Bhikṣunī) 師子月 XX: Lion-Moon. Siṃhacandra.

Shishisō (Buddha) 師子相 VII: Lion-Form. Siṃhadhvaja.

Shishiza 師子座 III: a lion-like seat.

Shishō 四生 XVIII. See *Keshō.* See *Four Kinds of Birth* in the English/Sanskrit Glossary.

Shishōbō 四攝法 XII. See *Four Ways to Attract Others* in the English/Sanskrit Glossary.

Shishōgon 四正勤 XXVII: the four right endeavors. See *Sanjūshichihon-jodōhō.* See *Thirty-Seven Ways to Enlightenment* in the English/Sanskrit Glossary.

Shishu 四衆 I. See *Shibushu, Biku. Bikuni, Ubasoku, Ubai.* See *Four Kinds of Devotees* in the English/Sanskrit Glossary.

Shisshō 濕生 XVIII: birth from moisture. See *Shishō.*

Shitai 四諦 I. See *Kutai, Jittai, Mettai, Dōtai, Hashōdō.* See *Four Truths* in the English/Sanskrit Glossary.

Shitchin 七珍 XII: the seven treasures. See *Shippō.*

Shitenge 四天下 XVIII: the four continents. See *Sumeru World* in the English/Sanskrit Glossary.

Shitennōgū 四天王宮 XI: the palaces of the four heavenly-kings. See *Sumeru World* in the English/Sanskrit Glossary.

Shiyui 四維 VII. See *Four Intermediate Quarters* in the English/Sanskrit Glossary.

Shō 生 VII: birth. One of the twelve causes. See *Jūni-innen*

Shō-ō 小王 I: the kings of small countries.

Shō-okunen 正憶念 XIII: to memorize correctly.

Shōbō 小法 II: the teachings of the Lesser Vehicle.

Shōbō 正法 I: the right teachings.

Shobusshū-sammai 諸佛集三昧 XXVII: the samādhi for the assembly of Buddhas.

Shōgaku 正覺 VII: perfect enlightenment.

Shōge 障礙 III: obstacle, hindrance.

Shōgonnō (Bodhisattva) 莊嚴王 XXIV: Adornment-King. Śubhavyūharāja.

Shōgonnō-sammai 莊嚴王三昧 XXIV: the samādhi for the Adornment-King.

Shōhenchi 正徧知 I: the Perfectly Enlightened One. One of the ten epithets of the Buddha. See *Jūgō.*

Shohōjakumetsu-sō 諸法寂滅相 II: the state of tranquil extinction of all things.

Shohōjissō 諸法實相 I: the reality of all things.

Shōja 精舎 XVII: a monastery.

Shōji 生死 I: birth and death.

Shōjin 精進 I: to make efforts; II: strenuous; VIII: endeavor.

Shōjō 小乘 II: the Lesser Vehicle. See *Hīnayāna* in the English/Sanskrit Glossary.

Shōjōju 正定聚 XXVIII: the stage of steadiness in proceeding to enlightenment.

Shōjōsammai 清淨三昧 XXIV: the samādhi for purity.

Shōken 正見 V: the right view.

Shōkō 小劫 I: a small kalpa. See *Kō.*

Shōkō 燒香 VI: incense to burn.

Shōku 章句 X: a phrase.

Shōmon 聲聞 I. See *Shudaon, Shidagon, Anagon, Arakan, Gaku, Mugaku.* See *Śrāvaka* in the English/Sanskrit Glossary.

Shōmonji 聲聞地 VII: Śrāvakahood.

Shōmyō 證明 XI: to prove the truthfulness (of the Dharma).

Shōnin 聖人 XIX: enlightened ones.

Shōrōbyōshi 生老病死 I: birth, old age, disease, and death.

Shōsengai 小千界 XVIII: one thousand Sumeru-worlds. See *Sumeru World* in the English/Sanskrit Glossary.

Shōsenkokudo 小千國土 XVII: one thousand Sumeru-worlds. See *Sumeru World* in the English/Sanskrit Glossary.

Shosha 書寫 X: to copy.

Shōshinjinyo 清信士女 X: men and women of pure faith. See *Ubasoku, Ubai.* See *Upāsaka, Upāsikā* in the English/Sanskrit Glossary.

Shōshishi 聖師子 II: the Lion-Like Saint. An epithet of the Buddha.

Shōshu 聖主 I: the Saintly Master. An epithet of the Buddha.

Shōtetchisen 小鐵圍山 XXIII: the Small Surrounding Iron Mountains. See *Sumeru World* in the English/Sanskrit Glossary.

Shu 取 VII: grasping. One of the twelve causes. See *Jūni-innen.*

Shu 銖 XXIII: a unit of the Chinese weights, about 0.67 grams.

Shū-issaikudoku-sammai 集一切功德三昧 XXIV: the samādhi by which one can collect all merits.

Shu 咒 XXVI: spells.

Shubodai 須菩提 I: Subhūti. See *Śākyamuni* in the English/Sanskrit Glossary.

Shuda 周陀 VIII: Cunda. See *Śākyamuni* in the English/Sanskrit Glossary.

Shudaon 須陀洹 XVIII: Srota-āpanna. See *Shōmon.* See *Śrāvaka* in the English/Sanskrit Glossary.

Shujō 衆生 I: living beings.

Shujōjoku 衆生濁 II: defilement by the deterioration of living beings. See *Gojoku.*

Shukke 出家 I: to renounce the world; VII: to leave home; X: a monk.

Shūkongōjin 執金剛神 XXV: the Vajra-Holding God. Vajrapāṇi. More properly, Vajradhara.

Shukuōke (Bodhisattva) 宿王華 XXIII: Star-King-Flower. Nakṣatrarājasaṃkusumitābhijña.

Shukuōke-sammai 宿王戲三昧 XXIV: the samādhi for the traveling of the king of the stars.

Shukuse 宿世 IV: previous existence.

Shuman 須曼 XVII. See *Shumanna.*

Shumanna 須曼那 XIX: sumanas. A plant.

Shumi (Mountain) 須彌 VII: Sumeru. See *Sumeru World* in the English/Sanskrit Glossary.

Shumichō (Buddha) 須彌頂 VII: Sumeru-Peak. Merukūṭa.

Shumisō (Buddha) 須彌相 VII: Sumeru-Form. Merukalpa.

Shusse 出世 XVI: to appear in a world.

Shutara 修多羅 II: prose. This is a transliteration of sūtra, but in this translation the word sūtra stands for a Buddhist scripture. See *Kubuhō.*

Shutsugen 出現 II: to appear; XI: to show oneself.

Sō 僧 I: the Saṃgha. The Buddhist community.

Sōbō 僧房 XVII: a monastery.

Soku 觸 VII: touch. One of the twelve causes. See *Jūni-innen.*

Somanake-yutō 蘇摩那華油燈 XXVI: lamps of sumanas-flower oil.

Sondarananda 孫陀羅難陀 I: Sundarananda. See *Śākyamuni* in the English/Sanskrit Glossary.

Sonja 尊者 XII: the Venerable.

Sotō 蘇燈 酥燈 XXIII: lamps of butter oil.
Soyu 蘇油 酥湯 XIX: the oil taken from sumanas-flowers.

T

Tada-akado 多陀阿伽度 I: Tathāgata. One of the ten epithets of the Buddha. See *Jūgō.*
Tahō (Buddha) 多寳 XIX: Many-Treasures. Prabhūtaratna.
Tahotsu (Rakṣasī) 多髮 XXVI: Many-Hairs. Keśini.
Taishaku 帝釋 XII: King Śakra. See *Sumeru World* in the English/Sanskrit Glossary.
Taisō (Buddha) 帝相 VII: Emperor-Form. Indradhvaja.
Taiten 退轉 I: to falter.
Takara 多伽羅 XIX: a tree.
Tamaraba 多摩羅跋 XIX: tamālapattra. A tree.
Tamaraba-sendankō-jinzū (Buddha) 多摩羅跋栴檀香神通 VII: Tamālapattracandana-Fragrance-Supernatural-Power. Tamālapattracandanagandhābhijña.
Tamaraba-sendankō (Buddha) 多摩羅跋栴檀香 VI: Tamālapattracandana-Fragrance. Tamālapattracandanagandha.
Tamon 多聞 III: to hear much; VIII: learned; IX: to learn much.
Tara 多羅 XVII: Tāla. A tree.
Tembōrin 轉法輪 II: to turn the wheel of the Dharma, to expound the teachings of the Buddha.
Ten 天 I: heaven, a heaven, a god.
Tenchūten 天中天 I: the God of Gods. An epithet of the Buddha.
Tendaishōgun 天大將軍 XXIV: a great general in heaven. An attendant of Brahman. See *Sumeru World* in the English/Sanskrit Glossary.
Tendō (World) 天道 XII: Heavenly-Way. Devasopāna.
Tenji 天子 I: a god.
Tenjin 天神 VII: a god.
Tennin 天人 I: gods and men.
Tenninshi 天人師 I: the Teacher of Gods and Men. One of the ten epithets of the Buddha. See *Jūgō.*
Tenninshobuson 天人所奉尊 I: the Gods-And-Men-Honored One. An epithet of the Buddha.
Tenninson 天人尊 VII: the Most Honorable of Gods and Men. An epithet of the Buddha.
Tennō (Buddha) 天王 XII: Heavenly-King. Devarāja.
Tennyo 天女 XIX: a goddess.
Tenrinjō-ō 轉輪聖王 I. See *Wheel-Turning-Holy-King, Sumeru World* in the English/Sanskrit Glossary.
Tenrinnō 轉輪王 XIX. See *Wheel-Turning-Holy-King* in the English/Sanskrit Glossary.
Tentaishaku (God) 天帝釋 II: the Heavenly-King Śakra. King Śakra. See *Sumeru World* in the English/Sanskrit Glossary.
Tetchisen 鐵圍山 XI: the Surrounding Iron Mountains. See *Sumeru World* in the English/Sanskrit Glossary.
Tō 塔 I. See *Stūpa* in the English/Sanskrit Glossary.

Tōji 塔寺 XIII: a monastery; XVII: a stūpa.

Tokudaisei (Bodhisattva) 得大勢 I: Great-Power-Obtainer. Mahāsthāmaprāpta.

Tokudo 得度 III: to save; VII: to attain enlightenment.

Tokudō 得道 IV: to attain enlightenment.

Tokugonshōjinriki (Bodhisattva) 得勤精進力 XXIV: Endeavor-Power-obtainer.

Tokushaka (Dragon-King) 德叉迦 I: Takṣaka.

Tokuzō (Bodhisattva) 德藏 I: Virtue-Store. Śrīgarbha.

Tōmyō 塔廟 I: a stūpa-mausoleum.

Tonjaku 貪著 I: to be attached.

Tōri-shoten 忉利諸天 VII: the trāyastriṃśa gods. The thirty-three gods. See *Sumeru World* in the English/Sanskrit Glossary.

Tōriten 忉利天 XXVIII: The Heaven of the Trāyastriṃśa Gods.

Toruba 兜樓婆 XXIII: a plant.

Tōshippōke (Buddha) 蹈七寶華 IX: Stepping-on-Flower-of-Seven-Treasures. Saptaratnapadmavikrāntagāmin.

Tōshōgaku 等正覺 VI: perfect enlightenment.

Tosotsu 兜率 XXVIII: Tuṣita. See *Sumeru World* in the English/Sanskrit Glossary.

U

U 有 II: existence; III: property; V: the bonds of existence. One of the twelve causes. See *Jūni-innen.*

Ubadaishakyō 優波提舍經 II: upadeśa. A discourse. See *Kubuhō.*

Ubai 優婆夷 I: a female lay devotee.

Ubakke 優鉢華 XVIII: utpala-flowers.

Ubasoku 優婆塞 I: a male lay devotee.

Uchō (Heaven) 有頂 I: the Highest Heaven. See *Sumeru World* in the English/Sanskrit Glossary.

Udai 優陀夷 VIII: Udāyin. See *Śākyamuni* in the English/Sanskrit Glossary.

Udombakke 優曇鉢華 優曇鉢花 II: udumbara-flowers.

Udombara 優曇波羅 VII: udumbara. Also uḍumbara. A plant.

Udonge 優曇華 優曇花 II: udumbara-flowers.

Uhatsura (Dragon-King) 優鉢羅 I: Utpalaka.

Uhatsurake-yutō 優鉢羅華油燈 XXVI: lamps of utpala-flower oil.

Uhō (Kalpa) 有寶 VI: Having-Treasures. Ratnaprabhāsa.

Ui 有爲 XIV: things subject to causality.

Ui (Prince) 有意 I: Having-Intention. Mati.

Umarogya 烏摩勒伽 XXVI: Umāraka. A devil.

Unjizai (Buddha) 雲自在 VII: Cloud-Freedom. Meghasvarapradīpa.

Unjizai-ō (Buddha) 雲自在王 VII: Cloud-Freedom-King. Meghasvararāja.

Unjizaitō-ō (Buddha) 雲自在燈王 XX: Cloud-Freedom-Light-King. Meghasvararāja.

Unrai-onnō (Buddha) 雲雷音王 XXIV: Cloud-Thunder-Sound-King. Meghadundubhisvararāja.

Unrai-onshuku-ōkechi (Buddha) 雲雷音宿王華智 XXVII: Cloud-Thunderpeal-Star-King-Flower-Wisdom. Jaladharagarjitaghoṣasusvaranakṣatrarājasaṃkusumitābhijña.

Uro 有漏 XVIII: āsrava. See *Ro*.

Urubinra-kashō 優樓頻螺迦葉 I: Uruvilvā-Kāśyapa. See *Śākyamuni* in the English/Sanskrit Glossary.

Uyo-nehan 有餘涅槃 IV: the Nirvāṇa-with-remainder.

W

Washukitsu (Dragon-King) 和修吉 I: Vāsuki.

Y

Yakujō (Bodhisattva) 藥上 XXVII: Medicine-Superior. Bhaiṣajyasamudgata.

Yakuō (Bodhisattva) 藥王 I: Medicine-King. Bhaiṣajyarāja.

Yasha 夜叉 I: yakṣa. A devil.

Yasha-kissha 夜叉吉蔗 夜叉吉遮 XXVI: yakṣa-kṛtya. A devil.

Yashutara 耶輸陀羅 I: Yaśodharā. See *Śākyamuni* in the English/Sanskrit Glossary.

Yujun 由旬 I: yojana. The distance of a day's journey by the chariot of a king.

Yuze (Bodhisattva) 勇施 I: Brave-In-Giving. Pradānaśūra.

Z

Zaigō 罪業 VII: sinful karmas; XV: a sin.

Zaihō 罪報 III: to punish; XX: retributions.

Zaike 在家 X: a layman.

Zaise 在世 III: a lifetime.

Zangi 慚愧 II: to be ashamed of oneself.

Zazen 坐禪 XIV: sitting in dhyāna.

Zembaramitsu 禪波羅蜜 XVII: the dhyāna-pāramitā. Meditation. See *Rokuharamitsu*.

Zempon 善本 I: the roots of good.

Zen 禪 I: dhyāna. Meditation.

Zenchishiki 善知識 XII: a teacher. Originally, a good friend.

Zengon 善根 I: the roots of good.

Zenjakuriki 善寂力 XX: the power of good tranquility.

Zenjō 禪定 I: dhyāna-concentration.

Zenjō (World) 善浄 VIII: Good-Purity. Suviśuddha.

Zenkutsu 禪窟 XVIII: a cave for the practice of dhyāna.

Zenni (Prince) 善意 I: Good-Intention. Sumati.

Zense 前世 XX: previous existence.

Zenzei 善逝 I: the Well-Gone. One of the ten epithets of the Buddha. See *Jūgō*.

Zō-i (Prince) 增意 I: Increasing-Intention. Viśeṣamati.

Zōbō 像法 III: the counterfeit of the right teachings.

Zōgai 繒蓋 VI: a canopy.

Zōjōman 增上慢 I: arrogant; XXVIII: arrogance from self-assumed acquisition of virtues.

Zokurui 囑累 XXI: to transmit.

Zuda 頭陀 XI. See *Dhūta* in the English/Sanskrit Glossary.

INDEX

A

Ābhāsvara (Heaven) 368
Abhidharma-piṭaka 369
Abhirati (World) 351
Abhyudgatarāja (Kalpa) 351
Acalā (Rakṣasī) 351
Accumulated-Treasure (Bodhisattva) 2
Accumulated-Wisdom (Bodhisattva) 203-205, 207-208
Accumulated-Wisdom (Prince) 132
Adbhuta 351
Adhimātrakāruṇika (Brahman) 351
Adornment-King (Bodhisattva) 351
Ajātaśatru (King) 3
Ajita 240-242, 256, 260, 263-266, 269, 271-272
Ājñāta-Kauṇḍinya (Arhat) 1, 28, 166
Ākāśapratiṣṭhita (Buddha) 351
Akṣayamati (Bodhisattva) 351
Akṣobhya (Buddha) 146
All-Pure-Light-Adornment (World) 351
All-Saving (Brahman) 134
Always-Raising-Banner-Of-Victory (World) 170
Amitāyus (Buddha) 147, 312
Ānanda 1, 169-173
Anantacāritra (Bodhisattva) 352
Anantamati (Prince) 352
Anantavikrāmin (Bodhisattva) 352
Anavanāmitavaijayantī (World) 352
Anavatapta (Dragon-King) 2
Anikṣiptadhura (Bodhisattva) 352
Aniruddha (Arhat) 1, 163
Antara (Kalpa) 358
Aparagodānīya 355
Appearance-Of-All-Worlds (World) 352
Aśaikṣa 352
Asita 201
Aśvajit (Bhikṣu) 364
Aupamya 352
Avabhāsaprāptā (World) 352
Avalokitasvara (Bodhisattva) 352
Avalokiteśvara (Bodhisattva) 372

B

Bakkula (Arhat) 1, 163
Balin (Asura-King) 3
Beautiful (Gandharva-King) 3
Beautiful-Form (Buddha) 121-122
Beautiful-Moon (God) 2
Beautiful-Voice (Gandharva-King) 3
Bhadra (Kalpa) 353
Bhadrapāla (Bodhisattva) 2, 294
Bhadrika (Bhikṣu) 364
Bhaiṣajyarāja (Bodhisattva) 353
Bhaiṣajyasamudgata (Bodhisattva) 353
Bharadvāja 14
Bhavāgra (Heaven) 368
Bhīṣmagarjitasvararāja (Buddha) 353

Bimbisāra (King) 364
Black-Teeth (Rākṣasī) 335
Brahma-Form (Buddha) 147
Brahmadvaja (Buddha) 353
Brahman 2, 16, 46, 54, 60, 105 114, 131, 134-141,143, 150-151, 196, 207, 216, 218, 257, 259-260, 260, 264, 266, 271, 274, 278, 280, 283, 285-286, 298, 301, 311, 319, 325, 331
Brave-In-Giving (Bodhisattva) 2, 316, 321, 333
Burning-Light (Buddha) 16, 21, 248

C

Cakravāḍa-parvata 367
Cakravartin 353
Candra (God) 353
Candrasvararāja (Buddha) 353
Candravimalasūryaprabhāsaśrī (Buddha) 353
Cloud-Freedom (Buddha) 147
Cloud-Freedom-King (Buddha) 147
Cloud-Freedom-Light-King (Buddha) 293
Cloud-Thunder-Sound-King (Buddha) 319
Cloud-Thunderpeal-Star-King-Flower-Wisdom (Buddha) 337-341
Constant-Endeavor (Bodhisattva) 2, 275-276, 279, 284, 287-288
Crooked-Teeth (Rākṣasī) 335
Cunda (Arhat) 163

D

Daśabala-Kāśyapa (Bhikṣu) 364
Devadatta 202-203, 336
Devarāja (Buddha) 354
Devasopāna (World) 354
Dharaṇiṃdhara (Bodhisattva) 354
Dharma 369
Dharma (Kiṃnara-King) 2
Dharma-Brightness (Buddha) 158, 161
Dharma-Keeping (Kiṃnara-King) 2
Dharmadhara (Kiṃnara-King) 354
Dharmagaganābhyudgatarāja (Buddha) 354
Dharmamati (Prince) 354
Dharmaprabhāsa (Buddha) 354
Dhṛtarāṣṭra (Heavenly-King) 355
Dhṛtiparipūrṇa (Bodhisattva) 354
Dīpaṃkara (Buddha) 354
Druma 354

E

Earth-Holding (Bodhisattva) 331
Eliminating-Fear-Of-All-Worlds (Buddha) 147
Emitting-Ten-Million-Rays-Of-Light (Buddha) 211
Emperor-Form (Buddha) 147
Endeavor-Power-Obtainer (Bodhisattva) 321
Endless-Intent (Bodhisattva) 323-327
Eternal-Extinction (Buddha) 147

F

Fame-Seeking (Bodhisattva) 16-17, 22
Flower-Foot-Easy-Walking (Buddha) 58
Flower-Light (Buddha) 57-59
Flower-Teeth (Rākṣasī) 335
Flower-Virtue (Bodhisattva) 319-322, 342
Free-At-Will (Garuḍa-King) 3
Free-From-Decay (Kalpa) 291
Free-From-Taint (World) 57-58
Freedom (God) 2, 286, 319, 325
Full-Moon (Bodhisattva) 2

G

Gadgadasvara (Bodhisattva) 356
Gautama 364
Gautamī (Bhikṣuṇī) 210
Gavāṃpati (Arhat) 1
Gayā (City) 242-244, 247
Gayā-Kāśyapa (Arhat) 1, 163
Ghoṣamati (Prince) 356
Gladly-Seen (Kalpa) 319, 337
Gladly-Seen-By-All-Beings (Bodhisattva) 306-310
Gladly-Seen-By-All-Beings (Buddha) 210,
Good-Purity (World) 159, 162
Gośīrṣacandana 357
Gṛdhrakūṭa (Mountain) 1
Great Kātyāyana (Arhat) 124
Great-Achievement (World) 291
Great-Adornment (Kalpa) 118
Great-Body (Garuḍa-King) 3
Great-Compassion (Brahman) 136
Great-Dharma (Kiṃnara-King) 2
Great-Eloquence (Bodhisattva) 187-188, 209
Great-Form (Kalpa) 129
Great-Freedom (God) 2, 46, 286, 320, 325
Great-Fulfillment (Garuḍa-King) 3
Great-Height-King (Kalpa) 341
Great-Light (World) 341
Great Maudgalyāyana 1, 120, 125-126
Great-Power (Bodhisattva) 2,
Great-Power-Obtainer (Bodhisattva) 2, 291-294
Great-Power-Virtue (Garuḍa-King) 3
Great-Treasure-Adornment (Kalpa) 57-58
Great-Universal-Wisdom-Excellence (Buddha) 129-132, 134-141, 143, 149

H

Happiness (World) 312
Hārītī (Rakṣasī) 357
Having-Treasures (Kalpa) 121
Heavenly-King (Buddha) 202-203
Hīnayāna 357

I

Immeasurable-Power (Bodhisattva) 2
Indradhvaja (Buddha) 357
Insatiable (Rākṣasī) 357
Īśvara (God) 357
Itivṛttaka 357

J

Jaladharagarjitaghoṣasusvaranakṣatrarājasaṃkusumitābhijña (Buddha) 358
Jambudvīpa 270, 292, 306, 313, 345, 346
Jāmbūnada-Gold-Light (Buddha) 124
Jāmbūnadaprabhāsa (Buddha) 358
Jātaka 358
Jīvaka 365
Jñānākara (Prince) 358
Joy (World) 146
Joyfulness (Kalpa) 126
Jyotiṣprabha (Brahman) 358

K

Kālodāyin (Arhat) 163
Kamaladalavimalanakṣatrarājasaṃkusumitābhijña (Buddha) 358
Kanakamuni (Buddha) 366
Kapilavastu 364
Kapphina (Arhat) 1, 163

Kapphiṇa (Arhat) 358
Kāśi 364
Kāśyapa (Bhikṣu) 108-111, 117, 119, 164
Kāśyapa (Buddha) 366
Kātyāyana (Arhat) 125
Kauṇḍinya (Bhikṣu) 163
Keśini (Rakṣasī) 359
Kharaskandha (Asura-King) 3
King-House (City) 1
Koli 364
Krakucchanda (Buddha) 366
Kuntī (Rakṣasī) 335-336
Kūṭadanti (Rakṣasī) 359

L

Lambā (Rakṣasī) 335
Leading-Teacher (Bodhisattva) 2
Light (Brahman) 2
Light (Buddha) 118, 120
Light-Adornment (World) 337
Light-Adornment-Appearance (Bodhisattva) 342
Light-Virtue (World) 118
Limitless-Practice (Bodhisattva) 236
Lion-Form (Buddha) 146
Lion-Moon (Bhikṣunī) 294
Lion-Voice (Buddha) 146

M

Madhura (Gandharva-King) 359
Madhurasvara (Gandharva-King) 359
Magadha 364
Mahā-Kāśyapa (Arhat) 1, 90, 96, 108, 118, 162
Mahā-Kātyāyana (Arhat) 1, 90, 120
Mahā-Kauṣṭhila (Arhat) 1
Mahā-Maudgalyāyana (Arhat) 90
Mahā-Prajāpatī (Bhikṣunī) 1, 210-211
Mahā-Pratibhāna (Bodhisattva) 360
Mahābhijñājñānābhibhū (Buddha) 360
Mahākāya (Garuḍa-King) 360
Mahānāman (Bhikṣu) 364
Mahāpūrṇa (Garuḍa-King) 360
Mahāratnapratimaṇḍita (Kalpa) 360
Maharddhiprāpta (Garuḍa-King) 360
Mahārūpa (Kalpa) 360
Mahāsaṃbhavā (World) 360
Mahāsthāmaprāpta (Bodhisattva) 360
Mahātejas (Garuḍa-King) 360
Mahāvikrāmin (Bodhisattva) 360
Mahāyāna 360
Maheśvara (God) 360
Maitrāyaṇī 1, 157
Maitreya (Bodhisattva) 2, 4, 5, 13-15, 17, 237, 240-244, 247-248, 256, 258, 260, 269-270, 346
Maitreya (Buddha) 22
Makuṭadanti (Rakṣasī) 360
Mālādhārī (Rakṣasī) 360
Manasvin (Dragon-King) 2
Mañjuśrī (Bodhisattva) 2, 4-5, 7-8, 11-13, 17, 23, 204-206, 216-217, 221-222, 224-228, 298, 316-317, 319, 321
Manobhirāma (World) 360
Manojña (Gandharva-King) 360
Manojñaśabdābhigarjita (Kalpa) 360
Manojñasvara (Gandharva-King) 360
Many-Hairs (Rakṣasī) 335
Many-Treasures (Buddha) 187-189, 191-195, 203, 206, 235, 257, 299, 301, 304, 313, 317-319, 321, 327
Māra (God) 9, 16, 55-56, 108, 118, 131, 140, 143, 207, 227-229, 286, 312-313, 318, 344, 347
Mati (Prince) 361
Māyā 364
Medicine-King (Bodhisattva) 2, 176, 180-183, 209, 305, 310, 312-313, 316, 321, 332-333, 342
Medicine-Superior (Bodhisattva) 316, 342
Meghadundubhisvararāja (Buddha) 361

Meghasvarapradīpa (Buddha) 361
Meghasvararāja (Buddha) 361
Merukalpa (Buddha) 361
Merukūṭa (Buddha) 361
Mind-Happiness (World) 126-127
Moon (God) 310
Moon-Light (Bodhisattva) 2
Mother-Of-Devils (Rakṣasī) 335
Mountain-Sea-Wisdom-Supernatural-Power-King (Buddha) 169-170, 172
Musical (Gandharva-King) 3
Musical-Voice (Gandharva-King) 3

N

Nadi-Kāśyapa (Arhat) 1, 163
Nāga 361
Nakṣatrarājasaṃkusumitābhijña (Bodhisattva) 361
Nanda (Bhikṣu) 1
Nanda (Dragon-King) 2
Necklace-Holding (Rākṣasī) 335
Never-Despising (Bodhisattva) 292-297
Never-Resting (Bodhisattva) 2
Nidāna 361
Nine Elements of Sūtras 362
Nirgrantha Jñātiputra 362
Nirmāṇarati (Heaven) 367
Nityaparinirvṛta (Buddha) 362
Nityodyukta (Bodhisattva) 362

P

Padmaprabha (Buddha) 362
Padmaśrī (Bodhisattva) 362
Padmavṛṣabhavikrāmin (Buddha) 362
Parable of a burning house 62-76
Parable of a magic city 148-149, 154-155
Parable of a poor man 91-102
Parable of an excellent physician 250-252, 255
Parable of the gem in the top-knot of a king 227-229
Parable of the gem inside a garment 165-167
Paranirmitavaśavartin (Heaven) 367
Pilindavatsa (Arhat) 1
Plunderer-Of-Energy-Of-All-Beings (Rākṣasī) 335
Powerful-Voice-King (Buddha) 291-294
Prabhūtaratna (Buddha) 363
Pradānaśūra (Bodhisattva) 363
Prajñakūṭa (Bodhisattva) 363
Pratyayabuddha 353
Pratyekabuddha 14, 24, 26, 28, 34, 66, 82, 146, 176, 203, 224, 248, 276, 280, 285, 287, 291, 310-312, 320, 325
Priyadarśana (Kalpa) 363
Pure-Body (Buddha) 16, 21
Pure-Eyes (Prince) 337-338, 340
Pure-Flower-Star-King-Wisdom (Buddha) 315-319, 321
Pure-Practice (Bodhisattva) 236
Pure-Store (Prince) 337-338, 340
Pure-Virtue (Queen) 337, 340, 342
Pūrṇa (Arhat) 1, 157-160, 162
Pūrṇacandra (Bodhisattva) 363
Pūrvavideha 355
Puṣpadantī (Rakṣasī) 363

R

Rāhu (Asura-King) 3
Rāhula (Arhat) 1, 169, 172-173, 210
Rājagṛha (City) 363
Raśmiprabhāsa (Buddha) 363
Raśmiśatasahasraparipūrṇadhvaja (Buddha) 363
Ratiprapūrṇa (Kalpa) 363
Ratnacandra (Bodhisattva) 363
Ratnākara (Bodhisattva) 363
Ratnaketurāja (Buddha) 363
Ratnamati (Prince) 363
Ratnapāṇi (Bodhisattva) 363

Ratnaprabha (Bodhisattva) 363
Ratnaprabha (God) 363
Ratnaprabhāsa (Kalpa) 363
Ratnasaṃbhava (World) 363
Ratnatejobhyudgatarāja (Buddha) 363
Ratnāvabhāsa (Kalpa) 364
Ratnaviśuddha (World) 364
Resolution-Fulfillment (Bodhisattva) 58
Revata (Arhat) 1, 163

S

Sacred Eagle (Mountain) 204, 253
Sadāparibhūta (Bodhisattva) 364
Sāgara (Dragon-King) 2, 204-205
Sāgaravaradharabuddhivikrīḍitābhijña (Buddha) 364
Śaikṣa 366
Śakra (God) 46, 114, 207, 259, 271, 274, 285, 311, 319, 325
Śakra-Devānām-Indra (God) 2, 60, 280
Śākyamuni (Buddha) 47, 147, 186-192, 203, 205-206, 234-237, 240, 247, 257, 298, 299, 303-304, 312, 314-319, 321-322, 327, 333, 343, 346
Sāla-Tree-King (Buddha) 341
Śālendrarāja (Buddha) 365
Samantabhadra (Bodhisattva) 365
Samantagandha (God) 365
Samantaprabhāsa (Buddha) 365
Saṃbhavā (World) 365
Saptaratnapadmavikrāntagāmin (Buddha) 365
Śāriputra (Arhat) 1, 24-35, 38-39, 45, 47-53, 56-58, 60-68, 76, 78-79, 81-82, 86-87, 89-90, 206-208, 304, 348
Sarvalokabhayacchambhitatva-vidhvaṃsanakara (Buddha) 365
Sarvalokadhātūpadravodvega-pratyuttīrṇa (Buddha) 365
Sarvarūpasaṃdarśanā (World) 365
Sarvasattvapriyadarśana (Bodhisattva) 365
Sarvasattvatrātar (Brahman) 365
Sarvasattvojohārī (Rakṣasī) 365
Śaśiketu (Buddha) 366
Saving-All-Worlds-From-Suffering (Buddha) 366
Siddhārtha 364
Śikhin (Brahman) 2, 141
Śikhin (Buddha) 366
Siṃhacandra (Bhikṣunī) 366
Siṃhadhvaja (Buddha) 366
Siṃhaghoṣa (Buddha) 366
Six pāramitās 14, 22, 41, 152, 200, 202, 204, 260-262, 265, 291
Sky-Dwelling (Buddha) 146
Spotless (World) 207
Śrāvaka 1, 14, 19, 24, 28, 30, 37, 50, 52, 56, 66, 78, 82, 91, 95-96, 101, 105, 116-118, 120, 122-127, 131, 144-147, 153, 158-160, 162, 164-165, 169, 171, 173-176, 182-183, 191, 204, 207, 209-210, 217, 222, 248, 264-265, 276, 280, 285, 287-288, 291, 304-306, 309, 311-312, 320, 325, 341, 348
Śrīgarbha (Bodhisattva) 366
Star-King-Flower (Bodhisattva) 305, 310-314, 316
Steadily-Established-Practice (Bodhisattva) 236
Śubhakṛtsna (Heaven) 368
Śubhavyūha (King) 367
Śubhavyūharāja (Bodhisattva) 367
Subhūti (Arhat) 1, 90, 120-122
Śuddhodana 265, 364
Sudharma (Brahman) 367
Sugatacetanā (Upāsaka) 401
Sukhāvatī (World) 367
Sumati (Prince) 367
Sumeru-Form (Buddha) 147
Sumeru-Peak (Buddha) 146
Sun (God) 311
Sun-Moon-Light (Buddha) 14-17, 19, 293
Sun-Moon-Pure-Bright-Virtue (Buddha) 305-309
Sundarananda (Arhat) 1
Superior-Practice (Bodhisattva) 236, 300, 304

Superior-Practice-Intent (Bodhisattva) 316
Suprabuddha 364
Supratiṣṭhitacārita (Bodhisattva) 368
Sūtra-piṭaka 369
Suviśuddha (World) 368
Svāgata (Arhat) 163

T

Takṣaka (Dragon-King) 2
Tamālapattracandana-Fragrance (Buddha) 126, 127
Tamālapattracandana-Fragrance-Supernatural-Power (Buddha) 147
Tamālapattracandanagandha (Buddha) 368
Tamālapattracandanagandhabhijña (Buddha) 368
Thinking-Of-Buddha (Upāsaka) 294
Three Vehicles 66
Trailokyavikrāmin (Bodhisattva) 369
Transcending-Triple-World (Bodhisattva) 2
Treasure-Born (World) 122
Treasure-Brightness (Kalpa) 159, 162
Treasure-Form (Buddha) 173-174
Treasure-Light (God) 2
Treasure-Moon (Bodhisattva) 2
Treasure-Palm (Bodhisattva) 2
Treasure-Power-Virtue-Superior-King (Buddha) 343
Treasure-Purity (World) 187
Tripiṭaka 369
Twelve Causes 144

U

Udāna 370
Udāyin (Arhat) 163
Universal-Brightness (Buddha) 163-164
Universal-Fragrance (God) 2
Universal-Sage (Bodhisattva) 343-348
Upāli (Arhat) 365
Upananda (Dragon-King) 2
Uruvilvā 364
Uruvilvā-Kāśyapa (Arhat) 1, 163
Utpalaka (Dragon-King) 2
Uttarakuru 367

V

Vaidehī 3
Vaipulya 370
Vairocanaraśmipratimaṇḍitā (World) 371
Vairocanaraśmipratimaṇḍitadhvajarāja (Bodhisattva) 371
Vaiśravaṇa (Heavenly-King) 371
Vajra 371
Vajra-Holding (God) 326
Vajradhara (God) 371
Vajrapāṇi (God) 371
Vārāṇasī (City) 48, 60
Varaprabha (Bodhisattva) 371
Vāsuki (Dragon-King) 2
Vemacitrin (Asura-King) 3
Vilambā (Rakṣasī) 335
Vimalā (World) 371
Vimaladatta (King) 371
Vimaladattā (Queen) 371
Vimalagarbha (Prince) 371
Vimalanetra (Buddha) 371
Vimatisamudghātin (Prince) 371
Vinaya-piṭaka 369
Vinirbhoga (Kalpa) 371
Vipaśyin (Buddha) 366
Viraja (World) 371
Virtue-Store (Bodhisattva) 16, 21
Virūḍhaka (God) 371
Virūpākṣa (Heavenly-King) 367

Viśeṣamati (Prince) 371
Viśiṣṭacāritra (Bodhisattva) 371
Vistīrṇavati (World) 371
Viśuddhacāritra (Bodhisattva) 371
Viśvabhū (Buddha) 366
Void-King (Buddha) 171
Vyākaraṇa 371

W

Walking-On-Flowers-of-Seven-Treasures (Buddha) 172
Well-Composed (World) 129, 135, 137, 139, 141
Wonderful-Adornment (King) 337, 340-342
Wonderful-Dharma (Brahman) 138
Wonderful-Dharma (Kiṃnara-King) 2
Wonderful-Light (Bodhisattva) 16, 17, 19-22
Wonderful-Voice (Bodhisattva) 315-322
Wonderful-Voice-Resounding-Everywhere (Kalpa) 170
World-Holding (God) 334
World-Voice-Perceiver (Bodhisattva) 2, 323-331

Y

Yama (Heaven) 367
Yaśaskāma (Bodhisattva) 372
Yaśodharā (Bhikṣuṇī) 1, 210-211

BIBLIOGRAPHY

Hokekyō (The Saddharmapuṇḍarīka-sūtra), Iwanami Bunko, Jō, 6531-6534 (1962); Chū, 6535-6538 (1964); Ge, 6539-6543 (1967). Translated into Japanese with notes by Yukio Sakamoto and Yutaka Iwamoto.

Saddharmapuṇḍarīka-sūtram, Romanized and revised text of the Bibliotheca Buddica, publication by consulting a Skt. MS & Tibetan and Chinese translations by Prof. U. Wogihara and C. Tsuchida, Tokyo, 1958.

The Saddharma-puṇḍarīka or the Lotus of the True Law, translated by H. Kern, Sacred Books of the East, Vol. XXI, Oxford, 1909.

Hokekyō No Seiritsu To Tenkai (The Lotus Sutra and the Development of Buddhist Thought), edited by Yensho Kanakura, Kyoto, 1972.

Hokekyō No Chūgokuteki Tenkai (The Lotus Sūtra and Chinese Buddhism), edited by Yukio Sakamoto, Kyoto, 1972.

Bukkyō Daijiten (Great Buddhist Dictionary), edited by Shinko Mochizuki, Tokyo, 1933.

Konsaisu Bukkyō Jiten (Concise Buddhist Dictionary), edited by Hakuju Ui, Tokyo, 1938.

Bukkyōgaku Jiten (A Dictionary of Buddhist Studies), Kyoto, 1955.

Shin Bukkyō Jiten (New Buddhist Dictionary), edited by Hajime Nakamaura, Tokyo, 1962.

Bonkan Taiyaku Bukkyō Jiten (The Sanskrit-Chinese Dictionary of Buddhist Technical Terms), based on the Mahāvyutpatti, by Unrai Wogahara, Tokyo, 1959.

A Dictionary of Chinese Buddhist Terms with Sanskrit and English Equivalents and a Sanskrit-Pali Index, compiled by William Edward Soothill and Lewis Hodous, London, 1937.

Japanese-English Buddhist Dictionary, published by Daito Shuppansha, Tokyo, 1965.

Buddhist Hybrid Sanskrit Grammar and Dictionary, by Franklin Edgerton, New Haven, Yale University Press, 1953.

CPSIA information can be obtained
at www.ICGtesting.com
Printed in the USA
BVHW042253270822
645705BV00003B/238

9 780971 964563